Generation X

X

AMERICANS
BORN 1965 to 1976

7th EDITION

Generation X

AMERICANS BORN 1965 to 1976

7th EDITION

The American
Generations Series

BY THE NEW STRATEGIST EDITORS

New Strategist Publications, Inc.
Ithaca, New York

New Strategist Publications, Inc.
P.O. Box 242, Ithaca, New York 14851
800/848-0842; 607/273-0913
www.newstrategist.com

ISBN 978-1-937737-04-7 (hardcover)
ISBN 978-1-937737-05-4 (paper)

Printed in the United States of America

Table of Contents

Chapter 10. Time Use

Chapter 11. Wealth

Tables

Illustrations

Chapter 6. Labor Force

Chapter 7. Living Arrangements

Chapter 8. Population

Chapter 9. Spending

Chapter 10. Time Use

Chapter 11. Wealth

Introduction

Generation X gained fame simply by following the Baby-Boom generation onto the stage of youth decades ago, a stage Boomers created and made the center of the nation's attention. Generation X was everything Boomers were not—small in number, cynical rather than idealistic, they were expected to make their way easily through life because of the swath Boomers had carved. But it didn't turn out that way. Gen Xers have struggled to compete with the masses of Boomers ahead of them and the large Millennial generation at their heels. Perhaps no generation has been hit as hard by the Great Recession and collapse of the housing market as Generation X. Now they face a tough job market, especially as Boomers postpone retirement. The seventh edition of *Generation X: Americans Born 1965 to 1976* tells the sometimes grim story of the small generation spanning the ages of 35 to 46 in 2012.

Although their numbers are small, lifestage dictates that Generation X is a vital part of the nation's commerce and culture. People in their thirties and forties are in the crowded-nest years. They are supposed to be advancing in their careers, their incomes should be growing, and their spending should climb because of the expenses of children and teens. *Generation X: Americans Born 1965 to 1976* shows how Gen Xers are coping with these demands and what to expect in the future.

Gen Xers are a diverse segment of the population, with minorities accounting for a large share of the whole. One issue binds together this diversity: the struggle to reach and remain in the middle class. While other generations face the same issue, getting ahead and staying there is proving more difficult for Generation X because of their position between two larger generations. Only 16 percent of Americans are Gen Xers, while 25 percent are Boomers and another 25 percent are Millennials (see the Population chapter). In part because they are overshadowed by others, Gen Xers are suffering economically. The percentage of men in their thirties and forties who have worked for their current employer for 10 or more years has fallen (see the Labor Force chapter). The median income of men aged 35 to 44 is lower today than it was in 1990, after adjusting for inflation (see the Income chapter).

It is not easy to study Generation Xers. Few government surveys focus on the generation, and the ages spanned by the members of the generation make it difficult to tease them out of the government's traditional five- or ten-year age categories. This time around, however, we got lucky. Generation X—which spanned the ages of 34 to 45 in 2010 (the date for most of the data in this book)—fits almost perfectly into the 35-to-44 age group. Consequently, *Generation X: Americans Born 1965 to 1976* provides real insight into the status of this struggling generation as it steers the next generation of children into adulthood.

Generation X is your guide to how well they are doing.

How to use this book

Generation X: Americans Born 1965 to 1976 is designed for easy use. It is divided into 11 chapters, organized alphabetically: Attitudes, Education, Health, Housing, Income, Labor Force, Living Arrangements, Population, Spending, Time Use, and Wealth.

The seventh edition of *Generation X* includes the latest data on the changing demographics of homeownership, based on the Census Bureau's 2011 Housing Vacancies and Homeownership Survey. The Income chapter, with 2010 income statistics, reveals the struggle of so many Americans to stay afloat. The Spending chapter reveals trends in Gen X spending through 2010, and examines how their spending changed after the Great Recession. *Generation X* includes the latest labor force numbers, including the government's projections that show rising participation among the Baby-Boom generation—not good news for Gen Xers anxious to advance in their careers. The Wealth chapter presents data from the Survey of Consumer Finances that reveal the impact of the Great Recession on household wealth, with a look at 2007-to-2009 trends. The Health chapter includes up-to-date statistics on health insurance coverage. The Attitudes chapter, based on New Strategist's analysis of the 2010 General Social Survey, compares and contrasts the perspectives of the generations.

Most of the tables in *Generation X* are based on data collected by the federal government, in particular the Bureau of the Census, the Bureau of Labor Statistics, the National Center for Education Statistics, the National Center for Health Statistics, and the Federal Reserve Board. The federal government is the best source of up-to-date, reliable information on the changing characteristics of Americans. By having *Generation X* on your bookshelf, you can get the answers to your questions faster than you can online. Even better, visit newstrategist.com and download the PDF version of *Generation X* with links to each table in Excel.

The chapters of *Generation X* present the demographic and lifestyle data most important to researchers. Within each chapter, most of the tables are based on data collected by the federal government, but they are not simply reproductions of government spreadsheets—as is the case in many reference books. Instead, each table is individually compiled and created by New Strategist's editors, with calculations designed to reveal the trends. The task of extracting and processing data from the government's web sites to create a single table can require hours of effort. New Strategist has done the work for you, each table telling a story about Gen Xers—a story explained by the accompanying text and chart, which analyze the data and highlight future trends. If you need more information than the tables and text provide, you can plumb the original source listed at the bottom of each table.

The book contains a comprehensive table list to help you locate the information you need. For a more detailed search, see the index at the back of the book. Also at the back of the book is the glossary, which defines the terms commonly used and describes the many surveys referenced in the tables and text.

With *Generation X: Americans Born 1965 to 1976* on your bookshelf, an in-depth understanding of this influential and struggling generation is at hand.

1

Attitudes

■ Older Americans are the most trusting. Forty-four percent of older Americans say most people can be trusted. In contrast, only 18 percent of Millennials say others can be trusted.

■ Older Americans are most satisfied with their finances. They are also the only generation in which the majority calls itself middle class.

■ Older Americans are by far most likely to think they are better off than their parents were at the same age (73 percent). Generation Xers are least likely to agree (52 percent).

■ The majority of Gen Xers, Boomers, and older Americans think two children is ideal. Among Millennials, only 39 percent think two is ideal and a larger 48 percent think three, four, or more children is ideal.

■ Only 33 percent of Millennials identify themselves as Protestant compared with 59 percent of older Americans.

■ The 62 percent majority of Millennials thinks gays and lesbians should have the right to marry. Millennials are the only generation in which the majority supports gay marriage.

■ Millennials are more liberal than Gen Xers, Boomers, or older Americans. They are the only generation in which liberals outnumber conservatives (31 versus 27 percent).

■ Most Boomers and Millennials favor legalizing marijuana.

Boomers Are Most Likely to Say They Are Not Too Happy

Fewer than one in three Americans is very happy.

When asked how happy they are, only 29 percent of Americans aged 18 or older say they are very happy. The majority says it feels only pretty happy. The Millennial generation is least likely to report being very happy (25 percent), but Boomers are most likely to report being not too happy (17 percent).

The 63 percent majority of married Americans say they are very happily married. Interestingly, older Americans are least likely to report being very happily married (59 percent), while Gen Xers are most likely (66 percent).

The majority of the public thinks life is exciting (52 percent). The only generation that does not feel this way is older Americans, with only 42 percent finding life exciting and the 53 percent majority finding it pretty routine.

Few believe most people can be trusted. Only 32 percent of the public says most can be trusted. Younger generations are far less trusting than older Americans. Only 18 percent of Millennials believe most people can be trusted compared with 44 percent of people aged 65 or older.

■ Younger generations of Americans are struggling with a deteriorating economy, which reduces their happiness and increases their distrust.

Few Millennials trust others

(percent of people aged 18 or older who think most people can be trusted, by generation, 2010)

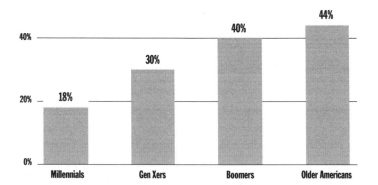

Table 1.1 General Happiness, 2010

"Taken all together, how would you say things are these days—
would you say that you are very happy, pretty happy, or not too happy?"

(percent of people aged 18 or older responding by generation, 2010)

	very happy	pretty happy	not too happy
Total people	**28.8%**	**57.0%**	**14.2%**
Millennial generation (18 to 33)	25.0	62.8	12.2
Generation X (34 to 45)	32.9	54.2	13.0
Baby Boom (46 to 64)	27.2	55.5	17.4
Older Americans (65 or older)	32.8	54.5	12.7

Source: Survey Documentation and Analysis, Computer-assisted Survey Methods Program, University of California, Berkeley, General Social Surveys, 1972–2010 Cumulative Data Files, Internet site http://sda.berkeley.edu/cgi-bin32/hsda?harcsda+gss10; calculations by New Strategist

Table 1.2 Happiness of Marriage, 2010

"Taking all things together, how would you describe your marriage?"

(percent of currently married people aged 18 or older responding by generation, 2010)

	very happy	pretty happy	not too happy
Total married people	**63.0%**	**34.3%**	**2.6%**
Millennial generation (18 to 33)	60.3	37.2	2.5
Generation X (34 to 45)	66.2	30.8	3.0
Baby Boom (46 to 64)	63.9	33.6	2.5
Older Americans (65 or older)	58.9	38.4	2.7

Source: Survey Documentation and Analysis, Computer-assisted Survey Methods Program, University of California, Berkeley, General Social Surveys, 1972–2010 Cumulative Data Files, Internet site http://sda.berkeley.edu/cgi-bin32/hsda?harcsda+gss10; calculations by New Strategist

Table 1.3 Is Life Exciting, Routine, or Dull, 2010

"In general, do you find life exciting, pretty routine, or dull?"

(percent of people aged 18 or older responding by generation, 2010)

	exciting	pretty routine	dull
Total people	**52.1%**	**43.3%**	**4.6%**
Millennial generation (18 to 33)	56.2	40.3	3.5
Generation X (34 to 45)	50.1	43.7	6.2
Baby Boom (46 to 64)	54.6	40.7	4.7
Older Americans (65 or older)	42.5	53.2	4.3

Note: Numbers do not sum to total because "don't know" is not shown.
Source: Survey Documentation and Analysis, Computer-assisted Survey Methods Program, University of California, Berkeley, General Social Surveys, 1972–2010 Cumulative Data Files, Internet site http://sda.berkeley.edu/cgi-bin32/hsda?harcsda+gss10; calculations by New Strategist

Table 1.4 Trust in Others, 2010

"Generally speaking, would you say that most people can be trusted or that you can't be too careful in life?"

(percent of people aged 18 or older responding by generation, 2010)

	can trust	cannot trust	depends
Total people	**32.2%**	**62.5%**	**5.3%**
Millennial generation (18 to 33)	17.8	76.9	5.3
Generation X (34 to 45)	30.4	64.4	5.2
Baby Boom (46 to 64)	40.2	54.8	5.1
Older Americans (65 or older)	43.7	50.6	5.7

Source: Survey Documentation and Analysis, Computer-assisted Survey Methods Program, University of California, Berkeley, General Social Surveys, 1972–2010 Cumulative Data Files, Internet site http://sda.berkeley.edu/cgi-bin32/hsda?harcsda+gss10; calculations by New Strategist

Belief in Hard Work Is Strong Across Generations

Millennials are most likely to believe hard work is the key to success.

How do people get ahead? More than two-thirds of Americans say it is by hard work. Only 10 percent believe luck alone gets people ahead. Millennials (73 percent) believe most strongly in hard work to get ahead.

Not surprisingly, Millennials are most likely to live in the same city as they did when they were 16 (48 percent), mostly because they have had less time to move than older generations. Older Americans are most likely to live in a different state (43 percent).

■ Older Americans are most likely to say (24 percent) that people get ahead through hard work and luck equally.

Many Americans live in the same city as they did when a teenager

(percent of people aged 18 or older who live in the same city/town/county as they did at age 16, by generation, 2010)

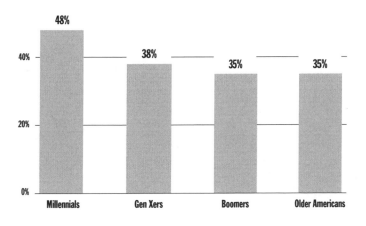

Table 1.5 How People Get Ahead, 2010

"Some people say that people get ahead by their own hard work; others say that lucky breaks or help from other people are more important. Which do you think is most important?"

(percent of people aged 18 or older responding by generation, 2010)

	hard work	both equally	luck
Total people	**69.6%**	**20.4%**	**10.0%**
Millennial generation (18 to 33)	72.7	17.4	9.9
Generation X (34 to 45)	68.4	19.8	11.8
Baby Boom (46 to 64)	69.4	21.6	9.1
Older Americans (65 or older)	67.0	24.0	9.0

Source: Survey Documentation and Analysis, Computer-assisted Survey Methods Program, University of California, Berkeley, General Social Surveys, 1972–2010 Cumulative Data Files, Internet site http://sda.berkeley.edu/cgi-bin32/hsda?harcsda+gss10; calculations by New Strategist

Table 1.6 Geographic Mobility since Age 16, 2010

"When you were 16 years old, were you living in this same (city / town / county)?"

(percent of people aged 18 or older responding by generation, 2010)

	same city	same state, different city	different state
Total people	**39.4%**	**25.7%**	**34.9%**
Millennial generation (18 to 33)	48.3	23.9	27.9
Generation X (34 to 45)	38.1	26.5	35.3
Baby Boom (46 to 64)	35.0	28.8	36.2
Older Americans (65 or older)	34.8	21.8	43.3

Source: Survey Documentation and Analysis, Computer-assisted Survey Methods Program, University of California, Berkeley, General Social Surveys, 1972–2010 Cumulative Data Files, Internet site http://sda.berkeley.edu/cgi-bin32/hsda?harcsda+gss10; calculations by New Strategist

Older Americans Are Doing Far Better than Middle-Aged or Younger Ones

People aged 65 or older are the only ones likely to say they are middle class.

The 60 percent majority of Americans aged 65 or older call themselves middle class compared with only 36 to 41 percent of younger generations, who are more likely to label themselves working class than middle class. Is the preference of younger generations for the label working class simply a matter of semantics or does it record a slippage in the standard of living among people under age 65?

Only 43 percent of Americans believe their family's income is average, down from 49 percent in 2000. Fully 36 percent say they make less than average, up from 26 percent in 2000. Older Americans are the ones least likely to say they have below average incomes and (along with Baby Boomers) most likely to say they have above average incomes.

The share of people who are satisfied with their financial situation fell to 23 percent in 2010, down from 31 percent in 2000. Satisfaction with personal finances is greatest among older Americans, only 18 percent of whom are not at all satisfied. The dissatisfied share is a much larger 32 to 35 percent among the younger generations.

When asked whether they are satisfied with the work they do—either at a job or at home, older Americans are much more likely than middle-aged or younger people to say they are very satisfied. Seventy percent of Americans aged 65 or older are very satisfied, as are the majority of Boomers and Gen Xers. Only 36 percent of Millennials are very satisfied with their work.

■ Older Americans, buoyed by the security of Medicare and Social Security, are the only ones who have managed to hold on to their middle-class status as the Great Recession swept through the economy.

Older Americans are least likely to be dissatisfied with their finances

(percent of people aged 18 or older who say they are not at all satisfied with their financial situation, by generation, 2010)

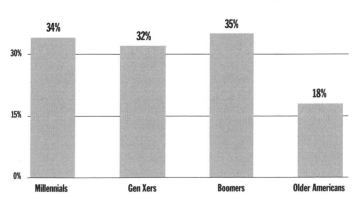

Table 1.7 Social Class Membership, 2010

"If you were asked to use one of four names for your social class, which would you say you belong in: the lower class, the working class, the middle class, or the upper class?"

(percent of people aged 18 or older responding by generation, 2010)

	lower	working	middle	upper
Total people	**8.2%**	**46.8%**	**42.4%**	**2.5%**
Millennial generation (18 to 33)	9.8	52.7	35.6	2.0
Generation X (34 to 45)	7.9	51.8	39.7	0.6
Baby Boom (46 to 64)	8.6	46.8	41.0	3.6
Older Americans (65 or older)	5.0	31.1	60.1	3.8

Source: Survey Documentation and Analysis, Computer-assisted Survey Methods Program, University of California, Berkeley, General Social Surveys, 1972–2010 Cumulative Data Files, Internet site http://sda.berkeley.edu/cgi-bin32/hsda?harcsda+gss10; calculations by New Strategist

Table 1.8 Family Income Relative to Others, 2010

"Compared with American families in general, would you say your family income is far below average, below average, average, above average, or far above average?"

(percent of people aged 18 or older responding by generation, 2010)

	far below average	below average	average	above average	far above average
Total people	**6.8%**	**28.8%**	**43.5%**	**18.4%**	**2.5%**
Millennial generation (18 to 33)	7.0	30.6	46.6	13.7	2.0
Generation X (34 to 45)	7.9	27.4	44.2	17.8	2.7
Baby Boom (46 to 64)	8.0	30.8	37.3	20.6	3.3
Older Americans (65 or older)	2.6	23.6	49.4	23.1	1.2

Source: Survey Documentation and Analysis, Computer-assisted Survey Methods Program, University of California, Berkeley, General Social Surveys, 1972–2010 Cumulative Data Files, Internet site http://sda.berkeley.edu/cgi-bin32/hsda?harcsda+gss10; calculations by New Strategist

Table 1.9 Satisfaction with Financial Situation, 2010

"So far as you and your family are concerned, would you say that you are pretty well satisfied with your present financial situation, more or less satisfied, or not satisfied at all?"

(percent of people aged 18 or older responding by generation, 2010)

	satisfied	more or less satisfied	not at all satisfied
Total people	**23.3%**	**45.2%**	**31.5%**
Millennial generation (18 to 33)	20.3	45.4	34.3
Generation X (34 to 45)	19.8	47.8	32.4
Baby Boom (46 to 64)	19.9	44.8	35.3
Older Americans (65 or older)	39.9	41.9	18.1

Source: Survey Documentation and Analysis, Computer-assisted Survey Methods Program, University of California, Berkeley, General Social Surveys, 1972–2010 Cumulative Data Files, Internet site http://sda.berkeley.edu/cgi-bin32/hsda?harcsda+gss10; calculations by New Strategist

Table 1.10 Job Satisfaction, 2010

"On the whole, how satisfied are you with the work you do—would you say you are very satisfied, moderately satisfied, a little dissatisfied, or very dissatisfied?"

(percent of people aged 18 or older responding by generation, 2010)

	very satisfied	moderately satisfied	a little dissatisfied	very dissatisfied
Total people	**49.8%**	**36.2%**	**10.3%**	**3.7%**
Millennial generation (18 to 33)	36.2	45.6	14.9	3.3
Generation X (34 to 45)	52.4	33.8	10.0	3.8
Baby Boom (46 to 64)	54.6	32.8	8.4	4.3
Older Americans (65 or older)	69.9	24.5	3.8	1.8

Note: Question refers to job or housework.
Source: Survey Documentation and Analysis, Computer-assisted Survey Methods Program, University of California, Berkeley, General Social Surveys, 1972–2010 Cumulative Data Files, Internet site http://sda.berkeley.edu/cgi-bin32/hsda?harcsda+gss10; calculations by New Strategist

The American Standard of Living Is Falling

Fewer Americans believe they are better off than their parents.

When comparing their own standard of living now with that of their parents when they were the same age, 59 percent of respondents say they are better off. The figure was 67 percent 10 years earlier. Older Americans are by far most likely to think they are better off than their parents were at the same age (73 percent). Generation Xers are least likely to feel that way (52 percent).

When asked whether they think they have a good chance of improving their standard of living, 58 percent of Americans say yes. This is down sharply from 77 percent a decade earlier. Not surprisingly, Millennials—with most of their life ahead of them—are most hopeful (65 percent). Disturbingly, Boomers are least hopeful (52 percent).

Fifty-nine percent of parents believe their children will have a better standard of living when they reach the respondent's present age. The share is 73 percent among Millennials, 60 percent among Xers, 53 percent among Boomers, and just 47 percent among older Americans. Apparently, many older Americans are aware of the declining standard of living among the younger generations. A substantial 27 percent of older Americans believe their children will be worse off in the years ahead.

■ The Americans who now have the least (Millennials) are most likely to believe things will be better in the future.

Most still believe their children will be better off

(percent of people aged 18 or older with children who think their children's standard of living will be somewhat or much better than theirs is now, by generation, 2010)

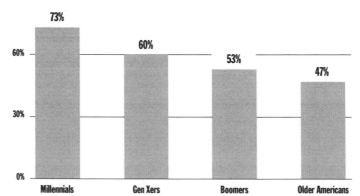

Table 1.11 Parents' Standard of Living, 2010

"Compared to your parents when they were the age you are now, do you think your own standard of living now is much better, somewhat better, about the same, somewhat worse, or much worse than theirs was?"

(percent of people aged 18 or older responding by generation, 2010)

	much better	somewhat better	about the same	somewhat worse	much worse
Total people	**29.2%**	**29.7%**	**24.8%**	**12.1%**	**4.2%**
Millennial generation (18 to 33)	27.6	32.3	25.6	10.4	4.0
Generation X (34 to 45)	25.6	26.0	29.1	16.5	2.9
Baby Boom (46 to 64)	27.8	27.7	23.7	14.9	5.9
Older Americans (65 or older)	39.2	34.0	19.6	4.6	2.6

Source: Survey Documentation and Analysis, Computer-assisted Survey Methods Program, University of California, Berkeley, General Social Surveys, 1972–2010 Cumulative Data Files, Internet site http://sda.berkeley.edu/cgi-bin32/hsda?harcsda+gss10; calculations by New Strategist

Table 1.12 Standard of Living Will Improve, 2010

"The way things are in America, people like me and my family have a good chance of improving our standard of living. Do you agree or disagree?"

(percent of people aged 18 or older responding by generation, 2010)

	strongly agree	agree	neither	disagree	strongly disagree
Total people	**13.1%**	**44.9%**	**16.2%**	**21.6%**	**4.2%**
Millennial generation (18 to 33)	15.5	49.7	16.9	15.9	2.0
Generation X (34 to 45)	18.5	38.4	16.3	22.4	4.4
Baby Boom (46 to 64)	10.7	41.6	16.4	25.0	6.2
Older Americans (65 or older)	7.4	50.8	14.1	23.5	4.2

Source: Survey Documentation and Analysis, Computer-assisted Survey Methods Program, University of California, Berkeley, General Social Surveys, 1972–2010 Cumulative Data Files, Internet site http://sda.berkeley.edu/cgi-bin32/hsda?harcsda+gss10; calculations by New Strategist

Table 1.13 Children's Standard of Living, 2010

"When your children are at the age you are now, do you think their standard of living will be much better, somewhat better, about the same, somewhat worse, or much worse than yours is now?"

(percent of people aged 18 or older with children responding by generation, 2010)

	much better	somewhat better	about the same	somewhat worse	much worse
Total people with children	**27.4%**	**32.0%**	**20.6%**	**15.0%**	**5.1%**
Millennial generation (18 to 33)	38.0	34.6	16.6	9.0	1.8
Generation X (34 to 45)	32.4	27.7	19.1	14.7	6.1
Baby Boom (46 to 64)	19.8	33.1	22.4	18.5	6.2
Older Americans (65 or older)	17.0	30.3	25.9	19.2	7.8

Source: Survey Documentation and Analysis, Computer-assisted Survey Methods Program, University of California, Berkeley, General Social Surveys, 1972–2010 Cumulative Data Files, Internet site http://sda.berkeley.edu/cgi-bin32/hsda?harcsda+gss10; calculations by New Strategist

Two Children Are Most Popular

Many Millennials think three children is the ideal number, however.

Across generations a plurality of Americans thinks two is the ideal number of children. The majority of Gen Xers, Boomers, and older Americans say two is ideal. Among Millennials, a smaller 39 percent think two is the ideal number, and a hefty 48 percent think three, four, or more is best. With a new baby bust in force because of the Great Recession, it is doubtful that Millennials will act on their larger family ideal.

Regardless of their number, most children are subject to a good, hard spanking when they misbehave. Sixty-nine percent of Americans believe children sometimes must be spanked, with little difference by generation.

As older Americans exit the stage, the preference for traditional sex roles has fallen below 50 percent even among people aged 65 or older. Only 48 percent of older Americans believe it is better for everyone involved if the man is the achiever outside the home and the woman takes care of the home and family. Among younger generations, the figure is just 31 to 35 percent. Most of the oldest generation now agrees with young and middle-aged adults that a working mother can have just as warm and secure a relationship with her children as a mother who does not work.

Support for the view that government should help people who are sick and in need is strongest among Millennials (58 percent). Ironically, those least likely to feel this way are older Americans—the only age group with government-provided health insurance. Just 35 percent believe government should help.

■ Many older Americans may not understand that Medicare is a government-provided health insurance program.

Even among older Americans, a minority thinks traditional sex roles are best

(percent of people aged 18 or older who think traditional sex roles are best, by generation, 2010)

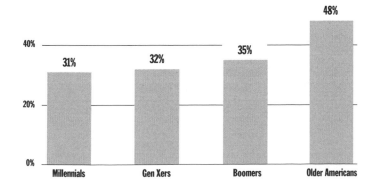

Table 1.14 Ideal Number of Children, 2010

"What do you think is the ideal number of children for a family to have?"

(percent of people aged 18 or older responding by generation, 2010)

	none	one	two	three	four or more	as many as want
Total people	**0.3%**	**2.5%**	**48.4%**	**26.3%**	**12.0%**	**10.5%**
Millennial generation (18 to 33)	0.1	2.1	39.3	32.4	15.8	10.3
Generation X (34 to 45)	0.3	1.2	54.0	23.9	11.1	9.5
Baby Boom (46 to 64)	0.5	3.4	51.7	22.1	11.3	11.0
Older Americans (65 or older)	0.2	3.0	51.7	26.3	8.0	10.8

Source: Survey Documentation and Analysis, Computer-assisted Survey Methods Program, University of California, Berkeley, General Social Surveys, 1972–2010 Cumulative Data Files, Internet site http://sda.berkeley.edu/cgi-bin32/hsda?harcsda+gss10; calculations by New Strategist

Table 1.15 Spanking Children, 2010

"Do you strongly agree, agree, disagree, or strongly disagree that it is sometimes necessary to discipline a child with a good, hard, spanking?"

(percent of people aged 18 or older responding by generation, 2010)

	strongly agree	agree	disagree	strongly disagree
Total people	**23.6%**	**45.4%**	**23.5%**	**7.5%**
Millennial generation (18 to 33)	21.3	48.1	24.0	6.7
Generation X (34 to 45)	26.6	43.9	22.6	6.8
Baby Boom (46 to 64)	22.2	45.1	23.6	9.0
Older Americans (65 or older)	25.7	43.4	23.6	7.3

Source: Survey Documentation and Analysis, Computer-assisted Survey Methods Program, University of California, Berkeley, General Social Surveys, 1972–2010 Cumulative Data Files, Internet site http://sda.berkeley.edu/cgi-bin32/hsda?harcsda+gss10; calculations by New Strategist

Table 1.16 Better for Man to Work, Woman to Tend Home, 2010

"Do you strongly agree, agree, disagree, or strongly disagree with the statement: It is much better for everyone involved if the man is the achiever outside the home and the woman takes care of the home and family?"

(percent of people aged 18 or older responding by generation, 2010)

	agree			disagree		
	total	strongly agree	agree	total	disagree	strongly disagree
Total people	**35.4%**	**6.8%**	**28.6%**	**64.7%**	**43.5%**	**21.2%**
Millennial generation (18 to 33)	31.1	5.5	25.6	68.9	42.7	26.2
Generation X (34 to 45)	31.6	5.9	25.7	68.4	42.9	25.5
Baby Boom (46 to 64)	34.8	5.5	29.3	65.2	46.5	18.7
Older Americans (65 or older)	48.5	12.8	35.7	51.5	40.0	11.5

Source: Survey Documentation and Analysis, Computer-assisted Survey Methods Program, University of California, Berkeley, General Social Surveys, 1972–2010 Cumulative Data Files, Internet site http://sda.berkeley.edu/cgi-bin32/

Table 1.17 Working Mother's Relationship with Children, 2010

"Do you strongly agree, agree, disagree, or strongly disagree with the statement: A working mother can establish just as warm and secure a relationship with her children as a mother who does not work?"

(percent of people aged 18 or older responding by generation, 2010)

	agree			disagree		
	total	strongly agree	agree	total	disagree	strongly disagree
Total people	**74.7%**	**28.8%**	**45.9%**	**25.2%**	**20.1%**	**5.1%**
Millennial generation (18 to 33)	76.0	30.2	45.8	24.0	19.5	4.5
Generation X (34 to 45)	78.4	32.6	45.8	21.6	17.0	4.6
Baby Boom (46 to 64)	74.7	28.5	46.2	25.3	19.7	5.6
Older Americans (65 or older)	68.9	22.4	46.5	31.1	25.4	5.7

Source: Survey Documentation and Analysis, Computer-assisted Survey Methods Program, University of California, Berkeley, General Social Surveys, 1972–2010 Cumulative Data Files, Internet site http://sda.berkeley.edu/cgi-bin32/ hsda?harcsda+gss10; calculations by New Strategist

Table 1.18 Should Government Help the Sick, 2010

"Some people think that it is the responsibility of the government in Washington to see to it that people have help in paying for doctors and hospital bills; they are at point 1. Others think that these matters are not the responsibility of the federal government and that people should take care of these things themselves; they are at point 5. Where would you place yourself on this scale?"

(percent of people aged 18 or older responding by generation, 2010)

	1 government should help	2	3 agree with both	4	5 people should help themselves
Total people	**30.5%**	**16.4%**	**31.9%**	**11.1%**	**10.1%**
Millennial generation (18 to 33)	35.7	21.9	27.2	9.7	5.5
Generation X (34 to 45)	27.3	12.1	37.1	15.5	8.0
Baby Boom (46 to 64)	31.6	16.6	30.3	10.0	11.6
Older Americans (65 or older)	23.3	11.7	37.1	10.1	17.7

Source: Survey Documentation and Analysis, Computer-assisted Survey Methods Program, University of California, Berkeley, General Social Surveys, 1972–2010 Cumulative Data Files, Internet site http://sda.berkeley.edu/cgi-bin32/hsda?harcsda+gss10; calculations by New Strategist

Religious Diversity Is on the Rise

Share of Protestants dwindles with each successive generation.

Asked whether science makes our way of life change too fast, the 51 percent majority of Americans disagrees with the statement. Most Millennials, Gen Xers, and Boomers disagree. But among Americans aged 65 or older, the 56 percent majority agrees that things are changing too fast.

The 56 percent majority of Americans now believes in evolution, up from an even split in 2006. The majority in every generation believes in evolution, the proportion being highest among Millennials.

Among older Americans, 59 percent are Protestants. Among Baby Boomers, the figure is 53 percent. The figure falls to 44 percent among Generation Xers and to just 33 percent among Millennials. Conversely, the share of people with no religious preference climbs from a mere 9 percent among older Americans to a substantial 27 percent among Millennials. Older Americans are twice as likely as members of younger generations to describe themselves as very religious and they are more likely to see the Bible as the word of God.

The majority of Americans disapproves of the Supreme Court decision barring local governments from requiring religious readings in public schools. While the slight majority of Millennials and nearly half the Generation Xers support the decision, only 39 percent of Baby Boomers and just 37 percent of older Americans back the Supreme Court's decision.

■ Along with the growing racial and ethnic diversity of the American population, religious preferences are also growing more diverse.

Younger generations are less likely to be Protestant

(percent of people aged 18 or older whose religious preference is Protestant, by generation, 2010)

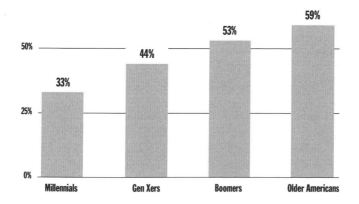

Table 1.19 Attitude toward Science, 2010

"Do you strongly agree, agree, disagree, or strongly disagree with the statement: Science makes our way of life change too fast?"

(percent of people aged 18 or older responding by generation, 2010)

	strongly agree	agree	disagree	strongly disagree
Total people	**7.2%**	**41.5%**	**43.2%**	**8.1%**
Millennial generation (18 to 33)	8.5	40.5	45.4	5.5
Generation X (34 to 45)	8.7	39.0	47.4	5.0
Baby Boom (46 to 64)	6.3	39.4	41.1	13.2
Older Americans (65 or older)	4.7	51.4	38.7	5.2

Source: Survey Documentation and Analysis, Computer-assisted Survey Methods Program, University of California, Berkeley, General Social Surveys, 1972–2010 Cumulative Data Files, Internet site http://sda.berkeley.edu/cgi-bin32/hsda?harcsda+gss10; calculations by New Strategist

Table 1.20 Attitude toward Evolution, 2010

"True or false: Human beings, as we know them today, developed from earlier species of animals?"

(percent of people aged 18 or older responding by generation, 2010)

	true	false
Total people	**55.7%**	**44.3%**
Millennial generation (18 to 33)	59.5	40.5
Generation X (34 to 45)	57.7	42.3
Baby Boom (46 to 64)	52.7	47.3
Older Americans (65 or older)	52.7	47.3

Source: Survey Documentation and Analysis, Computer-assisted Survey Methods Program, University of California, Berkeley, General Social Surveys, 1972–2010 Cumulative Data Files, Internet site http://sda.berkeley.edu/cgi-bin32/hsda?harcsda+gss10; calculations by New Strategist

Table 1.21 Religious Preference, 2010

"What is your religious preference?"

(percent of people aged 18 or older responding by generation, 2010)

	Protestant	Catholic	Jewish	none	other
Total people	**46.7%**	**25.2%**	**1.6%**	**17.8%**	**8.7%**
Millennial generation (18 to 33)	33.3	26.7	0.5	26.7	12.8
Generation X (34 to 45)	44.4	26.9	1.6	18.0	9.1
Baby Boom (46 to 64)	53.3	22.7	2.1	15.0	6.9
Older Americans (65 or older)	59.1	25.4	2.6	9.4	3.5

Source: Survey Documentation and Analysis, Computer-assisted Survey Methods Program, University of California, Berkeley, General Social Surveys, 1972–2010 Cumulative Data Files, Internet site http://sda.berkeley.edu/cgi-bin32/ hsda?harcsda+gss10; calculations by New Strategist

Table 1.22 Degree of Religiosity, 2010

"To what extent do you consider yourself a religious person?"

(percent of people aged 18 or older responding by generation, 2010)

	very religious	moderately relgious	slightly religious	not religious
Total people	**16.8%**	**41.5%**	**23.6%**	**18.1%**
Millennial generation (18 to 33)	10.8	35.8	27.8	25.6
Generation X (34 to 45)	15.0	41.0	25.9	18.1
Baby Boom (46 to 64)	20.1	42.0	22.3	15.6
Older Americans (65 or older)	22.2	51.0	16.1	10.7

Source: Survey Documentation and Analysis, Computer-assisted Survey Methods Program, University of California, Berkeley, General Social Surveys, 1972–2010 Cumulative Data Files, Internet site http://sda.berkeley.edu/cgi-bin32/ hsda?harcsda+gss10; calculations by New Strategist

Table 1.23 Belief in the Bible, 2010

"Which of these statements comes closest to describing your feelings about the Bible? 1) The Bible is the actual word of God and is to be taken literally, word for word; 2) The Bible is the inspired word of God but not everything in it should be taken literally, word for word; 3) The Bible is an ancient book of fables, legends, history, and moral precepts recorded by men."

(percent of people aged 18 or older responding by generation, 2010)

	word of God	inspired word	book of fables	other
Total people	**34.1%**	**43.6%**	**20.6%**	**1.7%**
Millennial generation (18 to 33)	30.7	44.3	23.3	1.7
Generation X (34 to 45)	31.8	45.6	21.3	1.3
Baby Boom (46 to 64)	35.3	42.7	19.9	2.1
Older Americans (65 or older)	39.9	42.0	16.5	1.6

Source: Survey Documentation and Analysis, Computer-assisted Survey Methods Program, University of California, Berkeley, General Social Surveys, 1972–2010 Cumulative Data Files, Internet site http://sda.berkeley.edu/cgi-bin32/hsda?harcsda+gss10; calculations by New Strategist

Table 1.24 Bible in the Public Schools, 2010

"The United States Supreme Court has ruled that no state or local government may require the reading of the Lord's Prayer or Bible verses in public schools. What are your views on this? Do you approve or disapprove of the court ruling?"

(percent of people aged 18 or older responding by generation, 2010)

	approve	disapprove
Total people	**44.1%**	**55.9%**
Millennial generation (18 to 33)	52.4	47.6
Generation X (34 to 45)	47.0	53.0
Baby Boom (46 to 64)	39.1	60.9
Older Americans (65 or older)	37.0	63.0

Source: Survey Documentation and Analysis, Computer-assisted Survey Methods Program, University of California, Berkeley, General Social Surveys, 1972–2010 Cumulative Data Files, Internet site http://sda.berkeley.edu/cgi-bin32/hsda?harcsda+gss10; calculations by New Strategist

Growing Tolerance of Sexual Behavior

Americans are more accepting of homosexuality.

The share of Americans who believe premarital sex is not wrong at all grew from 42 percent in 2000 to 53 percent in 2010. While the majority of Boomers and younger generations see nothing wrong with premarital sex, the share is just 37 percent among older Americans.

When it comes to sexual relations between adults of the same sex, the trend of growing tolerance is apparent as well. Each successive generation is less likely to condemn homosexuality. The 54 percent majority of Millennials sees nothing wrong with same-sex sexual relations, but support dwindles to 43 percent among Xers, 39 percent among Boomers, and a mere 30 percent among older Americans. Millennials are the only generation in which the majority (62 percent) believes gays and lesbians should have the right to marry.

■ Acceptance of gays and lesbians will grow as tolerant Millennials replace older, less tolerant generations in the population.

Most Millennials support gay marriage

(percent of people aged 18 or older who think gays and lesbians should have the right to marry, by generation, 2010)

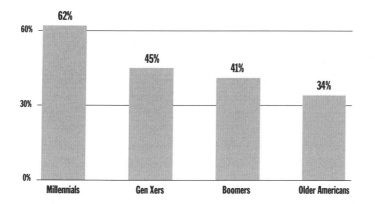

Table 1.25 Premarital Sex, 2010

"If a man and woman have sex relations before marriage,
do you think it is always wrong, almost always wrong,
wrong only sometimes, or not wrong at all?"

(percent of people aged 18 or older responding by generation, 2010)

	always wrong	almost always wrong	sometimes wrong	not wrong at all
Total people	**21.3%**	**7.8%**	**17.8%**	**53.1%**
Millennial generation (18 to 33)	15.0	5.3	20.1	59.6
Generation X (34 to 45)	16.7	8.5	17.9	56.8
Baby Boom (46 to 64)	25.0	5.3	16.4	53.4
Older Americans (65 or older)	30.9	15.7	16.5	36.9

Source: Survey Documentation and Analysis, Computer-assisted Survey Methods Program, University of California, Berkeley, General Social Surveys, 1972–2010 Cumulative Data Files, Internet site http://sda.berkeley.edu/cgi-bin32/hsda?harcsda+gss10; calculations by New Strategist

Table 1.26 Homosexual Relations, 2010

"What about sexual relations between two adults of the same sex?"

(percent of people aged 18 or older responding by generation, 2010)

	always wrong	almost always wrong	sometimes wrong	not wrong at all
Total people	**45.7%**	**3.7%**	**7.9%**	**42.7%**
Millennial generation (18 to 33)	29.6	4.6	11.5	54.3
Generation X (34 to 45)	48.1	2.5	6.1	43.3
Baby Boom (46 to 64)	50.4	3.0	7.2	39.4
Older Americans (65 or older)	58.5	5.4	6.0	30.1

Source: Survey Documentation and Analysis, Computer-assisted Survey Methods Program, University of California, Berkeley, General Social Surveys, 1972–2010 Cumulative Data Files, Internet site http://sda.berkeley.edu/cgi-bin32/hsda?harcsda+gss10; calculations by New Strategist

Table 1.27 Gay Marriage, 2010

"Do you agree or disagree: Homosexual couples should have the right to marry one another?"

(percent of people aged 18 or older responding by generation, 2010)

| | agree | | | | disagree | | |
	total	strongly agree	agree	neither	total	disagree	strongly disagree
Total people	**46.5%**	**21.1%**	**25.4%**	**12.8%**	**40.7%**	**15.6%**	**25.1%**
Millennial generation (18 to 33)	62.2	30.8	31.4	19.7	18.0	10.2	7.8
Generation X (34 to 45)	45.0	20.7	24.3	13.6	41.4	14.2	27.2
Baby Boom (46 to 64)	41.1	17.1	24.0	7.6	51.3	17.3	34.0
Older Americans (65 or older)	34.4	14.5	19.9	11.8	53.8	22.7	31.1

Source: Survey Documentation and Analysis, Computer-assisted Survey Methods Program, University of California, Berkeley, General Social Surveys, 1972–2010 Cumulative Data Files, Internet site http://sda.berkeley.edu/cgi-bin32/ hsda?harcsda+gss10; calculations by New Strategist

Television News Is Most Important

The Internet ranks second in importance.

Nearly half of Americans get most of their news from television, 22 percent from the Internet, and 18 percent from newspapers. Together these three news outlets are the main source of news for 88 percent of the public. But there are big differences by generation. Millennials and Gen Xers are far more likely than older generations to depend on the Internet. Twenty-eight percent of Millennials and 33 percent of Gen Xers say the Internet is their most important source of news. This compares with 20 percent of Boomers and just 2 percent of older Americans. Millennials and Gen Xers are more likely to get their news from radio than newspapers.

When asked about their political leanings, the largest share of Americans likes to point to the moderate middle (38 percent). A smaller 29 percent say they are liberal, and 34 percent identify themselves as conservative. Millennials are the only generation in which liberals outnumber conservatives (31 versus 27 percent). An examination of Americans by political party identification shows that self-identified Democrats far outnumber Republicans (46 versus 33 percent). This is the case in every generation.

■ Television remains the primary source of news for every generation of Americans.

News sources differ dramatically by generation

(percent of people aged 18 or older who identify medium as their primary source for news, by generation, 2010)

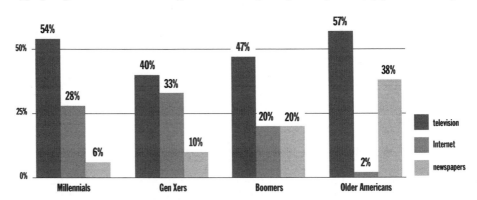

Table 1.28 Main Source of Information about Events in the News, 2010

"We are interested in how people get information about events in the news. Where do you get most of your information about current news events?"

(percent of people aged 18 or older responding by generation, 2010)

	television	Internet	newspapers	radio	family, friends, colleagues	books, magazines, other
Total people	**49.1%**	**21.6%**	**17.7%**	**7.7%**	**2.2%**	**1.7%**
Millennial generation (18 to 33)	54.3	28.3	5.7	8.4	3.3	0.0
Generation X (34 to 45)	40.2	33.5	9.8	12.2	2.9	1.4
Baby Boom (46 to 64)	47.2	19.7	20.2	6.7	2.2	4.0
Older Americans (65 or older)	56.7	1.8	38.4	3.2	0.0	0.0

Source: Survey Documentation and Analysis, Computer-assisted Survey Methods Program, University of California, Berkeley, General Social Surveys, 1972–2010 Cumulative Data Files, Internet site http://sda.berkeley.edu/cgi-bin32/ hsda?harcsda+gss10; calculations by New Strategist

Table 1.29 Political Leanings, 2010

"We hear a lot of talk these days about liberals and conservatives. On a seven-point scale from extremely liberal (1) to extremely conservative (7), where would you place yourself?"

(percent of people aged 18 or older responding by generation, 2010)

	1 extremely liberal	2 liberal	3 slightly liberal	4 moderate	5 slightly conservative	6 conservative	7 extremely conservative
Total people	**3.8%**	**12.9%**	**11.9%**	**37.6%**	**12.8%**	**16.6%**	**4.4%**
Millennial generation (18 to 33)	4.0	15.7	11.1	42.0	11.5	13.2	2.6
Generation X (34 to 45)	1.4	14.6	12.7	37.1	13.8	15.0	5.5
Baby Boom (46 to 64)	4.6	10.4	11.9	37.3	12.5	18.0	5.2
Older Americans (65 or older)	4.8	10.8	12.2	31.8	14.4	21.6	4.4

Source: Survey Documentation and Analysis, Computer-assisted Survey Methods Program, University of California, Berkeley, General Social Surveys, 1972–2010 Cumulative Data Files, Internet site http://sda.berkeley.edu/cgi-bin32/ hsda?harcsda+gss10; calculations by New Strategist

Table 1.30 Political Party Affiliation, 2010

"Generally speaking, do you usually think of yourself as a Republican, Democrat, independent, or what?"

(percent of people aged 18 or older responding by generation, 2010)

	strong Democrat	not strong Democrat	independent, near Democrat	independent	independent, near Republican	not strong Republican	strong Republican	other
Total people	**16.5%**	**15.7%**	**13.5%**	**18.8%**	**10.0%**	**13.4%**	**9.6%**	**2.6%**
Millennial generation (18 to 33)	12.1	18.2	15.3	23.9	10.3	12.1	5.1	3.1
Generation X (34 to 45)	13.1	15.9	13.6	19.5	10.0	15.1	9.4	3.3
Baby Boom (46 to 64)	17.7	13.2	14.6	16.7	10.0	13.4	12.2	2.3
Older Americans (65 or older)	25.3	16.3	8.0	13.4	9.7	13.2	12.2	1.8

Source: Survey Documentation and Analysis, Computer-assisted Survey Methods Program, University of California, Berkeley, General Social Surveys, 1972–2010 Cumulative Data Files, Internet site http://sda.berkeley.edu/cgi-bin32/ hsda?harcsda+gss10; calculations by New Strategist

Most Support Abortion if a Mother's Health Is Endangered

The majority of Millennials and Boomers favor legalizing marijuana.

Although opposition to capital punishment has grown slightly over the past decade, the great majority still supports the death penalty. In 2000, 30 percent of the public opposed the death penalty for persons convicted of murder. In 2010, the figure had increased slightly to 32 percent. The majority in every generation favors the death penalty.

Most Americans support requiring a permit for gun ownership, and there is little variation by generation. Nearly half the public supports legalizing marijuana—48 percent are for it and 52 percent are against it. More than 50 percent of Millennials and Boomers want to legalize marijuana compared with 43 percent of Gen Xers and 32 percent of older Americans.

Support for legal abortion under certain circumstances is overwhelming. Nearly 9 out of 10 Americans want abortion to be legal if a women's health is in serious danger, and three-quarters want it legal if a pregnancy is the result of rape or there is a chance of serious defect in the baby. Economic and lifestyle reasons garner substantially lower approval ratings.

The two-thirds majority of Americans favor the right of the terminally ill to die with a doctor's assistance. Support is strongest in the younger generations and weakest among Boomers and older Americans.

■ Attitudinal differences between older and younger generations have become more complex, with Gen Xers standing apart on some issues such as the legalization of marijuana.

Fewer than half of Americans in every generation favor allowing abortion for any reason

(percent of people aged 18 or older who favor legal abortion for any reason, by generation, 2010)

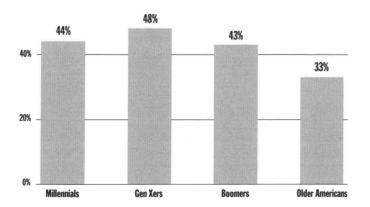

Table 1.31 Favor or Oppose Death Penalty for Murder, 2010

"Do you favor or oppose the death penalty for persons convicted of murder?"

(percent of people aged 18 or older responding by generation, 2010)

	favor	oppose
Total people	**67.8%**	**32.2%**
Millennial generation (18 to 33)	63.6	36.4
Generation X (34 to 45)	69.5	30.5
Baby Boom (46 to 64)	69.2	30.8
Older Americans (65 or older)	70.3	29.7

Source: Survey Documentation and Analysis, Computer-assisted Survey Methods Program, University of California, Berkeley, General Social Surveys, 1972–2010 Cumulative Data Files, Internet site http://sda.berkeley.edu/cgi-bin32/hsda?harcsda+gss10; calculations by New Strategist

Table 1.32 Favor or Oppose Gun Permits, 2010

"Would you favor or oppose a law which would require a person to obtain a police permit before he or she could buy a gun?"

(percent of people aged 18 or older responding by generation, 2010)

	favor	oppose
Total people	**74.3%**	**25.7%**
Millennial generation (18 to 33)	76.4	23.6
Generation X (34 to 45)	68.8	31.2
Baby Boom (46 to 64)	73.8	26.2
Older Americans (65 or older)	79.4	20.6

Source: Survey Documentation and Analysis, Computer-assisted Survey Methods Program, University of California, Berkeley, General Social Surveys, 1972–2010 Cumulative Data Files, Internet site http://sda.berkeley.edu/cgi-bin32/hsda?harcsda+gss10; calculations by New Strategist

Table 1.33 Legalization of Marijuana, 2010

"Do you think the use of marijuana should be made legal or not?"

(percent of people aged 18 or older responding by generation, 2010)

	made legal	not legal
Total people	**48.4%**	**51.6%**
Millennial generation (18 to 33)	55.6	44.4
Generation X (34 to 45)	43.5	56.5
Baby Boom (46 to 64)	53.9	46.1
Older Americans (65 or older)	31.9	68.1

Source: Survey Documentation and Analysis, Computer-assisted Survey Methods Program, University of California, Berkeley, General Social Surveys, 1972–2010 Cumulative Data Files, Internet site http://sda.berkeley.edu/cgi-bin32/hsda?harcsda+gss10; calculations by New Strategist

Table 1.34 Support for Legal Abortion by Reason, 2010

"Please tell me whether or not you think it should be possible
for a pregnant woman to obtain a legal abortion if..."

(percent of people aged 18 or older responding by generation, 2010)

	her health is seriously endangered	pregnancy is the result of rape	there is a serious defect in the baby	she cannot afford more children	she does not want more children	she is single and does not want to marry the man	she wants it for any reason
Total people	**86.4%**	**79.1%**	**73.9%**	**47.7%**	**44.9%**	**41.9%**	**42.9%**
Millennial generation (18 to 33)	84.7	82.3	70.9	44.2	47.3	41.2	44.4
Generation X (34 to 45)	86.4	80.9	74.1	46.2	52.1	46.6	48.2
Baby Boom (46 to 64)	87.7	75.7	74.0	46.7	50.0	44.1	42.6
Older Americans (65 or older)	86.2	78.6	78.2	39.5	36.7	31.0	33.4

Source: Survey Documentation and Analysis, Computer-assisted Survey Methods Program, University of California, Berkeley, General Social Surveys, 1972–2010 Cumulative Data Files, Internet site http://sda.berkeley.edu/cgi-bin32/hsda?harcsda+gss10; calculations by New Strategist

Table 1.35 Doctor-Assisted Suicide, 2010

"When a person has a disease that cannot be cured, do you think doctors should be allowed by law to end the patient's life by some painless means if the patient and his family request it?"

(percent of people aged 18 or older responding by generation, 2010)

	yes	no
Total people	**68.4%**	**31.6%**
Millennial generation (18 to 33)	71.5	28.5
Generation X (34 to 45)	73.0	27.0
Baby Boom (46 to 64)	64.6	35.4
Older Americans (65 or older)	64.9	35.1

Source: Survey Documentation and Analysis, Computer-assisted Survey Methods Program, University of California, Berkeley, General Social Surveys, 1972–2010 Cumulative Data Files, Internet site http://sda.berkeley.edu/cgi-bin32/ hsda?harcsda+gss10; calculations by New Strategist

2

Education

■ The percentage of Americans with a college degree peaks among Generation Xers and Millennials. One-third of people aged 35 to 44 have a bachelor's degree or more education, which makes them one of the best educated generations.

■ The women of Generation X are better educated than their male counterparts. Thirty-four percent of women aged 35 to 44 have at least a bachelor's degree. Among men in the age group, 32 percent are college graduates.

■ Among Gen Xers, Asians are by far the best educated. Nearly two-thirds of Asian men aged 35 to 44 have a bachelor's degree. In contrast, only 62 percent of Hispanic men in the age group have even graduated from high school.

■ People aged 35 to 44 account for only 7 percent of the nation's undergraduates, but they are 16 percent of graduate students.

Generation X Is Highly Educated

Boomers are in third place among the generations.

The percentage of Americans with a college degree peaks among Generation Xers (aged 34 to 45 in 2010). Just over 33 percent of people aged 35 to 44 have a bachelor's degree or more education, which makes them the best educated among the generations. Millennials are not far behind, at 32.8 percent. Boomers were once the best-educated generation, but younger adults have surpassed them. Thirty percent of Boomers have at least a bachelor's degree. Among Americans aged 65 or older, only 23 percent are college graduates.

Although Generation X is better educated than Boomers overall, the oldest Boomer men are better educated than the men of Generation X. Among Boomer men aged 60 to 64, for example, 37 percent have a bachelor's degree—thanks in part to draft deferments offered to college students during the Vietnam War. Among the men of Generation X, only 32 percent have a bachelor's degree.

■ The women of Generation X are better educated than Boomer women, pushing the percentage of Generation Xers with a college degree above that of Boomers.

Generation X is better educated than Boomers

(percent of people aged 25 or older with a bachelor's degree, by age and generation, 2010)

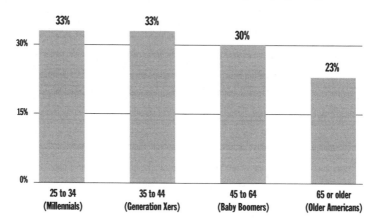

Table 2.1 Educational Attainment by Generation, 2010

(number and percent distribution of people aged 25 or older by highest level of education, by generation, 2010; numbers in thousands)

	total 25 or older	Millennials (25 to 34)	Generation X (35 to 44)	Boomers (45 to 64)	Older Americans (65 or older)
Total people	**199,928**	**41,085**	**40,447**	**79,782**	**38,613**
Not a high school graduate	25,711	4,763	4,715	8,316	7,917
High school graduate	62,456	11,186	11,582	25,632	14,057
Some college, no degree	33,662	7,752	6,593	13,569	5,748
Associate's degree	18,259	3,903	4,180	7,975	2,201
Bachelor's degree	38,784	9,840	8,857	15,022	5,066
Master's degree	15,203	2,773	3,298	6,730	2,402
Professional degree	3,074	494	649	1,297	635
Doctoral degree	2,779	373	575	1,243	588
High school graduate or more	174,217	36,321	35,734	71,468	30,697
Some college or more	111,761	25,135	24,152	45,836	16,640
Associate's degree or more	78,099	17,383	17,559	32,267	10,892
Bachelor's degree or more	59,840	13,480	13,379	24,292	8,691
Total people	**100.0%**	**100.0%**	**100.0%**	**100.0%**	**100.0%**
Not a high school graduate	12.9	11.6	11.7	10.4	20.5
High school graduate	31.2	27.2	28.6	32.1	36.4
Some college, no degree	16.8	18.9	16.3	17.0	14.9
Associate's degree	9.1	9.5	10.3	10.0	5.7
Bachelor's degree	19.4	24.0	21.9	18.8	13.1
Master's degree	7.6	6.7	8.2	8.4	6.2
Professional degree	1.5	1.2	1.6	1.6	1.6
Doctoral degree	1.4	0.9	1.4	1.6	1.5
High school graduate or more	87.1	88.4	88.3	89.6	79.5
Some college or more	55.9	61.2	59.7	57.5	43.1
Associate's degree or more	39.1	42.3	43.4	40.4	28.2
Bachelor's degree or more	29.9	32.8	33.1	30.4	22.5

Source: Bureau of the Census, Educational Attainment in the United States: 2010, detailed tables, Internet site http://www .census.gov/hhes/socdemo/education/data/cps/2010/tables.html; calculations by New Strategist

Most Gen Xers Have Been to College

One-third are college graduates.

Generation X followed the Baby-Boom generation onto the nation's college campuses. Overall, the 60 percent majority of Gen Xers have been to college—16 percent have college experience but no degree, 10 percent have an associate's degree, 22 percent have a bachelor's degree, and 11 percent have a graduate degree.

Although Generation X is better educated than Boomers, the oldest Boomer men are better educated than Generation X men. Among Boomer men aged 60 to 64, for example, 37 percent have a bachelor's degree—thanks in part to draft deferments offered to college students during the Vietnam War. Among the men of Generation X, only 32 percent have a bachelor's degree. In contrast, Gen X women are better educated than Boomer women. Thirty-four percent of Gen X women have at least a bachelor's degree versus 30 percent of Baby-Boom women.

■ Because most Gen Xers have college experience, they will be eager to see their children go to college as well.

Among Generation Xers, more than one in 10 have a graduate degree

(percent distribution of people aged 35 to 44 by educational attainment, 2010)

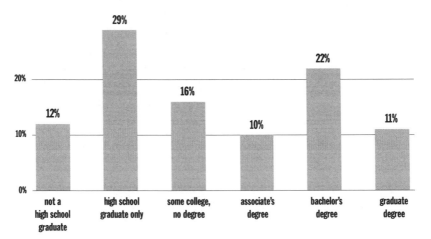

Table 2.2 Educational Attainment of Generation Xers, 2010

(number and percent distribution of people aged 25 or older, aged 35 to 44, and aged 35 to 44 in five-year age groups, by highest level of education, 2010; numbers in thousands)

		aged 35 to 44		
	total 25 or older	total	35 to 39	40 to 44
Total people	**199,928**	**40,447**	**19,888**	**20,559**
Not a high school graduate	25,711	4,715	2,336	2,378
High school graduate	62,456	11,582	5,361	6,220
Some college, no degree	33,662	6,593	3,328	3,265
Associate's degree	18,259	4,180	2,063	2,116
Bachelor's degree	38,784	8,857	4,521	4,336
Master's degree	15,203	3,298	1,662	1,636
Professional degree	3,074	649	330	319
Doctoral degree	2,779	575	286	288
High school graduate or more	174,217	35,734	17,551	18,180
Some college or more	111,761	24,152	12,190	11,960
Associate's degree or more	78,099	17,559	8,862	8,695
Bachelor's degree or more	59,840	13,379	6,799	6,579
Total people	**100.0%**	**100.0%**	**100.0%**	**100.0%**
Not a high school graduate	12.9	11.7	11.7	11.6
High school graduate	31.2	28.6	27.0	30.3
Some college, no degree	16.8	16.3	16.7	15.9
Associate's degree	9.1	10.3	10.4	10.3
Bachelor's degree	19.4	21.9	22.7	21.1
Master's degree	7.6	8.2	8.4	8.0
Professional degree	1.5	1.6	1.7	1.6
Doctoral degree	1.4	1.4	1.4	1.4
High school graduate or more	87.1	88.3	88.2	88.4
Some college or more	55.9	59.7	61.3	58.2
Associate's degree or more	39.1	43.4	44.6	42.3
Bachelor's degree or more	29.9	33.1	34.2	32.0

Source: Bureau of the Census, Educational Attainment in the United States: 2010, detailed tables, Internet site http://www .census.gov/hhes/socdemo/education/data/cps/2010/tables.html; calculations by New Strategist

Nearly 32 Percent of Gen X Men Are College Graduates

Some of those still without a college degree will get one later in life.

The men of Generation X are well educated, although not as highly educated as Baby-Boom men. Eighty-seven percent of men aged 35 to 44 are high school graduates, which means 13 percent do not have a high school diploma. These men will have a difficult time making ends meet in an economy that rewards the well educated.

Fifty-six percent of men aged 35 to 44 have attended college. Thirty-two percent have at least a bachelor's degree—meaning many men who start college drop out before getting their degree. Some are likely to return to school as older students to complete their education.

■ Most men are aware of the importance of education for their career. Even if they do not obtain a college degree, attending college for a year or two is likely to boost their earnings.

Most men aged 35 to 44 have at least some college experience

(percent distribution of men aged 35 to 44 by educational attainment, 2010)

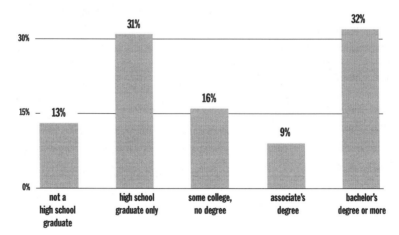

Table 2.3 Educational Attainment of Generation X Men, 2010

(number and percent distribution of men aged 25 or older, aged 35 to 44, and aged 35 to 44 in five-year age groups, by highest level of education, 2010; numbers in thousands)

		aged 35 to 44		
	total 25 or older	total	35 to 39	40 to 44
Total men	**96,325**	**20,074**	**9,902**	**10,172**
Not a high school graduate	12,914	2,566	1,268	1,298
High school graduate	30,682	6,269	2,983	3,286
Some college, no degree	15,908	3,117	1,611	1,506
Associate's degree	7,662	1,729	861	868
Bachelor's degree	18,674	4,262	2,145	2,117
Master's degree	6,859	1,470	703	767
Professional degree	1,861	311	159	152
Doctoral degree	1,763	351	172	179
High school graduate or more	83,409	17,509	8,634	8,875
Some college or more	52,727	11,240	5,651	5,589
Associate's degree or more	36,819	8,123	4,040	4,083
Bachelor's degree or more	29,157	6,394	3,179	3,215
Total men	**100.0%**	**100.0%**	**100.0%**	**100.0%**
Not a high school graduate	13.4	12.8	12.8	12.8
High school graduate	31.9	31.2	30.1	32.3
Some college, no degree	16.5	15.5	16.3	14.8
Associate's degree	8.0	8.6	8.7	8.5
Bachelor's degree	19.4	21.2	21.7	20.8
Master's degree	7.1	7.3	7.1	7.5
Professional degree	1.9	1.5	1.6	1.5
Doctoral degree	1.8	1.7	1.7	1.8
High school graduate or more	86.6	87.2	87.2	87.2
Some college or more	54.7	56.0	57.1	54.9
Associate's degree or more	38.2	40.5	40.8	40.1
Bachelor's degree or more	30.3	31.9	32.1	31.6

Source: Bureau of the Census, Educational Attainment in the United States: 2010, detailed tables, Internet site http://www .census.gov/hhes/socdemo/education/data/cps/2010/tables.html; calculations by New Strategist

Gen X Women Are Better Educated than Gen X Men

They are more likely to have attended and completed college.

As educational opportunities for women broadened over the years, increasing numbers of women took advantage of them. Women aged 35 to 44 are better educated than their male counterparts.

The women of Generation X, in fact, are some of the best-educated people in the nation. Fully 36 percent of women aged 35 to 39 have at least a bachelor's degree, and 65 percent have college experience. Among men aged 35 to 39, a smaller 32 percent have at least a bachelor's degree while 57 percent have college experience.

The higher educational attainment of Baby-Boom and younger women is the driving factor behind the changing role of women in society. Having been better educated than their forebears, today's women expect to work and are eager to advance in their careers.

■ With women being better educated than men among Gen Xers, the earnings gap between men and women in the generation should become much smaller.

Most women aged 35 to 44 have at least some college experience

(percent distribution of women aged 35 to 44 by educational attainment, 2010)

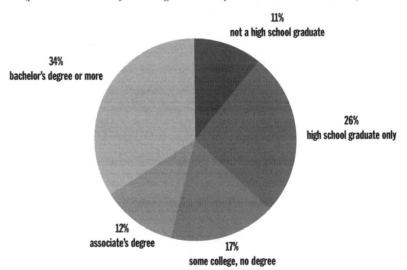

11%
not a high school graduate

34%
bachelor's degree or more

26%
high school graduate only

12%
associate's degree

17%
some college, no degree

Table 2.4 Educational Attainment of Generation X Women, 2010

(number and percent distribution of women aged 25 or older, aged 35 to 44, and aged 35 to 44 in five-year age groups, by highest level of education, 2010; numbers in thousands)

		aged 35 to 44		
	total 25 or older	total	35 to 39	40 to 44
Total women	**103,603**	**20,373**	**9,986**	**10,387**
Not a high school graduate	12,797	2,147	1,067	1,080
High school graduate	31,774	5,313	2,378	2,935
Some college, no degree	17,753	3,476	1,717	1,759
Associate's degree	10,597	2,451	1,203	1,248
Bachelor's degree	20,110	4,595	2,376	2,219
Master's degree	8,344	1,827	958	869
Professional degree	1,213	338	171	167
Doctoral degree	1,015	224	115	109
High school graduate or more	90,806	18,224	8,918	9,306
Some college or more	59,032	12,911	6,540	6,371
Associate's degree or more	41,279	9,435	4,823	4,612
Bachelor's degree or more	30,682	6,984	3,620	3,364
Total women	**100.0%**	**100.0%**	**100.0%**	**100.0%**
Not a high school graduate	12.4	10.5	10.7	10.4
High school graduate	30.7	26.1	23.8	28.3
Some college, no degree	17.1	17.1	17.2	16.9
Associate's degree	10.2	12.0	12.0	12.0
Bachelor's degree	19.4	22.6	23.8	21.4
Master's degree	8.1	9.0	9.6	8.4
Professional degree	1.2	1.7	1.7	1.6
Doctoral degree	1.0	1.1	1.2	1.0
High school graduate or more	87.6	89.5	89.3	89.6
Some college or more	57.0	63.4	65.5	61.3
Associate's degree or more	39.8	46.3	48.3	44.4
Bachelor's degree or more	29.6	34.3	36.3	32.4

Source: Bureau of the Census, Educational Attainment in the United States: 2010, detailed tables, Internet site http://www .census.gov/hhes/socdemo/education/data/cps/2010/tables.html; calculations by New Strategist

Among Gen Xers, Asian Men Have the Highest Educational Attainment

Hispanics are least likely to have completed high school or college.

There are substantial socioeconomic differences among Americans by race and Hispanic origin. Differences in educational attainment are the primary reason for the disparity.

Among Gen X men, Asians are by far the best educated. Fully 77 percent of Asian men aged 35 to 44 have college experience and nearly two-thirds have at least a bachelor's degree. Among non-Hispanic white men in the age group, 63 percent have college experience and 37 percent have a bachelor's degree.

Hispanics are the least educated. Only 62 percent of Hispanic men aged 35 to 44 have even graduated from high school. Just 13 percent have a bachelor's degree. Black Gen X men are much better educated than Hispanics. Forty-nine percent have college experience, and 21 percent have a bachelor's degree.

■ The educational attainment of Hispanics is low because many are recent immigrants from countries with little educational opportunity.

Education gaps point to continued socioeconomic differences

(percent of men aged 35 to 44 with a bachelor's degree or more, by race and Hispanic origin, 2010)

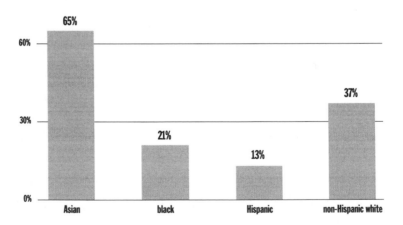

Table 2.5 Educational Attainment of Generation X Men by Race and Hispanic Origin, 2010

(number and percent distribution of men aged 35 to 44 by educational attainment, race, and Hispanic origin, 2010; numbers in thousands)

	total	Asian	black	Hispanic	non-Hispanic white
Total men aged 35 to 44	**20,074**	**1,169**	**2,348**	**3,750**	**12,621**
Not a high school graduate	2,566	80	206	1,428	846
High school graduate only	6,269	190	993	1,193	3,814
Some college, no degree	3,117	96	440	415	2,100
Associate's degree	1,729	46	223	214	1,234
Bachelor's degree	4,262	396	359	366	3,124
Master's degree	1,470	243	108	101	1,015
Professional degree	311	38	15	6	254
Doctoral degree	351	80	5	28	234
High school graduate or more	17,509	1,089	2,143	2,323	11,775
Some college or more	11,240	899	1,150	1,130	7,961
Associate's degree or more	8,123	803	710	715	5,861
Bachelor's degree or more	6,394	757	487	501	4,627
Total men aged 35 to 44	**100.0%**	**100.0%**	**100.0%**	**100.0%**	**100.0%**
Not a high school graduate	12.8	6.8	8.8	38.1	6.7
High school graduate only	31.2	16.3	42.3	31.8	30.2
Some college, no degree	15.5	8.2	18.7	11.1	16.6
Associate's degree	8.6	3.9	9.5	5.7	9.8
Bachelor's degree	21.2	33.9	15.3	9.8	24.8
Master's degree	7.3	20.8	4.6	2.7	8.0
Professional degree	1.5	3.3	0.6	0.2	2.0
Doctoral degree	1.7	6.8	0.2	0.7	1.9
High school graduate or more	87.2	93.2	91.3	61.9	93.3
Some college or more	56.0	76.9	49.0	30.1	63.1
Associate's degree or more	40.5	68.7	30.2	19.1	46.4
Bachelor's degree or more	31.9	64.8	20.7	13.4	36.7

Note: Asians and blacks are those who identify themselves as being of the race alone and those who identify themselves as being of the race in combination with other races. Non-Hispanic whites are those who identify themselves as being white alone and not Hispanic. Numbers do not add to total because not all races are shown and Hispanics may be of any race.
Source: Bureau of the Census, Educational Attainment in the United States: 2010, detailed tables, Internet site http://www .census.gov/hhes/socdemo/education/data/cps/2010/tables.html; calculations by New Strategist

Among Women, Hispanics Are Least Likely to Be High School Graduates

Asians are most likely to be college graduates.

Although the educational attainment of women has been rising for decades, substantial gaps persist among Gen Xers by race and Hispanic origin. From 88 to 95 percent of Asian, black, and non-Hispanic white women aged 35 to 44 have graduated from high school versus only 67 percent of Hispanic women in the age group. The majority of Asian, black, and non-Hispanic white women have college experience compared with only 38 percent of their Hispanic counterparts.

Among Gen X women, Asians are the best educated. Fully 55 percent have at least a bachelor's degree. Among non-Hispanic white women in the age group, the proportion is 39 percent. Twenty-four percent of black women aged 35 to 44 have a bachelor's degree, while the figure is just 16 percent for Hispanics.

■ The educational attainment of Hispanics will remain low as long as immigrants are a large share of the Hispanic population.

Among Gen X women, Asians have the highest educational attainment

(percent of women aged 35 to 44 with a bachelor's degree or more, by race and Hispanic origin, 2010)

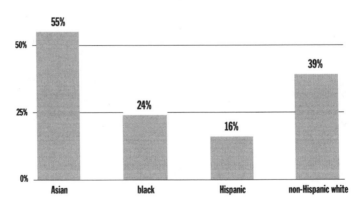

Table 2.6 Educational Attainment of Generation X Women by Race and Hispanic Origin, 2010

(number and percent distribution of women aged 35 to 44 by educational attainment, race, and Hispanic origin, 2010; numbers in thousands)

	total	Asian	black	Hispanic	non-Hispanic white
Total women aged 35 to 44	**20,373**	**1,301**	**2,902**	**3,318**	**12,716**
Not a high school graduate	2,147	114	352	1,095	603
High school graduate only	5,313	234	853	956	3,220
Some college, no degree	3,476	115	638	469	2,216
Associate's degree	2,451	117	355	260	1,690
Bachelor's degree	4,595	439	497	387	3,243
Master's degree	1,827	206	168	115	1,333
Professional degree	338	45	26	20	245
Doctoral degree	224	32	10	16	163
High school graduate or more	18,224	1,188	2,547	2,223	12,110
Some college or more	12,911	954	1,694	1,267	8,890
Associate's degree or more	9,435	839	1,056	798	6,674
Bachelor's degree or more	6,984	722	701	538	4,984
Total women aged 35 to 44	**100.0%**	**100.0%**	**100.0%**	**100.0%**	**100.0%**
Not a high school graduate	10.5	8.8	12.1	33.0	4.7
High school graduate only	26.1	18.0	29.4	28.8	25.3
Some college, no degree	17.1	8.8	22.0	14.1	17.4
Associate's degree	12.0	9.0	12.2	7.8	13.3
Bachelor's degree	22.6	33.7	17.1	11.7	25.5
Master's degree	9.0	15.8	5.8	3.5	10.5
Professional degree	1.7	3.5	0.9	0.6	1.9
Doctoral degree	1.1	2.5	0.3	0.5	1.3
High school graduate or more	89.5	91.3	87.8	67.0	95.2
Some college or more	63.4	73.3	58.4	38.2	69.9
Associate's degree or more	46.3	64.5	36.4	24.1	52.5
Bachelor's degree or more	34.3	55.5	24.2	16.2	39.2

Note: Asians and blacks are those who identify themselves as being of the race alone and those who identify themselves as being of the race in combination with other races. Non-Hispanic whites are those who identify themselves as being white alone and not Hispanic. Numbers do not add to total because not all races are shown and Hispanics may be of any race.
Source: Bureau of the Census, Educational Attainment in the United States: 2010, detailed tables, Internet site http://www
.census.gov/hhes/socdemo/education/data/cps/2010/tables.html; calculations by New Strategist

Some Gen Xers Are Still in School

Nearly 2 million people aged 35 to 44 are students.

School is a major part of life for many people in their twenties and early thirties. But taking classes becomes much less common in the 35-to-44 age group. In 2010, just 5 percent of 35-to-44-year-olds were in school.

Because women are more likely to go to college than men, a larger proportion of women than men are enrolled in school. Six percent of women aged 35 to 44 are students compared with 3 percent of men.

■ Among students aged 35 to 44, women outnumber men by more than 500,000.

Among 35-to-44-year-olds, women outnumber men in school

(number of people aged 35 to 44 enrolled in school, by sex, 2010)

Table 2.7 School Enrollment by Sex and Age, 2010

(total number of people aged 3 or older, and number and percent enrolled in school by sex and age, 2010; numbers in thousands)

		enrolled	
	total	number	percent
Total people	**292,233**	**78,519**	**26.9%**
Under age 35	132,749	75,150	56.6
Aged 35 to 44	39,980	1,885	4.7
Aged 35 to 39	19,449	1,131	5.8
Aged 40 to 44	20,531	754	3.7
Aged 45 or older	119,503	1,486	1.2
Total females	**149,234**	**39,778**	**26.7**
Under age 35	65,594	37,637	57.4
Aged 35 to 44	20,222	1,194	5.9
Aged 35 to 39	9,832	682	6.9
Aged 40 to 44	10,390	512	4.9
Aged 45 or older	63,420	946	1.5
Total males	**142,999**	**38,741**	**27.1**
Under age 35	67,156	37,508	55.9
Aged 35 to 44	19,759	691	3.5
Aged 35 to 39	9,617	449	4.7
Aged 40 to 44	10,142	242	2.4
Aged 45 or older	56,083	539	1.0

Source: Bureau of the Census, School Enrollment—Social and Economic Characteristics of Students: October 2010, Internet site http://www.census.gov/hhes/school/data/cps/2010/tables.html; calculations by New Strategist

Gen Xers Account for Few College Students

They are a significant share of graduate students, however.

Although the college enrollment of older people has grown over the years, young adults still dominate the nation's college campuses. In 2010, only 16 percent of college students were aged 35 or older. People aged 35 to 44 accounted for 9 percent of college students, while another 7 percent were people aged 45 or older.

Students aged 35 to 44 account for 7 percent of all undergraduates. The age group accounts for a larger 16 percent of graduate students.

■ Generation Xers are disappearing on college campuses, but many are still in graduate school.

More than half a million graduate students are aged 35 to 44

(number of graduate students by age, 2010)

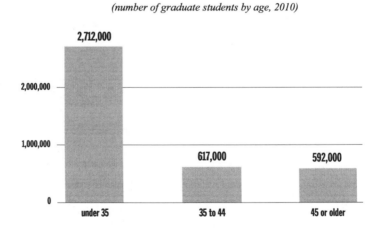

Table 2.8 College Students by Age and Enrollment Level, 2010

(number and percent distribution of people aged 15 or older enrolled in institutions of higher education by age and level of enrollment, 2010; numbers in thousands)

	total	undergraduate	graduate school
Total enrolled	**20,275**	**16,354**	**3,921**
Under age 35	17,067	14,355	2,712
Aged 35 to 44	1,800	1,183	617
Aged 35 to 39	1,080	681	399
Aged 40 to 44	720	502	218
Aged 45 or older	1,409	817	592
PERCENT DISTRIBUTION BY LEVEL OF ENROLLMENT			
Total enrolled	**100.0%**	**80.7%**	**19.3%**
Under age 35	100.0	84.1	15.9
Aged 35 to 44	100.0	65.7	34.3
Aged 35 to 39	100.0	63.1	36.9
Aged 40 to 44	100.0	69.7	30.3
Aged 45 or older	100.0	58.0	42.0
PERCENT DISTRIBUTION BY AGE			
Total enrolled	**100.0%**	**100.0%**	**100.0%**
Under age 35	84.2	87.8	69.2
Aged 35 to 44	8.9	7.2	15.7
Aged 35 to 39	5.3	4.2	10.2
Aged 40 to 44	3.6	3.1	5.6
Aged 45 or older	6.9	5.0	15.1

Source: Bureau of the Census, School Enrollment—Social and Economic Characteristics of Students: October 2010, Internet site http://www.census.gov/hhes/school/data/cps/2010/tables.html; calculations by New Strategist

3

Health

■ The 55 percent majority of Americans aged 18 or older say their health is excellent or very good. Among 35-to-44-year-olds the figure is 60 percent.

■ Americans have a weight problem, and Gen Xers are no exception. The average Gen X man weighs nearly 200 pounds. The average Gen X woman weighs more than 160 pounds.

■ Gen X men have had a median of six opposite-sex partners in their lifetime. Women in the age group have had a median of three partners.

■ The women of Generation X accounted for only 14 percent of the nation's births in 2010.

■ Many Gen Xers do not have health insurance. In 2010, nearly 22 percent of people aged 35 to 44 were without health insurance coverage.

■ Twenty-five percent of Americans aged 18 to 44 have experienced lower back pain for at least one full day in the past three months, making it the most common health condition in the age group.

■ Most Gen Xers had a prescription drug expense in the past year, spending a median of $213 on drugs—22 percent of which they paid out-of-pocket.

Most 35-to-44-Year-Olds Say Their Health Is Very Good or Excellent

The proportion that reports very good or excellent health declines with age.

Overall, the 55 percent majority of Americans aged 18 or older say their health is "excellent" or "very good." The figure peaks at 63 percent among adults under age 35. Among people aged 35 to 44 in 2010 (Gen Xers were aged 34 to 45 in that year), fully 60 percent say they are in very good or excellent health. The figure falls with increasing age as chronic conditions become common.

Fewer than half of people aged 65 or older report that their health is excellent or very good. Nevertheless, the proportion that is in poor health remains below 8 percent, regardless of age. Among people aged 65 or older, the proportion saying their health is excellent or very good (41 percent) surpasses the proportion saying their health is only fair or poor (25 percent).

■ Medical advances that allow people to manage chronic conditions should boost the proportions of people reporting excellent or very good health in the years ahead.

Sixty percent of 35-to-44-year-olds say their health is excellent or very good

(percent of people aged 18 or older who say their health is excellent or very good, by age, 2010)

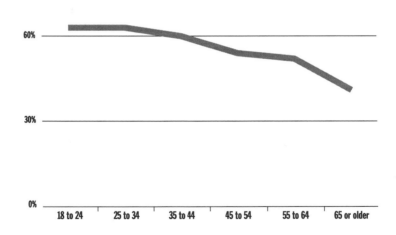

Table 3.1 Health Status by Age, 2010

(percent distribution of people aged 18 or older by self-reported health status, by age, 2010)

| | total | excellent or very good | | | good | fair or poor | | |
		total	excellent	very good		total	fair	poor
Total people	**100.0%**	**54.8%**	**20.2%**	**34.6%**	**29.8%**	**14.9%**	**10.9%**	**4.0%**
Aged 18 to 24	100.0	62.6	25.0	37.6	27.5	6.7	5.6	1.1
Aged 25 to 34	100.0	62.9	25.0	37.9	28.8	9.0	7.5	1.5
Aged 35 to 44	100.0	60.2	23.0	37.2	28.6	10.6	8.2	2.4
Aged 45 to 54	100.0	54.4	20.0	34.4	29.0	15.1	10.7	4.4
Aged 55 to 64	100.0	51.7	17.6	34.1	30.3	19.0	13.2	5.8
Aged 65 or older	100.0	40.7	12.1	28.6	33.9	24.7	17.7	7.0

Source: Centers for Disease Control and Prevention, Behavioral Risk Factor Surveillance System Prevalence Data, 2010, Internet site http://apps.nccd.cdc.gov/brfss/

Weight Problems Are the Norm for Gen Xers

Most men and women are overweight.

Americans have a weight problem, and Gen Xers are no exception. The average Gen X man weighs nearly 200 pounds. The average Gen X woman weighs more than 160 pounds. More than 80 percent of Gen X men and 64 percent of Gen X women are overweight, and more than one-third are obese.

Although many people say they exercise, only 20 percent of adults meet federal physical activity guidelines. The proportion that meets the guidelines falls with age to fewer than 10 percent of people aged 65 or older. The guidelines are fairly complex and demanding, however, which might explain why so few can meet them.

■ Most Gen Xers lack the willpower to eat less or exercise more—fueling a diet and weight loss industry that never lacks for customers.

Most Gen Xers weigh more than they should

(percent distribution of people aged 35 to 44 by weight status, by sex, 2007–10)

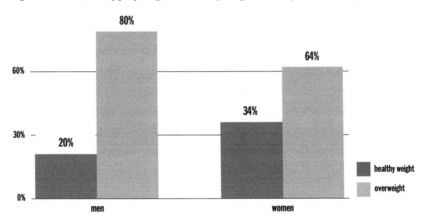

Table 3.2 Average Measured Weight by Age and Sex, 2003–06

(average weight in pounds of people aged 20 or older by age and sex, 2003–06)

	men	women
Total aged 20 or older	**194.7**	**164.7**
Aged 20 to 29	188.3	155.9
Aged 30 to 39	194.1	164.7
Aged 40 to 49	202.3	171.3
Aged 50 to 59	198.8	172.1
Aged 60 to 69	198.3	170.5
Aged 70 to 79	187.4	155.6
Aged 80 or older	168.1	142.2

Note: Data are based on measured weight of a sample of the civilian noninstitutionalized population.
Source: National Center for Health Statistics, Anthropometric Reference Data for Children and Adults: United States, 2003–2006, National Health Statistics Reports, Number 10, 2008, Internet site http://www.cdc.gov/nchs/products/pubs/pubd/nhsr/nhsr.htm; calculations by New Strategist

Table 3.3 Weight Status by Sex and Age, 2007–10

(percent distribution of people aged 20 or older by weight status, sex, and age, 2007–10)

	total	healthy weight	overweight total	overweight obese
Total people	**100.0%**	**29.6%**	**68.7%**	**34.9%**
Total men	**100.0**	**25.8**	**73.2**	**33.9**
Aged 20 to 34	100.0	37.5	61.1	27.1
Aged 35 to 44	100.0	19.8	80.2	37.2
Aged 45 to 54	100.0	21.8	76.8	36.6
Aged 55 to 64	100.0	19.4	79.8	37.3
Aged 65 to 74	100.0	21.6	77.5	41.5
Aged 75 or older	100.0	25.4	73.2	26.6
Total women	**100.0**	**33.2**	**64.5**	**35.9**
Aged 20 to 34	100.0	41.1	55.4	30.4
Aged 35 to 44	100.0	34.4	63.9	37.1
Aged 45 to 54	100.0	30.7	66.2	36.9
Aged 55 to 64	100.0	26.7	72.2	43.4
Aged 65 to 74	100.0	23.9	74.2	40.3
Aged 75 or older	100.0	35.4	63.2	28.7

Note: Data are based on measured height and weight of a sample of the civilian noninstitutionalized population. "Overweight" is defined as a body mass index of 25 or higher. "Obese" is defined as a body mass index of 30 or higher. Body mass index is calculated by dividing weight in kilograms by height in meters squared. Percentages do not add to 100 because "underweight" is not shown.
Source: National Center for Health Statistics, Health, United States, 2011, Internet site http://www.cdc.gov/nchs/hus.htm

Table 3.4 Leisure-Time Physical Activity Level by Sex and Age, 2010

(percent distribution of people aged 18 or older by leisure-time physical activity level, by sex and age, 2010)

	total	physically inactive	met at least one guideline	met aerobic and muscle-strengthening guidelines
Total people	**100.0%**	**49.5%**	**30.1%**	**20.4%**
Aged 18 to 24	100.0	39.4	31.0	29.6
Aged 25 to 44	100.0	44.4	31.3	24.3
Aged 45 to 54	100.0	48.9	31.9	19.2
Aged 55 to 64	100.0	53.7	30.4	15.9
Aged 65 or older	100.0	64.6	25.0	10.4
Total men	**100.0**	**43.8**	**31.1**	**25.1**
Aged 18 to 44	100.0	37.1	31.1	31.8
Aged 45 to 54	100.0	45.2	33.9	20.9
Aged 55 to 64	100.0	50.1	30.8	19.1
Aged 65 to 74	100.0	55.6	27.8	16.6
Aged 75 or older	100.0	62.8	28.1	9.1
Total women	**100.0**	**54.0**	**29.5**	**16.5**
Aged 18 to 44	100.0	49.0	31.4	19.6
Aged 45 to 54	100.0	52.4	30.1	17.5
Aged 55 to 64	100.0	57.0	29.9	13.1
Aged 65 to 74	100.0	63.6	25.4	11.0
Aged 75 or older	100.0	75.3	20.1	4.6

Note: The federal government recommends that adults perform at least 150 minutes (2 hours and 30 minutes) a week of moderate-intensity, or 75 minutes (1 hour and 15 minutes) a week of vigorous-intensity aerobic physical activity, or an equivalent combination. Aerobic activity should be performed in episodes of at least 10 minutes, and preferably should be spread throughout the week. It also recommends that adults perform muscle-strengthening activities that are moderate or high intensity and involve all major muscle groups on two or more days a week.
Source: National Center for Health Statistics, Health United States, 2011, Internet site http://www.cdc.gov/nchs/hus.htm

Americans Report on Their Sexual Behavior

Gen X men have had a median of six opposite-sex partners, while Gen X women have had a median of three.

Every few years the federal government fields the National Survey of Family Growth (NSFG), which examines the sexual behavior, contraceptive use, and childbearing patterns of Americans aged 15 to 44. Results from the 2006–08 survey are now available from the National Center for Health Statistics.

Overall, about nine of ten men and women aged 15 to 44 have had at least one opposite-sex partner in their lifetime. Even among 15-to-19-year-olds, 57 percent of men and 52 percent of women are sexually experienced. Men in the broad 15-to-44 age group have had a median of 5.1 opposite-sex partners in their lifetime, and women have had a median of 3.2 partners.

More than 93 percent of men and a smaller 83 percent of women aged 15 to 44 identify themselves as attracted only to the opposite sex. A tiny 2 percent of men and 1 percent of women identify themselves as homosexual, and another 1 percent of men and 3.5 percent of women say they are bisexual. Self-identified homosexuality is likely to be underreported. Evidence of underreporting can be found in the fact that a larger 5 percent of men and 12.5 percent of women report sexual activity with a same-sex partner in their lifetime.

■ Twenty-one percent of men and 8 percent of women report having 15 or more opposite-sex partners in their lifetime.

Women are more likely than men to report some same-sex attraction

(percent distribution of men and women aged 15 to 44 by sexual attraction, 2006–08)

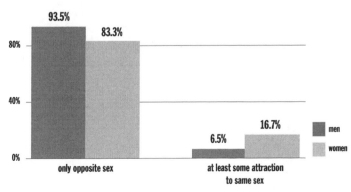

Table 3.5 Lifetime Sexual Activity of 15-to-44-Year-Olds by Sex, 2006–08

(number of people aged 15 to 44 and percent distribution by sexual experience with opposite-sex partners during lifetime, by sex and age, 2006–08; numbers in thousands)

	total		number of opposite-sex partners in lifetime							
	number	percent	none	1 or more	1	2	3 to 6	7 to 14	15 or more	median
Total men 15–44	**62,199**	**100.0%**	**11.4%**	**88.6%**	**15.0%**	**7.6%**	**26.5%**	**18.1%**	**21.4%**	**5.1**
Aged 15 to 19	10,777	100.0	43.3	56.7	21.2	9.4	17.6	5.4	3.1	1.8
Aged 20 to 24	10,404	100.0	14.4	85.5	19.1	8.0	26.1	18.1	14.2	4.1
Aged 25 to 29	10,431	100.0	3.8	96.2	11.8	8.9	29.5	22.9	23.1	5.7
Aged 30 to 34	9,575	100.0	3.1	96.9	14.2	6.1	26.6	21.7	28.3	6.4
Aged 35 to 39	10,318	100.0	1.4	98.8	13.3	5.6	29.7	19.6	30.6	6.2
Aged 40 to 44	10,695	100.0	1.3	98.8	10.3	7.2	29.7	21.6	30.0	6.4
Total women 15–44	**61,865**	**100.0**	**11.3**	**88.8**	**22.2**	**10.7**	**31.6**	**16.0**	**8.3**	**3.2**
Aged 15 to 19	10,431	100.0	48.1	51.8	22.7	8.2	15.7	4.1	1.1	1.4
Aged 20 to 24	10,140	100.0	12.6	87.5	24.5	12.5	31.6	11.7	7.2	2.6
Aged 25 to 29	10,250	100.0	3.4	96.6	20.0	12.4	31.0	20.4	12.8	3.6
Aged 30 to 34	9,587	100.0	1.9	98.1	20.9	10.6	31.9	21.3	13.4	4.2
Aged 35 to 39	10,475	100.0	0.9	99.1	22.2	9.9	38.3	20.8	7.9	3.5
Aged 40 to 44	10,982	100.0	0.4	99.7	22.4	10.8	40.5	18.0	8.0	3.4

Source: National Center for Health Statistics, Sexual Behavior, Sexual Attraction, and Sexual Identity in the United States: Data from the 2006–2008 National Survey of Family Growth, National Health Statistics Reports, No. 36, 2011, Internet site http://www.cdc.gov/nchs/nsfg/new_nsfg.htm; calculations by New Strategist

Table 3.6 Sexual Attraction among 18-to-44-Year-Olds, 2006–08

(number of people aged 18 to 44 and percent distribution by sexual attraction, by sex and age, 2006–08; numbers in thousands)

	total		only opposite sex	mostly opposite sex	equally to both	mostly same sex	only same sex	not sure
	number	percent						
Total men 18 to 44	**55,399**	**100.0%**	**93.5%**	**3.7%**	**0.5%**	**0.7%**	**1.2%**	**0.4%**
Aged 18 to 19	4,460	100.0	91.7	5.7	–	0.7	1.1	0.6
Aged 20 to 24	9,883	100.0	91.3	5.8	1.1	0.5	0.7	0.7
Aged 25 to 29	9,226	100.0	94.3	3.1	0.3	0.7	1.3	0.4
Aged 30 to 34	10,138	100.0	95.3	2.7	–	0.5	0.8	0.4
Aged 35 to 44	21,692	100.0	93.6	3.1	0.4	0.9	1.7	0.2
Total women 18 to 44	**56,032**	**100.0**	**83.3**	**11.9**	**2.8**	**0.6**	**0.8**	**0.7**
Aged 18 to 19	4,598	100.0	82.4	9.4	4.8	0.9	1.3	1.2
Aged 20 to 24	10,140	100.0	77.6	16.7	3.7	0.8	0.8	0.4
Aged 25 to 29	10,250	100.0	81.4	12.9	3.8	0.5	1.1	0.4
Aged 30 to 34	9,587	100.0	81.4	13.0	2.8	0.7	0.9	1.2
Aged 35 to 44	21,457	100.0	87.9	9.1	1.4	0.4	0.5	0.6

Note: "–" means sample is too small to make a reliable estimate.
Source: National Center for Health Statistics, Sexual Behavior, Sexual Attraction, and Sexual Identity in the United States: Data from the 2006–2008 National Survey of Family Growth, National Health Statistics Reports, No. 36, 2011, Internet site http://www.cdc.gov/nchs/nsfg/new_nsfg.htm; calculations by New Strategist

Table 3.7 Sexual Orientation of 18-to-44-Year-Olds, 2006–08

(number of people aged 18 to 44 and percent distribution by sexual orientation, by sex and age, 2006–08; numbers in thousands)

	total		heterosexual	homosexual	
	number	percent	or straight	or gay	bisexual
Total men 18 to 44	**55,399**	**100.0%**	**95.7%**	**1.7%**	**1.1%**
Aged 18 to 19	4,460	100.0	96.6	1.6	1.1
Aged 20 to 24	9,883	100.0	95.1	1.2	2.0
Aged 25 to 29	9,226	100.0	96.3	1.7	0.8
Aged 30 to 34	10,138	100.0	96.2	1.5	0.6
Aged 35 to 44	21,692	100.0	95.2	2.1	1.0
Total women 18 to 44	**56,032**	**100.0**	**93.7**	**1.1**	**3.5**
Aged 18 to 19	4,598	100.0	90.1	1.9	5.8
Aged 20 to 24	10,140	100.0	90.4	1.3	6.3
Aged 25 to 29	10,250	100.0	91.9	1.2	5.4
Aged 30 to 34	9,587	100.0	94.4	1.1	2.9
Aged 35 to 44	21,457	100.0	96.6	0.7	1.1

Note: Numbers do not add to 100 percent because "something else" and "not reported" are not shown.
Source: National Center for Health Statistics, Sexual Behavior, Sexual Attraction, and Sexual Identity in the United States: Data from the 2006–2008 National Survey of Family Growth, National Health Statistics Reports, No. 36, 2011, Internet site http://www.cdc.gov/nchs/nsfg/new_nsfg.htm; calculations by New Strategist

Table 3.8 Lifetime Same-Sex Sexual Activity of 15-to-44-Year-Olds, 2006–08

(percent of people aged 15 to 44 reporting any sexual activity with same-sex partners in their lifetime, by age and sex, 2006–08)

	men	women
Total aged 15 to 44	**5.2%**	**12.5%**
Aged 15 to 19	2.5	11.0
Aged 20 to 24	5.6	15.8
Aged 25 to 29	5.2	15.0
Aged 30 to 34	4.0	14.2
Aged 35 to 39	5.7	11.5
Aged 40 to 44	8.1	7.9

Source: National Center for Health Statistics, Sexual Behavior, Sexual Attraction, and Sexual Identity in the United States: Data from the 2006–2008 National Survey of Family Growth, National Health Statistics Reports, No. 36, 2011, Internet site http://www.cdc.gov/nchs/nsfg/new_nsfg.htm; calculations by New Strategist

Fertility Rates Are Falling

Rate had been rising among women in their thirties.

The women of Generation X (aged 34 to 45) are in their late childbearing years. Because many went to college and delayed marrying, their childbearing was postponed. Many waited until their thirties to have children. Consequently, over the past two decades, the fertility rate among women aged 30 or older has increased, while the rate among women under age 30 has fallen. Then the Great Recession hit, driving down the fertility rate among women in their thirties as well. The rate is still rising (although from a low level) among women aged 40 or older.

Whether the current downturn in fertility is permanent or temporary remains to be seen. Studies show that economic uncertainty lowers fertility, and the Great Recession has caused much uncertainty, which continues despite the recession's end.

■ The birth rate among women aged 20 to 24 fell to an all-time low in 2010.

Birth rate peaks in the 25-to-29 age group

(births per 1,000 women in age group, 2010)

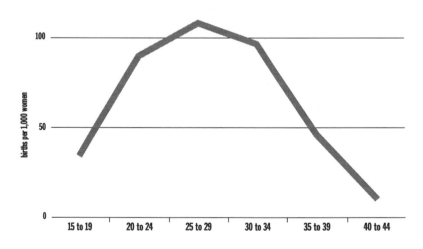

Table 3.9 Fertility Rate by Age, 1990 to 2010

(number of births per 1,000 women aged 15 to 44, and per 1,000 women in specified age group, 1990 to 2010; percent change for selected years)

	total	15 to 19	20 to 24	25 to 29	30 to 34	35 to 39	40 to 44	45 to 49
2010	64.1	34.3	90.0	108.3	96.6	45.9	10.2	0.7
2009	66.2	37.9	96.2	111.5	97.5	46.1	10.0	0.7
2008	68.6	41.5	103.0	115.1	99.3	46.9	9.8	0.7
2007	69.5	42.5	106.3	117.5	99.9	47.5	9.5	0.6
2006	68.5	41.9	105.9	116.7	97.7	47.3	9.4	0.6
2005	66.7	40.4	102.2	115.6	95.9	46.3	9.1	0.6
2004	66.3	41.1	101.7	115.5	95.3	45.4	8.9	0.5
2003	66.1	41.6	102.6	115.6	95.1	43.8	8.7	0.5
2002	64.8	43.0	103.6	113.6	91.5	41.4	8.3	0.5
2001	65.3	45.3	106.2	113.4	91.9	40.6	8.1	0.5
2000	65.9	47.7	109.7	113.5	91.2	39.7	8.0	0.5
1999	64.4	48.8	107.9	111.2	87.1	37.8	7.4	0.4
1998	64.3	50.3	108.4	110.2	85.2	36.9	7.4	0.4
1997	63.6	51.3	107.3	108.3	83.0	35.7	7.1	0.4
1996	64.1	53.5	107.8	108.6	82.1	34.9	6.8	0.3
1995	64.6	56.0	107.5	108.8	81.1	34.0	6.6	0.3
1994	65.9	58.2	109.2	111.0	80.4	33.4	6.4	0.3
1993	67.0	59.0	111.3	113.2	79.9	32.7	6.1	0.3
1992	68.4	60.3	113.7	115.7	79.6	32.3	5.9	0.3
1991	69.3	61.8	115.3	117.2	79.2	31.9	5.5	0.2
1990	70.9	59.9	116.5	120.2	80.8	31.7	5.5	0.2

Percent change

	total	15 to 19	20 to 24	25 to 29	30 to 34	35 to 39	40 to 44	45 to 49
2007 to 2010	−7.8%	−19.3%	−15.3%	−7.8%	−3.3%	−3.4%	7.4%	16.7%
2000 to 2010	−2.7	−28.1	−18.0	−4.6	5.9	15.6	27.5	40.0
1990 to 2010	−9.6	−42.7	−22.7	−9.9	19.6	44.8	85.5	250.0

Source: National Center for Health Statistics, Birth Data, Internet site http://www.cdc.gov/nchs/births.htm; calculations by New Strategist

Most Women Are Mothers by Age 30

Among women aged 35 to 44, the largest share has had two children.

The proportion of women who have never had a child falls from 95 percent among 15-to-19-year-olds to a much smaller (but still substantial) 19 percent among women aged 40 to 44. Overall, 53 percent of women aged 15 to 44 have had at least one child. The largest share (20 percent) has had two.

Six percent of women aged 15 to 44 had a baby in the past year, according to a 2010 survey. Women aged 25 to 29 are most likely to have had a baby in the past year, with nearly 10 percent giving birth. By race and Hispanic origin, Hispanics are most likely to have had a baby in the past year, at 7 percent. Six percent of native-born women aged 15 to 44 had a child in the past year. Among foreign-born women, the figure is a larger 8 percent.

■ The two-child family has been the norm in the United States for several decades.

Most women aged 25 or older have had at least one child

(percent of women aged 15 to 44 who have had one or more children, by age, 2010)

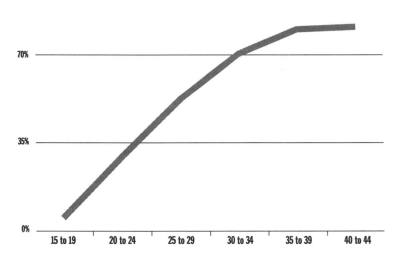

Table 3.10 Number of Children Born to Women Aged 15 to 44, 2010

(total number of women aged 15 to 44, and percent distribution by number of children ever borne, by age, 2010; numbers in thousands)

	total		number of children							
	number	percent	none	one or more	one	two	three	four	five or six	seven or more
Total aged 15 to 44	**61,481**	**100.0%**	**47.1%**	**52.9%**	**16.9%**	**20.4%**	**10.4%**	**3.4%**	**1.5%**	**0.3%**
Aged 15 to 19	10,273	100.0	94.6	5.3	4.4	0.6	0.3	0.0	0.0	0.0
Aged 20 to 24	10,493	100.0	70.5	29.5	18.1	9.0	2.0	0.3	0.1	0.0
Aged 25 to 29	10,501	100.0	47.6	52.4	22.7	18.7	7.8	2.3	0.8	0.1
Aged 30 to 34	9,923	100.0	29.7	70.4	19.2	29.2	14.3	5.2	2.1	0.4
Aged 35 to 39	9,917	100.0	19.7	80.2	18.5	32.6	19.7	5.9	3.1	0.4
Aged 40 to 44	10,374	100.0	18.8	81.2	18.5	33.3	19.1	6.8	2.7	0.8

Source: Bureau of the Census, Fertility of American Women: 2010, Detailed Tables, Internet site http://www.census.gov/hhes/ fertility/data/cps/2010.html

Table 3.11 Women Giving Birth in the Past Year, 2010

(total number of women aged 15 to 44, number and percent who gave birth in the past year, and number and percent who had a first birth in past year, by age, 2010; numbers in thousands)

	total	gave birth in past year		first birth in past year	
		number	percent	number	percent
Total aged 15 to 44	**61,481**	**3,686**	**6.0%**	**1,467**	**2.4%**
Age					
Aged 15 to 19	10,273	301	2.9	229	2.2
Aged 20 to 24	10,493	916	8.7	462	4.4
Aged 25 to 29	10,501	1,014	9.7	405	3.9
Aged 30 to 34	9,923	820	8.3	225	2.3
Aged 35 to 39	9,917	503	5.1	126	1.3
Aged 40 to 44	10,374	131	1.3	20	0.2
Race and Hispanic origin					
Asian	3,616	251	6.9	102	2.8
Black	9,468	600	6.3	202	2.1
Hispanic	10,845	756	7.0	296	2.7
Non-Hispanic white	37,271	2,069	5.6	868	2.3
Nativity status					
Native born	51,981	2,952	5.7	1,221	2.3
Foreign born	9,501	734	7.7	246	2.6
Region					
Northeast	10,942	648	5.9	254	2.3
Midwest	13,124	802	6.1	308	2.3
South	22,799	1,345	5.9	545	2.4
West	14,617	891	6.1	360	2.5

Note: Numbers by race and Hispanic origin do not add to total because Asians and blacks are those who identify themselves as being of the race alone and those who identify themselves as being of the race in combination with other races, and because Hispanics may be of any race. Non-Hispanic whites are those who identify themselves as being white alone and not Hispanic.
Source: Bureau of the Census, Fertility of American Women: 2010, Detailed Tables, Internet site http://www.census.gov/hhes/fertility/data/cps/2010.html

Generation X Is at the End of the Childbearing Years

Most babies are born to women under age 30.

Despite an increase in the number of older mothers during the past few decades, the great majority of women who give birth are under age 30. Women aged 35 or older accounted for only 14 percent of the nation's births in 2010 (Generation X was aged 34 to 45 in that year).

The age at which women give birth varies by race and Hispanic origin. Among blacks and Hispanics, women aged 35 to 44 account for only 11 to 13 percent of births. Among Asians, the women of Generation X account for a substantial 24 percent of births. Many Asian women postpone childbearing until their thirties because most spend much of their twenties in college.

Among women aged 35 to 44 who gave birth in 2010, only 23 percent were having their first child. A larger 31 percent were having their second child, and the 45 percent plurality was having a third or subsequent child.

■ The Millennial generation has replaced Generation X as the dominant group entering parenthood.

The women of Generation X account for few births

(percent distribution of births by age of mother, 2010)

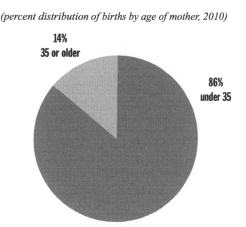

14%
35 or older

86%
under 35

Table 3.12 Births by Age, Race, and Hispanic Origin, 2010

(number and percent distribution of births by age, race, and Hispanic origin, 2010)

	total	American Indian	Asian	non-Hispanic black	Hispanic	non-Hispanic white
Total births	**4,000,279**	**46,760**	**246,915**	**589,139**	**946,000**	**2,161,669**
Under age 15	4,500	100	50	1,572	1,811	967
Aged 15 to 19	367,752	7,409	6,263	88,142	121,849	143,984
Aged 20 to 24	951,900	15,746	27,738	187,754	254,868	464,645
Aged 25 to 29	1,134,008	12,223	68,379	147,549	255,236	648,473
Aged 30 to 34	962,420	7,310	85,304	100,697	191,595	574,479
Aged 35 to 44	571,954	3,934	58,410	62,445	119,445	324,616
Aged 35 to 39	464,943	3,212	48,095	49,693	97,652	264,044
Aged 40 to 44	107,011	722	10,315	12,752	21,793	60,572
Aged 45 to 54	7,744	38	770	980	1,196	4,504

PERCENT DISTRIBUTION BY RACE AND HISPANIC ORIGIN

	total	American Indian	Asian	non-Hispanic black	Hispanic	non-Hispanic white
Total births	**100.0%**	**1.2%**	**6.2%**	**14.7%**	**23.6%**	**54.0%**
Under age 15	100.0	2.2	1.1	34.9	40.2	21.5
Aged 15 to 19	100.0	2.0	1.7	24.0	33.1	39.2
Aged 20 to 24	100.0	1.7	2.9	19.7	26.8	48.8
Aged 25 to 29	100.0	1.1	6.0	13.0	22.5	57.2
Aged 30 to 34	100.0	0.8	8.9	10.5	19.9	59.7
Aged 35 to 44	100.0	0.7	10.2	10.9	20.9	56.8
Aged 35 to 39	100.0	0.7	10.3	10.7	21.0	56.8
Aged 40 to 44	100.0	0.7	9.6	11.9	20.4	56.6
Aged 45 to 54	100.0	0.5	9.9	12.7	15.4	58.2

PERCENT DISTRIBUTION BY AGE

	total	American Indian	Asian	non-Hispanic black	Hispanic	non-Hispanic white
Total births	**100.0%**	**100.0%**	**100.0%**	**100.0%**	**100.0%**	**100.0%**
Under age 15	0.1	0.2	0.0	0.3	0.2	0.0
Aged 15 to 19	9.2	15.8	2.5	15.0	12.9	6.7
Aged 20 to 24	23.8	33.7	11.2	31.9	26.9	21.5
Aged 25 to 29	28.3	26.1	27.7	25.0	27.0	30.0
Aged 30 to 34	24.1	15.6	34.5	17.1	20.3	26.6
Aged 35 to 44	14.3	8.4	23.7	10.6	12.6	15.0
Aged 35 to 39	11.6	6.9	19.5	8.4	10.3	12.2
Aged 40 to 44	2.7	1.5	4.2	2.2	2.3	2.8
Aged 45 to 54	0.2	0.1	0.3	0.2	0.1	0.2

Note: Births by race and Hispanic origin do not add to total because Hispanics may be of any race and "not stated" is not shown.
Source: National Center for Health Statistics, Births: Preliminary Data for 2010, National Vital Statistics Reports, Vol. 60, No. 2, 2011, Internet site http://www.cdc.gov/nchs/births.htm; calculations by New Strategist

Table 3.13 Births by Age of Mother and Birth Order, 2010

(number and percent distribution of births by age of mother and birth order, 2010)

	total	first child	second child	third child	fourth or later child
Total births	**4,000,279**	**1,604,181**	**1,248,376**	**654,769**	**461,280**
Under age 15	4,500	4,375	74	7	2
Aged 15 to 19	367,752	298,160	57,181	8,392	1,158
Aged 20 to 24	951,900	472,391	309,206	118,836	43,964
Aged 25 to 29	1,134,008	420,183	371,861	204,848	128,631
Aged 30 to 34	962,420	277,963	328,686	194,903	153,525
Aged 35 to 44	571,954	129,034	179,424	126,465	131,680
Aged 35 to 39	464,943	105,097	149,453	104,573	101,547
Aged 40 to 44	107,011	23,937	29,971	21,892	30,133
Aged 45 to 54	7,744	2,075	1,945	1,317	2,319
PERCENT DISTRIBUTION BY BIRTH ORDER					
Total births	**100.0%**	**40.1%**	**31.2%**	**16.4%**	**11.5%**
Under age 15	100.0	97.2	1.6	0.2	0.0
Aged 15 to 19	100.0	81.1	15.5	2.3	0.3
Aged 20 to 24	100.0	49.6	32.5	12.5	4.6
Aged 25 to 29	100.0	37.1	32.8	18.1	11.3
Aged 30 to 34	100.0	28.9	34.2	20.3	16.0
Aged 35 to 44	100.0	22.6	31.4	22.1	23.0
Aged 35 to 39	100.0	22.6	32.1	22.5	21.8
Aged 40 to 44	100.0	22.4	28.0	20.5	28.2
Aged 45 to 54	100.0	26.8	25.1	17.0	29.9
PERCENT DISTRIBUTION BY AGE					
Total births	**100.0%**	**100.0%**	**100.0%**	**100.0%**	**100.0%**
Under age 15	0.1	0.3	0.0	0.0	0.0
Aged 15 to 19	9.2	18.6	4.6	1.3	0.3
Aged 20 to 24	23.8	29.4	24.8	18.1	9.5
Aged 25 to 29	28.3	26.2	29.8	31.3	27.9
Aged 30 to 34	24.1	17.3	26.3	29.8	33.3
Aged 35 to 44	14.3	8.0	14.4	19.3	28.5
Aged 35 to 39	11.6	6.6	12.0	16.0	22.0
Aged 40 to 44	2.7	1.5	2.4	3.3	6.5
Aged 45 to 54	0.2	0.1	0.2	0.2	0.5

Note: Numbers do not add to total because "not stated" is not shown.
Source: National Center for Health Statistics, Births: Preliminary Data for 2010, National Vital Statistics Reports, Vol. 60, No. 2, 2011, Internet site http://www.cdc.gov/nchs/births.htm; calculations by New Strategist

Many Generation X Mothers Are Not Married

Out-of-wedlock births fall with age.

Nearly 41 percent of babies born in 2010 had a mother who was not married. There are sharp differences by age in the percentage of new mothers who are not married, however. The younger the woman, the more likely she is to give birth out of wedlock.

Among babies born to women under age 25 in 2010, most were born to single mothers. The figure falls to 34 percent in the 25-to-29 age group. Among babies born to women aged 30 or older, from 20 to 22 percent had a single mother.

■ Out-of-wedlock childbearing has increased enormously over the past few decades and has become common even among older mothers.

One in five babies born to women aged 30 or older is out-of-wedlock

(percent of babies born to unmarried women, by age, 2010)

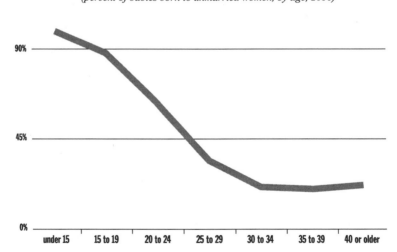

Table 3.14 Births to Unmarried Women by Age, 2010

(total number of births and number and percent to unmarried women, by age, 2010)

		unmarried women		
	total	number	percent distribution	percent of total
Total births	**4,000,279**	**1,633,785**	**100.0%**	**40.8%**
Under age 15	4,500	4,467	0.3	99.3
Aged 15 to 19	367,752	323,922	19.8	88.1
Aged 20 to 24	951,900	600,971	36.8	63.1
Aged 25 to 29	1,134,008	384,955	23.6	33.9
Aged 30 to 34	962,420	203,527	12.5	21.1
Aged 35 to 39	464,943	91,085	5.6	19.6
Aged 40 or older	114,755	24,858	1.5	21.7

Source: National Center for Health Statistics, Births: Preliminary Data for 2010, National Vital Statistics Reports, Vol. 60, No. 2, 2011, Internet site http://www.cdc.gov/nchs/births.htm; calculations by New Strategist

Eighteen Percent of 35-to-44-Year-Olds Smoke Cigarettes

Smoking rate peaks among 25-to-34-year-olds.

The percentage of Americans who smoke cigarettes has declined sharply from what it was a few decades ago. Nevertheless, a substantial 17 percent of people aged 18 or older were current smokers in 2010. Among people aged 35 to 44, a slightly larger 18 percent smoke cigarettes. Another 18 percent of 35-to-44-year-olds are former smokers.

Drinking is much more popular than smoking. Overall, 55 percent of people aged 18 or older have had an alcoholic beverage in the past month. The proportion peaks at 61 percent in the broad 25-to-34 age group, then falls to 60 percent in the 35-to-44 age group.

Although many Gen Xers have experience with illicit drugs, particularly marijuana, few continue to use them. Only 7 to 8 percent of people aged 35 to 44 have used illicit drugs in the past month. But most people between the ages of 19 and 59 have used illicit drugs at some point in their lives. About half of 35-to-44-year-olds have used marijuana in the past, although only 5 to 6 percent have used it in the past month.

■ As Gen Xers age and health concerns become increasingly important, the proportion of smokers and drinkers will decline.

Most Gen Xers have never smoked

(percent distribution of people aged 35 to 44 by cigarette smoking status, 2010)

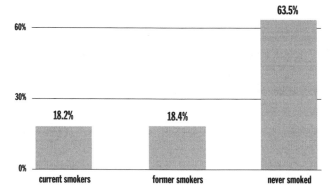

Table 3.15 Cigarette Smoking Status by Age, 2010

(percent distribution of people aged 18 or older by age and cigarette smoking status, 2010)

	total	current smokers total	smoke every day	smoke some days	former smoker	never smoked
Total people	**100.0%**	**17.2%**	**12.4%**	**4.8%**	**25.1%**	**56.6%**
Aged 18 to 24	100.0	19.7	12.9	6.8	6.6	73.0
Aged 25 to 34	100.0	23.9	16.9	7.0	16.8	58.5
Aged 35 to 44	100.0	18.2	13.2	5.0	18.4	63.5
Aged 45 to 54	100.0	19.4	14.7	4.7	24.4	54.7
Aged 55 to 64	100.0	15.9	11.9	4.0	34.5	49.0
Aged 65 or older	100.0	8.5	6.3	2.2	43.6	47.9

Source: Centers for Disease Control and Prevention, Behavioral Risk Factor Surveillance System Prevalence Data, 2010, Internet site http://apps.nccd.cdc.gov/brfss/

Table 3.16 Alcohol Use by Age, 2010

(percent distribution of people aged 18 or older by whether they have had at least one drink of alcohol within the past 30 days, by age, 2010)

	total	yes	no
Total people	**100.0%**	**54.6%**	**45.4%**
Aged 18 to 24	100.0	48.3	51.7
Aged 25 to 34	100.0	61.0	39.0
Aged 35 to 44	100.0	60.2	39.8
Aged 45 to 54	100.0	57.7	42.3
Aged 55 to 64	100.0	53.6	46.4
Aged 65 or older	100.0	40.5	59.5

Source: Centers for Disease Control and Prevention, Behavioral Risk Factor Surveillance System Prevalence Data, 2010, Internet site http://apps.nccd.cdc.gov/brfss/

Table 3.17 Illicit Drug Use by People Aged 12 or Older, 2010

(percent of people aged 12 or older who ever used any illicit drug, who used an illicit drug in the past year, and who used an illicit drug in the past month, by age, 2010)

	ever used	used in past year	used in past month
Total people	**47.1%**	**15.3%**	**8.9%**
Aged 12	10.0	6.6	3.2
Aged 13	15.5	10.5	4.8
Aged 14	20.1	14.7	7.2
Aged 15	30.2	22.9	11.3
Aged 16	34.3	26.7	14.9
Aged 17	41.9	33.4	18.4
Aged 18	49.0	37.8	22.1
Aged 19	53.6	38.9	24.7
Aged 20	56.1	36.5	22.5
Aged 21	58.5	37.5	23.1
Aged 22	58.6	35.1	22.1
Aged 23	59.7	32.5	20.1
Aged 24	60.4	30.7	19.1
Aged 25	62.1	29.8	17.6
Aged 26 to 29	62.3	25.4	14.8
Aged 30 to 34	57.5	19.9	12.9
Aged 35 to 39	53.6	14.2	8.1
Aged 40 to 44	57.2	12.8	6.9
Aged 45 to 49	60.0	12.5	7.2
Aged 50 to 54	60.5	11.7	7.2
Aged 55 to 59	54.8	9.2	4.1
Aged 60 to 64	39.6	4.7	2.7
Aged 65 or older	16.0	1.7	1.1

Note: Illicit drugs include marijuana, hashish, cocaine (including crack), heroin, hallucinogens, inhalants, or any prescription-type psychotherapeutic used nonmedically.
Source: SAMHSA, Office of Applied Studies, 2010 National Survey on Drug Use and Health, Detailed Tables, Internet site http://www.samhsa.gov/data/NSDUH/2k10ResultsTables/Web/HTML/TOC.htm

Table 3.18 Marijuana Use by People Aged 12 or Older, 2010

(percent of people aged 12 or older who ever used marijuana, who used marijuana in the past year, and who used marijuana in the past month, by age, 2010)

	ever used	used in past year	used in past month
Total people	**41.9%**	**11.5%**	**6.9%**
Aged 12	1.0	0.9	0.2
Aged 13	4.7	4.0	1.5
Aged 14	10.6	9.1	4.2
Aged 15	20.2	17.0	8.6
Aged 16	27.0	21.8	12.4
Aged 17	36.2	29.2	16.2
Aged 18	42.6	32.9	19.3
Aged 19	47.4	33.7	21.6
Aged 20	49.6	31.7	20.0
Aged 21	53.3	31.8	19.3
Aged 22	53.1	30.1	19.3
Aged 23	55.0	27.9	17.1
Aged 24	54.3	25.5	16.4
Aged 25	55.7	23.6	14.0
Aged 26 to 29	56.6	20.0	11.4
Aged 30 to 34	51.6	15.5	9.8
Aged 35 to 39	46.9	9.8	5.8
Aged 40 to 44	51.8	8.3	4.9
Aged 45 to 49	56.2	8.4	5.0
Aged 50 to 54	56.2	7.3	4.9
Aged 55 to 59	50.2	6.5	3.1
Aged 60 to 64	36.5	3.3	1.9
Aged 65 or older	12.3	1.0	0.5

Source: SAMHSA, Office of Applied Studies, 2010 National Survey on Drug Use and Health, Detailed Tables, Internet site http://www.samhsa.gov/data/NSDUH/2k10ResultsTables/Web/HTML/TOC.htm

Twenty-two Percent of Generation Xers Lack Health Insurance

The figure is even higher among younger adults.

More than one in five 35-to-44-year-olds is without health insurance. While Gen Xers are more likely to have health insurance than 18-to-34-year-olds, many are at risk of medical bankruptcy.

Most Americans obtain health insurance coverage through their employer. Among 35-to-44-year-olds, 64 percent had employment-based coverage in 2010. But only 45 percent had their own employment-based coverage.

Not surprisingly, health care expenses rise with age. Median health care expenses for Gen Xers exceed $1,000 annually. Most of their health care expenses are paid for by private insurance. Gen Xers account for only 12 percent of total health care spending.

■ The Great Recession has inflated the percentage of Gen Xers without health insurance.

Many Americans under age 65 do not have health insurance coverage

(percent of people aged 18 or older without health insurance, by age, 2010)

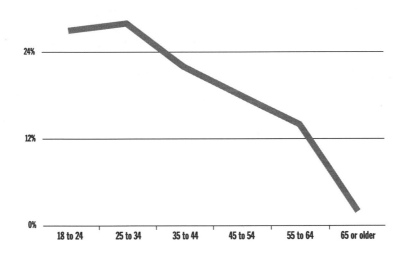

Table 3.19 Health Insurance Coverage by Age, 2010

(number and percent distribution of people by age and health insurance coverage status, 2010; numbers in thousands)

	total	with health insurance total	private	government	not covered
Total people	**306,110**	**256,206**	**195,874**	**95,003**	**49,904**
Under age 65	266,931	217,819	173,206	58,374	49,112
Under age 18	74,916	67,609	44,620	28,385	7,307
Aged 18 to 24	29,651	21,573	17,407	5,579	8,078
Aged 25 to 34	41,584	29,780	25,314	5,746	11,804
Aged 35 to 44	39,842	31,149	27,426	5,046	8,692
Aged 45 to 54	43,954	36,035	31,695	6,110	7,919
Aged 55 to 64	36,984	31,672	26,743	7,509	5,312
Aged 65 or older	39,179	38,387	22,668	36,629	792

PERCENT DISTRIBUTION BY COVERAGE STATUS

	total	total	private	government	not covered
Total people	**100.0%**	**83.7%**	**64.0%**	**31.0%**	**16.3%**
Under age 65	100.0	81.6	64.9	21.9	18.4
Under age 18	100.0	90.2	59.6	37.9	9.8
Aged 18 to 24	100.0	72.8	58.7	18.8	27.2
Aged 25 to 34	100.0	71.6	60.9	13.8	28.4
Aged 35 to 44	100.0	78.2	68.8	12.7	21.8
Aged 45 to 54	100.0	82.0	72.1	13.9	18.0
Aged 55 to 64	100.0	85.6	72.3	20.3	14.4
Aged 65 or older	100.0	98.0	57.9	93.5	2.0

PERCENT DISTRIBUTION BY AGE

	total	total	private	government	not covered
Total people	**100.0%**	**100.0%**	**100.0%**	**100.0%**	**100.0%**
Under age 65	87.2	85.0	88.4	61.4	98.4
Under age 18	24.5	26.4	22.8	29.9	14.6
Aged 18 to 24	9.7	8.4	8.9	5.9	16.2
Aged 25 to 34	13.6	11.6	12.9	6.0	23.7
Aged 35 to 44	13.0	12.2	14.0	5.3	17.4
Aged 45 to 54	14.4	14.1	16.2	6.4	15.9
Aged 55 to 64	12.1	12.4	13.7	7.9	10.6
Aged 65 or older	12.8	15.0	11.6	38.6	1.6

Note: Numbers may not add to total because some people have more than one type of health insurance coverage.
Source: Bureau of the Census, Health Insurance, Internet site http://www.census.gov/hhes/www/cpstables/032011/health/toc
.htm; calculations by New Strategist

Table 3.20 Private Health Insurance Coverage by Age, 2010

(number and percent distribution of people by age and private health insurance coverage status, 2010; numbers in thousands)

| | | with private health insurance | | | |
| | | total | employment based | | |
	total	total	total	own	direct purchase
Total people	**306,110**	**195,874**	**169,264**	**87,471**	**30,147**
Under age 65	266,931	173,206	156,536	77,875	18,880
Under age 18	74,916	44,620	41,083	179	4,291
Aged 18 to 24	29,651	17,407	13,612	3,671	1,987
Aged 25 to 34	41,584	25,314	23,221	17,341	2,478
Aged 35 to 44	39,842	27,426	25,573	18,080	2,604
Aged 45 to 54	43,954	31,695	29,201	21,014	3,600
Aged 55 to 64	36,984	26,743	23,846	17,591	3,922
Aged 65 or older	39,179	22,668	12,728	9,597	11,267

PERCENT DISTRIBUTION BY COVERAGE STATUS

Total people	**100.0%**	**64.0%**	**55.3%**	**28.6%**	**9.8%**
Under age 65	100.0	64.9	58.6	29.2	7.1
Under age 18	100.0	59.6	54.8	0.2	5.7
Aged 18 to 24	100.0	58.7	45.9	12.4	6.7
Aged 25 to 34	100.0	60.9	55.8	41.7	6.0
Aged 35 to 44	100.0	68.8	64.2	45.4	6.5
Aged 45 to 54	100.0	72.1	66.4	47.8	8.2
Aged 55 to 64	100.0	72.3	64.5	47.6	10.6
Aged 65 or older	100.0	57.9	32.5	24.5	28.8

PERCENT DISTRIBUTION BY AGE

Total people	**100.0%**	**100.0%**	**100.0%**	**100.0%**	**100.0%**
Under age 65	87.2	88.4	92.5	89.0	62.6
Under age 18	24.5	22.8	24.3	0.2	14.2
Aged 18 to 24	9.7	8.9	8.0	4.2	6.6
Aged 25 to 34	13.6	12.9	13.7	19.8	8.2
Aged 35 to 44	13.0	14.0	15.1	20.7	8.6
Aged 45 to 54	14.4	16.2	17.3	24.0	11.9
Aged 55 to 64	12.1	13.7	14.1	20.1	13.0
Aged 65 or older	12.8	11.6	7.5	11.0	37.4

Note: Numbers may not add to total because some people have more than one type of health insurance coverage.
Source: Bureau of the Census, Health Insurance, Internet site http://www.census.gov/hhes/www/cpstables/032011/health/toc .htm; calculations by New Strategist

Table 3.21 Government Health Insurance Coverage by Age, 2010

(number and percent distribution of people by age and government health insurance coverage status, 2010; numbers in thousands)

	total	with government health insurance			
		total	Medicaid	Medicare	military
Total people	**306,110**	**95,003**	**48,580**	**44,327**	**12,848**
Under age 65	266,931	58,374	44,993	7,870	9,666
Under age 18	74,916	28,385	26,067	602	2,461
Aged 18 to 24	29,651	5,579	4,516	257	1,035
Aged 25 to 34	41,584	5,746	4,249	610	1,244
Aged 35 to 44	39,842	5,046	3,449	900	1,172
Aged 45 to 54	43,954	6,110	3,607	1,901	1,553
Aged 55 to 64	36,984	7,509	3,105	3,600	2,201
Aged 65 or older	39,179	36,629	3,587	36,457	3,182

PERCENT DISTRIBUTION BY COVERAGE STATUS

	total	total	Medicaid	Medicare	military
Total people	**100.0%**	**31.0%**	**15.9%**	**14.5%**	**4.2%**
Under age 65	100.0	21.9	16.9	2.9	3.6
Under age 18	100.0	37.9	34.8	0.8	3.3
Aged 18 to 24	100.0	18.8	15.2	0.9	3.5
Aged 25 to 34	100.0	13.8	10.2	1.5	3.0
Aged 35 to 44	100.0	12.7	8.7	2.3	2.9
Aged 45 to 54	100.0	13.9	8.2	4.3	3.5
Aged 55 to 64	100.0	20.3	8.4	9.7	6.0
Aged 65 or older	100.0	93.5	9.2	93.1	8.1

PERCENT DISTRIBUTION BY AGE

	total	total	Medicaid	Medicare	military
Total people	**100.0%**	**100.0%**	**100.0%**	**100.0%**	**100.0%**
Under age 65	87.2	61.4	92.6	17.8	75.2
Under age 18	24.5	29.9	53.7	1.4	19.2
Aged 18 to 24	9.7	5.9	9.3	0.6	8.1
Aged 25 to 34	13.6	6.0	8.7	1.4	9.7
Aged 35 to 44	13.0	5.3	7.1	2.0	9.1
Aged 45 to 54	14.4	6.4	7.4	4.3	12.1
Aged 55 to 64	12.1	7.9	6.4	8.1	17.1
Aged 65 or older	12.8	38.6	7.4	82.2	24.8

Note: Numbers may not add to total because some people have more than one type of health insurance coverage.
Source: Bureau of the Census, Health Insurance, Internet site http://www.census.gov/hhes/www/cpstables/032011/health/toc
.htm; calculations by New Strategist

Table 3.22 Spending on Health Care by Age, 2009

(percent of people with health care expense, median expense per person, total expenses, and percent distribution of total expenses by source of payment, by age, 2009)

	total (thousands)	percent with expense	median expense per person	total expenses amount (millions)	total expenses percent distribution
Total people	**306,661**	**84.6%**	**$1,301**	**$1,259,456**	**100.0%**
Under age 18	74,836	86.5	548	143,261	11.4
Aged 18 to 24	29,787	74.0	665	54,682	4.3
Aged 25 to 34	40,861	74.3	920	96,666	7.7
Aged 35 to 44	40,495	79.7	1,174	126,885	10.1
Aged 45 to 49	21,892	83.3	1,492	90,712	7.2
Aged 50 to 54	22,699	88.8	1,958	104,769	8.3
Aged 55 to 59	19,335	91.6	2,314	123,052	9.8
Aged 60 to 64	16,417	90.9	3,129	126,709	10.1
Aged 65 or older	40,338	96.6	4,542	392,721	31.2

	total	out of pocket	private insurance	Medicare	Medicaid	other
			percent distribution by source of payment			
Total people	**100.0%**	**14.6%**	**42.6%**	**23.8%**	**9.7%**	**9.3%**
Under age 18	100.0	12.9	57.3	1.2	21.7	6.9
Aged 18 to 24	100.0	17.6	48.5	0.7	20.2	13.0
Aged 25 to 34	100.0	16.6	55.3	2.7	14.8	10.5
Aged 35 to 44	100.0	16.1	59.5	6.3	9.2	8.8
Aged 45 to 49	100.0	15.8	55.4	9.5	8.4	10.9
Aged 50 to 54	100.0	16.6	52.3	11.7	9.9	9.5
Aged 55 to 59	100.0	15.2	56.2	10.1	8.3	10.1
Aged 60 to 64	100.0	15.1	52.5	12.6	7.8	12.0
Aged 65 or older	100.0	12.5	14.8	60.6	4.2	7.8

Note: "Other" insurance includes Department of Veterans Affairs (except Tricare), American Indian Health Service, state and local clinics, worker's compensation, homeowner's and automobile insurance, etc.
Source: Agency for Healthcare Research and Quality, Medical Expenditure Panel Survey, 2009, Internet site http://meps.ahrq .gov/mepsweb/survey_comp/household.jsp; calculations by New Strategist

Table 3.23 Spending on Health Care by Generation, 2009

(percent of people with health care expense, median expense per person, total expenses, and percent distribution of total expenses by source of payment, by generation, 2009)

	total (thousands)	percent with expense	median expense per person	total expenses amount (millions)	total expenses percent distribution
Total people	**306,661**	**84.6%**	**$1,301**	**$1,259,456**	**100.0%**
iGeneration (under 15)	62,153	87.2	531	120,682	9.6
Millennials (15 to 32)	75,919	75.6	748	155,210	12.3
Generation X (33 to 44)	47,907	79.0	1,157	145,601	11.6
Baby Boomers (45 to 63)	77,800	88.3	2,108	426,592	33.9
Older Americans (64 or older)	42,882	96.3	4,477	411,371	32.7

	percent distribution by source of payment total	out of pocket	private insurance	Medicare	Medicaid	other
Total people	**100.0%**	**14.6%**	**42.6%**	**23.8%**	**9.7%**	**9.3%**
iGeneration (under 15)	100.0	12.0	58.3	1.3	21.9	6.5
Millennials (15 to 32)	100.0	17.3	53.1	1.3	16.7	11.6
Generation X (33 to 44)	100.0	16.1	58.3	6.2	10.8	8.6
Baby Boomers (45 to 63)	100.0	15.7	54.5	10.6	8.6	10.7
Older Americans (64 or older)	100.0	12.6	16.2	58.9	4.4	8.0

Note: "Other" insurance includes Department of Veterans Affairs (except Tricare), American Indian Health Service, state and local clinics, worker's compensation, homeowner's and automobile insurance, etc.
Source: Agency for Healthcare Research and Quality, Medical Expenditure Panel Survey, 2009, Internet site http://meps.ahrq .gov/mepsweb/survey_comp/household.jsp; calculations by New Strategist

Health Problems Are Few in the 18-to-44 Age Group

Lower back pain is by far the most common health condition in the age group.

Twenty-five percent of Americans aged 18 to 44 have experienced lower back pain for at least one full day in the past three months, making it the most common health condition in the age group. Migraines or severe headaches are second, with 20 percent having the problem. Chronic joint symptoms are third, with 17 percent reporting this problem. The 18-to-44 age group accounts for more than half of those ever experiencing asthma.

A substantial one in five Gen X men has high blood pressure, as does a smaller 14 percent of women in the 35-to-44 age group. High cholesterol is about equally as common. Only 4 percent have doctor-diagnosed diabetes.

More than 1 million Americans have been diagnosed with AIDS over the decades. The largest share were diagnosed in their thirties—the age group now filled with Generation X.

■ As Generation X ages into its late forties and fifties, the percentage with chronic health problems will rise.

The percent of people with diabetes rises with age

(percent of people with diabetes, by age, 2010)

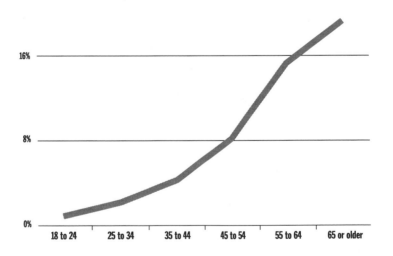

Table 3.24 Number of Adults with Health Conditions by Age, 2010

(number of people aged 18 or older with selected health conditions, by type of condition and age, 2010; numbers in thousands)

	total	18 to 44	45 to 64	aged 65 or older total	65 to 74	75 or older
Total people aged 18 or older	**229,505**	**110,615**	**80,198**	**38,692**	**21,291**	**17,401**
Selected circulatory diseases						
Heart disease, all types	27,066	4,897	10,568	11,601	5,173	6,428
Coronary	15,262	1,494	5,803	7,965	3,508	4,457
Hypertension	59,259	10,303	27,521	21,425	11,485	9,940
Stroke	6,226	664	2,403	3,158	1,302	1,856
Selected respiratory conditions						
Emphysema	4,314	361	1,703	2,250	1,153	1,097
Asthma, ever	29,057	15,020	9,723	4,314	2,492	1,822
Asthma, still	18,734	8,902	6,704	3,128	1,849	1,279
Hay fever	17,937	6,656	8,638	2,642	1,684	958
Sinusitis	29,821	11,584	13,025	5,213	3,240	1,973
Chronic bronchitis	9,882	3,265	4,247	2,371	1,279	1,092
Selected types of cancer						
Any cancer	19,441	2,427	7,939	9,075	4,343	4,732
Breast cancer	3,169	91	1,387	1,691	803	888
Cervical cancer	1,448	675	581	193	108	85
Prostate cancer	2,457	0	634	1,817	679	1,138
Other selected diseases and conditions						
Diabetes	20,974	3,022	9,676	8,276	4,563	3,713
Ulcers	14,992	4,591	6,418	3,983	2,241	1,742
Kidney disease	3,931	804	1,578	1,549	740	809
Liver disease	3,288	978	1,835	476	309	167
Arthritis	51,948	7,838	24,292	19,817	10,426	9,391
Chronic joint symptoms	67,024	18,794	30,801	17,429	9,572	7,857
Migraines or severe headaches	37,529	22,580	12,485	2,464	1,578	886
Pain in neck	36,177	14,459	16,002	5,717	3,292	2,425
Pain in lower back	66,106	27,811	26,007	12,288	6,923	5,365
Pain in face or jaw	11,460	5,460	4,779	1,221	725	496
Selected sensory problems						
Hearing	37,117	7,448	15,193	14,476	6,630	7,846
Vision	21,516	6,825	9,298	5,393	2,591	2,802
Absence of all natural teeth	17,539	2,322	5,817	9,400	4,096	5,304

Note: The conditions shown are those that have ever been diagnosed by a doctor, except as noted. Hay fever, sinusitis, and chronic bronchitis have been diagnosed in the past 12 months. Kidney and liver diseases have been diagnosed in the past 12 months and exclude kidney stones, bladder infections, and incontinence. Chronic joint symptoms are shown if respondent had pain, aching, or stiffness in or around a joint (excluding back and neck) and the condition began more than three months ago. Migraines and pain in neck, lower back, face, or jaw are shown only if pain lasted a whole day or more.
Source: National Center for Health Statistics, Summary Health Statistics for U.S. Adults: National Health Interview Survey, 2010, Vital and Health Statistics, Series 10, No. 252, 2012, Internet site http://www.cdc.gov/nchs/nhis.htm

Table 3.25 Distribution of Health Conditions among Adults by Age, 2010

(percent distribution of people aged 18 or older with selected health conditions, by type of condition and age, 2010)

	total	18 to 44	45 to 64	aged 65 or older total	65 to 74	75 or older
Total people aged 18 or older	**100.0%**	**48.2%**	**34.9%**	**16.9%**	**9.3%**	**7.6%**
Selected circulatory diseases						
Heart disease, all types	100.0	18.1	39.0	42.9	19.1	23.7
Coronary	100.0	9.8	38.0	52.2	23.0	29.2
Hypertension	100.0	17.4	46.4	36.2	19.4	16.8
Stroke	100.0	10.7	38.6	50.7	20.9	29.8
Selected respiratory conditions						
Emphysema	100.0	8.4	39.5	52.2	26.7	25.4
Asthma, ever	100.0	51.7	33.5	14.8	8.6	6.3
Asthma, still	100.0	47.5	35.8	16.7	9.9	6.8
Hay fever	100.0	37.1	48.2	14.7	9.4	5.3
Sinusitis	100.0	38.8	43.7	17.5	10.9	6.6
Chronic bronchitis	100.0	33.0	43.0	24.0	12.9	11.1
Selected types of cancer						
Any cancer	100.0	12.5	40.8	46.7	22.3	24.3
Breast cancer	100.0	2.9	43.8	53.4	25.3	28.0
Cervical cancer	100.0	46.6	40.1	13.3	7.5	5.9
Prostate cancer	100.0	0.0	25.8	74.0	27.6	46.3
Other selected diseases and conditions						
Diabetes	100.0	14.4	46.1	39.5	21.8	17.7
Ulcers	100.0	30.6	42.8	26.6	14.9	11.6
Kidney disease	100.0	20.5	40.1	39.4	18.8	20.6
Liver disease	100.0	29.7	55.8	14.5	9.4	5.1
Arthritis	100.0	15.1	46.8	38.1	20.1	18.1
Chronic joint symptoms	100.0	28.0	46.0	26.0	14.3	11.7
Migraines or severe headaches	100.0	60.2	33.3	6.6	4.2	2.4
Pain in neck	100.0	40.0	44.2	15.8	9.1	6.7
Pain in lower back	100.0	42.1	39.3	18.6	10.5	8.1
Pain in face or jaw	100.0	47.6	41.7	10.7	6.3	4.3
Selected sensory problems						
Hearing	100.0	20.1	40.9	39.0	17.9	21.1
Vision	100.0	31.7	43.2	25.1	12.0	13.0
Absence of all natural teeth	100.0	13.2	33.2	53.6	23.4	30.2

Note: The conditions shown are those that have ever been diagnosed by a doctor, except as noted. Hay fever, sinusitis, and chronic bronchitis have been diagnosed in the past 12 months. Kidney and liver diseases have been diagnosed in the past 12 months and exclude kidney stones, bladder infections, and incontinence. Chronic joint symptoms are shown if respondent had pain, aching, or stiffness in or around a joint (excluding back and neck) and the condition began more than three months ago. Migraines and pain in neck, lower back, face, or jaw are shown only if pain lasted a whole day or more.
Source: National Center for Health Statistics, Summary Health Statistics for U.S. Adults: National Health Interview Survey, 2010, Vital and Health Statistics, Series 10, No. 252, 2012, Internet site http://www.cdc.gov/nchs/nhis.htm

Table 3.26 Percent of Adults with Health Conditions by Age, 2010

(percent of people aged 18 or older with selected health conditions, by type of condition and age, 2010)

| | | | | aged 65 or older | | |
	total	18 to 44	45 to 64	total	65 to 74	75 or older
Total people aged 18 or older	100.0%	100.0%	100.0%	100.0%	100.0%	100.0%
Selected circulatory diseases						
Heart disease, all types	11.8	4.4	13.2	30.0	24.3	37.1
Coronary	6.7	1.4	7.2	20.6	16.5	25.8
Hypertension	25.9	9.3	34.4	55.4	54.2	57.3
Stroke	2.7	0.6	3.0	8.2	6.1	10.7
Selected respiratory conditions						
Emphysema	1.9	0.3	2.1	5.8	5.4	6.3
Asthma, ever	12.7	13.6	12.1	11.1	11.7	10.5
Asthma, still	8.2	8.1	8.4	8.1	8.7	7.4
Hay fever	7.8	6.0	10.8	6.8	7.9	5.5
Sinusitis	13.0	10.5	16.3	13.5	15.2	11.4
Chronic bronchitis	4.2	3.0	5.3	6.1	6.0	6.3
Selected types of cancer						
Any cancer	8.5	2.2	9.9	23.5	20.4	27.2
Breast cancer	1.4	0.1	1.7	4.4	3.8	5.1
Cervical cancer	1.2	0.6	1.4	0.5	0.9	0.8
Prostate cancer	2.2	0.0	1.6	4.7	6.9	16.4
Other selected diseases and conditions						
Diabetes	9.3	2.8	12.3	21.4	22.0	21.7
Ulcers	6.5	4.2	8.0	10.3	10.5	10.0
Kidney disease	1.7	0.7	2.0	4.0	3.5	4.7
Liver disease	1.4	0.9	2.3	1.2	1.5	1.0
Arthritis	22.7	7.1	30.3	51.2	49.0	54.1
Chronic joint symptoms	29.2	17.0	38.4	45.0	45.0	45.3
Migraines or severe headaches	16.4	20.4	15.6	6.4	7.4	5.1
Pain in neck	15.8	13.1	20.0	14.8	15.5	14.0
Pain in lower back	28.8	25.2	32.4	31.8	32.5	30.9
Pain in face or jaw	5.0	4.9	6.0	3.2	3.4	2.9
Selected sensory problems						
Hearing	16.2	6.7	18.9	37.4	31.2	45.1
Vision	9.4	6.2	11.6	13.9	12.2	16.1
Absence of all natural teeth	7.6	2.1	7.3	24.3	19.3	30.5

Note: The conditions shown are those that have ever been diagnosed by a doctor, except as noted. Hay fever, sinusitis, and chronic bronchitis have been diagnosed in the past 12 months. Kidney and liver diseases have been diagnosed in the past 12 months and exclude kidney stones, bladder infections, and incontinence. Chronic joint symptoms are shown if respondent had pain, aching, or stiffness in or around a joint (excluding back and neck) and the condition began more than three months ago. Migraines and pain in neck, lower back, face, or jaw are shown only if pain lasted a whole day or more.
Source: National Center for Health Statistics, Summary Health Statistics for U.S. Adults: National Health Interview Survey, 2010, Vital and Health Statistics, Series 10, No. 252, 2012, Internet site http://www.cdc.gov/nchs/nhis.htm

Table 3.27 Hypertension by Sex and Age, 1988–94 to 2007–10

(percent of people aged 20 to 74 with hypertension by sex and age, 1988–94 to 2007–10; and percentage point change, 1988–94 to 2007–10)

	2007–10	1988–94	percentage point change
Total aged 20 or older	**32.2%**	**24.1%**	**8.1**
Men aged 20 or older	**31.7**	**23.8**	**7.9**
Aged 20 to 34	6.8	7.1	–0.3
Aged 35 to 44	20.7	17.1	3.6
Aged 45 to 54	35.5	29.2	6.3
Aged 55 to 64	49.5	40.6	8.9
Aged 65 to 74	64.1	54.4	9.7
Aged 75 or older	71.7	60.4	11.3
Women aged 20 or older	**32.8**	**24.4**	**8.4**
Aged 20 to 34	3.8	2.9	0.9
Aged 35 to 44	14.2	11.2	3.0
Aged 45 to 54	31.2	23.9	7.3
Aged 55 to 64	50.4	42.6	7.8
Aged 65 to 74	69.3	56.2	13.1
Aged 75 or older	81.3	73.6	7.7

Note: Hypertension is defined as a systolic pressure of at least 140 mmHg or a diastolic pressure of at least 90 mmHg; in addition, anyone who takes antihypertensive medication is considered to have hypertension.
Source: National Center for Health Statistics, Health, United States, 2011, Internet site http://www.cdc.gov/nchs/hus.htm; calculations by New Strategist

Table 3.28 High Cholesterol by Sex and Age, 1988–94 to 2007–10

(percent of people aged 20 or older with high serum cholesterol by sex and age, 1988–94 to 2007–10; and percentage point change, 1988–94 to to 2007–10)

	2007–10	1988–94	percentage point change
Total aged 20 or older	**28.7%**	**21.5%**	**7.2**
Men aged 20 or older	**28.7**	**19.6**	**9.1**
Aged 20 to 34	8.5	8.2	0.3
Aged 35 to 44	22.5	21.0	1.5
Aged 45 to 54	34.0	29.6	4.4
Aged 55 to 64	46.2	30.8	15.4
Aged 65 to 74	48.9	27.4	21.5
Aged 75 or older	45.2	24.4	20.8
Women aged 20 or older	**28.7**	**23.2**	**5.5**
Aged 20 to 34	6.8	7.3	–0.5
Aged 35 to 44	15.7	13.5	2.2
Aged 45 to 54	29.1	28.2	0.9
Aged 55 to 64	51.4	45.8	5.6
Aged 65 to 74	53.3	46.9	6.4
Aged 75 or older	52.5	41.2	11.3

Note: High cholesterol is defined as 240 mg/dL or more.
Source: National Center for Health Statistics, Health, United States, 2011, Internet site http://www.cdc.gov/nchs/hus.htm; calculations by New Strategist

Table 3.29 **Diabetes Diagnosis by Age, 2010**

(percent distribution of people aged 18 or older by age and diabetes diagnosis status, 2010)

| | diagnosed with diabetes by a doctor | | |
	total	yes	no
Total people	**100.0%**	**8.7%**	**91.3%**
Aged 18 to 24	100.0	0.9	99.1
Aged 25 to 34	100.0	2.2	97.8
Aged 35 to 44	100.0	4.3	95.7
Aged 45 to 54	100.0	8.2	91.8
Aged 55 to 64	100.0	15.3	84.7
Aged 65 or older	100.0	19.3	80.7

Source: Centers for Disease Control and Prevention, Behavioral Risk Factor Surveillance System Prevalence Data, 2010, Internet site http://apps.nccd.cdc.gov/brfss/

Table 3.30 **Cumulative Number of AIDS Cases by Sex and Age, through 2009**

(cumulative number and percent distribution of AIDS cases by sex and age at diagnosis, through 2009)

	number	percent distribution
Total cases	**1,108,611**	**100.0%**
Sex		
Males 13 or older	878,366	79.2
Females 13 or older	220,795	19.9
Age		
Under age 13	9,448	0.9
Aged 13 to 14	1,321	0.1
Aged 15 to 19	7,214	0.7
Aged 20 to 24	42,920	3.9
Aged 25 to 29	129,639	11.7
Aged 30 to 34	214,149	19.3
Aged 35 to 39	234,575	21.2
Aged 40 to 44	193,237	17.4
Aged 45 to 49	126,380	11.4
Aged 50 to 54	72,327	6.5
Aged 55 to 59	39,025	3.5
Aged 60 to 64	20,633	1.9
Aged 65 or older	17,743	1.6

Source: Centers for Disease Control and Prevention, Cases of HIV/AIDS and AIDS in the United States and Dependent Areas, 2009, Internet site http://www.cdc.gov/hiv/surveillance/resources/reports/2009report/; calculations by New Strategist

Prescription Drug Use Is Increasing

More Americans use a growing number of prescriptions.

The use of prescription drugs to treat a variety of illnesses, particularly chronic conditions, increased substantially between 1988–94 and 2005–08. The percentage of people who too at least one drug in the past month rose from 38 to 48 percent during those years. The percentage using three or more prescription drugs in the past month climbed from 11 to 21 percent.

Most adults aged 25 or older have incurred a prescription drug expense during the past year, according to the federal government's Medical Expenditure Panel Survey. Expenses for prescription drugs rise with age, to nearly $1,300 for people aged 65 or older. The 58 percent majority of Gen Xers had a prescription drug expense in 2009, spending a median of $213 on drugs. Gen Xers paid 22 percent of that cost out-of-pocket.

■ Behind the increase in the use of prescriptions is the introduction and marketing of new drugs to treat chronic health problems.

Most Gen Xers have prescription drug expenses

(percent of people with prescription drug expenses, by generation, 2009)

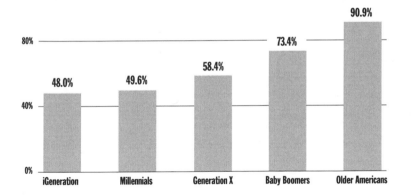

Table 3.31 Prescription Drug Use by Sex and Age, 1988–94 to 2005–08

(percent of people aged 18 or older taking at least one or three or more prescription drugs in the past month, by sex and age, 1988–94 to 2005–08; percentage point change, 1988–94 to 2005–08)

	at least one			three or more		
	2005–08	1988–94	percentage point change	2005–08	1988–94	percentage point change
Total people	**47.9%**	**37.8%**	**10.1**	**21.4%**	**11.0%**	**10.4**
Under age 18	25.3	20.5	4.8	4.4	2.4	2.0
Aged 18 to 44	37.8	31.3	6.5	9.8	5.7	4.1
Aged 45 to 64	64.8	54.8	10.0	34.1	20.0	14.1
Aged 65 or older	90.1	73.6	16.5	65.0	35.3	29.7
Total females	**53.9**	**44.6**	**9.3**	**24.8**	**13.6**	**11.2**
Under age 18	25.2	20.6	4.6	3.8	2.3	1.5
Aged 18 to 44	47.9	40.7	7.2	13.3	7.6	5.7
Aged 45 to 64	70.2	62.0	8.2	39.4	24.7	14.7
Aged 65 or older	90.5	78.3	12.2	65.3	38.2	27.1
Total males	**41.7**	**30.6**	**11.1**	**17.8**	**8.3**	**9.5**
Under age 18	25.3	20.4	4.9	5.0	2.6	2.4
Aged 18 to 44	27.5	21.5	6.0	6.2	3.6	2.6
Aged 45 to 64	59.3	47.2	12.1	28.6	15.1	13.5
Aged 65 or older	89.7	67.2	22.5	64.6	31.3	33.3

Source: National Center for Health Statistics, Health, United States, 2011, Internet site http://www.cdc.gov/nchs/hus.htm; calculations by New Strategist

Table 3.32 Spending on Prescription Medications by Age, 2009

(percent of people with prescription medication expense, median expense per person, total expenses, and percent distribution of total expenses by source of payment, by age, 2009)

	total (thousands)	percent with expense	median expense per person	total expenses	
				amount (millions)	percent distribution
Total people	**306,661**	**62.5%**	**$310**	**$257,593**	**100.0%**
Under age 18	74,836	48.2	65	17,806	6.9
Aged 18 to 24	29,787	47.9	103	6,974	2.7
Aged 25 to 34	40,861	51.9	123	14,919	5.8
Aged 35 to 39	19,571	56.6	192	10,800	4.2
Aged 40 to 44	20,924	61.5	274	15,877	6.2
Aged 45 to 54	44,591	68.9	427	47,363	18.4
Aged 55 to 64	35,753	79.9	794	56,853	22.1
Aged 65 or older	40,338	91.2	1,290	87,001	33.8

	percent distribution by source of payment					
	total	out of pocket	private insurance	Medicare	Medicaid	other
Total people	**100.0%**	**21.7%**	**39.3%**	**24.0%**	**8.7%**	**6.3%**
Under age 18	100.0	12.3	47.2	3.7	33.3	3.5
Aged 18 to 24	100.0	25.9	44.3	2.5	20.0	7.2
Aged 25 to 34	100.0	23.5	48.1	8.3	15.9	4.2
Aged 35 to 39	100.0	21.2	57.7	8.4	8.4	4.2
Aged 40 to 44	100.0	23.4	46.6	10.8	13.2	6.0
Aged 45 to 54	100.0	21.1	46.8	16.1	9.2	6.9
Aged 55 to 64	100.0	21.5	53.1	12.2	6.9	6.3
Aged 65 or older	100.0	23.4	19.0	49.1	1.6	7.0

Note: "Other" insurance includes Department of Veterans Affairs (except Tricare), American Indian Health Service, state and local clinics, worker's compensation, homeowner's and automobile insurance, etc.
Source: Agency for Healthcare Research and Quality, Medical Expenditure Panel Survey, 2009, Internet site http://meps.ahrq .gov/mepsweb/survey_comp/household.jsp; calculations by New Strategist

Table 3.33 Spending on Prescription Medications by Generation, 2009

(percent of people with prescription medication expense, median expense per person, total expenses, and percent distribution of total expenses by source of payment, by generation, 2009)

	total (thousands)	percent with expense	median expense per person	total expenses amount (millions)	total expenses percent distribution
Total people	**306,661**	**62.5%**	**$310**	**$257,593**	**100.0%**
iGeneration (under age 15)	62,153	48.0	62	14,000	5.4
Millennials (15 to 32)	75,919	49.6	107	22,049	8.6
Generation X (33 to 44)	47,907	58.4	213	30,328	11.8
Baby Boomers (45 to 63)	77,800	73.4	557	99,132	38.5
Older Americans (64 or older)	42,882	90.9	1,281	92,085	35.7

		percent distribution by source of payment				
	total	out of pocket	private insurance	Medicare	Medicaid	other
Total people	**100.0%**	**21.7%**	**39.3%**	**24.0%**	**8.7%**	**6.3%**
iGeneration (under age 15)	100.0	11.7	43.8	4.2	36.5	3.7
Millennials (15 to 32)	100.0	23.8	51.0	4.0	16.2	5.1
Generation X (33 to 44)	100.0	21.8	49.2	10.7	13.3	5.0
Baby Boomers (45 to 63)	100.0	21.3	50.8	13.6	7.8	6.6
Older Americans (64 or older)	100.0	23.3	20.0	47.5	2.1	7.0

Note: Other insurance includes Department of Veterans Affairs (except Tricare), American Indian Health Service, state and local clinics, worker's compensation, homeowner's and automobile insurance, etc.
Source: Agency for Healthcare Research and Quality, Medical Expenditure Panel Survey, 2009, Internet site http://meps.ahrq .gov/mepsweb/survey_comp/household.jsp; calculations by New Strategist

Adults Aged 25 to 44 Account for One in Five Physician Visits

Among 25-to-44-year-olds, more than two out of three physician visits are made by women.

In 2009, Americans visited a physician more than 1 billion times. Among the broad age groups examined by the National Center for Health Statistics, people aged 25 to 44 accounted for 20 percent of physician visits. The age group also accounts for 24 percent of visits to hospital outpatient departments and for a larger 28 percent of visits to emergency departments.

When adults who visited a doctor or health care clinic are asked to rate the care they received, only half give it the highest rating (a 9 or 10 on a scale of 0 to 10). The proportion that rates the experience a 9 or 10 is lowest among the Millennial generation (40 percent) and not much higher among Gen Xers (43 percent). It rises to a peak of 64 percent among older Americans, virtually all of whom are on Medicare.

■ As Gen Xers age, the frequency of their visits to the doctor will rise.

People aged 25 to 44 see a doctor between two and three times a year

(average number of physician visits per person per year, by age, 2009)

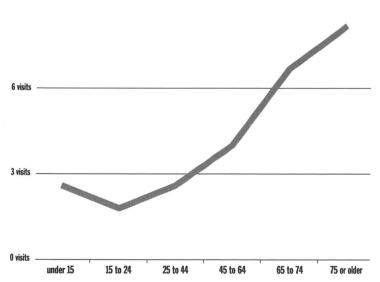

Table 3.34 Physician Office Visits by Sex and Age, 2009

(total number, percent distribution, and number of physician office visits per person per year, by sex and age, 2009; numbers in thousands)

	total	percent distribution	average visits per year
Total visits	**1,037,796**	**100.0%**	**3.4**
Under age 15	158,907	15.3	2.6
Aged 15 to 24	74,080	7.1	1.8
Aged 25 to 44	208,901	20.1	2.6
Aged 45 to 64	316,395	30.5	4.0
Aged 65 or older	279,514	26.9	7.4
Aged 65 to 74	137,452	13.2	6.7
Aged 75 or older	142,062	13.7	8.2
Visits by females	**611,064**	**58.9**	**4.0**
Under age 15	72,243	7.0	2.4
Aged 15 to 24	48,029	4.6	2.3
Aged 25 to 44	144,022	13.9	3.5
Aged 45 to 64	184,994	17.8	4.6
Aged 65 to 74	75,428	7.3	6.8
Aged 75 or older	86,348	8.3	8.2
Visits by males	**426,732**	**41.1**	**2.9**
Under age 15	86,664	8.4	2.7
Aged 15 to 24	26,052	2.5	1.2
Aged 25 to 44	64,879	6.3	1.6
Aged 45 to 64	131,400	12.7	3.4
Aged 65 to 74	62,023	6.0	6.5
Aged 75 or older	55,713	5.4	8.1

Source: National Center for Health Statistics, National Ambulatory Medical Care Survey: 2009 Summary Tables, Internet site http://www.cdc.gov/nchs/ahcd/web_tables.htm#2009

Table 3.35 Hospital Outpatient Department Visits by Age and Reason, 2008

(number and percent distribution of visits to hospital outpatient departments by age and major reason for visit, 2008; numbers in thousands)

| | total | | | major reason for visit | | | | | |
	number	percent distribution	total	new problem	chronic problem, routine	chronic problem, flare-up	pre- or post-surgery or injury follow-up	preventive care	unknown
Total visits	109,889	100.0%	100.0%	38.1%	30.3%	6.1%	4.7%	19.2%	1.6%
Under age 15	22,332	20.3	100.0	51.9	16.2	2.6	1.5	26.3	1.5
Aged 15 to 24	11,563	10.5	100.0	42.8	18.5	4.2	3.1	30.2	1.2
Aged 25 to 44	26,186	23.8	100.0	40.9	25.8	6.5	4.6	21.2	1.1
Aged 45 to 64	31,150	28.3	100.0	31.4	40.3	7.8	6.4	12.3	1.6
Aged 65 or older	18,658	17.0	100.0	26.1	43.8	8.3	6.7	12.5	2.5
Aged 65 to 74	10,273	9.3	100.0	26.8	42.3	8.1	7.3	13.5	2.0
Aged 75 or older	835	0.8	100.0	25.4	45.6	8.5	6.1	11.3	3.2

Source: National Center for Health Statistics, National Ambulatory Medical Care Survey: 2008 Outpatient Department Summary Tables, Internet site http://www.cdc.gov/nchs/ahcd/web_tables.htm#2009

Table 3.36 Emergency Department Visits by Age and Urgency of Problem, 2008

(number of visits to emergency rooms and percent distribution by urgency of problem, by age, 2008; numbers in thousands)

| | total | | percent distribution by urgency of problem | | | | | | |
	number	percent distribution	total	immediate	emergent	urgent	semiurgent	nonurgent	unknown
Total visits	123,761	100.0%	100.0%	3.7%	11.9%	38.9%	21.2%	8.0%	16.3%
Under age 15	23,157	18.7	100.0	1.9	8.3	36.0	25.1	8.8	20.0
Aged 15 to 24	19,823	16.0	100.0	2.6	9.2	37.0	24.9	9.8	16.5
Aged 25 to 44	35,185	28.4	100.0	3.1	10.1	39.0	23.0	9.1	15.7
Aged 45 to 64	26,335	21.3	100.0	5	14.0	40.2	18.4	7.1	15.3
Aged 65 or older	19,261	15.6	100.0	6.2	19.5	42.2	13.5	4.6	14.0
Aged 65 to 74	7,479	6.0	100.0	5.2	19.3	41.3	15.3	5.5	13.3
Aged 75 or older	11,781	9.5	100.0	6.9	19.7	42.8	12.4	4.0	14.4

Note: "Immediate" is a visit in which the patient should be seen immediately. "Emergent" is a visit in which the patient should be seen within 1 to 14 minutes; "urgent" is a visit in which the patient should be seen within 15 to 60 minutes; "semiurgent" is a visit in which the patient should be seen within 61 to 120 minutes; "nonurgent" is a visit in which the patient should be seen within 121 minutes to 24 hours; "unknown" is a visit with no mention of immediacy or triage or the patient was dead on arrival.
Source: National Center for Health Statistics, National Ambulatory Medical Care Survey: 2008 Emergency Department Summary Tables, Internet site http://www.cdc.gov/nchs/ahcd/web_tables.htm#2009

Table 3.37 Rating of Health Care Received from Doctor's Office or Clinic by Age, 2009

(number of people aged 18 or older visiting a doctor or health care clinic in past 12 months, and percent distribution by rating for health care received on a scale from 0 (worst) to 10 (best), by age, 2009; people in thousands)

	with health care visit		rating		
	number	percent	9 to 10	7 to 8	0 to 6
Total adults	**155,909**	**100.0%**	**50.1%**	**36.5%**	**12.2%**
Aged 18 to 29	26,931	100.0	40.2	42.3	16.4
Aged 30 to 39	24,107	100.0	41.0	44.0	13.8
Aged 40 to 44	13,415	100.0	44.6	42.1	12.0
Aged 45 to 49	14,379	100.0	48.9	36.4	14.1
Aged 50 to 54	15,980	100.0	48.2	35.9	14.9
Aged 55 to 59	15,259	100.0	52.7	34.8	11.5
Aged 60 to 64	12,989	100.0	58.7	31.7	7.8
Aged 65 or older	32,847	100.0	64.0	26.8	7.5

Source: Agency for Healthcare Research and Quality, Medical Expenditure Panel Survey, 2009, Internet site http://meps.ahrq .gov/mepsweb/survey_comp/household.jsp; calculations by New Strategist

---

Table 3.38 Rating of Health Care Received from Doctor's Office or Clinic by Generation, 2009

(number of people aged 18 or older visiting a doctor or health care clinic in past 12 months, and percent distribution by rating for health care received on a scale from 0 (worst) to 10 (best), by generation, 2009; people in thousands)

	with health care visit		rating		
	number	percent	9 to 10	7 to 8	0 to 6
Total adults	**155,909**	**100.0%**	**50.1%**	**36.5%**	**12.2%**
Millennials (18 to 32)	34,072	100.0	39.9	42.8	16.1
Generation X (33 to 44)	30,382	100.0	43.1	43.0	12.6
Baby Boomers (45 to 63)	56,573	100.0	51.5	35.0	12.5
Older Americans (64 or older)	34,883	100.0	63.9	27.0	7.3

Source: Agency for Healthcare Research and Quality, Medical Expenditure Panel Survey, 2009, Internet site http://meps.ahrq .gov/mepsweb/survey_comp/household.jsp; calculations by New Strategist

Many Americans Turn to Alternative Medicine

People in their fifties are most likely to seek alternative therapies.

Alternative medicine is a big business. In 2007, fully 38 percent of Americans aged 18 or older used a complementary or alternative medicine or therapy, according to a study by the National Center for Health Statistics. Alternative treatments range from popular regimens such as the South Beach Diet to chiropractic care, yoga, and acupuncture.

Middle-aged adults are most likely to use alternative medicine. Forty-four percent of people aged 50 to 59 used alternative medicine in 2007. Among Gen Xers (people in their thirties and forties) 40 percent used alternative medicine in the past year—20 percent used biologically based therapies (which include special diets) and 20 percent used mind-body therapy (which includes meditation and yoga).

■ The use of alternative medicine falls steeply with age as health problems become more severe.

The use of alternative medicine peaks in middle age

(percent of people aged 18 or older who have used alternative medicine in the past 12 months, by age, 2007)

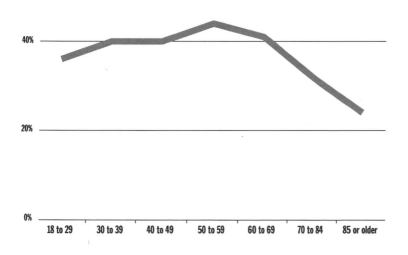

Table 3.39 Adults Who Use Complementary and Alternative Medicine by Age, 2007

(percent of people aged 18 or older who used complementary or alternative medicine in the past 12 months, by age, 2007)

	any use	biologically based therapies	mind-body therapies	alternative medical systems	manipulative and body-based therapies
Total adults	**38.3%**	**19.9%**	**19.2%**	**3.4%**	**15.2%**
Aged 18 to 29	36.3	15.9	21.3	3.2	15.1
Aged 30 to 39	39.6	19.8	19.9	3.6	17.2
Aged 40 to 49	40.1	20.4	19.7	4.6	17.4
Aged 50 to 59	44.1	24.2	22.9	4.9	17.3
Aged 60 to 69	41.0	25.4	17.3	2.8	13.8
Aged 70 to 84	32.1	19.3	11.9	1.8	9.9
Aged 85 or older	24.2	13.7	9.8	1.9	7.0

Definitions: Biologically based therapies include chelation therapy, nonvitamin, nonmineral, natural products and diet-based therapies. Mind-body therapies include biofeedback meditation, guided imagery, progressive relaxation, deep breathing exercises, hypnosis, yoga, tai chi, and qi gong. Alternative medical systems include acupuncture, ayurveda, homeopathic treatment, naturopathy, and traditional healers. Manipulative body-based therapies include chiropractic or osteopathic manipulation, massage, and movement therapies.
Source: National Center for Health Statistics, Complementary and Alternative Medicine Use Among Adults and Children: United States, 2007, National Health Statistics Report, No. 12, 2008, Internet site http://www.cdc.gov/nchs/products/nhsr.htm

Many Deaths of Younger Adults Are Preventable

Accidents are the leading killers of 25-to-44-year-olds.

When adults under age 45 die, it is often preventable. Accidents are the leading cause of death among 25-to-44-year-olds, and they account for 25 percent of the total. Suicide ranks fourth among 25-to-44-year-olds, and homicide is fifth. Cancer is the second-most-important cause of death in the age group, followed by heart disease. HIV infection ranks seventh—a cause that no longer ranks among the top 15 for the population as a whole.

Although more could be done to reduce deaths among young adults, some progress has been made. The life expectancy of Americans continues to rise. At age 35, life expectancy is another 45 years. At age 40, another 41 years of life remain—marking the true age of middle age.

■ As Gen Xers age, heart disease and cancer will become the two leading causes of death.

Cancer and heart disease are important causes of death among 25-to-44-year-olds

(percent of deaths among 25-to-44-year-olds caused by top-three causes of death, 2010)

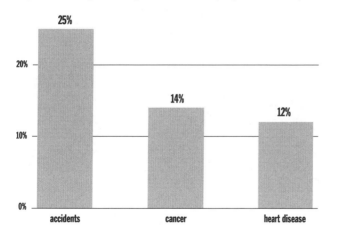

Table 3.40 Leading Causes of Death among People Aged 25 to 44, 2010

(total number of deaths, number and and percent distribution of deaths among people aged 25 to 44, and age group share of total, for the 10 leading causes of death among people aged 25 to 44, 2010)

			aged 25 to 44		
		total	number	percent distribution	share of total
	All causes	**2,465,932**	**112,177**	**100.0%**	**4.5%**
1.	Accidents (unintentional injuries) (5)	118,043	28,149	25.1	23.8
2.	Malignant neoplasms (cancer) (2)	573,855	15,389	13.7	2.7
3.	Diseases of the heart (1)	595,444	13,447	12.0	2.3
4.	Suicide (10)	37,793	12,119	10.8	32.1
5.	Homicide (15)	16,065	6,674	5.9	41.5
6.	Chronic liver disease and cirrhosis (12)	31,802	2,900	2.6	9.1
7.	Human immunodeficiency virus infection	8,352	2,638	2.4	31.6
8.	Cerebrovascular diseases (4)	129,180	2,396	2.1	1.9
9.	Diabetes mellitus (7)	68,905	2,365	2.1	3.4
10.	Influenza and pneumonia (9)	50,003	1,146	1.0	2.3
	All other causes	836,490	24,954	22.2	3.0

Note: Number in parentheses shows cause of death rank for total population if cause is one of top 15.
Source: National Center for Health Statistics, Deaths: Preliminary Data for 2010, National Vital Statistics Reports, Vol. 60, No. 4, 2012, Internet site http://www.cdc.gov/nchs/deaths.htm; calculations by New Strategist

Table 3.41 Life Expectancy by Age and Sex, 2010

(expected years of life remaining at selected ages, by sex, 2010)

	total	females	males
At birth	78.7	81.1	76.2
Aged 1	78.2	80.5	75.7
Aged 5	74.3	76.6	71.8
Aged 10	69.3	71.6	66.8
Aged 15	64.4	66.7	61.9
Aged 20	59.5	61.8	57.1
Aged 25	54.8	56.9	52.4
Aged 30	50.0	52.0	47.8
Aged 35	45.3	47.2	43.1
Aged 40	40.6	42.5	38.5
Aged 45	36.0	37.8	33.9
Aged 50	31.5	33.2	29.6
Aged 55	27.2	28.8	25.4
Aged 60	23.1	24.5	21.5
Aged 65	19.2	20.3	17.7
Aged 70	15.5	16.5	14.2
Aged 75	12.2	12.9	11.0
Aged 80	9.2	9.7	8.2
Aged 85	6.6	7.0	5.9
Aged 90	4.7	4.9	4.1
Aged 95	3.3	3.4	2.9
Aged 100	2.4	2.4	2.1

Source: National Center for Health Statistics, Deaths: Preliminary Data for 2010, National Vital Statistics Reports, Vol. 60, No. 4, 2012, Internet site http://www.cdc.gov/nchs/deaths.htm; calculations by New Strategist

4

Housing

■ The homeownership rate in the United States reached a peak of 69.0 percent in 2004. Since then, the rate has fallen by 2.9 percentage points. Among Gen Xers, those aged 35 to 39 have been hurt the most.

■ The 2011 homeownership rate of householders aged 35 to 44 was 4.6 percentage points below the rate of 2000.

■ Among Gen Xers, the homeownership rate is above 50 percent only for married couples and male-headed families.

■ Homeownership surpasses 50 percent among non-Hispanic whites in the 25-to-34 age group. Among Asians, the majority owns a home in the 35-to-44 age group. Among blacks and Hispanics, the percentage reaches at least 50 percent in the 45-to-54 age group.

■ The majority of American households (69 percent) live in single-family homes or duplexes (one unit detached or attached). Householders aged 35 to 64 are most likely to live in this type of home, at 74 percent.

■ Twelve percent of Americans aged 1 or older moved between March 2010 and March 2011, but the proportion was a slightly smaller 11 percent among people aged 35 to 44.

Homeownership Rate Has Declined

Since 2004, rate has fallen steeply among 35-to-44-year-olds.

The homeownership rate in the United States reached a peak of 69.0 percent in 2004. Since then, the rate has fallen by 2.9 percentage points, to 66.1 percent in 2011, because of the Great Recession and the collapse of the housing market. Among Gen Xers, those aged 35 to 39 have been hurt the most. The homeownership rate of 35-to-39-year-olds fell by more than 6 percentage points between 2004 and 2011.

The overall homeownership rate of 2011 was 1.4 percentage points below the rate of 2000. For 35-to-44-year-olds, the homeownership rate was nearly 5 percentage points lower in 2011 than in 2000. The homeownership rate of Gen Xers has fallen, in part, because some have lost their homes in the economic downturn.

■ When jobs become plentiful again, the homeownership rate among Gen Xers will rise.

After peaking in 2004, the homeownership rate is down among 35-to-44-year-olds

(percentage point change in homeownership rate for householders aged 35 to 44, by age, 2004 and 2011)

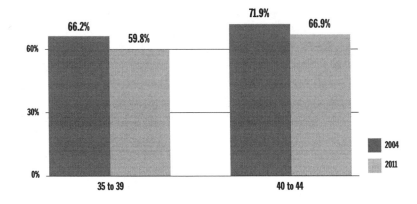

Table 4.1 Homeownership by Age of Householder, 2000 to 2011

(percentage of householders who own their home by age of householder, 2000 to 2011; percentage point change, 2004–11 and 2000–11)

					percentage point change	
	2011	2010	2004	2000	2004–11	2000–11
Total households	**66.1%**	**66.8%**	**69.0%**	**67.5%**	**–2.9**	**–1.4**
Under age 25	22.6	22.8	25.2	21.7	–2.6	0.9
Aged 25 to 29	34.6	36.8	40.2	38.1	–5.6	–3.5
Aged 30 to 34	49.8	51.6	57.4	54.6	–7.6	–4.8
Aged 35 to 44	63.5	65.0	69.2	68.0	–5.8	–4.6
Aged 35 to 39	59.8	61.9	66.2	65.0	–6.4	–5.2
Aged 40 to 44	66.9	67.8	71.9	70.6	–5.0	–3.7
Aged 45 to 54	72.7	73.5	77.2	76.5	–4.5	–3.8
Aged 55 to 64	78.5	79.0	81.7	80.3	–3.2	–1.8
Aged 65 or older	80.9	80.5	81.1	80.5	–0.2	0.4

Source: Bureau of the Census, Housing Vacancies and Homeownership, Internet site http://www.census.gov/hhes/www/housing/ hvs/hvs.html; calculations by New Strategist

Homeownership Rises with Age

Most householders aged 35 to 44 own their home.

Most of Generation X has made the transition from renting to home owning, although some are losing their homes in the economic downturn. The 60 percent majority of householders aged 35 to 39 were homeowners in 2011 (Gen Xers were aged 35 to 46 in that year). Among householders aged 40 to 44, the proportion who own their home rises to 67 percent.

Overall, 63 percent of householders aged 35 to 44 are homeowners and 37 percent are renters. The 35-to-44 age group accounts for 17 percent of the nation's homeowners and 19 percent of its renters.

■ The rental market is getting a boost as Gen Xers delay buying houses and the large Millennial generation fills the young-adult age groups.

Homeownership becomes the norm in the 35-to-39 age group

(percent distribution of householders aged 35 to 44 by homeownership status, 2011)

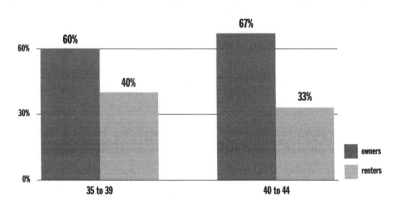

Table 4.2 Owners and Renters by Age of Householder, 2011

(number and percent distribution of householders by homeownership status, and owner and renter share of total, by age of householder, 2011; numbers in thousands)

	total	owners			renters		
		number	percent distribution	share of total	number	percent distribution	share of total
Total households	**113,534**	**75,091**	**100.0%**	**66.1%**	**38,443**	**100.0%**	**33.9%**
Under age 25	6,079	1,373	1.8	22.6	4,706	12.2	77.4
Aged 25 to 29	9,062	3,134	4.2	34.6	5,928	15.4	65.4
Aged 30 to 34	9,957	4,958	6.6	49.8	4,999	13.0	50.2
Aged 35 to 44	20,182	12,808	17.1	63.5	7,374	19.2	36.5
Aged 35 to 39	9,667	5,777	7.7	59.8	3,890	10.1	40.2
Aged 40 to 44	10,515	7,031	9.4	66.9	3,484	9.1	33.1
Aged 45 to 54	23,234	16,886	22.5	72.7	6,348	16.5	27.3
Aged 55 to 64	20,689	16,240	21.6	78.5	4,449	11.6	21.5
Aged 65 or older	24,330	19,693	26.2	80.9	4,637	12.1	19.1

Source: Bureau of the Census, Housing Vacancies and Homeownership Survey, Internet site http://www.census.gov/hhes/www/ housing/hvs/historic/index.html; calculations by New Strategist

Married Couples Are Most Likely to Be Homeowners

Homeownership rates are highest in the Midwest.

The homeownership rate among all married couples stood at 81.5 percent in 2011, much higher than the 66.1 percent for all households. Among Gen X couples, the homeownership rate was 77 percent. Homeownership is much lower for other types of households and lowest for female-headed families, at 48.1 percent in 2011. Among Gen Xers, only married couples and male-headed families are likely to be homeowners.

Nationally, the homeownership rate is highest in the Midwest and lowest in the West. This is also true among Gen Xers, whose homeownership rate ranges from a high of 69 percent in the Midwest to a low of 55 percent in the West.

■ The lax lending standards of the housing bubble era did not eliminate differences in homeownership rates by household type.

More than 70 percent of couples aged 35 to 44 own their home

(percent of married-couple householders who own their home, by age, 2011)

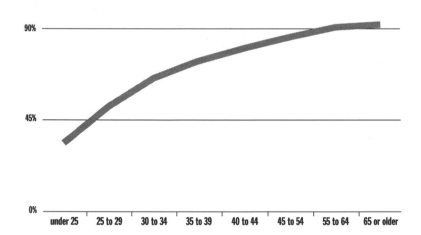

Table 4.3 Homeownership Rate by Age of Householder and Type of Household, 2011

(percent of households owning their home, by age of householder and type of household, 2011)

	total	married couples	female family householder, no spouse present	male family householder, no spouse present	people living alone	
					females	males
Total households	**66.1%**	**81.5%**	**48.1%**	**55.6%**	**58.5%**	**50.6%**
Under age 25	22.6	33.7	25.9	40.3	10.6	14.5
Aged 25 to 29	34.6	51.7	22.0	36.4	19.4	26.3
Aged 30 to 34	49.8	65.5	28.6	43.5	35.6	34.4
Aged 35 to 44	63.5	77.4	42.4	54.4	43.8	44.1
Aged 35 to 39	59.8	74.1	37.4	51.3	42.1	41.5
Aged 40 to 44	66.9	80.4	47.3	57.5	45.3	46.4
Aged 45 to 54	72.7	85.9	58.4	65.8	53.9	53.2
Aged 55 to 64	78.5	90.7	66.2	74.5	64.8	59.1
Aged 65 or older	80.9	92.1	80.5	80.4	70.9	68.9

Source: Bureau of the Census, Housing Vacancies and Homeownership, Internet site http://www.census.gov/hhes/www/housing/hvs/hvs.html; calculations by New Strategist

Table 4.4 Homeownership Rate by Age of Householder and Region, 2011

(percent of households owning their home, by age of householder and region, 2011)

	total	Northeast	Midwest	South	West
Total households	**66.1%**	**63.6%**	**70.2%**	**68.3%**	**60.5%**
Under age 25	22.6	21.9	23.2	23.6	20.7
Aged 25 to 29	34.6	28.9	40.3	36.8	29.4
Aged 30 to 34	49.8	45.8	58.0	50.4	44.1
Aged 35 to 44	63.5	61.6	69.3	66.2	55.0
Aged 35 to 39	59.8	56.8	65.4	63.2	51.2
Aged 40 to 44	66.9	65.7	72.9	69.0	58.6
Aged 45 to 54	72.7	70.2	77.5	74.4	66.9
Aged 55 to 64	78.5	75.1	81.5	81.1	74.0
Aged 65 or older	80.9	73.7	82.0	85.3	78.9

Source: Bureau of the Census, Housing Vacancies and Homeownership, Internet site http://www.census.gov/hhes/www/housing/hvs/hvs.html; calculations by New Strategist

Most Black and Hispanic Gen Xers Are Not Yet Homeowners

Among Asians aged 35 to 44, the majority owns a home.

The homeownership rate of Asians, blacks, and Hispanics is below average. According to the 2010 census, the homeownership rate was 65.1 percent for all households in 2010. Among Asians, the rate was 58.0 percent. Among blacks it was 44.3 percent, and the Hispanic homeownership rate was 47.3 percent. In contrast, an above-average 72.2 percent of non-Hispanic whites owned their home in 2010.

Homeownership surpasses the 50 percent threshold among non-Hispanic whites in the 25-to-34 age group. Among Asians, the majority owns a home in the 35-to-44 age group. Among blacks and Hispanics, the percentage reaches at least 50 percent in the 45-to-54 age group.

■ Although Hispanics outnumber blacks in the United States, black and Hispanic homeowners are nearly equal in number.

More than 70 percent of non-Hispanic white householders aged 35 to 44 own their home

(homeownership rate of householders aged 35 to 44, by race and Hispanic origin, 2010)

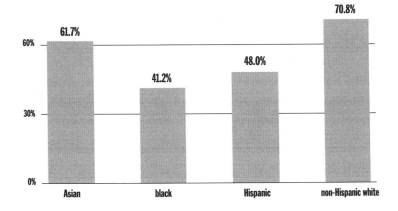

Table 4.5 Homeownership by Age, Race, and Hispanic Origin, 2010

(number and percent of households thath own their home, by age, race, and Hispanic origin of householder, 2010; numbers in thousands)

	total	Asian	black	Hispanic	non-Hispanic white
Total households	**116,716**	**4,632**	**14,130**	**13,461**	**82,333**
Under age 25	5,401	217	802	885	3,333
Aged 25 to 34	17,957	924	2,466	3,122	11,003
Aged 35 to 44	21,291	1,145	2,890	3,457	13,362
Aged 45 to 54	24,907	1,002	3,190	2,808	17,438
Aged 55 to 64	21,340	720	2,450	1,693	16,129
Aged 65 or older	25,820	624	2,331	1,496	21,069
Aged 65 to 74	13,505	371	1,374	883	10,692
Aged 75 to 84	8,716	191	722	476	7,238
Aged 85 or older	3,599	62	235	136	3,139
HOMEOWNERS					
Total households	**75,986**	**2,689**	**6,261**	**6,368**	**59,484**
Under age 25	870	26	63	133	622
Aged 25 to 34	7,547	319	557	976	5,538
Aged 35 to 44	13,256	706	1,190	1,659	9,461
Aged 45 to 54	17,804	701	1,594	1,611	13,601
Aged 55 to 64	16,503	530	1,398	1,048	13,285
Aged 65 or older	20,007	407	1,460	941	16,977
Aged 65 to 74	10,834	260	851	558	9,028
Aged 75 to 84	6,789	114	463	303	5,844
Aged 85 or older	2,384	33	146	80	2,105
HOMEOWNERSHIP RATE					
Total households	**65.1%**	**58.0%**	**44.3%**	**47.3%**	**72.2%**
Under age 25	16.1	12.1	7.8	15.1	18.7
Aged 25 to 34	42.0	34.5	22.6	31.3	50.3
Aged 35 to 44	62.3	61.7	41.2	48.0	70.8
Aged 45 to 54	71.5	69.9	50.0	57.4	78.0
Aged 55 to 64	77.3	73.6	57.0	61.9	82.4
Aged 65 or older	77.5	65.2	62.6	62.9	80.6
Aged 65 to 74	80.2	70.2	61.9	63.2	84.4
Aged 75 to 84	77.9	59.4	64.2	63.5	80.7
Aged 85 or older	66.2	52.9	62.3	59.1	67.1

Note: Asians and blacks are those who identify themselves as being of the race alone. Hispanics may be of any race. Non-Hispanic whites are those who identify themselves as being white alone and not Hispanic.
Source: Bureau of the Census, 2010 Census, American Factfinder,Internet site http://factfinder2.census .gov/faces/nav/jsf/ pages/index.xhtml; calculations by New Strategist

The Middle Aged Are Most Likely to Live in Single-Family Homes

Only 20 percent of householders aged 35 to 64 live in multi-unit buildings.

The majority of American households (69 percent) live in single-family homes or duplexes (one unit detached or attached). Householders aged 35 to 64 are most likely to live in this type of home, at 74 percent. Not surprisingly, homeowners are much more likely than renters to live in a single-family home. Among householders aged 35 to 64, fully 89 percent of homeowners live in a single-family home versus 38 percent of renters.

Apartment living is most popular among younger adults. Forty-five percent of householders under age 35 live in a multi-unit building, while just under half live in a single-family home or duplex. Interestingly, however, adults aged 65 or older are more likely than middle-aged or younger adults to live in a building with 50 or more units. Behind this figure is the movement of older adults into multi-unit retirement complexes and assisted living facilities.

Six percent of households live in mobile homes, boats, RVs, and so on. This category is dominated by mobile homes. The proportion of householders who live in a mobile home does not vary much by age.

■ The demand for single-family homes helped to fuel the housing bubble, resulting in the Great Recession.

Most of the middle aged are in single-family homes

(percent of households living in single-family homes, by age of householder, 2010)

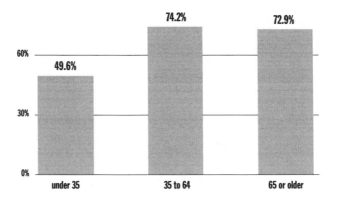

Table 4.6 Number of Units in Structure by Age of Householder and Homeownership Status, 2010

(number and percent distribution of households by age of householder, homeownership status, and number of units in structure, 2010; numbers in thousands)

	total	one detached or attached	multi-unit building total	2 to 4	5 to 19	20 to 49	50 or more	mobile home, boat, RV, etc.
Total households	114,567	79,080	28,507	9,032	10,094	3,906	5,475	6,979
Under age 35	22,695	11,267	10,160	3,060	4,214	1,424	1,462	1,267
Aged 35 to 64	66,998	49,692	13,247	4,665	4,705	1,687	2,190	4,061
Aged 65 or older	24,874	18,121	5,100	1,307	1,175	795	1,823	1,651
Owner-occupied	74,873	65,779	3,986	1,590	1,034	493	869	5,108
Under age 35	8,062	6,837	602	191	208	77	126	622
Aged 35 to 64	47,265	42,140	2,100	906	536	234	424	3,026
Aged 65 or older	19,546	16,802	1,284	493	290	182	319	1,460
Renter-occupied	39,694	13,301	24,521	7,442	9,060	3,413	4,606	1,871
Under age 35	14,633	4,430	9,558	2,869	4,006	1,347	1,336	645
Aged 35 to 64	19,733	7,552	11,147	3,759	4,169	1,453	1,766	1,035
Aged 65 or older	5,328	1,319	3,816	814	885	613	1,504	191

PERCENT DISTRIBUTION BY UNITS IN STRUCTURE

	total	one detached or attached	multi-unit building total	2 to 4	5 to 19	20 to 49	50 or more	mobile home, boat, RV, etc.
Total households	100.0%	69.0%	24.9%	7.9%	8.8%	3.4%	4.8%	6.1%
Under age 35	100.0	49.6	44.8	13.5	18.6	6.3	6.4	5.6
Aged 35 to 64	100.0	74.2	19.8	7.0	7.0	2.5	3.3	6.1
Aged 65 or older	100.0	72.9	20.5	5.3	4.7	3.2	7.3	6.6
Owner-occupied	100.0	87.9	5.3	2.1	1.4	0.7	1.2	6.8
Under age 35	100.0	84.8	7.5	2.4	2.6	1.0	1.6	7.7
Aged 35 to 64	100.0	89.2	4.4	1.9	1.1	0.5	0.9	6.4
Aged 65 or older	100.0	86.0	6.6	2.5	1.5	0.9	1.6	7.5
Renter-occupied	100.0	33.5	61.8	18.7	22.8	8.6	11.6	4.7
Under age 35	100.0	30.3	65.3	19.6	27.4	9.2	9.1	4.4
Aged 35 to 64	100.0	38.3	56.5	19.0	21.1	7.4	8.9	5.2
Aged 65 or older	100.0	24.8	71.6	15.3	16.6	11.5	28.2	3.6

Source: Bureau of the Census, 2010 American Community Survey, Internet site http://factfinder2.census.gov/faces/nav/jsf/pages/index.xhtml; calculations by New Strategist

About One in 10 Gen Xers Moves Annually

Most move for housing-related reasons.

Twelve percent of Americans aged 1 or older moved between March 2010 and March 2011, but the proportion was a slightly smaller 11 percent among people aged 35 to 44. Among all movers, the majority stays within the same county. Only 14 percent of people who moved between 2010 and 2011 went to a different state.

Regardless of age, housing is the primary motivation for moving. The 47 percent plurality of movers aged 30 to 44 say housing was the main reason for the move. Family reasons ranked second as a motivation for moving, and employment ranked third. Among those who moved between 2010 and 2011 because of foreclosure, about one in four were aged 30 to 44.

■ Mobility has been declining in the United States for decades, and the Great Recession lowered mobility rates even further.

Twelve percent of 35-to-39-year-olds moved between 2010 and 2011

(percent of people who moved between March 2010 and March 2011, by age)

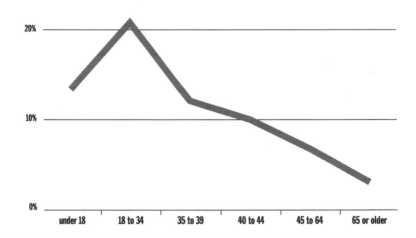

Table 4.7 Geographic Mobility by Age and Type of Move, 2010–11

(total number of people aged 1 or older, and number and percent who moved between March 2010 and March 2011, by age and type of move; numbers in thousands)

	total	total movers	same county	different county, same state	different state total	different state same region	different state different region	movers from abroad
Total, aged 1 or older	**302,005**	**35,075**	**23,325**	**5,912**	**4,779**	**2,323**	**2,456**	**1,058**
Under age 18	70,811	9,465	6,591	1,494	1,162	554	608	216
Aged 18 to 34	71,234	14,796	9,777	2,564	1,956	975	981	499
Aged 35 to 44	39,842	4,387	2,917	696	617	291	326	157
Aged 35 to 39	19,255	2,330	1,549	373	307	138	169	101
Aged 40 to 44	20,587	2,057	1,368	323	310	153	157	56
Aged 45 to 64	80,939	5,513	3,311	950	796	409	387	134
Aged 65 or older	39,178	1,233	729	209	246	92	154	51

PERCENT DISTRIBUTION BY MOBILITY STATUS

	total	total movers	same county	different county, same state	different state total	different state same region	different state different region	movers from abroad
Total, aged 1 or older	**100.0%**	**11.6%**	**7.7%**	**2.0%**	**1.6%**	**0.8%**	**0.8%**	**0.4%**
Under age 18	100.0	13.4	9.3	2.1	1.6	0.8	0.9	0.3
Aged 18 to 34	100.0	20.8	13.7	3.6	2.7	1.4	1.4	0.7
Aged 35 to 44	100.0	11.0	7.3	1.7	1.5	0.7	0.8	0.4
Aged 35 to 39	100.0	12.1	8.0	1.9	1.6	0.7	0.9	0.5
Aged 40 to 44	100.0	10.0	6.6	1.6	1.5	0.7	0.8	0.3
Aged 45 to 64	100.0	6.8	4.1	1.2	1.0	0.5	0.5	0.2
Aged 65 or older	100.0	3.1	1.9	0.5	0.6	0.2	0.4	0.1

PERCENT DISTRIBUTION OF MOVERS BY TYPE OF MOVE

	total	total movers	same county	different county, same state	different state total	different state same region	different state different region	movers from abroad
Total, aged 1 or older	–	**100.0%**	**66.5%**	**16.9%**	**13.6%**	**6.6%**	**7.0%**	**3.0%**
Under age 18	–	100.0	69.6	15.8	12.3	5.9	6.4	2.3
Aged 18 to 34	–	100.0	66.1	17.3	13.2	6.6	6.6	3.4
Aged 35 to 44	–	100.0	66.5	15.9	14.1	6.6	7.4	3.6
Aged 35 to 39	–	100.0	66.5	16.0	13.2	5.9	7.3	4.3
Aged 40 to 44	–	100.0	66.5	15.7	15.1	7.4	7.6	2.7
Aged 45 to 64	–	100.0	60.1	17.2	14.4	7.4	7.0	2.4
Aged 65 or older	–	100.0	59.1	17.0	20.0	7.5	12.5	4.1

Note: "–" means not applicable.
Source: Bureau of the Census, Geographic Mobility: 2010 to 2011, Detailed Tables, Internet site http://www.census.gov/hhes/migration/data/cps/cps2011.html; calculations by New Strategist

Table 4.8 Reason for Moving among People Aged 30 to 44, 2010–11

(number and percent distribution of movers aged 30 to 44 by primary reason for move and share of total movers between March 2010 and March 2011; numbers in thousands)

	total movers	movers aged 30 to 44		
		number	percent distribution	share of total
Total movers	**35,075**	**7,783**	**100.0%**	**22.2%**
Family reasons	**9,784**	**2,037**	**26.2**	**20.8**
Change in marital status	1,949	511	6.6	26.2
To establish own household	3,334	648	8.3	19.4
Other familiy reasons	4,501	878	11.3	19.5
Employment reasons	**6,481**	**1,616**	**20.8**	**24.9**
New job or job transfer	2,829	784	10.1	27.7
To look for work or lost job	924	230	3.0	24.9
To be closer to work/easier commute	2,081	467	6.0	22.4
Retired	108	6	0.1	5.6
Other job-related reason	539	129	1.7	23.9
Housing reasons	**15,736**	**3,641**	**46.8**	**23.1**
Wanted own home, not rent	1,530	393	5.0	25.7
Wanted better home/apartment	5,665	1,371	17.6	24.2
Wanted better neighborhood/less crime	1,360	350	4.5	25.7
Wanted cheaper housing	3,684	792	10.2	21.5
Foreclosure/eviction	412	100	1.3	24.3
Other housing reasons	3,085	635	8.2	20.6
Other reasons	**3,073**	**488**	**6.3**	**15.9**
To attend or leave college	890	64	0.8	7.2
Change of climate	149	41	0.5	27.5
Health reasons	564	79	1.0	14.0
Natural disaster	31	3	0.0	9.7
Other reasons	1,439	301	3.9	20.9

Source: Bureau of the Census, Geographic Mobility: 2010 to 2011, Detailed Tables, Internet site http://www.census.gov/hhes/migration/data/cps/cps2011.html; calculations by New Strategist

5

Income

■ Between 2000 and 2010, the median income of households headed by people aged 35 to 44 fell by a substantial 9 percent, after adjusting for inflation.

■ The median income of households headed by Asians aged 35 to 44 stood at $79,596 in 2010, exceeding the median income of non-Hispanic whites by nearly $8,000.

■ Among Gen Xers, married couples have the highest incomes by far. In 2010 married couples headed by people aged 35 to 44 had a median income of $82,537.

■ The median income of men aged 35 to 44 fell 12 percent between 2000 and 2010, after adjusting for inflation. The median income of women in the age group climbed 5 percent during the decade.

■ Generation Xers are less likely to be poor than the average American, but a substantial one in eight is poor. Overall, 15.1 percent of Americans lived in poverty in 2010. Among people aged 35 to 44, a smaller 12.6 percent were poor.

Household Incomes of Gen Xers Have Declined

Incomes are lower than they were in 1990.

Between 2000 and 2010, the median income of households headed by people aged 35 to 44 fell by a substantial 9 percent, after adjusting for inflation. (Generation Xers were aged 34 to 45 in 2010.) Most of the decline occurred since 2007.

The Great Recession has been so severe that the household incomes of young and middle-aged adults are now lower than the incomes of their counterparts two decades ago. Between 1990 and 2010, householders aged 35 to 44 have seen their median household income slip by 1 percent.

■ The $61,644 median income of householders aged 35 to 44 is 25 percent greater than the overall household median of $49,445.

Since 2000, the median household income of Gen Xers has fallen by more than $6,000

(median income of households headed by people aged 35 to 44, 2000 and 2010, in 2010 dollars)

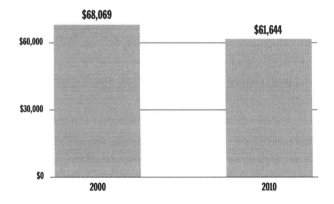

Table 5.1 Median Income of Households Headed by People Aged 35 to 44, 1990 to 2010

(median income of total households and households headed by people aged 35 to 44, and index of age group to total, 1990 to 2010; percent change for selected years; in 2010 dollars)

	total households	35 to 44	index, 35–44 to total
2010	$49,445	$61,644	125
2009	50,599	62,091	123
2008	50,939	63,750	125
2007	52,823	65,327	124
2006	52,124	65,321	125
2005	51,739	64,871	125
2004	51,174	65,427	128
2003	51,353	65,254	127
2002	51,398	64,865	126
2001	52,005	65,666	126
2000	53,164	68,069	128
1999	53,252	66,486	125
1998	51,944	64,723	125
1997	50,123	62,793	125
1996	49,112	61,466	125
1995	48,408	61,746	128
1994	46,937	60,617	129
1993	46,419	60,715	131
1992	46,646	60,680	130
1991	47,032	61,431	131
1990	48,423	62,360	129
Percent change			
2007 to 2010	−6.4%	−5.6%	–
2000 to 2010	−7.0	−9.4	–
1990 to 2010	2.1	−1.1	–

Note: The index is calculated by dividing the median income of the age group by the national median and multiplying by 100. "–" means not applicable.
Source: Bureau of the Census, Historical Income Statistics—Households, Internet site http://www.census.gov/hhes/www/income/data/historical/household/; calculations by New Strategist

Household Income Rises with Age

Household income is nearing its peak in the 40-to-44 age group.

The median income of householders aged 35 to 44 was $61,644 in 2010, well above the national median of $49,445. The median income of householders aged 40 to 44, at $63,198, was only a few dollars below the household income peak of $63,233 reached in the 45-to-49 age group.

In the nation as a whole, 24 million households had incomes of $100,000 or more in 2010. One-fourth of those householders were aged 35 to 44. (Gen Xers were aged 34 to 45 in 2010.) Among all households, 20 percent have incomes of $100,000 or more. Among householders aged 35 to 44, the figure is a higher 26 percent.

■ Gen Xers are likely to see little income growth in the years ahead as Boomers postpone retirement and clog up the promotion pipeline.

Householders aged 35 to 44 have above-average incomes

(median income of total households and households headed by people aged 35 to 44, 2010)

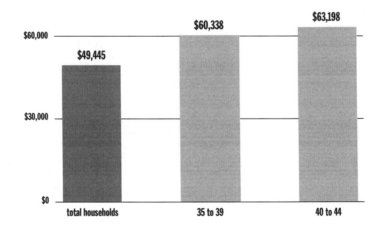

Table 5.2 Income of Households Headed by People Aged 35 to 44, 2010: Total Households

(number and percent distribution of total households and households headed by people aged 35 to 44, by income, 2010; households in thousands as of 2011)

		aged 35 to 44		
	total	total	35 to 39	40 to 44
Total households	**118,682**	**21,250**	**10,334**	**10,917**
Under $10,000	9,231	1,218	620	599
$10,000 to $19,999	14,321	1,548	774	773
$20,000 to $29,999	13,667	1,904	950	953
$30,000 to $39,999	12,055	2,006	995	1,011
$40,000 to $49,999	10,557	1,844	933	911
$50,000 to $59,999	9,291	1,755	858	897
$60,000 to $69,999	7,991	1,590	777	813
$70,000 to $79,999	6,887	1,468	697	771
$80,000 to $89,999	5,823	1,247	631	616
$90,000 to $99,999	4,626	1,054	497	557
$100,000 or more	24,234	5,618	2,602	3,016
$100,000 to $124,999	9,008	2,163	1,019	1,146
$125,000 to $149,999	5,294	1,202	543	661
$150,000 to $174,999	3,386	722	325	396
$175,000 to $199,999	1,919	442	228	212
$200,000 or more	4,627	1,089	487	601
Median income	$49,445	$61,644	$60,338	$63,198
Total households	**100.0%**	**100.0%**	**100.0%**	**100.0%**
Under $10,000	7.8	5.7	6.0	5.5
$10,000 to $19,999	12.1	7.3	7.5	7.1
$20,000 to $29,999	11.5	9.0	9.2	8.7
$30,000 to $39,999	10.2	9.4	9.6	9.3
$40,000 to $49,999	8.9	8.7	9.0	8.3
$50,000 to $59,999	7.8	8.3	8.3	8.2
$60,000 to $69,999	6.7	7.5	7.5	7.4
$70,000 to $79,999	5.8	6.9	6.7	7.1
$80,000 to $89,999	4.9	5.9	6.1	5.6
$90,000 to $99,999	3.9	5.0	4.8	5.1
$100,000 or more	20.4	26.4	25.2	27.6
$100,000 to $124,999	7.6	10.2	9.9	10.5
$125,000 to $149,999	4.5	5.7	5.3	6.1
$150,000 to $174,999	2.9	3.4	3.1	3.6
$175,000 to $199,999	1.6	2.1	2.2	1.9
$200,000 or more	3.9	5.1	4.7	5.5

Source: Bureau of the Census, 2011 Current Population Survey, Internet site http://www.census.gov/hhes/www/cpstables/032011/hhinc/toc.htm; calculations by New Strategist

Incomes Are Highest for Asian Households

Among Gen Xers, the incomes of Asians are far higher than those of other racial or ethnic groups.

The median income of households headed by Asians aged 35 to 44 stood at $79,596 in 2010. (Gen Xers were aged 34 to 45 in that year.) Among Asian householders aged 35 to 39, median income was an even higher $80,097. The median income of non-Hispanic whites aged 35 to 44, at $71,708, was lower than that of Asians. The median incomes of Hispanic and black householders aged 35 to 44 were much lower—$42,370 and $40,353, respectively.

One factor behind the income differences by race and Hispanic origin is the number of earners per household. Because Asian and non-Hispanic white households are more likely than black households to be two-earner married couples, their incomes are considerably higher. Education also accounts for some of the gap, especially for Hispanic households.

■ Blacks will not close the household income gap with non-Hispanic whites until dual-earner couples make up a larger share of their households. Hispanics will not close the gap until their educational attainment rises.

The household incomes of Gen Xers vary by race and Hispanic origin

(median income of households headed by people aged 35 to 44, by race and Hispanic origin, 2010)

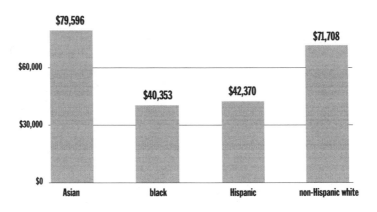

Table 5.3 Income of Households Headed by People Aged 35 to 44, 2010: Asian Households

(number and percent distribution of total Asian households and Asian households headed by people aged 35 to 44, by income, 2010; households in thousands as of 2011)

	total	aged 35 to 44 total	35 to 39	40 to 44
Total Asian households	**5,040**	**1,163**	**649**	**513**
Under $10,000	353	58	30	28
$10,000 to $19,999	406	58	31	28
$20,000 to $29,999	460	68	41	26
$30,000 to $39,999	358	63	40	22
$40,000 to $49,999	382	87	38	48
$50,000 to $59,999	376	97	56	41
$60,000 to $69,999	387	85	43	41
$70,000 to $79,999	265	67	45	23
$80,000 to $89,999	243	54	33	21
$90,000 to $99,999	213	40	22	19
$100,000 or more	1,594	487	271	215
$100,000 to $124,999	508	144	90	53
$125,000 to $149,999	335	88	43	46
$150,000 to $174,999	258	77	44	31
$175,000 to $199,999	135	57	40	18
$200,000 or more	358	121	54	67
Median income	$63,726	$79,596	$80,097	$77,939
Total Asian households	**100.0%**	**100.0%**	**100.0%**	**100.0%**
Under $10,000	7.0	5.0	4.6	5.5
$10,000 to $19,999	8.1	5.0	4.8	5.5
$20,000 to $29,999	9.1	5.8	6.3	5.1
$30,000 to $39,999	7.1	5.4	6.2	4.3
$40,000 to $49,999	7.6	7.5	5.9	9.4
$50,000 to $59,999	7.5	8.3	8.6	8.0
$60,000 to $69,999	7.7	7.3	6.6	8.0
$70,000 to $79,999	5.3	5.8	6.9	4.5
$80,000 to $89,999	4.8	4.6	5.1	4.1
$90,000 to $99,999	4.2	3.4	3.4	3.7
$100,000 or more	31.6	41.9	41.8	41.9
$100,000 to $124,999	10.1	12.4	13.9	10.3
$125,000 to $149,999	6.6	7.6	6.6	9.0
$150,000 to $174,999	5.1	6.6	6.8	6.0
$175,000 to $199,999	2.7	4.9	6.2	3.5
$200,000 or more	7.1	10.4	8.3	13.1

Note: Asians are those who identify themselves as being of the race alone and those who identify themselves as being of the race in combination with other races.
Source: Bureau of the Census, 2011 Current Population Survey, Internet site http://www.census.gov/hhes/www/cpstables/032011/hhinc/toc.htm; calculations by New Strategist

Table 5.4 Income of Households Headed by People Aged 35 to 44, 2010: Black Households

(number and percent distribution of total black households and black households headed by people aged 35 to 44, by income, 2010; households in thousands as of 2011)

	total	aged 35 to 44		
		total	35 to 39	40 to 44
Total black households	**15,613**	**3,008**	**1,514**	**1,494**
Under $10,000	2,564	351	183	168
$10,000 to $19,999	2,573	345	175	170
$20,000 to $29,999	2,208	405	204	200
$30,000 to $39,999	1,770	387	212	175
$40,000 to $49,999	1,454	309	173	136
$50,000 to $59,999	1,063	222	117	106
$60,000 to $69,999	836	200	89	111
$70,000 to $79,999	777	187	76	111
$80,000 to $89,999	507	131	77	54
$90,000 to $99,999	354	84	35	48
$100,000 or more	1,509	387	172	214
$100,000 to $124,999	675	205	93	113
$125,000 to $149,999	345	96	38	57
$150,000 to $174,999	213	20	10	9
$175,000 to $199,999	84	20	7	13
$200,000 or more	192	46	24	22
Median income	$32,106	$40,353	$38,257	$41,773
Total black households	**100.0%**	**100.0%**	**100.0%**	**100.0%**
Under $10,000	16.4	11.7	12.1	11.2
$10,000 to $19,999	16.5	11.5	11.6	11.4
$20,000 to $29,999	14.1	13.5	13.5	13.4
$30,000 to $39,999	11.3	12.9	14.0	11.7
$40,000 to $49,999	9.3	10.3	11.4	9.1
$50,000 to $59,999	6.8	7.4	7.7	7.1
$60,000 to $69,999	5.4	6.6	5.9	7.4
$70,000 to $79,999	5.0	6.2	5.0	7.4
$80,000 to $89,999	3.2	4.4	5.1	3.6
$90,000 to $99,999	2.3	2.8	2.3	3.2
$100,000 or more	9.7	12.9	11.4	14.3
$100,000 to $124,999	4.3	6.8	6.1	7.6
$125,000 to $149,999	2.2	3.2	2.5	3.8
$150,000 to $174,999	1.4	0.7	0.7	0.6
$175,000 to $199,999	0.5	0.7	0.5	0.9
$200,000 or more	1.2	1.5	1.6	1.5

Note: Blacks are those who identify themselves as being of the race alone and those who identify themselves as being of the race in combination with other races.
Source: Bureau of the Census, 2011 Current Population Survey, Internet site http://www.census.gov/hhes/www/cpstables/032011/hhinc/toc.htm; calculations by New Strategist

Table 5.5 Income of Households Headed by People Aged 35 to 44, 2010: Hispanic Households

(number and percent distribution of total Hispanic households and Hispanic households headed by people aged 35 to 44, by income, 2010; households in thousands as of 2011)

	total	aged 35 to 44 total	35 to 39	40 to 44
Total Hispanic households	**13,665**	**3,367**	**1,739**	**1,628**
Under $10,000	1,363	259	140	119
$10,000 to $19,999	1,967	392	213	179
$20,000 to $29,999	2,100	480	231	248
$30,000 to $39,999	1,678	443	236	207
$40,000 to $49,999	1,329	369	184	184
$50,000 to $59,999	1,132	281	134	147
$60,000 to $69,999	895	254	136	117
$70,000 to $79,999	679	207	109	98
$80,000 to $89,999	564	160	79	81
$90,000 to $99,999	391	91	40	52
$100,000 or more	1,563	431	237	195
$100,000 to $124,999	665	173	90	84
$125,000 to $149,999	390	99	53	46
$150,000 to $174,999	211	63	31	31
$175,000 to $199,999	97	29	22	8
$200,000 or more	200	67	41	26
Median income	$37,759	$42,370	$41,835	$43,275
Total Hispanic households	**100.0%**	**100.0%**	**100.0%**	**100.0%**
Under $10,000	10.0	7.7	8.1	7.3
$10,000 to $19,999	14.4	11.6	12.2	11.0
$20,000 to $29,999	15.4	14.3	13.3	15.2
$30,000 to $39,999	12.3	13.2	13.6	12.7
$40,000 to $49,999	9.7	11.0	10.6	11.3
$50,000 to $59,999	8.3	8.3	7.7	9.0
$60,000 to $69,999	6.5	7.5	7.8	7.2
$70,000 to $79,999	5.0	6.1	6.3	6.0
$80,000 to $89,999	4.1	4.8	4.5	5.0
$90,000 to $99,999	2.9	2.7	2.3	3.2
$100,000 or more	11.4	12.8	13.6	12.0
$100,000 to $124,999	4.9	5.1	5.2	5.2
$125,000 to $149,999	2.9	2.9	3.0	2.8
$150,000 to $174,999	1.5	1.9	1.8	1.9
$175,000 to $199,999	0.7	0.9	1.3	0.5
$200,000 or more	1.5	2.0	2.4	1.6

Source: Bureau of the Census, 2011 Current Population Survey, Internet site http://www.census.gov/hhes/www/ cpstables/032011/hhinc/toc.htm; calculations by New Strategist

Table 5.6 Income of Households Headed by People Aged 35 to 44, 2010: Non-Hispanic White Households

(number and percent distribution of total non-Hispanic white households and non-Hispanic white households headed by people aged 35 to 44, by income, 2010; households in thousands as of 2011)

| | | aged 35 to 44 | | |
	total	total	35 to 39	40 to 44
Total non-Hispanic white households	**83,471**	**13,560**	**6,340**	**7,220**
Under $10,000	4,859	535	256	279
$10,000 to $19,999	9,247	762	361	401
$20,000 to $29,999	8,796	932	463	470
$30,000 to $39,999	8,157	1,087	487	600
$40,000 to $49,999	7,312	1,071	532	538
$50,000 to $59,999	6,650	1,138	542	596
$60,000 to $69,999	5,813	1,037	497	539
$70,000 to $79,999	5,116	1,000	468	532
$80,000 to $89,999	4,455	897	440	457
$90,000 to $99,999	3,641	827	396	430
$100,000 or more	19,425	4,273	1,898	2,377
$100,000 to $124,999	7,093	1,609	726	883
$125,000 to $149,999	4,187	921	407	514
$150,000 to $174,999	2,686	558	238	321
$175,000 to $199,999	1,596	330	158	173
$200,000 or more	3,863	855	369	486
Median income	$54,620	$71,708	$70,616	$72,486
Total non-Hispanic white households	**100.0%**	**100.0%**	**100.0%**	**100.0%**
Under $10,000	5.8	3.9	4.0	3.9
$10,000 to $19,999	11.1	5.6	5.7	5.6
$20,000 to $29,999	10.5	6.9	7.3	6.5
$30,000 to $39,999	9.8	8.0	7.7	8.3
$40,000 to $49,999	8.8	7.9	8.4	7.5
$50,000 to $59,999	8.0	8.4	8.5	8.3
$60,000 to $69,999	7.0	7.6	7.8	7.5
$70,000 to $79,999	6.1	7.4	7.4	7.4
$80,000 to $89,999	5.3	6.6	6.9	6.3
$90,000 to $99,999	4.4	6.1	6.2	6.0
$100,000 or more	23.3	31.5	29.9	32.9
$100,000 to $124,999	8.5	11.9	11.5	12.2
$125,000 to $149,999	5.0	6.8	6.4	7.1
$150,000 to $174,999	3.2	4.1	3.8	4.4
$175,000 to $199,999	1.9	2.4	2.5	2.4
$200,000 or more	4.6	6.3	5.8	6.7

Note: Non-Hispanic whites are those who identify themselves as being white alone and not Hispanic.
Source: Bureau of the Census, 2011 Current Population Survey, Internet site http://www.census.gov/hhes/www/cpstables/032011/hhinc/toc.htm; calculations by New Strategist

Married Couples Have the Highest Incomes

Female-headed families have the lowest incomes.

The incomes of households headed by people aged 35 to 44 vary sharply by household type. Married couples have the highest incomes by far. Among households headed by people aged 35 to 44 (Gen Xers were aged 34 to 45 in 2010), married couples had a median income of $82,537 in 2010. Behind the high incomes of couples is the fact that most are dual earners.

Female-headed families in the 35-to-44 age group had a median income of only $33,426 in 2010. Most are single parents. The median income of women in the age group who live alone was almost identical, at $33,602. The median income of men aged 35 to 44 who live alone was not much higher, at $38,154. Male-headed families had a much higher median of $51,637 in 2010.

■ Female-headed families have low incomes because their households usually include only one earner.

Incomes of Gen X couples are above average

(median income of householders aged 35 to 44 by household type, 2010)

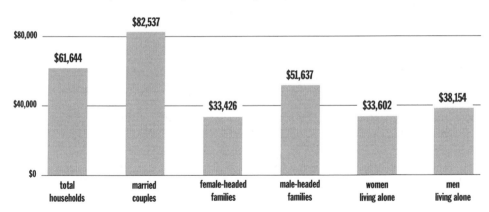

Table 5.7 Income of Households by Household Type, 2010: Aged 35 to 44

(number and percent distribution of households headed by people aged 35 to 44, by income and household type, 2010; households in thousands as of 2011)

| | | family households | | | nonfamily households | | | |
| | | | female householder, no spouse present | male householder, no spouse present | female householder | | male householder | |
	total	married couples			total	living alone	total	living alone
Total households headed by 35-to-44-year-olds	**21,250**	**12,087**	**3,480**	**1,141**	**1,680**	**1,390**	**2,862**	**2,162**
Under $10,000	1,218	196	434	50	260	248	279	255
$10,000 to $19,999	1,548	411	535	84	229	207	288	258
$20,000 to $29,999	1,904	693	567	135	171	156	339	286
$30,000 to $39,999	2,006	741	530	148	207	179	380	324
$40,000 to $49,999	1,844	842	371	121	166	138	345	284
$50,000 to $59,999	1,755	958	273	135	159	123	230	174
$60,000 to $69,999	1,590	930	187	96	138	106	240	181
$70,000 to $79,999	1,468	935	171	91	90	65	180	104
$80,000 to $89,999	1,247	913	95	78	50	42	111	64
$90,000 to $99,999	1,054	834	62	39	40	18	77	35
$100,000 or more	5,618	4,634	252	163	171	109	395	197
$100,000 to $124,999	2,163	1,687	128	79	76	48	193	99
$125,000 to $149,999	1,202	996	52	47	34	18	72	36
$150,000 to $174,999	722	615	26	19	14	12	48	27
$175,000 to $199,999	442	386	15	4	11	8	23	11
$200,000 or more	1,089	950	31	14	36	23	59	24
Median income	$61,644	$82,537	$33,426	$51,637	$37,459	$33,602	$44,047	$38,154
Total households headed by 35-to-44-year-olds	**100.0%**	**100.0%**	**100.0%**	**100.0%**	**100.0%**	**100.0%**	**100.0%**	**100.0%**
Under $10,000	5.7	1.6	12.5	4.4	15.5	17.8	9.7	11.8
$10,000 to $19,999	7.3	3.4	15.4	7.4	13.6	14.9	10.1	11.9
$20,000 to $29,999	9.0	5.7	16.3	11.8	10.2	11.2	11.8	13.2
$30,000 to $39,999	9.4	6.1	15.2	13.0	12.3	12.9	13.3	15.0
$40,000 to $49,999	8.7	7.0	10.7	10.6	9.9	9.9	12.1	13.1
$50,000 to $59,999	8.3	7.9	7.8	11.8	9.5	8.8	8.0	8.0
$60,000 to $69,999	7.5	7.7	5.4	8.4	8.2	7.6	8.4	8.4
$70,000 to $79,999	6.9	7.7	4.9	8.0	5.4	4.7	6.3	4.8
$80,000 to $89,999	5.9	7.6	2.7	6.8	3.0	3.0	3.9	3.0
$90,000 to $99,999	5.0	6.9	1.8	3.4	2.4	1.3	2.7	1.6
$100,000 or more	26.4	38.3	7.2	14.3	10.2	7.8	13.8	9.1
$100,000 to $124,999	10.2	14.0	3.7	6.9	4.5	3.5	6.7	4.6
$125,000 to $149,999	5.7	8.2	1.5	4.1	2.0	1.3	2.5	1.7
$150,000 to $174,999	3.4	5.1	0.7	1.7	0.8	0.9	1.7	1.2
$175,000 to $199,999	2.1	3.2	0.4	0.4	0.7	0.6	0.8	0.5
$200,000 or more	5.1	7.9	0.9	1.2	2.1	1.7	2.1	1.1

Source: Bureau of the Census, 2011 Current Population Survey, Internet site http://www.census.gov/hhes/www/cpstables/032011/hhinc/toc.htm; calculations by New Strategist

Table 5.8 Income of Households by Household Type, 2010: Aged 35 to 39

(number and percent distribution of households headed by people aged 35 to 39, by income and household type, 2010; households in thousands as of 2011)

| | total | family households | | | nonfamily households | | | |
| | | | | | female householder | | male householder | |
		married couples	female householder, no spouse present	male householder, no spouse present	total	living alone	total	living alone
Total households headed by 35-to-39-year-olds	**10,334**	**5,820**	**1,780**	**572**	**783**	**654**	**1,379**	**1,028**
Under $10,000	620	97	251	24	123	116	124	118
$10,000 to $19,999	774	224	286	40	97	87	126	110
$20,000 to $29,999	950	337	266	88	79	77	182	153
$30,000 to $39,999	995	348	316	69	89	75	172	152
$40,000 to $49,999	933	424	196	66	74	66	173	139
$50,000 to $59,999	858	469	135	60	84	63	112	82
$60,000 to $69,999	777	448	90	50	77	60	112	84
$70,000 to $79,999	697	452	75	47	36	25	88	50
$80,000 to $89,999	631	448	45	46	30	29	62	32
$90,000 to $99,999	497	398	22	16	13	6	48	16
$100,000 or more	2,602	2,176	99	65	82	54	180	94
$100,000 to $124,999	1,019	824	47	30	35	20	83	47
$125,000 to $149,999	543	437	21	25	20	13	39	18
$150,000 to $174,999	325	280	12	6	7	7	20	9
$175,000 to $199,999	228	205	8	2	2	0	11	6
$200,000 or more	487	430	11	2	18	14	27	14
Median income	$60,338	$81,683	$32,032	$49,826	$40,209	$36,022	$45,334	$38,557
Total households headed by 35-to-39-year-olds	**100.0%**	**100.0%**	**100.0%**	**100.0%**	**100.0%**	**100.0%**	**100.0%**	**100.0%**
Under $10,000	6.0	1.7	14.1	4.2	15.7	17.7	9.0	11.5
$10,000 to $19,999	7.5	3.8	16.1	7.0	12.4	13.3	9.1	10.7
$20,000 to $29,999	9.2	5.8	14.9	15.4	10.1	11.8	13.2	14.9
$30,000 to $39,999	9.6	6.0	17.8	12.1	11.4	11.5	12.5	14.8
$40,000 to $49,999	9.0	7.3	11.0	11.5	9.5	10.1	12.5	13.5
$50,000 to $59,999	8.3	8.1	7.6	10.5	10.7	9.6	8.1	8.0
$60,000 to $69,999	7.5	7.7	5.1	8.7	9.8	9.2	8.1	8.2
$70,000 to $79,999	6.7	7.8	4.2	8.2	4.6	3.8	6.4	4.9
$80,000 to $89,999	6.1	7.7	2.5	8.0	3.8	4.4	4.5	3.1
$90,000 to $99,999	4.8	6.8	1.2	2.8	1.7	0.9	3.5	1.6
$100,000 or more	25.2	37.4	5.6	11.4	10.5	8.3	13.1	9.1
$100,000 to $124,999	9.9	14.2	2.6	5.2	4.5	3.1	6.0	4.6
$125,000 to $149,999	5.3	7.5	1.2	4.4	2.6	2.0	2.8	1.8
$150,000 to $174,999	3.1	4.8	0.7	1.0	0.9	1.1	1.5	0.9
$175,000 to $199,999	2.2	3.5	0.4	0.3	0.3	0.0	0.8	0.6
$200,000 or more	4.7	7.4	0.6	0.3	2.3	2.1	2.0	1.4

Source: Bureau of the Census, 2011 Current Population Survey, Internet site http://www.census.gov/hhes/www/cpstables/032011/hhinc/toc.htm; calculations by New Strategist

Table 5.9 Income of Households by Household Type, 2010: Aged 40 to 44

(number and percent distribution of households headed by people aged 40 to 44, by income and household type, 2010; households in thousands as of 2011)

| | total | family households | | | nonfamily households | | | |
| | | | female householder, no spouse present | male householder, no spouse present | female householder | | male householder | |
		married couples			total	living alone	total	living alone
Total households headed by 40-to-44-year-olds	**10,917**	**6,267**	**1,700**	**569**	**897**	**736**	**1,484**	**1,134**
Under $10,000	599	99	183	27	137	132	154	139
$10,000 to $19,999	773	187	249	44	132	121	161	148
$20,000 to $29,999	953	357	301	48	92	79	157	133
$30,000 to $39,999	1,011	393	213	79	118	104	208	173
$40,000 to $49,999	911	418	175	55	92	72	173	146
$50,000 to $59,999	897	490	139	75	75	60	118	92
$60,000 to $69,999	813	481	97	46	61	46	127	97
$70,000 to $79,999	771	484	98	43	55	40	91	54
$80,000 to $89,999	616	465	50	31	20	13	49	32
$90,000 to $99,999	557	435	40	24	28	13	29	19
$100,000 or more	3,016	2,460	154	96	86	54	216	101
$100,000 to $124,999	1,146	863	81	50	40	29	111	52
$125,000 to $149,999	661	560	32	22	12	3	32	17
$150,000 to $174,999	396	336	14	11	7	5	28	17
$175,000 to $199,999	212	181	7	2	9	8	13	5
$200,000 or more	601	520	20	11	18	9	32	10
Median income	$63,198	$83,939	$36,090	$53,445	$36,154	$31,966	$42,420	$37,712
Total households headed by 40-to-44-year-olds	**100.0%**	**100.0%**	**100.0%**	**100.0%**	**100.0%**	**100.0%**	**100.0%**	**100.0%**
Under $10,000	5.5	1.6	10.8	4.7	15.3	17.9	10.4	12.3
$10,000 to $19,999	7.1	3.0	14.6	7.7	14.7	16.4	10.8	13.1
$20,000 to $29,999	8.7	5.7	17.7	8.4	10.3	10.7	10.6	11.7
$30,000 to $39,999	9.3	6.3	12.5	13.9	13.2	14.1	14.0	15.3
$40,000 to $49,999	8.3	6.7	10.3	9.7	10.3	9.8	11.7	12.9
$50,000 to $59,999	8.2	7.8	8.2	13.2	8.4	8.2	8.0	8.1
$60,000 to $69,999	7.4	7.7	5.7	8.1	6.8	6.3	8.6	8.6
$70,000 to $79,999	7.1	7.7	5.8	7.6	6.1	5.4	6.1	4.8
$80,000 to $89,999	5.6	7.4	2.9	5.4	2.2	1.8	3.3	2.8
$90,000 to $99,999	5.1	6.9	2.4	4.2	3.1	1.8	2.0	1.7
$100,000 or more	27.6	39.3	9.1	16.9	9.6	7.3	14.6	8.9
$100,000 to $124,999	10.5	13.8	4.8	8.8	4.5	3.9	7.5	4.6
$125,000 to $149,999	6.1	8.9	1.9	3.9	1.3	0.4	2.2	1.5
$150,000 to $174,999	3.6	5.4	0.8	1.9	0.8	0.7	1.9	1.5
$175,000 to $199,999	1.9	2.9	0.4	0.4	1.0	1.1	0.9	0.4
$200,000 or more	5.5	8.3	1.2	1.9	2.0	1.2	2.2	0.9

Source: Bureau of the Census, 2011 Current Population Survey, Internet site http://www.census.gov/hhes/www/ cpstables/032011/hhinc/toc.htm; calculations by New Strategist

Median Income of Men Aged 35 to 44 Is below 1990 Level

Women's incomes have grown.

The median income of men aged 35 to 44 fell 12 percent between 2000 and 2010, after adjusting for inflation. (Gen Xers were aged 34 to 45 in 2010.) The median income of women in the age group climbed 5 percent during the decade.

The Great Recession was only one factor behind the decline in men's incomes, because the decline began well before the recession hit. The median income of men aged 35 to 44 in 2010 was nearly $6,000 below the median income of their counterparts in 1990, after adjusting for inflation. Women in the age group made gains during the same time period because more had full-time jobs and their educational attainment was rising.

■ Men aged 35 to 44 made only 31 percent more than the average man in 2010, down from 47 percent more in 1990.

The median income of Gen X men has plummeted

(percent change in median income of people aged 35 to 44 by sex, 2000–10, in 2010 dollars)

Table 5.10 Median Income of Men Aged 35 to 44, 1990 to 2010

(median income of men aged 15 or older and aged 35 to 44, and index of age group to total, 1990 to 2010; percent change for selected years; in 2010 dollars)

	total men	35 to 44	index, 35–44 to total
2010	$32,137	$42,252	131
2009	32,715	42,921	131
2008	33,580	44,748	133
2007	34,908	47,339	136
2006	34,891	46,107	132
2005	34,929	45,751	131
2004	35,224	46,788	133
2003	35,483	46,465	131
2002	35,435	45,924	130
2001	35,839	47,217	132
2000	35,885	48,014	134
1999	35,714	47,627	133
1998	35,389	46,991	133
1997	34,149	44,496	130
1996	32,980	44,511	135
1995	32,051	44,635	139
1994	31,598	44,672	141
1993	31,354	45,084	144
1992	31,145	44,903	144
1991	31,956	45,744	143
1990	32,817	48,148	147

Percent change

2000 to 2010	−10.4%	−12.0%	–
1990 to 2010	−2.1	−12.2	–

Note: The index is calculated by dividing the median income of the age group by the national median and multiplying by 100. "–" means not applicable.
Source: Bureau of the Census, Historical Income Statistics—People, Internet site http://www.census.gov/hhes/www/income/ data/historical/people/; calculations by New Strategist

Table 5.11 Median Income of Women Aged 35 to 44, 1990 to 2010

(median income of women aged 15 or older and aged 35 to 44, and index of age group to total, 1990 to 2010; percent change for selected years; in 2010 dollars)

	total women	35 to 44	index, 35–44 to total
2010	$20,831	$29,447	141
2009	21,303	28,354	133
2008	21,131	27,717	131
2007	22,001	29,130	132
2006	21,643	28,514	132
2005	20,747	28,407	137
2004	20,393	28,167	138
2003	20,460	27,826	136
2002	20,375	27,053	133
2001	20,461	27,674	135
2000	20,338	27,952	137
1999	20,026	27,034	135
1998	19,276	27,097	141
1997	18,560	25,337	137
1996	17,733	25,526	144
1995	17,232	24,714	143
1994	16,681	23,552	141
1993	16,413	23,542	143
1992	16,313	23,474	144
1991	16,355	23,613	144
1990	16,285	23,455	144
Percent change			
2000 to 2010	2.4%	5.3%	–
1990 to 2010	27.9	25.5	–

Note: The index is calculated by dividing the median income of the age group by the national median and multiplying by 100. "–" means not applicable.
Source: Bureau of the Census, Historical Income Statistics—People, Internet site http://www.census.gov/hhes/www/income/data/historical/people/; calculations by New Strategist

Seventy Percent of Gen X Men Work Full-Time

Asian and Non-Hispanic white men have the highest incomes.

The incomes of men aged 35 to 44 are well above average. In 2010, men aged 35 to 44 had a median income of $42,252. Among the 70 percent who have a full-time job, median income is a higher $51,549.

Among men aged 35 to 44 who work full-time, Asians have the highest median income—$66,818 in 2010, nearly $10,000 more than the median income of their non-Hispanic white counterparts. Black men in the age group who work full-time had a median income of $41,044. Among Hispanics, median income was just $35,797. The percentage of men aged 35 to 44 with a full-time job ranges from a low of 59 percent among blacks to a high of 76 percent among Asians.

■ Hispanic men have the lowest incomes because they are the least educated.

Among men aged 35 to 44, Hispanics have the lowest incomes

(median income of men aged 35 to 44 who work full-time, by race and Hispanic origin, 2010)

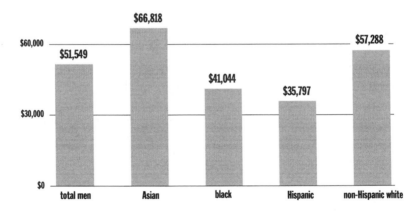

Table 5.12 Income of Men Aged 35 to 44, 2010: Total Men

(number and percent distribution of men aged 15 or older and men aged 35 to 44 by income and age, 2010; median income of men with income and of men working full-time, year-round; percent working full-time, year-round; men in thousands as of 2011)

	total	aged 35 to 44 total	aged 35 to 44 35 to 39	aged 35 to 44 40 to 44
Total men	**118,871**	**19,714**	**9,542**	**10,172**
Without income	13,520	1,043	526	517
With income	105,351	18,671	9,016	9,655
Under $5,000	7,350	633	317	316
$5,000 to $9,999	7,741	816	397	418
$10,000 to $14,999	8,933	1,027	483	544
$15,000 to $19,999	8,914	986	441	544
$20,000 to $24,999	8,525	1,384	689	695
$25,000 to $29,999	7,133	1,177	605	572
$30,000 to $34,999	6,846	1,283	624	659
$35,000 to $39,999	5,840	1,184	567	616
$40,000 to $44,999	5,714	1,206	606	600
$45,000 to $49,999	4,325	999	507	492
$50,000 to $54,999	4,978	1,108	514	594
$55,000 to $59,999	3,091	637	297	340
$60,000 to $64,999	3,416	841	434	407
$65,000 to $69,999	2,335	547	235	314
$70,000 to $74,999	2,371	603	282	321
$75,000 to $79,999	2,040	498	249	249
$80,000 to $84,999	1,979	475	211	264
$85,000 to $89,999	1,211	279	146	133
$90,000 to $94,999	1,362	343	163	180
$95,000 to $99,999	860	186	94	93
$100,000 or more	10,386	2,461	1,156	1,305
Median income				
Men with income	$32,137	$42,252	$41,999	$42,548
Working full-time	50,063	51,549	51,013	51,989
Percent full-time	47.5%	69.9%	70.7%	69.2%
PERCENT DISTRIBUTION				
Total men	**100.0%**	**100.0%**	**100.0%**	**100.0%**
Without income	11.4	5.3	5.5	5.1
With income	88.6	94.7	94.5	94.9
Under $15,000	20.2	12.6	12.5	12.6
$15,000 to $24,999	14.7	12.0	11.8	12.2
$25,000 to $34,999	11.8	12.5	12.9	12.1
$35,000 to $49,999	13.4	17.2	17.6	16.8
$50,000 to $74,999	13.6	19.0	18.5	19.4
$75,000 or more	15.0	21.5	21.2	21.9

Source: Bureau of the Census, 2011 Current Population Survey Annual Social and Economic Supplement, Internet site http://www.census.gov/hhes/www/cpstables/032011/perinc/toc.htm; calculations by New Strategist

Table 5.13 Income of Men Aged 35 to 44, 2010: Asian Men

(number and percent distribution of Asian men aged 15 or older and aged 35 to 44 by income and age, 2010; median income of men with income and of men working full-time, year-round; percent working full-time, year-round; men in thousands as of 2011)

| | | aged 35 to 44 | | |
	total	total	35 to 39	40 to 44
Asian men	**5,787**	**1,191**	**618**	**573**
Without income	865	62	33	29
With income	4,922	1,129	585	544
Under $5,000	356	29	14	15
$5,000 to $9,999	304	32	13	20
$10,000 to $14,999	401	57	30	26
$15,000 to $19,999	334	39	18	21
$20,000 to $24,999	395	88	46	42
$25,000 to $29,999	318	55	25	30
$30,000 to $34,999	314	72	31	40
$35,000 to $39,999	227	43	21	22
$40,000 to $44,999	210	59	32	27
$45,000 to $49,999	186	41	21	19
$50,000 to $54,999	202	48	26	22
$55,000 to $59,999	111	29	17	12
$60,000 to $64,999	195	56	41	14
$65,000 to $69,999	100	23	11	12
$70,000 to $74,999	135	34	18	16
$75,000 to $79,999	108	38	16	22
$80,000 to $84,999	100	37	13	24
$85,000 to $89,999	91	36	24	13
$90,000 to $94,999	78	27	11	16
$95,000 to $99,999	40	17	12	5
$100,000 or more	716	271	144	127
Median income				
Men with income	$35,622	$55,262	$57,985	$51,243
Working full-time	52,444	66,818	65,989	68,197
Percent full-time	53.0%	75.9%	75.2%	76.6%
PERCENT DISTRIBUTION				
Asian men	**100.0%**	**100.0%**	**100.0%**	**100.0%**
Without income	14.9	5.2	5.3	5.1
With income	85.1	94.8	94.7	94.9
Under $15,000	18.3	9.9	9.2	10.6
$15,000 to $24,999	12.6	10.7	10.4	11.0
$25,000 to $34,999	10.9	10.7	9.1	12.2
$35,000 to $49,999	10.8	12.0	12.0	11.9
$50,000 to $74,999	12.8	16.0	18.3	13.3
$75,000 or more	19.6	35.8	35.6	36.1

Note: Asians are those who identify themselves as being of the race alone and those who identify themselves as being of the race in combination with other races.
Source: Bureau of the Census, 2011 Current Population Survey Annual Social and Economic Supplement, Internet site http:// www.census.gov/hhes/www/cpstables/032011/perinc/toc.htm; calculations by New Strategist

Table 5.14 Income of Men Aged 35 to 44, 2010: Black Men

(number and percent distribution of black men aged 15 or older and aged 35 to 44 by income and age, 2010; median income of men with income and of men working full-time, year-round; percent working full-time, year-round; men in thousands as of 2011)

	total	aged 35 to 44		
	total	total	35 to 39	40 to 44
Black men	**14,101**	**2,336**	**1,141**	**1,195**
Without income	2,843	268	149	119
With income	11,258	2,068	992	1,076
Under $5,000	1,052	111	42	69
$5,000 to $9,999	1,471	166	77	89
$10,000 to $14,999	1,270	165	87	78
$15,000 to $19,999	1,035	105	48	57
$20,000 to $24,999	1,067	225	112	115
$25,000 to $29,999	831	150	81	69
$30,000 to $34,999	795	216	101	115
$35,000 to $39,999	617	121	52	68
$40,000 to $44,999	568	142	61	81
$45,000 to $49,999	432	136	76	60
$50,000 to $54,999	367	83	46	37
$55,000 to $59,999	252	57	25	32
$60,000 to $64,999	244	76	36	40
$65,000 to $69,999	195	47	18	28
$70,000 to $74,999	217	70	28	42
$75,000 to $79,999	122	34	19	15
$80,000 to $84,999	132	25	11	13
$85,000 to $89,999	55	16	9	8
$90,000 to $94,999	66	20	8	12
$95,000 to $99,999	51	10	5	6
$100,000 or more	418	92	51	41
Median income				
Men with income	$23,061	$31,722	$31,584	$31,852
Working full-time	37,805	41,044	40,352	41,605
Percent full-time	38.0%	59.2%	59.8%	58.7%
PERCENT DISTRIBUTION				
Black men	**100.0%**	**100.0%**	**100.0%**	**100.0%**
Without income	20.2	11.5	13.1	10.0
With income	79.8	88.5	86.9	90.0
Under $15,000	26.9	18.9	18.1	19.7
$15,000 to $24,999	14.9	14.1	14.0	14.4
$25,000 to $34,999	11.5	15.7	16.0	15.4
$35,000 to $49,999	11.5	17.1	16.6	17.5
$50,000 to $74,999	9.0	14.3	13.4	15.0
$75,000 or more	6.0	8.4	9.0	7.9

Note: Blacks are those who identify themselves as being of the race alone and those who identify themselves as being of the race in combination with other races.
Source: Bureau of the Census, 2011 Current Population Survey Annual Social and Economic Supplement, Internet site http:// www.census.gov/hhes/www/cpstables/032011/perinc/toc.htm; calculations by New Strategist

Table 5.15 Income of Men Aged 35 to 44, 2010: Hispanic Men

(number and percent distribution of Hispanic men aged 15 or older and aged 35 to 44 by income and age, 2010; median income of men with income and of men working full-time, year-round; percent working full-time, year-round; men in thousands as of 2011)

	total	aged 35 to 44 total	35 to 39	40 to 44
Hispanic men	**18,105**	**3,687**	**1,950**	**1,737**
Without income	3,140	256	152	104
With income	14,965	3,431	1,798	1,633
Under $5,000	1,094	135	67	68
$5,000 to $9,999	1,573	236	129	108
$10,000 to $14,999	1,918	321	152	170
$15,000 to $19,999	1,902	374	181	193
$20,000 to $24,999	1,669	395	204	191
$25,000 to $29,999	1,305	363	201	163
$30,000 to $34,999	1,041	235	122	113
$35,000 to $39,999	780	252	135	117
$40,000 to $44,999	711	185	110	75
$45,000 to $49,999	503	157	93	64
$50,000 to $54,999	516	153	75	78
$55,000 to $59,999	275	66	25	40
$60,000 to $64,999	328	112	62	50
$65,000 to $69,999	171	66	41	25
$70,000 to $74,999	168	46	30	17
$75,000 to $79,999	149	52	28	24
$80,000 to $84,999	147	47	25	22
$85,000 to $89,999	91	28	12	15
$90,000 to $94,999	71	20	8	11
$95,000 to $99,999	42	11	10	1
$100,000 or more	511	177	86	91
Median income				
Men with income	$22,233	$27,913	$28,852	$27,047
Working full-time	31,671	35,797	36,116	35,430
Percent full-time	46.3%	63.3%	64.4%	62.0%
PERCENT DISTRIBUTION				
Hispanic men	**100.0%**	**100.0%**	**100.0%**	**100.0%**
Without income	17.3	6.9	7.8	6.0
With income	82.7	93.1	92.2	94.0
Under $15,000	25.3	18.8	17.8	19.9
$15,000 to $24,999	19.7	20.9	19.7	22.1
$25,000 to $34,999	13.0	16.2	16.6	15.9
$35,000 to $49,999	11.0	16.1	17.3	14.7
$50,000 to $74,999	8.1	12.0	11.9	12.1
$75,000 or more	5.6	9.1	8.7	9.4

Source: Bureau of the Census, 2011 Current Population Survey Annual Social and Economic Supplement, Internet site http://www.census.gov/hhes/www/cpstables/032011/perinc/toc.htm; calculations by New Strategist

Table 5.16 Income of Men Aged 35 to 44, 2010: Non-Hispanic White Men

(number and percent distribution of non-Hispanic white men aged 15 or older and aged 35 to 44 by income and age, 2010; median income of men with income and of men working full-time, year-round; percent working full-time, year-round; men in thousands as of 2011)

	total	aged 35 to 44 total	35 to 39	40 to 44
Non-Hispanic white men	**80,108**	**12,354**	**5,765**	**6,589**
Without income	6,617	438	188	250
With income	73,491	11,916	5,577	6,339
Under $5,000	4,754	348	188	161
$5,000 to $9,999	4,356	378	172	206
$10,000 to $14,999	5,318	475	209	265
$15,000 to $19,999	5,542	462	191	270
$20,000 to $24,999	5,388	674	316	357
$25,000 to $29,999	4,633	602	297	305
$30,000 to $34,999	4,634	764	380	384
$35,000 to $39,999	4,169	748	346	402
$40,000 to $44,999	4,193	801	397	404
$45,000 to $49,999	3,165	664	317	346
$50,000 to $54,999	3,860	807	362	446
$55,000 to $59,999	2,412	478	225	253
$60,000 to $64,999	2,615	589	291	298
$65,000 to $69,999	1,868	418	168	250
$70,000 to $74,999	1,840	451	204	248
$75,000 to $79,999	1,650	368	186	183
$80,000 to $84,999	1,586	363	160	202
$85,000 to $89,999	968	198	102	96
$90,000 to $94,999	1,133	270	130	140
$95,000 to $99,999	718	144	64	80
$100,000 or more	8,691	1,913	872	1,042
Median income				
Men with income	$37,037	$50,175	$49,389	$50,517
Working full-time	54,192	57,288	56,703	58,240
Percent full-time	49.1%	73.4%	74.6%	72.5%
PERCENT DISTRIBUTION				
Non-Hispanic white men	**100.0%**	**100.0%**	**100.0%**	**100.0%**
Without income	8.3	3.5	3.3	3.8
With income	91.7	96.5	96.7	96.2
Under $15,000	18.0	9.7	9.9	9.6
$15,000 to $24,999	13.6	9.2	8.8	9.5
$25,000 to $34,999	11.6	11.1	11.7	10.5
$35,000 to $49,999	14.4	17.9	18.4	17.5
$50,000 to $74,999	15.7	22.2	21.7	22.7
$75,000 or more	18.4	26.4	26.3	26.5

Note: Non-Hispanic whites are those who identify themselves as being white alone and not Hispanic.
Source: Bureau of the Census, 2011 Current Population Survey Annual Social and Economic Supplement, Internet site http://www.census.gov/hhes/www/cpstables/032011/perinc/toc.htm; calculations by New Strategist

Nearly Half of Gen X Women Work Full-Time

Asian and Non-Hispanic white women have the highest incomes.

The incomes of women aged 35 to 44 are well above average. In 2010, women aged 35 to 44 had a median income of $29,447. Among the 49 percent who have a full-time job, median income is a higher $41,108.

Among women aged 35 to 44 who work full-time, Asians have the highest median income—$45,662 in 2010. Non-Hispanic whites are not far behind, with a median of $44,890. Black women in the age group who work full-time had a median income of $36,862. Among Hispanics, median income was just $30,860. The percentage of women aged 35 to 44 with a full-time job ranges from a low of 42 percent among Hispanics to a high of 53 percent among blacks.

■ Hispanic women have the lowest incomes because they are the least educated.

Among women aged 35 to 44, Hispanics have the lowest incomes

(median income of women aged 35 to 44 who work full-time, by race and Hispanic origin, 2010)

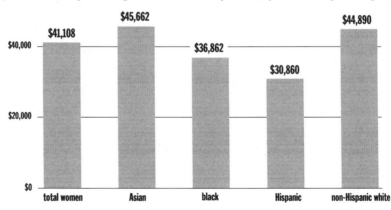

Table 5.17 Income of Women Aged 35 to 44, 2010: Total Women

(number and percent distribution of women aged 15 or older and women aged 35 to 44 by income and age, 2010; median income of women with income and of women working full-time, year-round; percent working full-time, year-round; women in thousands as of 2011)

	total	aged 35 to 44 total	35 to 39	40 to 44
Total women	**125,084**	**20,128**	**9,713**	**10,415**
Without income	18,942	2,576	1,293	1,283
With income	106,142	17,552	8,420	9,132
Under $5,000	12,538	1,832	936	896
$5,000 to $9,999	14,061	1,406	674	733
$10,000 to $14,999	13,672	1,541	713	828
$15,000 to $19,999	10,971	1,426	684	742
$20,000 to $24,999	8,842	1,523	745	778
$25,000 to $29,999	7,228	1,146	537	609
$30,000 to $34,999	6,582	1,370	679	691
$35,000 to $39,999	5,443	1,124	527	597
$40,000 to $44,999	4,778	995	459	536
$45,000 to $49,999	3,701	825	380	444
$50,000 to $54,999	3,527	812	377	435
$55,000 to $59,999	2,239	554	299	255
$60,000 to $64,999	2,276	561	282	279
$65,000 to $69,999	1,464	339	166	173
$70,000 to $74,999	1,492	360	161	200
$75,000 to $79,999	1,060	239	108	130
$80,000 to $84,999	971	238	115	124
$85,000 to $89,999	669	150	79	71
$90,000 to $94,999	619	142	68	74
$95,000 to $99,999	425	74	39	34
$100,000 or more	3,584	894	393	501
Median income				
Women with income	$20,831	$29,447	$29,090	$29,776
Working full-time	38,531	41,108	41,285	40,963
Percent full-time	34.2%	49.2%	47.8%	50.5%
PERCENT DISTRIBUTION				
Total women	**100.0%**	**100.0%**	**100.0%**	**100.0%**
Without income	15.1	12.8	13.3	12.3
With income	84.9	87.2	86.7	87.7
Under $15,000	32.2	23.7	23.9	23.6
$15,000 to $24,999	15.8	14.7	14.7	14.6
$25,000 to $34,999	11.0	12.5	12.5	12.5
$35,000 to $49,999	11.1	14.6	14.1	15.1
$50,000 to $74,999	8.8	13.0	13.2	12.9
$75,000 or more	5.9	8.6	8.3	9.0

Source: Bureau of the Census, 2011 Current Population Survey Annual Social and Economic Supplement, Internet site http://www.census.gov/hhes/www/cpstables/032011/perinc/toc.htm; calculations by New Strategist

Table 5.18 Income of Women Aged 35 to 44, 2010: Asian Women

(number and percent distribution of Asian women aged 15 or older and aged 35 to 44 by income, 2010; median income by work status, and percent working year-round, full-time; women in thousands as of 2011)

		aged 35 to 44		
	total	total	35 to 39	40 to 44
Asian women	**6,460**	**1,336**	**701**	**635**
Without income	1,413	199	113	85
With income	5,047	1,137	588	550
Under $5,000	694	157	78	80
$5,000 to $9,999	617	79	39	40
$10,000 to $14,999	518	79	33	45
$15,000 to $19,999	397	80	48	31
$20,000 to $24,999	380	86	45	41
$25,000 to $29,999	293	47	24	23
$30,000 to $34,999	333	66	30	36
$35,000 to $39,999	229	63	37	26
$40,000 to $44,999	250	81	34	47
$45,000 to $49,999	144	35	19	16
$50,000 to $54,999	188	46	22	23
$55,000 to $59,999	113	30	18	12
$60,000 to $64,999	146	32	14	18
$65,000 to $69,999	89	37	24	13
$70,000 to $74,999	92	31	18	13
$75,000 to $79,999	68	17	9	7
$80,000 to $84,999	76	23	13	10
$85,000 to $89,999	42	17	12	5
$90,000 to $94,999	58	18	3	15
$95,000 to $99,999	20	7	5	2
$100,000 or more	297	110	62	48
Median income				
Women with income	$23,664	$32,013	$33,841	$31,303
Working full-time	41,821	45,662	47,229	42,413
Percent full-time	36.6%	49.5%	47.5%	51.7%
PERCENT DISTRIBUTION				
Asian women	**100.0%**	**100.0%**	**100.0%**	**100.0%**
Without income	21.9	14.9	16.1	13.4
With income	78.1	85.1	83.9	86.6
Under $15,000	28.3	23.6	21.4	26.0
$15,000 to $24,999	12.0	12.4	13.3	11.3
$25,000 to $34,999	9.7	8.5	7.7	9.3
$35,000 to $49,999	9.6	13.4	12.8	14.0
$50,000 to $74,999	9.7	13.2	13.7	12.4
$75,000 or more	8.7	14.4	14.8	13.7

Note: Asians are those who identify themselves as being of the race alone and those who identify themselves as being of the race in combination with other races.
Source: Bureau of the Census, 2011 Current Population Survey Annual Social and Economic Supplement, Internet site http://www.census.gov/hhes/www/cpstables/032011/perinc/toc.htm; calculations by New Strategist

Table 5.19 Income of Women Aged 35 to 44, 2010: Black Women

(number and percent distribution of black women aged 15 or older and aged 35 to 44 by income and age, 2010; median income of women with income and of women working full-time, year-round; percent working full-time, year-round; women in thousands as of 2011)

| | | aged 35 to 44 | | |
	total	total	35 to 39	40 to 44
Black women	**16,879**	**2,883**	**1,419**	**1,464**
Without income	2,948	326	152	174
With income	13,931	2,557	1,267	1,290
Under $5,000	1,507	151	74	77
$5,000 to $9,999	2,173	240	119	121
$10,000 to $14,999	1,965	255	129	126
$15,000 to $19,999	1,402	226	104	121
$20,000 to $24,999	1,274	250	134	116
$25,000 to $29,999	1,086	187	89	99
$30,000 to $34,999	925	280	163	118
$35,000 to $39,999	730	174	93	80
$40,000 to $44,999	612	134	59	75
$45,000 to $49,999	452	132	69	63
$50,000 to $54,999	416	109	54	55
$55,000 to $59,999	242	85	45	40
$60,000 to $64,999	248	104	38	68
$65,000 to $69,999	128	42	16	25
$70,000 to $74,999	144	15	4	11
$75,000 to $79,999	108	38	16	21
$80,000 to $84,999	111	33	18	16
$85,000 to $89,999	60	17	1	16
$90,000 to $94,999	65	10	3	7
$95,000 to $99,999	36	4	3	1
$100,000 or more	247	71	36	35
Median income				
Women with income	$19,634	$28,958	$28,796	$29,087
Working full-time	33,918	36,862	36,101	38,036
Percent full-time	35.7%	53.1%	52.3%	54.0%
PERCENT DISTRIBUTION				
Black women	**100.0%**	**100.0%**	**100.0%**	**100.0%**
Without income	17.5	11.3	10.7	11.9
With income	82.5	88.7	89.3	88.1
Under $15,000	33.4	22.4	22.7	22.1
$15,000 to $24,999	15.9	16.5	16.8	16.2
$25,000 to $34,999	11.9	16.2	17.8	14.8
$35,000 to $49,999	10.6	15.3	15.6	14.9
$50,000 to $74,999	7.0	12.3	11.1	13.6
$75,000 or more	3.7	6.0	5.4	6.6

Note: Blacks are those who identify themselves as being of the race alone and those who identify themselves as being of the race in combination with other races.
Source: Bureau of the Census, 2011 Current Population Survey Annual Social and Economic Supplement, Internet site http://www.census.gov/hhes/www/cpstables/032011/perinc/toc.htm; calculations by New Strategist

Table 5.20 Income of Women Aged 35 to 44, 2010: Hispanic Women

(number and percent distribution of Hispanic women aged 15 or older and aged 35 to 44 by income and age, 2010; median income of women with income and of women working full-time, year-round; percent working full-time, year-round; women in thousands as of 2011)

| | | aged 35 to 44 | | |
	total	total	35 to 39	40 to 44
Hispanic women	**16,964**	**3,382**	**1,765**	**1,617**
Without income	4,842	814	421	393
With income	12,122	2,568	1,344	1,224
Under $5,000	1,654	249	155	93
$5,000 to $9,999	2,058	290	151	140
$10,000 to $14,999	1,901	344	146	199
$15,000 to $19,999	1,442	332	169	163
$20,000 to $24,999	1,165	258	131	127
$25,000 to $29,999	829	207	111	95
$30,000 to $34,999	713	200	108	91
$35,000 to $39,999	570	154	73	81
$40,000 to $44,999	410	137	66	71
$45,000 to $49,999	257	63	37	26
$50,000 to $54,999	270	79	43	35
$55,000 to $59,999	133	44	26	18
$60,000 to $64,999	154	46	33	13
$65,000 to $69,999	100	23	12	10
$70,000 to $74,999	68	20	16	4
$75,000 to $79,999	56	14	6	7
$80,000 to $84,999	59	18	7	11
$85,000 to $89,999	45	7	5	2
$90,000 to $94,999	33	12	8	5
$95,000 to $99,999	16	6	5	1
$100,000 or more	187	67	39	28
Median income				
Women with income	$16,269	$21,035	$21,655	$20,466
Working full-time	28,944	30,860	31,468	29,975
Percent full-time	30.5%	42.0%	41.7%	42.4%
PERCENT DISTRIBUTION				
Hispanic women	**100.0%**	**100.0%**	**100.0%**	**100.0%**
Without income	28.5	24.1	23.9	24.3
With income	71.5	75.9	76.1	75.7
Under $15,000	33.1	26.1	25.6	26.7
$15,000 to $24,999	15.4	17.4	17.0	17.9
$25,000 to $34,999	9.1	12.0	12.4	11.5
$35,000 to $49,999	7.3	10.5	10.0	11.0
$50,000 to $74,999	4.3	6.3	7.4	4.9
$75,000 or more	2.3	3.7	4.0	3.3

Source: Bureau of the Census, 2011 Current Population Survey Annual Social and Economic Supplement, Internet site http://www.census.gov/hhes/www/cpstables/032011/perinc/toc.htm; calculations by New Strategist

Table 5.21 Income of Women Aged 35 to 44, 2010: Non-Hispanic White Women

(number and percent distribution of non-Hispanic white women aged 15 or older and aged 35 to 44 by income and age, 2010; median income of women with income and of women working full-time, year-round; percent working full-time, year-round; women in thousands as of 2011)

	total	aged 35 to 44 total	35 to 39	40 to 44
Non-Hispanic white women	**84,028**	**12,433**	**5,766**	**6,668**
Without income	9,663	1,238	599	640
With income	74,365	11,195	5,167	6,028
Under $5,000	8,605	1,255	618	637
$5,000 to $9,999	9,108	783	358	426
$10,000 to $14,999	9,217	859	407	452
$15,000 to $19,999	7,665	790	355	435
$20,000 to $24,999	5,946	912	427	485
$25,000 to $29,999	4,964	691	303	389
$30,000 to $34,999	4,551	817	369	448
$35,000 to $39,999	3,868	721	321	399
$40,000 to $44,999	3,505	660	306	354
$45,000 to $49,999	2,820	590	255	335
$50,000 to $54,999	2,638	575	254	321
$55,000 to $59,999	1,738	392	207	185
$60,000 to $64,999	1,728	378	201	176
$65,000 to $69,999	1,129	234	112	122
$70,000 to $74,999	1,172	287	120	167
$75,000 to $79,999	826	172	76	96
$80,000 to $84,999	717	162	76	86
$85,000 to $89,999	518	108	61	47
$90,000 to $94,999	462	103	55	48
$95,000 to $99,999	344	57	27	30
$100,000 or more	2,844	645	255	390
Median income				
Women with income	$21,754	$31,274	$31,069	$31,442
Working full-time	41,307	44,890	45,268	44,166
Percent full-time	34.6%	50.2%	48.5%	51.6%
PERCENT DISTRIBUTION				
Non-Hispanic white women	**100.0%**	**100.0%**	**100.0%**	**100.0%**
Without income	11.5	10.0	10.4	9.6
With income	88.5	90.0	89.6	90.4
Under $15,000	32.0	23.3	24.0	22.7
$15,000 to $24,999	16.2	13.7	13.6	13.8
$25,000 to $34,999	11.3	12.1	11.7	12.6
$35,000 to $49,999	12.1	15.9	15.3	16.3
$50,000 to $74,999	10.0	15.0	15.5	14.6
$75,000 or more	6.8	10.0	9.5	10.5

Note: Non-Hispanic whites are those who identify themselves as being white alone and not Hispanic.
Source: Bureau of the Census, 2011 Current Population Survey Annual Social and Economic Supplement, Internet site http://www.census.gov/hhes/www/cpstables/032011/perinc/toc.htm; calculations by New Strategist

Earnings Rise with Education

The highest earners are men with professional degrees.

A college degree has been well worth the cost for Gen Xers. The higher their educational level, the greater their earnings. Among men aged 35 to 44 with full-time jobs, those with a professional degree (such as physicians and lawyers) had median earnings of $131,313. Among women as well, median earnings are highest for those with a professional degree, peaking at $91,211.

Among men aged 35 to 44 who did not finish high school, the earnings of those who work full-time ranged from just $24,746 to $29,112 in 2010. For male full-time workers with a bachelor's degree, median earnings are above $70,000. The pattern is the same for women. Among women aged 35 to 44 who did not finish high school, median annual earnings of those who work full-time range from $16,317 to $20,224. Among college graduates, median earnings are above $50,000.

■ The steeply rising cost of a college degree may reduce the financial return of a college education in the years ahead.

College bonus is big for Gen Xers

(median earnings of men aged 35 to 44 who work full-time, by education, 2010)

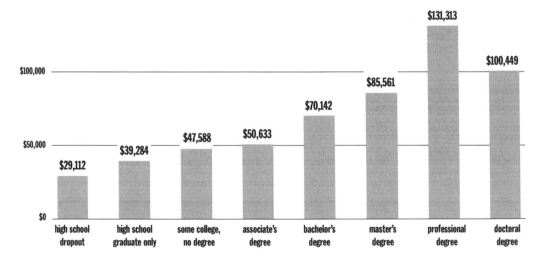

Table 5.22 Earnings of Men by Education, 2010: Men Aged 35 to 44

(number and percent distribution of men aged 35 to 44 who work full-time, year-round, by earnings and educational attainment, 2010; median earnings of men with earnings; men in thousands as of 2011)

	total	less than 9th grade	9th to 12th grade, no degree	high school graduate	some college	associate's degree	bachelor's degree or more				
							total	bachelor's degree	master's degree	professional degree	doctoral degree
Men aged 35 to 44 who work full-time	**13,773**	**451**	**693**	**3,804**	**2,162**	**1,357**	**5,305**	**3,432**	**1,296**	**250**	**328**
Under $5,000	75	5	7	25	14	5	19	15	2	2	0
$5,000 to $9,999	102	12	29	37	9	3	10	9	1	0	0
$10,000 to $14,999	301	68	42	79	39	21	50	34	10	0	7
$15,000 to $19,999	470	78	82	208	44	27	30	24	5	0	1
$20,000 to $24,999	830	65	98	400	134	60	74	54	17	1	1
$25,000 to $29,999	870	54	99	376	124	92	126	104	19	0	3
$30,000 to $34,999	1,019	40	68	436	195	77	202	165	32	1	5
$35,000 to $39,999	979	52	63	369	186	128	182	138	33	4	9
$40,000 to $44,999	1,061	19	49	372	239	146	236	182	45	4	4
$45,000 to $49,999	826	10	41	295	164	96	220	157	58	2	2
$50,000 to $54,999	1,009	9	36	274	200	115	375	272	78	8	16
$55,000 to $59,999	565	7	15	139	130	82	193	128	51	2	12
$60,000 to $64,999	771	13	23	200	107	85	342	263	61	8	11
$65,000 to $69,999	496	6	10	111	97	56	217	161	44	3	10
$70,000 to $74,999	537	1	10	100	106	65	256	184	46	9	16
$75,000 to $79,999	455	4	1	85	59	67	239	146	63	4	27
$80,000 to $84,999	442	2	8	67	83	47	237	153	74	3	8
$85,000 to $89,999	259	0	0	23	35	25	175	100	56	12	7
$90,000 to $94,999	329	0	3	33	59	36	199	128	52	10	9
$95,000 to $99,999	158	0	0	14	11	7	125	72	34	6	14
$100,000 or more	2,220	8	9	161	130	115	1,798	942	517	171	168
Median earnings	$51,052	$24,746	$29,112	$39,284	$47,588	$50,633	$76,523	$70,142	$85,561	$131,313	$100,449

PERCENT DISTRIBUTION

Men aged 35 to 44 who work full-time	100.0%	100.0%	100.0%	100.0%	100.0%	100.0%	100.0%	100.0%	100.0%	100.0%	100.0%
Under $15,000	3.5	18.8	11.3	3.7	2.9	2.1	1.5	1.7	1.0	0.8	2.1
$15,000 to $24,999	9.4	31.7	26.0	16.0	8.2	6.4	2.0	2.3	1.7	0.4	0.6
$25,000 to $34,999	13.7	20.8	24.1	21.3	14.8	12.5	6.2	7.8	3.9	0.4	2.4
$35,000 to $49,999	20.8	18.0	22.1	27.2	27.2	27.3	12.0	13.9	10.5	4.0	4.6
$50,000 to $74,999	24.5	8.0	13.6	21.7	29.6	29.7	26.1	29.4	21.6	12.0	19.8
$75,000 to $99,999	11.9	1.3	1.7	5.8	11.4	13.4	18.4	17.5	21.5	14.0	19.8
$100,000 or more	16.1	1.8	1.3	4.2	6.0	8.5	33.9	27.4	39.9	68.4	51.2

Note: Earnings include wages and salary only.
Source: Bureau of the Census, 2011 Current Population Survey Annual Social and Economic Supplement, Internet site http://www.census.gov/hhes/www/cpstables/032011/perinc/toc.htm; calculations by New Strategist

Table 5.23 Earnings of Women by Education, 2010: Aged 35 to 44

(number and percent distribution of women aged 35 to 44 who work full-time, year-round, by earnings and educational attainment, 2010; median earnings of women with earnings; women in thousands as of 2011)

	total	less than 9th grade	9th to 12th grade, no degree	high school graduate	some college	associate's degree	bachelor's degree or more total	bachelor's degree	master's degree	professional degree	doctoral degree
Women aged 35 to 44 who work full-time	**9,900**	**171**	**358**	**2,327**	**1,720**	**1,224**	**4,099**	**2,560**	**1,180**	**171**	**187**
Under $5,000	56	4	2	15	11	7	15	10	7	0	0
$5,000 to $9,999	71	5	7	28	12	8	11	3	8	0	0
$10,000 to $14,999	396	61	70	154	55	32	25	21	3	0	1
$15,000 to $19,999	648	41	97	270	131	52	59	47	11	0	1
$20,000 to $24,999	977	32	58	450	208	127	103	77	19	4	2
$25,000 to $29,999	774	10	51	282	204	93	135	105	27	1	3
$30,000 to $34,999	1,067	5	29	307	263	170	292	237	49	6	0
$35,000 to $39,999	859	6	6	231	193	151	270	197	66	0	6
$40,000 to $44,999	830	1	24	188	162	110	345	242	90	10	3
$45,000 to $49,999	730	2	4	135	133	77	380	277	88	7	8
$50,000 to $54,999	667	0	2	85	108	113	359	214	127	11	6
$55,000 to $59,999	433	2	2	29	68	73	258	144	94	10	12
$60,000 to $64,999	426	0	6	54	43	47	275	179	79	14	4
$65,000 to $69,999	278	0	0	13	20	43	202	116	69	6	10
$70,000 to $74,999	293	0	0	26	11	49	207	121	74	6	7
$75,000 to $79,999	206	0	0	16	22	14	154	81	45	5	22
$80,000 to $84,999	175	0	0	14	20	16	126	62	49	4	11
$85,000 to $89,999	126	0	0	7	14	12	93	59	28	0	7
$90,000 to $94,999	121	0	1	1	9	11	98	53	31	9	5
$95,000 to $99,999	63	0	0	0	2	3	57	27	20	4	6
$100,000 or more	705	1	0	26	32	13	633	290	195	75	72
Median earnings	$40,382	$16,317	$20,224	$29,272	$34,134	$37,856	$55,661	$50,890	$60,021	$91,211	$81,918

PERCENT DISTRIBUTION

Women aged 35 to 44 who work full-time	**100.0%**	**100.0%**	**100.0%**	**100.0%**	**100.0%**	**100.0%**	**100.0%**	**100.0%**	**100.0%**	**100.0%**	**100.0%**
Under $15,000	5.3	40.9	22.1	8.5	4.5	3.8	1.2	1.3	1.5	0.0	0.5
$15,000 to $24,999	16.4	42.7	43.3	30.9	19.7	14.6	4.0	4.8	2.5	2.3	1.6
$25,000 to $34,999	18.6	8.8	22.3	25.3	27.2	21.5	10.4	13.4	6.4	4.1	1.6
$35,000 to $49,999	24.4	5.3	9.5	23.8	28.4	27.6	24.3	28.0	20.7	9.9	9.1
$50,000 to $74,999	21.2	1.2	2.8	8.9	14.5	26.6	31.7	30.2	37.5	27.5	20.9
$75,000 to $99,999	7.0	0.0	0.3	1.6	3.9	4.6	12.9	11.0	14.7	12.9	27.3
$100,000 or more	7.1	0.6	0.0	1.1	1.9	1.1	15.4	11.3	16.5	43.9	38.5

Note: Earnings include wages and salary only.
Source: Bureau of the Census, 2011 Current Population Survey Annual Social and Economic Supplement, Internet site http:// www.census.gov/hhes/www/cpstables/032011/perinc/toc.htm; calculations by New Strategist

Poverty Rate Is below Average for Gen Xers

But more than one in eight Gen Xers is poor.

Generation Xers (aged 34 to 45 in 2010) are slightly less likely to be poor than the average American. Overall, 15.1 percent of Americans lived in poverty in 2010. Among people aged 35 to 44, the figure was 12.6 percent. Children under age 18 are most likely to be poor, with a poverty rate of 22.0 percent.

Black and Hispanic Generation Xers are more than twice as likely as Asian and non-Hispanic white Gen Xers to be poor. Among blacks aged 35 to 44, 19.8 percent live below the poverty level. The poverty rate is an even higher 22.9 percent among Hispanics in the age group. In contrast, 8.8 percent of Asians and 8.6 percent of non-Hispanic whites are poor.

■ Blacks are more likely to be poor than Asians or non-Hispanic whites because they are less likely to live in a married-couple family, the most affluent household type.

The poverty rate falls with age

(percent of people with incomes below poverty level, by age, 2010)

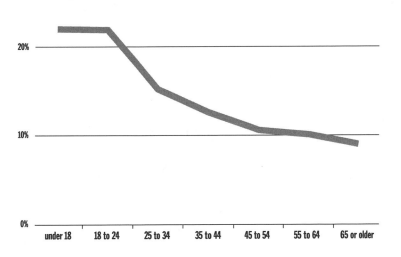

Table 5.24 People below Poverty Level by Age, Race, and Hispanic Origin, 2010

(number, percent, and percent distribution of people below poverty level by age, race, and Hispanic origin, 2010; people in thousands as of 2011)

	total	Asian	black	Hispanic	non-Hispanic white
NUMBER IN POVERTY					
Total people	**46,180**	**1,859**	**11,361**	**13,243**	**19,599**
Under age 18	16,401	547	4,817	6,110	5,002
Aged 18 to 24	6,507	296	1,514	1,547	3,132
Aged 25 to 34	6,333	255	1,485	1,917	2,682
Aged 35 to 44	5,028	223	1,032	1,618	2,129
Aged 45 to 54	4,662	181	1,039	968	2,421
Aged 55 to 59	1,972	89	445	308	1,095
Aged 60 to 64	1,755	56	393	261	1,024
Aged 65 or older	3,520	213	636	514	2,116
PERCENT IN POVERTY					
Total people	**15.1%**	**11.9%**	**27.4%**	**26.6%**	**9.9%**
Under age 18	22.0	13.6	38.2	35.0	12.4
Aged 18 to 24	21.9	19.8	31.9	26.8	17.8
Aged 25 to 34	15.2	10.2	25.1	23.6	10.8
Aged 35 to 44	12.6	8.8	19.8	22.9	8.6
Aged 45 to 54	10.6	8.7	19.0	18.1	7.9
Aged 55 to 59	10.1	10.2	20.5	17.1	7.6
Aged 60 to 64	10.1	8.0	21.2	18.0	7.7
Aged 65 or older	9.0	14.4	18.2	18.0	6.8
PERCENT DISTRIBUTION OF POOR BY AGE					
Total people	**100.0%**	**100.0%**	**100.0%**	**100.0%**	**100.0%**
Under age 18	35.5	29.4	42.4	46.1	25.5
Aged 18 to 24	14.1	15.9	13.3	11.7	16.0
Aged 25 to 34	13.7	13.7	13.1	14.5	13.7
Aged 35 to 44	10.9	12.0	9.1	12.2	10.9
Aged 45 to 54	10.1	9.7	9.1	7.3	12.4
Aged 55 to 59	4.3	4.8	3.9	2.3	5.6
Aged 60 to 64	3.8	3.0	3.5	2.0	5.2
Aged 65 or older	7.6	11.5	5.6	3.9	10.8
PERCENT DISTRIBUTION OF POOR BY RACE AND HISPANIC ORIGIN					
Total people	**100.0%**	**4.0%**	**24.6%**	**28.7%**	**42.4%**
Under age 18	100.0	3.3	29.4	37.3	30.5
Aged 18 to 24	100.0	4.5	23.3	23.8	48.1
Aged 25 to 34	100.0	4.0	23.4	30.3	42.3
Aged 35 to 44	100.0	4.4	20.5	32.2	42.3
Aged 45 to 54	100.0	3.9	22.3	20.8	51.9
Aged 55 to 59	100.0	4.5	22.6	15.6	55.5
Aged 60 to 64	100.0	3.2	22.4	14.9	58.3
Aged 65 or older	100.0	6.1	18.1	14.6	60.1

Note: Numbers will not add to total because Asians and blacks are those who identify themselves as being of the race alone and those who identify themselves as being of the race in combination with other races, because Hispanics may be of any race, and because not all races are shown. Non-Hispanic whites are those who identify themselves as being white alone and not Hispanic. Source: Bureau of the Census, 2011 Current Population Survey Annual Social and Economic Supplement, Internet site http:// www.census.gov/hhes/www/cpstables/032011/pov/toc.htm; calculations by New Strategist

6

Labor Force

■ Generation Xers are in their prime working years. But their labor force participation has declined, thanks to the weak economy in the aftermath of the Great Recession.

■ Eighty-three percent of people aged 35 to 44 were in the labor force in 2011 (Generation Xers were aged 35 to 46 in that year). Nine of ten Gen X men and three out of four Gen X women are in the labor force.

■ In 2011, only 4.3 percent of Asian men aged 35 to 44 were unemployed. The unemployment rate was 6.6 percent among white men, 8.7 percent among Hispanic men, and 14.9 percent among black men in the age group.

■ Sixty-nine percent of married couples aged 35 to 44 are dual earners, while the husband is the only one in the labor force in another 25 percent.

■ Job tenure (the median number of years a worker has been with the current employer) has been stable among men aged 35 to 44 over the past decade. Long-term employment has fallen, however.

■ Between 2010 and 2020, the small Generation X will fill the 45-to-54 age group (Gen Xers will be aged 44 to 55 in 2020). Consequently, the number of workers in the age group will decline by more than 2 million.

Gen Xers Are in Their Prime Working Years

But labor force participation rate has fallen for both men and women.

Generation Xers are at the career-building stage of their lives. But their labor force participation rate has declined because of the Great Recession and weak economy.

Typically, labor force participation peaks among men in their thirties and forties, and that is still true today. The 2011 labor force participation rate of men tops out in the 35-to-39 age group (Gen Xers were aged 35 to 46 in 2011) at 91.5 percent. This figure is 1.7 percentage points below the 93.2 percent of 2000. Among women aged 35 to 44, the labor force participation rate was 74 to 76 percent. These figures were 2 to 3 percentage points lower than in 2000.

■ Although labor force participation has declined for Generation Xers, the great majority of both men and women either have a job or are looking for work.

The labor force participation rate of men aged 35 to 44 has declined

(percent of men aged 35 to 44 in the labor force, 2000 and 2011)

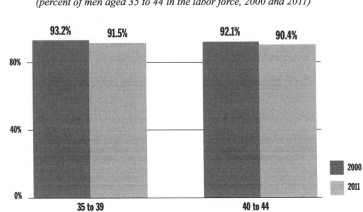

Table 6.1 Labor Force Participation Rate by Sex and Age, 2000 to 2011

(civilian labor force participation rate of people aged 16 or older, by sex and age, 2000 to 2011; percentage point change, 2000–11)

	2011	2010	2000	percentage point change 2000–11
Men aged 16 or older	**70.5%**	**71.2%**	**74.8%**	**–4.3**
Aged 16 to 17	20.4	21.8	40.9	–20.5
Aged 18 to 19	48.3	49.6	65.0	–16.7
Aged 20 to 24	74.7	74.5	82.6	–7.9
Aged 25 to 29	87.8	88.4	92.5	–4.7
Aged 30 to 34	90.6	91.1	94.2	–3.6
Aged 35 to 39	91.5	92.2	93.2	–1.7
Aged 40 to 44	90.4	90.7	92.1	–1.7
Aged 45 to 49	88.1	88.5	90.2	–2.1
Aged 50 to 54	84.2	85.1	86.8	–2.6
Aged 55 to 59	78.2	78.5	77.0	1.2
Aged 60 to 64	59.1	60.0	54.9	4.2
Aged 65 or older	22.8	22.1	17.7	5.1
Women aged 16 or older	**58.1**	**58.6**	**59.9**	**–1.8**
Aged 16 to 17	22.6	23.0	40.8	–18.2
Aged 18 to 19	47.4	48.6	61.3	–13.9
Aged 20 to 24	67.8	68.3	73.1	–5.3
Aged 25 to 29	74.4	75.6	76.7	–2.3
Aged 30 to 34	73.4	73.8	75.5	–2.1
Aged 35 to 39	73.7	74.1	75.7	–2.0
Aged 40 to 44	75.6	76.2	78.7	–3.1
Aged 45 to 49	76.5	76.8	79.1	–2.6
Aged 50 to 54	74.3	74.6	74.1	0.2
Aged 55 to 59	67.7	68.4	61.4	6.3
Aged 60 to 64	50.3	50.7	40.2	10.1
Aged 65 or older	14.0	13.8	9.4	4.6

Source: Bureau of Labor Statistics, Labor Force Statistics from the Current Population Survey, Internet site http://www.bls .gov/cps/tables.htm#empstat; calculations by New Strategist

More than 80 Percent of Gen Xers Are in the Labor Force

Among men, labor force participation is over 90 percent.

Eighty-three percent of people aged 35 to 44 were in the labor force in 2011. (Generation Xers were aged 35 to 46 in that year.) Labor force participation rates for men and women vary little within the age group, with nine of 10 Gen X men and three out of four Gen X women in the labor force.

Generation X men are less likely than the average male to be unemployed—7.4 percent of men aged 35 to 44 are unemployed versus 9.4 percent of all male workers in 2011. The unemployment rate among Gen X women is also below the average for all women, at 7.2 percent compared with a rate of 8.5 percent for all women. Gen Xers are less likely to be unemployed than workers under age 35, but more likely to be job hunting than workers in most of the older age groups.

■ Workers aged 35 to 44 account for 22 percent of the employed and 17 percent of the unemployed.

Most men and women of Generation X are in the labor force

(percent of people aged 35 to 44 in the labor force, by sex, 2011)

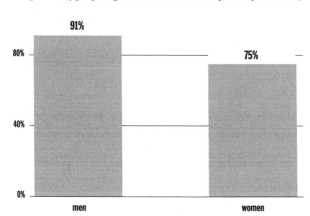

Table 6.2 Employment Status by Sex and Age, 2011

(number and percent of people aged 16 or older in the civilian labor force by sex and age, 2011; numbers in thousands)

	civilian noninstitutional population	civilian labor force			unemployed	
		total	percent of population	employed	number	percent of labor force
Total aged 16 or older	**239,618**	**153,617**	**64.1%**	**139,869**	**13,747**	**8.9%**
Aged 16 to 24	38,197	20,997	55.0	17,363	3,634	17.3
Aged 25 to 29	21,119	17,137	81.1	15,380	1,757	10.3
Aged 30 to 34	20,245	16,588	81.9	15,158	1,430	8.6
Aged 35 to 44	39,499	32,660	82.7	30,270	2,389	7.3
Aged 35 to 39	19,022	15,688	82.5	14,512	1,176	7.5
Aged 40 to 44	20,476	16,972	82.9	15,758	1,214	7.2
Aged 45 to 54	43,842	35,360	80.7	32,867	2,493	7.1
Aged 55 to 64	36,987	23,765	64.3	22,186	1,579	6.6
Aged 65 or older	39,729	7,112	17.9	6,647	465	6.5
Men aged 16 or older	**116,317**	**81,975**	**70.5**	**74,290**	**7,684**	**9.4**
Aged 16 to 24	19,426	10,996	56.6	8,934	2,061	18.7
Aged 25 to 29	10,666	9,364	87.8	8,347	1,017	10.9
Aged 30 to 34	10,045	9,105	90.6	8,327	779	8.6
Aged 35 to 44	19,446	17,686	90.9	16,370	1,316	7.4
Aged 35 to 39	9,373	8,578	91.5	7,949	630	7.3
Aged 40 to 44	10,073	9,108	90.4	8,421	686	7.5
Aged 45 to 54	21,451	18,483	86.2	17,113	1,370	7.4
Aged 55 to 64	17,810	12,350	69.3	11,469	882	7.1
Aged 65 or older	17,474	3,990	22.8	3,730	261	6.5
Women aged 16 or older	**123,300**	**71,642**	**58.1**	**65,579**	**6,063**	**8.5**
Aged 16 to 24	18,772	10,001	53.3	8,428	1,573	15.7
Aged 25 to 29	10,453	7,773	74.4	7,032	741	9.5
Aged 30 to 34	10,200	7,482	73.4	6,831	651	8.7
Aged 35 to 44	20,053	14,973	74.7	13,900	1,073	7.2
Aged 35 to 39	9,649	7,109	73.7	6,563	546	7.7
Aged 40 to 44	10,404	7,864	75.6	7,337	527	6.7
Aged 45 to 54	22,391	16,876	75.4	15,753	1,123	6.7
Aged 55 to 64	19,177	11,414	59.5	10,717	697	6.1
Aged 65 or older	22,255	3,121	14.0	2,917	204	6.5

Source: Bureau of Labor Statistics, Labor Force Statistics from the Current Population Survey, Internet site http://www.bls .gov/cps/tables.htm#empstat; calculations by New Strategist

Asians Are Least Likely to Be Unemployed

Nearly 15 percent of black men aged 35 to 44 were looking for work in 2011.

Most men of Generation X are in the labor force, but there are differences in labor force participation and unemployment by race and Hispanic origin. Among Asian, Hispanic, and white men aged 35 to 44, 92 percent are in the labor force. Among black men the figure is 84 percent.

Asian men aged 35 to 44 are less likely to be unemployed than others. In 2011, only 4.3 percent were unemployed, much lower than the 6.8 percent average for all Asian men and less than the 6.6 percent rate among white men in the age group. A larger 8.7 percent of Hispanic men aged 35 to 44 were unemployed. Among blacks in the age group, a substantial 14.9 percent were unemployed in 2011.

■ Higher unemployment among black men contributes to their lower labor force participation rate. Discouraged by the prospects for work in their communities, some black men give up looking for work.

Unemployment rate varies by race and Hispanic origin

(percent of men aged 35 to 44 who are unemployed, by race and Hispanic origin, 2011)

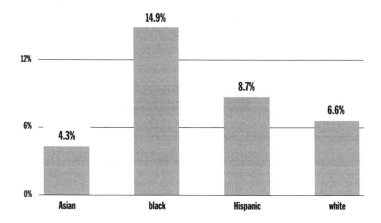

Table 6.3 Employment Status of Men by Race, Hispanic Origin, and Age, 2011

(number and percent of men aged 16 or older in the civilian labor force by race, Hispanic origin, and age, 2011; numbers in thousands)

	civilian noninstitutional population	civilian labor force			unemployed	
		total	percent of population	employed	number	percent of labor force
ASIAN MEN						
Total aged 16 or older	**5,429**	**3,972**	**73.2%**	**3,703**	**269**	**6.8%**
Aged 16 to 24	804	336	41.8	285	52	15.5
Aged 25 to 29	543	450	82.9	417	33	7.4
Aged 30 to 34	570	520	91.2	496	24	4.6
Aged 35 to 44	1,186	1,092	92.1	1,045	47	4.3
Aged 35 to 39	612	565	92.2	541	23	4.1
Aged 40 to 44	573	527	92.0	503	24	4.5
Aged 45 to 54	956	874	91.4	810	63	7.2
Aged 55 to 64	707	531	75.0	492	39	7.3
Aged 65 or older	663	169	25.5	158	11	6.4
BLACK MEN						
Total aged 16 or older	**13,164**	**8,454**	**64.2**	**6,953**	**1,502**	**17.8**
Aged 16 to 24	2,792	1,341	48.0	922	420	31.3
Aged 25 to 29	1,379	1,126	81.7	889	237	21.0
Aged 30 to 34	1,233	1,033	83.7	844	189	18.3
Aged 35 to 44	2,222	1,860	83.7	1,583	277	14.9
Aged 35 to 39	1,077	902	83.7	772	129	14.4
Aged 40 to 44	1,146	959	83.7	811	148	15.4
Aged 45 to 54	2,435	1,854	76.1	1,621	233	12.5
Aged 55 to 64	1,759	983	55.9	858	125	12.7
Aged 65 or older	1,344	257	19.1	236	21	8.2
HISPANIC MEN						
Total aged 16 or older	**17,753**	**13,576**	**76.5**	**12,049**	**1,527**	**11.2**
Aged 16 to 24	4,091	2,358	57.6	1,897	460	19.5
Aged 25 to 29	2,214	2,008	90.7	1,798	210	10.5
Aged 30 to 34	2,165	2,002	92.5	1,817	185	9.2
Aged 35 to 44	3,702	3,421	92.4	3,124	297	8.7
Aged 35 to 39	1,965	1,835	93.4	1,679	156	8.5
Aged 40 to 44	1,737	1,586	91.3	1,444	141	8.9
Aged 45 to 54	2,717	2,372	87.3	2,141	231	9.8
Aged 55 to 64	1,604	1,122	69.9	1,006	116	10.4
Aged 65 or older	1,260	293	23.3	266	28	9.5

	civilian noninstitutional population	civilian labor force			unemployed	
		total	percent of population	employed	number	percent of labor force
WHITE MEN						
Total aged 16 or older	**94,801**	**67,551**	**71.3%**	**61,920**	**5,631**	**8.3%**
Aged 16 to 24	15,095	8,925	59.1	7,433	1,494	16.7
Aged 25 to 29	8,412	7,506	89.2	6,804	701	9.3
Aged 30 to 34	7,921	7,280	91.9	6,744	535	7.4
Aged 35 to 44	15,540	14,317	92.1	13,366	951	6.6
Aged 35 to 39	7,424	6,892	92.8	6,434	458	6.6
Aged 40 to 44	8,117	7,425	91.5	6,932	493	6.6
Aged 45 to 54	17,602	15,400	87.5	14,370	1,030	6.7
Aged 55 to 64	15,018	10,629	70.8	9,932	697	6.6
Aged 65 or older	15,213	3,494	23.0	3,271	223	6.4

Note: People who selected more than one race are not included. Hispanics may be of any race.
Source: Bureau of Labor Statistics, Labor Force Statistics from the Current Population Survey, Internet site http://www.bls
.gov/cps/tables.htm#empstat; calculations by New Strategist

Labor Force Participation of Gen X Women Varies by Race and Hispanic Origin

Hispanic women are least likely to be in the labor force.

Black women aged 35 to 44 are more likely than Asian, Hispanic, or white women to be in the labor force. Seventy-eight percent of black women in the age group were working or looking for work in 2011. This figure compares with 74 percent of white women, 72 percent of Asian women, and 67 percent of Hispanic women in the age group.

Unemployment is greater among black and Hispanic women than among Asian or white women. Among black women aged 35 to 44, 11.6 percent were unemployed in 2011. Among their Hispanic counterparts, the figure was 9.9 percent. The unemployment rate was 6.3 percent for white women in the age group and 6.4 percent for Asians.

■ Hispanic women are less likely to work than black or white women because a larger proportion are married and caring for young children.

Labor force participation rate is highest among black women

(labor force participation rate of women aged 35 to 44, by race and Hispanic origin, 2011)

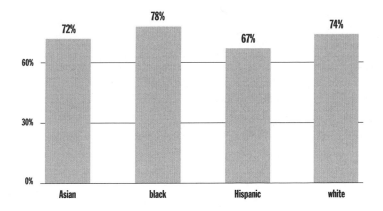

Table 6.4 Employment Status of Women by Race, Hispanic Origin, and Age, 2011

(number and percent of women aged 16 or older in the civilian labor force by race, Hispanic origin, and age, 2011; numbers in thousands)

	civilian noninstitutional population	civilian labor force			unemployed	
		total	percent of population	employed	number	percent of labor force
ASIAN WOMEN						
Total aged 16 or older	**6,011**	**3,414**	**56.8%**	**3,165**	**250**	**7.3%**
Aged 16 to 24	788	324	41.1	283	41	12.7
Aged 25 to 29	570	368	64.7	339	29	7.9
Aged 30 to 44	627	410	65.4	381	30	7.2
Aged 35 to 34	1,279	917	71.7	859	58	6.4
Aged 35 to 39	649	460	70.8	428	32	6.9
Aged 40 to 44	630	457	72.6	430	27	5.9
Aged 45 to 54	1,058	797	75.3	750	47	5.9
Aged 55 to 64	848	501	59.1	461	40	7.9
Aged 65 or older	841	97	11.6	92	5	5.3
BLACK WOMEN						
Total aged 16 or older	**15,950**	**9,427**	**59.1**	**8,098**	**1,329**	**14.1**
Aged 16 to 24	2,969	1,410	47.5	1,033	379	26.9
Aged 25 to 29	1,522	1,143	75.1	932	211	18.4
Aged 30 to 34	1,472	1,132	76.9	967	165	14.6
Aged 35 to 44	2,773	2,168	78.2	1,916	252	11.6
Aged 35 to 39	1,356	1,072	79.0	940	131	12.3
Aged 40 to 44	1,417	1,097	77.4	976	121	11.0
Aged 45 to 54	2,922	2,104	72.0	1,892	211	10.0
Aged 55 to 64	2,196	1,172	53.4	1,086	86	7.4
Aged 65 or older	2,096	298	14.2	272	25	8.5
HISPANIC WOMEN						
Total aged 16 or older	**16,685**	**9,322**	**55.9**	**8,220**	**1,102**	**11.8**
Aged 16 to 24	3,510	1,625	46.3	1,312	314	19.3
Aged 25 to 29	1,863	1,218	65.4	1,077	141	11.5
Aged 30 to 34	1,865	1,188	63.7	1,055	133	11.2
Aged 35 to 44	3,401	2,282	67.1	2,055	227	9.9
Aged 35 to 39	1,774	1,174	66.2	1,054	120	10.2
Aged 40 to 44	1,627	1,108	68.1	1,001	106	9.6
Aged 45 to 54	2,696	1,899	70.4	1,707	192	10.1
Aged 55 to 64	1,707	893	52.3	814	78	8.8
Aged 65 or older	1,643	217	13.2	200	17	8.0

	civilian noninstitutional population	civilian labor force				
		total	percent of population	employed	unemployed	
					number	percent of labor force
WHITE WOMEN						
Total aged 16 or older	**98,276**	**57,028**	**58.0%**	**52,770**	**4,257**	**7.5%**
Aged 16 to 24	14,285	7,908	55.4	6,833	1,077	13.6
Aged 25 to 29	8,025	6,027	75.1	5,558	468	7.8
Aged 30 to 34	7,778	5,700	73.3	5,270	430	7.5
Aged 35 to 44	15,490	11,517	74.4	10,789	728	6.3
Aged 35 to 39	7,370	5,377	73.0	5,015	363	6.7
Aged 40 to 44	8,120	6,140	75.6	5,775	365	5.9
Aged 45 to 54	17,925	13,636	76.1	12,806	829	6.1
Aged 55 to 64	15,781	9,559	60.6	9,005	554	5.8
Aged 65 or older	18,992	2,681	14.1	2,509	171	6.4

Note: People who selected more than one race are not included. Hispanics may be of any race.
Source: Bureau of Labor Statistics, Labor Force Statistics from the Current Population Survey, Internet site http://www.bls
.gov/cps/tables.htm#empstat; calculations by New Strategist

Most Generation X Couples Are Dual Earners

The husband is the sole support for only about one in four couples.

Dual incomes are by far the norm among married couples. Both husband and wife are in the labor force in 53 percent of the nation's couples. In another 22 percent, the husband is the only worker. Not far behind are the 17 percent of couples in which neither spouse is in the labor force. The wife is the sole worker in 7 percent of couples.

Sixty-nine percent of couples aged 35 to 44 are dual earners, while the husband is the only one in the labor force in another 25 percent. The dual-earner share falls to 50 percent among couples aged 55 to 64 as workers begin to retire.

■ The dual-earner share of couples will rise in the older age groups as early retirement becomes less common.

Few Generation X couples are supported solely by the husband

(percent distribution of married couples aged 35 to 44 by labor force status of husband and wife, 2011)

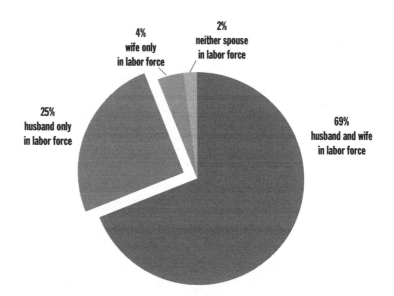

Table 6.5 Labor Force Status of Married-Couple Family Groups by Age, 2011

(number and percent distribution of married-couple family groups by age of reference person and labor force status of husband and wife, 2011; numbers in thousands)

	total	husband and wife in labor force	husband only in labor force	wife only in labor force	neither husband nor wife in labor force
Total married-couple family groups	**60,155**	**31,994**	**13,241**	**4,455**	**10,464**
Under age 35	10,252	6,495	3,170	359	229
Aged 35 to 44	12,478	8,609	3,098	494	277
Aged 35 to 39	5,994	4,079	1,562	226	127
Aged 40 to 44	6,484	4,530	1,536	268	150
Aged 45 to 54	14,017	9,609	2,963	869	577
Aged 55 to 64	12,158	6,035	2,601	1,615	1,906
Aged 65 or older	11,248	1,247	1,409	1,118	7,475

PERCENT DISTRIBUTION BY LABOR FORCE STATUS

	total	husband and wife in labor force	husband only in labor force	wife only in labor force	neither husband nor wife in labor force
Total married-couple family groups	**100.0%**	**53.2%**	**22.0%**	**7.4%**	**17.4%**
Under age 35	100.0	63.4	30.9	3.5	2.2
Aged 35 to 44	100.0	69.0	24.8	4.0	2.2
Aged 35 to 39	100.0	68.1	26.1	3.8	2.1
Aged 40 to 44	100.0	69.9	23.7	4.1	2.3
Aged 45 to 54	100.0	68.6	21.1	6.2	4.1
Aged 55 to 64	100.0	49.6	21.4	13.3	15.7
Aged 65 or older	100.0	11.1	12.5	9.9	66.5

PERCENT DISTRIBUTION BY AGE

	total	husband and wife in labor force	husband only in labor force	wife only in labor force	neither husband nor wife in labor force
Total married-couple family groups	**100.0%**	**100.0%**	**100.0%**	**100.0%**	**100.0%**
Under age 35	17.0	20.3	23.9	8.1	2.2
Aged 35 to 44	20.7	26.9	23.4	11.1	2.6
Aged 35 to 39	10.0	12.7	11.8	5.1	1.2
Aged 40 to 44	10.8	14.2	11.6	6.0	1.4
Aged 45 to 54	23.3	30.0	22.4	19.5	5.5
Aged 55 to 64	20.2	18.9	19.6	36.3	18.2
Aged 65 or older	18.7	3.9	10.6	25.1	71.4

Source: Bureau of the Census, America's Families and Living Arrangements: 2011, Internet site http://www.census.gov/population/www/socdemo/hh-fam/cps2011.html; calculations by New Strategist

Generation Xers Are Overrepresented in Some Jobs

They are more than one-third of computer and information system managers.

Only 22 percent of workers were aged 35 to 44 in 2011 (Generation X was aged 35 to 46 in that year), but the share varies widely by occupation. Workers in the 35-to-44 age group tend to be underrepresented in leadership positions and overrepresented in jobs requiring technical skills. The 35-to-44 age group accounts for only 19 percent of chief executives. But 36 percent of computer and information systems managers and 34 percent of telecommunications line installers and repairers are aged 35 to 44.

Generation Xers make up a large share of employees in jobs requiring physical stamina. Thirty-five percent of police are in the 35-to-44 age group, as are 32 percent of firefighters and physical therapists.

■ Generation X was raised on computers, explaining their disproportionate presence in high-tech jobs.

People aged 35 to 44 account for a relatively large share of some occupations

(percent of workers in the 35-to-44 age group, by occupation, 2011)

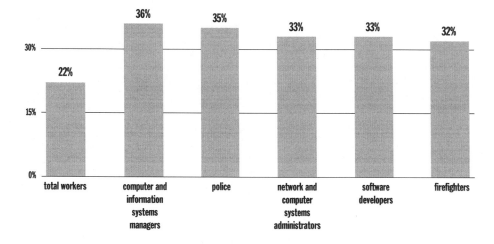

Table 6.6 Occupations of Workers Aged 35 to 44, 2011

(number of employed workers aged 16 or older and median age, number and percent distribution of workers aged 35 to 44, and 35-to-44-year-olds as share of total, by occupation, 2011; numbers in thousands)

	total	median age	aged 35 to 44		
			number	percent distribution	share of total
TOTAL WORKERS	**139,869**	**42.1**	**30,270**	**100.0%**	**21.6%**
Management and professional occupations	**52,547**	**44.2**	**12,574**	**41.5**	**23.9**
Management, business and financial operations	21,589	45.7	5,274	17.4	24.4
Management	15,250	46.7	3,724	12.3	24.4
Business and financial operations	6,339	43.3	1,550	5.1	24.5
Professional and related occupations	30,957	43.1	7,301	24.1	23.6
Computer and mathematical	3,608	40.5	1,034	3.4	28.7
Architecture and engineering	2,785	43.9	642	2.1	23.1
Life, physical, and social sciences	1,303	42.3	294	1.0	22.6
Community and social services	2,352	44.8	516	1.7	21.9
Legal	1,770	46.1	406	1.3	22.9
Education, training, and library	8,619	43.6	1,946	6.4	22.6
Arts, design, entertainment, sports, and media	2,779	40.9	586	1.9	21.1
Health care practitioner and technician	7,740	43.3	1,877	6.2	24.3
Service occupations	**24,787**	**37.6**	**4,722**	**15.6**	**19.1**
Health care support	3,359	38.8	675	2.2	20.1
Protective service	3,210	40.4	806	2.7	25.1
Food preparation and serving	7,747	29.3	1,119	3.7	14.4
Building and grounds cleaning and maintenance	5,492	43.8	1,128	3.7	20.5
Personal care and service	4,979	39.5	995	3.3	20.0
Sales and office occupations	**33,066**	**41.5**	**6,342**	**21.0**	**19.2**
Sales and related occupations	15,330	39.9	2,797	9.2	18.2
Office and administrative support	17,736	42.7	3,546	11.7	20.0
Natural resources, construction, and maintenance occupations	**13,009**	**41.0**	**3,069**	**10.1**	**23.6**
Farming, fishing, and forestry	1,001	37.0	189	0.6	18.9
Construction and extraction	7,125	40.4	1,756	5.8	24.6
Installation, maintenance, and repair	4,883	42.6	1,123	3.7	23.0
Production, transportation, and material-moving occupations	**16,461**	**42.8**	**3,563**	**11.8**	**21.6**
Production	8,142	43.1	1,812	6.0	22.3
Transportation and material-moving	8,318	42.6	1,751	5.8	21.1

Source: Bureau of Labor Statistics, unpublished data from the 2011 Current Population Survey; calculations by New Strategist

Table 6.7 Workers Aged 35 to 44 by Detailed Occupation, 2011

(number of employed workers aged 16 or older, median age, and number and percent aged 35 to 44, for detailed occupations with at least 100,000 workers, 2011; numbers in thousands)

	total workers	median age	aged 35 to 44 number	aged 35 to 44 percent of total
TOTAL WORKERS	**139,869**	**42.1**	**30,270**	**21.6%**
Chief executives	1,515	52.0	291	19.2
General and operations managers	978	45.4	253	25.9
Marketing and sales managers	1,009	42.1	301	29.8
Administrative services managers	128	48.9	25	19.5
Computer and information systems managers	553	43.1	199	36.0
Financial managers	1,107	43.6	308	27.8
Human resources managers	243	45.1	78	32.1
Industrial production managers	259	46.3	76	29.3
Purchasing managers	204	48.7	44	21.6
Transportation, storage, and distribution managers	254	43.8	71	28.0
Farmers, ranchers, and other agricultural managers	978	55.9	122	12.5
Construction managers	926	46.9	235	25.4
Education administrators	853	46.9	224	26.3
Architectural and engineering managers	106	47.6	30	28.3
Food service managers	1,051	39.7	232	22.1
Lodging managers	148	46.7	32	21.6
Medical and health services managers	529	49.6	121	22.9
Property, real estate, and community association managers	587	49.5	121	20.6
Social and community service managers	329	48.2	72	21.9
Managers, all other	3,173	46.6	812	25.6
Wholesale and retail buyers, except farm products	170	40.7	36	21.2
Purchasing agents, except wholesale, retail, and farm products	259	43.5	64	24.7
Claims adjusters, appraisers, examiners, and investigators	296	42.6	83	28.0
Compliance officers	198	45.9	57	28.8
Cost estimators	119	44.7	23	19.3
Human resources workers	595	42.4	169	28.4
Training and development specialists	130	45.0	36	27.7
Management analysts	707	46.6	151	21.4
Meeting, convention, and event planners	109	37.4	19	17.4
Market research analysts and marketing specialists	205	36.4	42	20.5
Business operations specialists, all other	281	43.6	71	25.3
Accountants and auditors	1,653	43.1	408	24.7
Personal financial advisors	371	43.9	88	23.7
Insurance underwriters	117	44.0	29	24.8
Credit counselors and loan officers	326	42.0	91	27.9
Tax preparers	110	50.2	17	15.5
Computer systems analysts	447	43.1	113	25.3
Computer programmers	459	41.8	131	28.5
Software developers, applications and systems software	1,044	39.4	340	32.6
Web developers	182	37.0	58	31.9
Computer support specialists	461	39.1	112	24.3
Database administrators	134	42.5	34	25.4
Network and computer systems administrators	233	40.6	77	33.0
Computer occupations, all other	306	40.8	74	24.2
Operations research analysts	116	41.3	30	25.9
Architects, except naval	181	46.7	36	19.9
Aerospace engineers	144	43.9	33	22.9

	total workers	median age	aged 35 to 44	
			number	percent of total
Civil engineers	383	42.5	87	22.7%
Electrical and electronics engineers	309	45.0	68	22.0
Industrial engineers, including health and safety	174	43.4	46	26.4
Mechanical engineers	322	42.5	78	24.2
Engineers, all other	337	43.3	74	22.0
Drafters	147	44.0	38	25.9
Engineering technicians, except drafters	376	46.5	83	22.1
Biological scientists	114	42.6	23	20.2
Medical scientists	156	39.5	46	29.5
Physical scientists, all other	152	40.4	41	27.0
Psychologists	197	48.3	46	23.4
Counselors	732	43.0	149	20.4
Social workers	769	42.6	206	26.8
Social and human service assistants	131	44.1	22	16.8
Clergy	414	52.5	73	17.6
Lawyers	1,085	47.2	263	24.2
Paralegals and legal assistants	404	42.8	79	19.6
Miscellaneous legal support workers	209	44.8	53	25.4
Postsecondary teachers	1,355	45.7	270	19.9
Preschool and kindergarten teachers	707	39.2	182	25.7
Elementary and middle school teachers	2,848	43.0	741	26.0
Secondary school teachers	1,136	43.2	279	24.6
Special education teachers	388	43.3	93	24.0
Other teachers and instructors	812	43.7	133	16.4
Librarians	198	52.0	29	14.6
Teacher assistants	950	44.9	175	18.4
Other education, training, and library workers	140	46.3	32	22.9
Artists and related workers	180	45.3	49	27.2
Designers	766	41.8	170	22.2
Producers and directors	149	40.3	30	20.1
Athletes, coaches, umpires, and related workers	272	30.8	41	15.1
Musicians, singers, and related workers	191	43.2	39	20.4
Public relations specialists	158	39.2	36	22.8
Editors	166	41.4	31	18.7
Writers and authors	218	46.1	40	18.3
Broadcast and sound engineering technicians and radio operators	106	39.7	28	26.4
Photographers	148	40.6	37	25.0
Dentists	181	51.0	44	24.3
Dietitians and nutritionists	102	47.7	18	17.6
Pharmacists	274	41.1	77	28.1
Physicians and surgeons	822	46.3	209	25.4
Occupational therapists	112	41.7	38	33.9
Physical therapists	222	40.5	71	32.0
Respiratory therapists	134	44.5	37	27.6
Speech-language pathologists	125	40.5	38	30.4
Therapists, all other	138	40.7	31	22.5
Registered nurses	2,706	44.7	641	23.7
Nurse practitioners	100	46.9	31	31.0
Clinical laboratory technologists and technicians	321	43.2	66	20.6
Dental hygienists	148	42.2	41	27.7
Diagnostic related technologists and technicians	342	42.1	84	24.6
Emergency medical technicians and paramedics	185	31.8	34	18.4
Health practitioner support technologists and technicians	511	34.8	93	18.2

	total workers	median age	aged 35 to 44 number	percent of total
Licensed practical and licensed vocational nurses	560	43.2	144	25.7%
Medical records and health information technicians	116	42.7	26	22.4
Nursing, psychiatric, and home health aides	1,981	40.3	401	20.2
Massage therapists	146	40.5	30	20.5
Dental assistants	307	36.3	73	23.8
Medical assistants	395	34.6	73	18.5
Phlebotomists	119	38.3	29	24.4
First-line supervisors of police and detectives	107	46.0	37	34.6
First-line supervisors of protective service workers, all other	111	47.2	22	19.8
Firefighters	305	37.3	97	31.8
Bailiffs, correctional officers, and jailers	446	39.7	127	28.5
Detectives and criminal investigators	151	42.3	52	34.4
Police and sheriff's patrol officers	668	39.3	234	35.0
Security guards and gaming surveillance officers	963	41.9	152	15.8
Lifeguards and other recreational, all other protective service workers	146	21.8	7	4.8
Chefs and head cooks	347	38.8	100	28.8
First-line supervisors of food preparation and serving workers	505	36.8	106	21.0
Cooks	1,990	33.8	356	17.9
Food preparation workers	784	28.0	99	12.6
Bartenders	392	31.8	72	18.4
Combined food preparation and serving workers, including fast food	326	28.1	38	11.7
Counter attendants, cafeteria, food concession, and coffee shop	255	21.4	13	5.1
Waiters and waitresses	2,059	26.1	222	10.8
Food servers, nonrestaurant	181	32.3	18	9.9
Dining room and cafeteria attendants and bartender helpers	347	25.4	42	12.1
Dishwashers	273	28.3	39	14.3
Hosts and hostesses, restaurant, lounge, and coffee shop	286	21.4	15	5.2
First-line supervisors of housekeeping and janitorial workers	292	48.9	70	24.0
First-line supervisors of landscaping, lawn service, and groundskeeping workers	274	43.5	77	28.1
Janitors and building cleaners	2,186	46.4	393	18.0
Maids and housekeeping cleaners	1,419	45.2	311	21.9
Grounds maintenance workers	1,247	37.1	256	20.5
First-line supervisors of gaming workers	120	40.6	31	25.8
First-line supervisors of personal service workers	192	43.1	61	31.8
Nonfarm animal caretakers	179	37.2	34	19.0
Gaming services workers	113	40.5	24	21.2
Miscellaneous entertainment attendants and related workers	182	26.4	19	10.4
Hairdressers, hairstylists, and cosmetologists	758	39.8	174	23.0
Miscellaneous personal appearance workers	251	40.8	80	31.9
Childcare workers	1,231	37.2	219	17.8
Personal care aides	1,057	43.9	189	17.9
Recreation and fitness workers	390	36.6	74	19.0
Personal care and service workers, all other	105	33.2	22	21.0
First-line supervisors of retail sales workers	3,217	42.6	676	21.0
First-line supervisors of nonretail sales workers	1,088	46.3	276	25.4
Cashiers	3,158	27.2	381	12.1
Counter and rental clerks	139	38.2	19	13.7
Parts salespersons	131	40.9	25	19.1
Retail salespersons	3,224	35.9	471	14.6
Advertising sales agents	254	39.6	56	22.0
Insurance sales agents	531	45.8	112	21.1
Securities, commodities, and financial services sales agents	267	41.7	63	23.6
Sales representatives, services, all other	503	40.7	122	24.3

	total workers	median age	aged 35 to 44	
			number	percent of total
Sales representatives, wholesale and manufacturing	1,297	44.6	314	24.2%
Real estate brokers and sales agents	811	50.3	153	18.9
Telemarketers	108	30.5	9	8.3
Door-to-door sales workers, news and street vendors, related workers	201	43.8	34	16.9
Sales and related workers, all other	226	44.2	53	23.5
First-line supervisors of office and administrative support workers	1,423	45.7	361	25.4
Bill and account collectors	211	38.9	44	20.9
Billing and posting clerks	471	42.2	100	21.2
Bookkeeping, accounting, and auditing clerks	1,300	48.5	278	21.4
Payroll and timekeeping clerks	168	46.1	46	27.4
Tellers	413	31.8	57	13.8
Customer service representatives	1,916	37.0	378	19.7
File Clerks	334	40.8	63	18.9
Hotel, motel, and resort desk clerks	135	30.1	20	14.8
Interviewers, except eligibility and loan	153	40.8	24	15.7
Library assistants, clerical	113	44.8	15	13.3
Loan interviewers and clerks	117	40.4	37	31.6
Order clerks	113	41.7	20	17.7
Receptionists and information clerks	1,259	38.3	210	16.7
Information and record clerks, all other	118	45.7	19	16.1
Couriers and messengers	249	46.5	57	22.9
Dispatchers	239	41.5	56	23.4
Postal service clerks	146	53.1	24	16.4
Postal service mail carriers	348	49.9	71	20.4
Production, planning, and expediting clerks	236	44.1	61	25.8
Shipping, receiving, and traffic clerks	559	40.0	130	23.3
Stock clerks and order fillers	1,503	34.2	228	15.2
Secretaries and administrative assistants	2,871	47.9	565	19.7
Computer operators	126	48.9	15	11.9
Data entry keyers	334	40.0	75	22.5
Word processors and typists	136	46.5	28	20.6
Insurance claims and policy processing clerks	246	41.7	51	20.7
Office clerks, general	1,061	42.2	198	18.7
Office and administrative support workers, all other	513	42.4	117	22.8
Miscellaneous agricultural workers	708	33.8	126	17.8
First-line supervisors of construction trades and extraction workers	634	45.2	159	25.1
Brickmasons, blockmasons, and stonemasons	146	41.8	35	24.0
Carpenters	1,330	41.4	358	26.9
Carpet, floor, and tile installers and finishers	189	37.0	48	25.4
Construction laborers	1,253	36.9	291	23.2
Operating engineers and other construction equipment operators	369	43.0	85	23.0
Drywall installers, ceiling tile installers, and tapers	150	37.6	50	33.3
Electricians	682	41.5	162	23.8
Painters, construction and maintenance	528	40.9	140	26.5
Pipelayers, plumbers, pipefitters, and steamfitters	519	41.4	138	26.6
Roofers	222	34.2	42	18.9
Sheet metal workers	126	40.0	21	16.7
Highway maintenance workers	105	45.3	19	18.1
First-line supervisors of mechanics, installers, and repairers	313	49.7	57	18.2
Computer, automated teller, and office machine repairers	305	40.6	70	23.0
Radio and telecommunications equipment installers and repairers	150	41.9	45	30.0
Aircraft mechanics and service technicians	164	44.0	40	24.4
Automotive body and related repairers	140	41.1	40	28.6
Automotive service technicians and mechanics	855	39.1	189	22.1

	total workers	median age	aged 35 to 44	
			number	percent of total
Bus and truck mechanics and diesel engine specialists	312	42.4	61	19.6%
Heavy vehicle and mobile equipment service technicians, mechanics	199	43.4	45	22.6
Heating, air conditioning, and refrigeration mechanics and installers	338	39.4	82	24.3
Industrial and refractory machinery mechanics	433	45.7	104	24.0
Maintenance and repair workers, general	422	48.4	90	21.3
Electrical power-line installers and repairers	124	40.6	26	21.0
Telecommunications line installers and repairers	201	39.8	68	33.8
Other installation, maintenance, and repair workers	215	41.8	56	26.0
First-line supervisors of production and operating workers	727	47.1	172	23.7
Electrical, electronics, and electromechanical assemblers	156	45.9	33	21.2
Miscellaneous assemblers and fabricators	860	41.5	195	22.7
Bakers	207	40.3	36	17.4
Butchers and other meat, poultry, and fish processing workers	342	39.0	67	19.6
Food processing workers, all other	115	41.0	29	25.2
Cutting, punching, and press machine setters, operators, and tenders, metal and plastic	100	40.0	24	24.0
Machinists	419	45.6	92	22.0
Welding, soldering, and brazing workers	505	40.9	119	23.6
Metal workers and plastic workers, all other	368	41.7	95	25.8
Printing press operators	217	43.6	45	20.7
Laundry and dry-cleaning workers	174	44.6	33	19.0
Sewing machine operators	169	48.0	40	23.7
Inspectors, testers, sorters, samplers, and weighers	647	43.6	145	22.4
Packaging and filling machine operators and tenders	288	39.1	60	20.8
Painting workers	120	40.8	34	28.3
Production workers, all other	777	42.2	185	23.8
Supervisors of transportation and material moving workers	228	44.3	57	25.0
Aircraft pilots and flight engineers	121	49.0	24	19.8
Bus drivers	573	52.6	98	17.1
Driver/sales workers and truck drivers	3,059	45.4	716	23.4
Taxi drivers and chauffeurs	342	48.8	63	18.4
Industrial truck and tractor operators	528	39.8	130	24.6
Cleaners of vehicles and equipment	331	32.7	70	21.1
Laborers and freight, stock, and material movers, hand	1,787	35.0	321	18.0
Packers and packagers, hand	393	37.9	77	19.6

Source: Bureau of Labor Statistics, unpublished tables from the 2011 Current Population Survey; calculations by New Strategist

Few Gen Xers Work Part-time

Part-time work is the rule only among teenagers aged 16 to 19.

Among employed men ranging in age from 25 to 54 in 2011, only 14 percent had part-time jobs. Among the part-time workers, a substantial 39 percent would have preferred full-time work but could not find it.

Among employed women aged 25 to 54, a larger 27 percent worked part-time. Twenty-three percent of the part-time workers were doing so for economic reasons—meaning they could not find a full-time job.

Older workers are more likely to work part-time. Among workers aged 55 or older, 23 percent of employed men and 35 percent of employed women had part-time jobs. The percentage of workers with part-time jobs peaks at 78 percent among 16-to-19-year-olds.

■ The percentage of workers who have part-time jobs because they cannot find full-time employment has been rising because of the Great Recession.

Some part-time workers want full-time jobs

(percent of employed men who work part-time but would prefer a full-time job, by age, 2011)

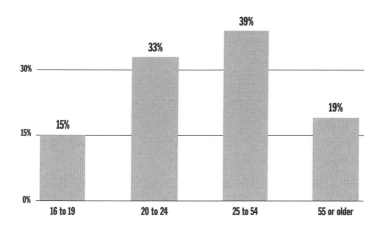

Table 6.8 Full-Time and Part-Time Workers by Age and Sex, 2011

(number and percent distribution of people aged 16 or older at work in nonagricultural industries by age, employment status, and sex, 2011; numbers in thousands)

	total			men			women		
	total	full-time	part-time	total	full-time	part-time	total	full-time	part-time
Total at work	**132,717**	**98,446**	**34,271**	**70,440**	**56,598**	**13,841**	**62,278**	**41,848**	**20,430**
Aged 16 to 19	4,065	888	3,178	1,951	534	1,417	2,114	353	1,761
Aged 20 to 24	12,515	7,226	5,289	6,543	4,097	2,446	5,972	3,129	2,843
Aged 25 to 54	89,430	71,366	18,064	47,964	41,213	6,751	41,466	30,153	11,313
Aged 55 or older	26,707	18,967	7,741	13,982	10,754	3,228	12,726	8,213	4,513

PERCENT DISTRIBUTION BY EMPLOYMENT STATUS

	total			men			women		
Total at work	**100.0%**	**74.2%**	**25.8%**	**100.0%**	**80.3%**	**19.6%**	**100.0%**	**67.2%**	**32.8%**
Aged 16 to 19	100.0	21.8	78.2	100.0	27.4	72.6	100.0	16.7	83.3
Aged 20 to 24	100.0	57.7	42.3	100.0	62.6	37.4	100.0	52.4	47.6
Aged 25 to 54	100.0	79.8	20.2	100.0	85.9	14.1	100.0	72.7	27.3
Aged 55 or older	100.0	71.0	29.0	100.0	76.9	23.1	100.0	64.5	35.5

PERCENT DISTRIBUTION BY AGE

	total			men			women		
Total at work	**100.0%**	**100.0%**	**100.0%**	**100.0%**	**100.0%**	**100.0%**	**100.0%**	**100.0%**	**100.0%**
Aged 16 to 19	3.1	0.9	9.3	2.8	0.9	10.2	3.4	0.8	8.6
Aged 20 to 24	9.4	7.3	15.4	9.3	7.2	17.7	9.6	7.5	13.9
Aged 25 to 54	67.4	72.5	52.7	68.1	72.8	48.8	66.6	72.1	55.4
Aged 55 or older	20.1	19.3	22.6	19.8	19.0	23.3	20.4	19.6	22.1

Note: "Part-time" work is less than 35 hours per week. Part-time workers exclude those who worked less than 35 hours in the previous week because of vacation, holidays, child care problems, weather issues, and other temporary, noneconomic reasons.
Source: Bureau of Labor Statistics, Labor Force Statistics from the Current Population Survey, Internet site http://www.bls .gov/cps/tables.htm#empstat; calculations by New Strategist

Table 6.9 Part-Time Workers by Sex, Age, and Reason, 2011

(total number of people aged 16 or older who work in nonagricultural industries part-time, and number and percent working part-time for economic reasons, by sex and age, 2011; numbers in thousands)

	total	working part-time for economic reasons	
		number	share of total
Men working part-time	**13,841**	**4,285**	**31.0%**
Aged 16 to 19	1,417	217	15.3
Aged 20 to 24	2,446	816	33.4
Aged 25 to 54	6,751	2,627	38.9
Aged 55 or older	3,228	625	19.4
Women working part-time	**20,430**	**4,138**	**20.3**
Aged 16 to 19	1,761	226	12.8
Aged 20 to 24	2,843	703	24.7
Aged 25 to 54	11,313	2,556	22.6
Aged 55 or older	4,513	653	14.5

Note: "Part-time" work is less than 35 hours per week. Part-time workers exclude those who worked less than 35 hours in the previous week because of vacation, holidays, child care problems, weather issues, and other temporary, noneconomic reasons. "Economic reasons" means a worker's hours have been reduced or worker cannot find full-time employment.
Source: Bureau of Labor Statistics, Labor Force Statistics from the Current Population Survey, Internet site http://www.bls .gov/cps/tables.htm#empstat; calculations by New Strategist

Self-Employment Is Uncommon among Gen Xers

Men are more likely than women to be self-employed.

Despite plenty of media hype about America's entrepreneurial spirit, few Americans are self-employed. Only 6.8 percent of the nation's workers were self-employed in 2011.

Men are more likely than women to be self-employed, and self-employment rises with age. Among 35-to-44-year-olds, 7.1 percent of men and 5.4 percent of women are self-employed. The figures peak among men and women aged 65 or older at 20 and 14 percent, respectively.

■ Self-employment is becoming a more difficult for Americans because the cost of buying private health insurance has become prohibitive.

Few Gen Xers are self-employed

(percent of workers who are self-employed, by age, 2011)

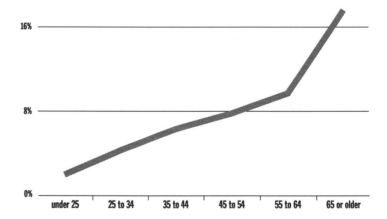

Table 6.10 Self-Employed Workers by Sex and Age, 2011

(number of employed workers aged 16 or older, number and percent who are self-employed, and percent distribution of self-employed, by age, 2011; numbers in thousands)

	total	self-employed number	self-employed percent	percent distribution of self-employed by age
Total aged 16 or older	**139,869**	**9,449**	**6.8%**	**100.0%**
Aged 16 to 24	17,363	355	2.0	3.8
Aged 25 to 34	30,538	1,312	4.3	13.9
Aged 35 to 44	30,271	1,906	6.3	20.2
Aged 45 to 54	32,867	2,567	7.8	27.2
Aged 55 to 64	22,186	2,141	9.7	22.7
Aged 65 or older	6,647	1,168	17.6	12.4
Total men	**74,290**	**5,894**	**7.9**	**100.0**
Aged 16 to 24	8,934	226	2.5	3.8
Aged 25 to 34	16,674	820	4.9	13.9
Aged 35 to 44	16,370	1,158	7.1	19.6
Aged 45 to 54	17,113	1,588	9.3	26.9
Aged 55 to 64	11,469	1,337	11.7	22.7
Aged 65 or older	3,729	764	20.5	13.0
Total women	**65,579**	**3,555**	**5.4**	**100.0**
Aged 16 to 24	8,428	129	1.5	3.6
Aged 25 to 34	13,864	492	3.5	13.8
Aged 35 to 44	13,901	748	5.4	21.0
Aged 45 to 54	15,753	980	6.2	27.6
Aged 55 to 64	10,717	803	7.5	22.6
Aged 65 or older	2,917	404	13.8	11.4

Source: Bureau of Labor Statistics, Labor Force Statistics from the Current Population Survey, Internet site http://www.bls .gov/cps/tables.htm#empstat; calculations by New Strategist

Job Tenure Has Been Stable for Men Aged 35 to 44

Long-term employment has fallen.

Job tenure (the median number of years a worker has been with the current employer) has been stable among men aged 35 to 44 over the past decade. In 2000 and in 2010, the average male worker aged 35 to 44 had been with the current employer for 5.3 years. Among women in the age group, job tenure grew during the time period from 4.3 to 4.9 years.

Long-term employment has fallen among men aged 35 to 44 but increased among women in the age group. Among men aged 35 to 39, the percentage who had been with their current employer for 10 or more years fell from 29.4 to 27.2 percent between 2000 and 2010. Among men aged 40 to 44, the figure fell from 40.2 to 37.5 percent. Their female counterparts saw a 1.7 percentage point increase in long-term employment during those years.

■ The decline in long-term employment among men is due to massive job cuts in many sectors.

Fewer men aged 35 to 44 have long-term jobs

(percent of men aged 35 to 44 who have worked for their current employer for 10 or more years, 2000 and 2010)

Table 6.11 Job Tenure by Sex and Age, 2000 and 2010

(median number of years workers aged 16 or older have been with their current employer by sex and age, 2000 and 2010; change in years, 2000–10)

	2010	2000	change in years 2000–10
Total employed men	**4.6**	**3.8**	**0.8**
Aged 16 to 17	0.7	0.6	0.1
Aged 18 to 19	1.0	0.7	0.3
Aged 20 to 24	1.6	1.2	0.4
Aged 25 to 34	3.2	2.7	0.5
Aged 35 to 44	5.3	5.3	0.0
Aged 45 to 54	8.5	9.5	–1.0
Aged 55 to 64	10.4	10.2	0.2
Aged 65 or older	9.7	9.0	0.7
Total employed women	**4.2**	**3.3**	**0.9**
Aged 16 to 17	0.7	0.6	0.1
Aged 18 to 19	1.0	0.7	0.3
Aged 20 to 24	1.5	1.0	0.5
Aged 25 to 34	3.0	2.5	0.5
Aged 35 to 44	4.9	4.3	0.6
Aged 45 to 54	7.1	7.3	–0.2
Aged 55 to 64	9.7	9.9	–0.2
Aged 65 or older	10.1	9.7	0.4

Source: Bureau of Labor Statistics, Employee Tenure, Internet site http://www.bls.gov/news.release/tenure.toc.htm; calculations by New Strategist

Table 6.12 Long-Term Employment by Sex and Age, 2000 and 2010

(percent of employed wage and salary workers aged 25 or older who have been with their current employer for 10 or more years, by sex and age, 2000 and 2010; percentage point change in share, 2000–10)

	2010	2000	percentage point change 2000–10
Total employed men	**34.3%**	**33.4%**	**0.9**
Aged 25 to 29	3.1	3.0	0.1
Aged 30 to 34	14.3	15.1	−0.8
Aged 35 to 39	27.2	29.4	−2.2
Aged 40 to 44	37.5	40.2	−2.7
Aged 45 to 49	43.7	49.0	−5.3
Aged 50 to 54	51.3	51.6	−0.3
Aged 55 to 59	53.6	53.7	−0.1
Aged 60 to 64	56.8	52.4	4.4
Aged 65 or older	51.9	48.6	3.3
Total employed women	**31.9**	**29.5**	**2.4**
Aged 25 to 29	1.6	1.9	−0.3
Aged 30 to 34	11.1	12.5	−1.4
Aged 35 to 39	24.0	22.3	1.7
Aged 40 to 44	32.9	31.2	1.7
Aged 45 to 49	38.0	41.4	−3.4
Aged 50 to 54	46.5	45.8	0.7
Aged 55 to 59	51.2	52.5	−1.3
Aged 60 to 64	52.2	53.6	−1.4
Aged 65 or older	54.3	51.0	3.3

Source: Bureau of Labor Statistics, Employee Tenure, Internet site http://www.bls.gov/news.release/tenure.toc.htm; calculations by New Strategist

Few Gen Xers Work for Minimum Wage

Only 3 percent of workers aged 35 to 44 earn minimum wage or less.

Among the nation's 74 million workers who were paid hourly rates in 2011, only 3.8 million (5 percent) made minimum wage or less, according to the Bureau of Labor Statistics. Nearly half of minimum-wage workers are under age 25.

Among workers aged 35 to 44 (Gen Xers were aged 35 to 46 in 2011) only 399,000 made minimum wage or less. The 35-to-44 age group accounts for 10 percent of all minimum wage workers.

■ Younger workers are most likely to earn minimum wage or less because many are in entry-level jobs.

Half of minimum-wage workers are under age 25

(percent distribution of workers who make minimum wage or less, by age, 2011)

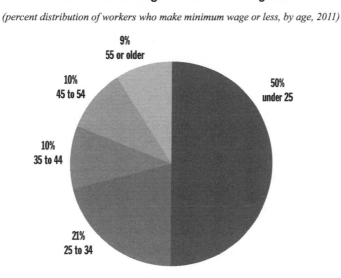

Table 6.13 Workers Earning Minimum Wage by Age, 2011

(number, percent, and percent distribution of workers paid hourly rates at or below minimum wage, by age, 2011; numbers in thousands)

	total paid hourly rates	at or below minimum wage		
		number	share of total	percent distribution
Total aged 16 or older	**73,926**	**3,829**	**5.2%**	**100.0%**
Aged 16 to 24	14,437	1,896	13.1	49.5
Aged 25 to 29	9,229	460	5.0	12.0
Aged 30 to 34	7,926	348	4.4	9.1
Aged 35 to 44	14,168	399	2.8	10.4
Aged 35 to 39	6,889	205	3.0	5.4
Aged 40 to 44	7,279	194	2.7	5.1
Aged 45 to 54	15,331	382	2.5	10.0
Aged 55 to 64	10,046	221	2.2	5.8
Aged 65 or older	2,790	123	4.4	3.2

Source: Bureau of Labor Statistics, Characteristics of Minimum Wage Workers, 2011, Internet site http://www.bls.gov/cps/ minwage2011.htm; calculations by New Strategist

Few 35-to-44-Year-Olds Are Represented by Unions

Men and women are almost equally likely to be represented by a union.

Union representation has fallen sharply over the past few decades. In 2011, only 13 percent of wage and salary workers were represented by a union.

The percentage of workers who are represented by a union peaks in the 55-to-64 age group at 17 percent. Among Gen Xers, only 14 percent are represented by a union. Union representation is slightly higher among Gen X men (15 percent) than women (13 percent).

■ Union representation may rise along with workers' concerns about job security and the cost of health care coverage.

Few workers are represented by a union

(percent of employed wage and salary workers who are represented by unions, by age, 2011)

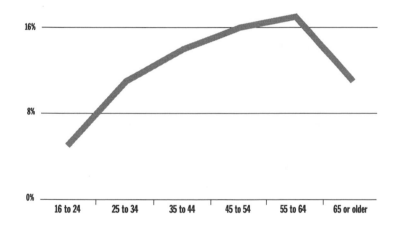

Table 6.14 Union Representation by Sex and Age, 2011

(number and percent of employed wage and salary workers aged 16 or older by union representation status, sex, and age, 2011; numbers in thousands)

	total employed	represented by unions	
		number	percent
Total aged 16 or older	**125,187**	**16,290**	**13.0%**
Aged 16 to 24	16,910	845	5.0
Aged 25 to 34	28,682	3,155	11.0
Aged 35 to 44	27,231	3,804	14.0
Aged 45 to 54	28,693	4,707	16.4
Aged 55 to 64	18,751	3,219	17.2
Aged 65 or older	4,920	559	11.4
Men aged 16 or older	**64,686**	**8,731**	**13.5**
Aged 16 to 24	8,636	486	5.6
Aged 25 to 34	15,465	1,706	11.0
Aged 35 to 44	14,412	2,114	14.7
Aged 45 to 54	14,415	2,513	17.4
Aged 55 to 64	9,212	1,623	17.6
Aged 65 or older	2,547	290	11.4
Women aged 16 or older	**60,502**	**7,558**	**12.5**
Aged 16 to 24	8,274	360	4.8
Aged 25 to 34	13,218	1,449	11.0
Aged 35 to 44	12,819	1,690	13.2
Aged 45 to 54	14,278	2,195	15.4
Aged 55 to 64	9,540	1,596	16.7
Aged 65 or older	2,373	269	10.7

Note: Workers represented by unions are either members of a labor union or similar employee association or workers who report no union affiliation but whose jobs are covered by a union or an employee association contract.
Source: Bureau of Labor Statistics, Labor Force Statistics from the Current Population Survey, Internet site http://www.bls .gov/cps/tables.htm#empstat; calculations by New Strategist

Number of Workers Aged 45 to 54 Will Decline

The number of workers aged 55 and older will grow.

Between 2010 and 2020, the small Generation X will fill the 45-to-54 age group (Gen Xers will be aged 44 to 55 in 2020). Consequently, the number of workers in the age group will decline by more than 2 million. The 35-to-44 age group, in contrast, will be filling with the larger Millennial generation, and the total number of workers aged 35 to 44 will expand by more than 1 million during the decade.

The number of older workers is projected to soar between 2010 and 2020 as Boomers enter the 65-or-older age group and many postpone retirement. The Bureau of Labor Statistics projects a 73 percent increase in the number of male workers aged 65 or older during those years. The number of older female workers is projected to increase by an even greater 90 percent.

■ Generation X may find it difficult to advance on the job as Boomers, working well into their sixties, clog the ranks of upper management.

Number of workers aged 45 to 54 will decline

(percent change in number of workers aged 25 to 54, by sex and age, 2010–20)

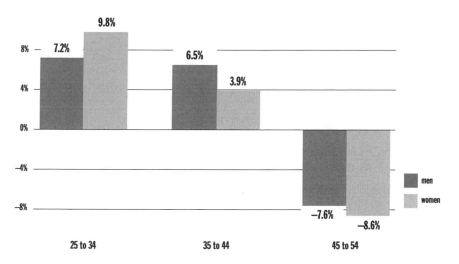

Table 6.15 Projections of the Labor Force by Sex and Age, 2010 and 2020

(number of people aged 16 or older in the civilian labor force by sex and age, 2010 and 2020; percent change, 2010–20; numbers in thousands)

	2010	2020	percent change
Total labor force	**153,889**	**164,360**	**6.8%**
Aged 16 to 24	20,934	18,331	−12.4
Aged 25 to 34	33,615	36,421	8.3
Aged 35 to 44	33,366	35,147	5.3
Aged 45 to 54	35,960	33,050	−8.1
Aged 55 to 64	23,297	29,299	25.8
Aged 65 or older	6,717	12,112	80.3
Total men in labor force	**81,985**	**87,128**	**6.3**
Aged 16 to 24	10,855	9,690	−10.7
Aged 25 to 34	18,352	19,667	7.2
Aged 35 to 44	18,119	19,303	6.5
Aged 45 to 54	18,856	17,415	−7.6
Aged 55 to 64	12,103	14,662	21.1
Aged 65 or older	3,700	6,391	72.7
Total women in labor force	**71,904**	**77,232**	**7.4**
Aged 16 to 24	10,079	8,641	−14.3
Aged 25 to 34	15,263	16,754	9.8
Aged 35 to 44	15,247	15,844	3.9
Aged 45 to 54	17,104	15,635	−8.6
Aged 55 to 64	11,194	14,637	30.8
Aged 65 or older	3,017	5,721	89.6

Source: Bureau of Labor Statistics, Employment Projections, Internet site http://www.bls.gov/emp/; calculations by New Strategist

Table 6.16 Projections of Labor Force Participation by Sex and Age, 2010 and 2020

(percent of people aged 16 or older in the civilian labor force by sex and age, 2010 and 2020; percentage point change, 2010–20)

	2010	2020	percentage point change
Total labor force participation rate	**64.7%**	**62.5%**	**–2.2**
Men in labor force	**71.2**	**68.2**	**–3.0**
Aged 16 to 19	34.9	27.9	–7.0
Aged 20 to 24	74.5	69.4	–5.1
Aged 25 to 34	90.3	86.9	–3.4
Aged 35 to 44	91.5	91.3	–0.2
Aged 45 to 54	86.8	86.0	–0.8
Aged 55 to 64	70.0	71.1	1.1
Aged 65 or older	22.1	26.7	4.6
Women in labor force	**58.6**	**57.1**	**–1.5**
Aged 16 to 19	35.0	25.2	–9.8
Aged 20 to 24	68.3	62.3	–6.0
Aged 25 to 34	74.7	74.2	–0.5
Aged 35 to 44	75.2	74.0	–1.2
Aged 45 to 54	75.7	75.7	0.0
Aged 55 to 64	60.2	66.6	6.4
Aged 65 or older	13.8	19.2	5.4

Source: Bureau of Labor Statistics, Employment Projections, Internet site http://www.bls.gov/emp/; calculations by New Strategist

7

Living Arrangements

■ The lives of Gen Xers revolve around marriage and children. Overall, 57 percent of households headed by 35-to-44-year-olds were married couples in 2011 (Gen Xers were aged 35 to 46 in that year).

■ Among all households headed by people aged 35 to 44, non-Hispanic whites head the 64 percent majority. But the figure varies greatly by type of household.

■ The average American household was home to 2.58 people in 2011. Household size peaks among householders aged 35 to 39, at 3.36 people.

■ More than 60 percent of households headed by people aged 35 to 44 include children under age 18.

■ Overall, 63 to 64 percent of men and women aged 35 to 44 are married and living with their spouse. Most Gen Xers have been married only once and are still married.

Married Couples Head the Majority of Gen X Households

In middle age, Gen Xers are in the most stable lifestage.

As people age from their thirties into their forties, life becomes more routine. Gen Xers are now at the stage of life when work, marriage, children, and home are the central focus.

Overall, 57 percent of households headed by 35-to-44-year-olds were married couples in 2011 (Gen Xers were aged 35 to 46 in that year). Another 16 percent were families headed by women and 5 percent were families headed by men.

This is a lifestage when few women live by themselves. Among women aged 35 to 44, fewer than 7 percent live alone. One in 10 men aged 35 to 44 lives alone.

■ Gen X is in the lifestage when people look for stability as they raise their children.

Married couples dominate Gen X households

(percent distribution of households headed by people aged 35 to 44, by type, 2011)

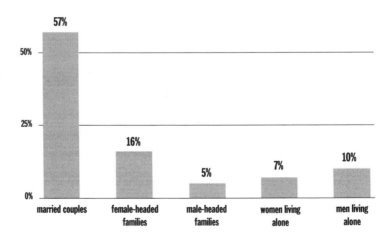

Table 7.1 Households Headed by People Aged 35 to 44 by Household Type, 2011: Total Households

(number and percent distribution of total households and households headed by people aged 35 to 44, by household type, 2011; numbers in thousands)

	total	aged 35 to 44 total	35 to 39	40 to 44
TOTAL HOUSEHOLDS	**118,682**	**21,251**	**10,334**	**10,917**
Family households	**78,613**	**16,708**	**8,172**	**8,536**
Married couples	58,036	12,087	5,820	6,267
Female householder, no spouse present	15,019	3,480	1,780	1,700
Male householder, no spouse present	5,559	1,141	572	569
Nonfamily households	**40,069**	**4,542**	**2,161**	**2,381**
Female householder	21,234	1,680	783	897
Living alone	18,184	1,390	654	736
Male householder	18,835	2,863	1,379	1,484
Living alone	14,539	2,162	1,028	1,134
Percent distribution by type				
TOTAL HOUSEHOLDS	**100.0%**	**100.0%**	**100.0%**	**100.0%**
Family households	**66.2**	**78.6**	**79.1**	**78.2**
Married couples	48.9	56.9	56.3	57.4
Female householder, no spouse present	12.7	16.4	17.2	15.6
Male householder, no spouse present	4.7	5.4	5.5	5.2
Nonfamily households	**33.8**	**21.4**	**20.9**	**21.8**
Female householder	17.9	7.9	7.6	8.2
Living alone	15.3	6.5	6.3	6.7
Male householder	15.9	13.5	13.3	13.6
Living alone	12.3	10.2	9.9	10.4
Percent distribution by age				
Total households	**100.0%**	**17.9%**	**8.7%**	**9.2%**
Family households	**100.0**	**21.3**	**10.4**	**10.9**
Married couples	100.0	20.8	10.0	10.8
Female householder, no spouse present	100.0	23.2	11.9	11.3
Male householder, no spouse present	100.0	20.5	10.3	10.2
Nonfamily households	**100.0**	**11.3**	**5.4**	**5.9**
Female householder	100.0	7.9	3.7	4.2
Living alone	100.0	7.6	3.6	4.0
Male householder	100.0	15.2	7.3	7.9
Living alone	100.0	14.9	7.1	7.8

Source: Bureau of the Census, America's Families and Living Arrangements: 2011, Internet site http://www.census.gov/population/www/socdemo/hh-fam/cps2011.html; calculations by New Strategist

Hispanics and Blacks Head Many Gen X Households

Non-Hispanic whites head fewer than half of female-headed families.

Non-Hispanic whites head the 64 percent majority of households headed by people aged 35 to 44, but the figure varies greatly by type of household. Non-Hispanic whites account for only 47 percent of female-headed families in the 35-to-44 age group, for example, but they account for 68 percent of married couples.

Married couples dominate households headed by Asian Gen Xers, and account for nearly 69 percent of the total. The figure is 61 percent among non-Hispanic whites and 57 percent among Hispanics. Among households headed by black Gen Xers, however, only 33 percent are married couples. A larger 35 percent are female-headed families.

■ The non-Hispanic white share of households will continue to shrink as more-diverse younger generations replace older people in the population.

Nearly one in three Gen X couples are Asian, black, or Hispanic

(percent distribution of married couples aged 35 to 44 by race and Hispanic origin, 2011)

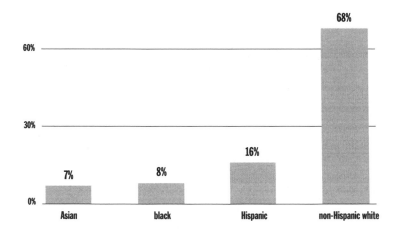

Table 7.2 Households Headed by People Aged 35 to 44 by Household Type, Race, and Hispanic Origin, 2011

(number and percent distribution of households headed by people aged 35 to 44, by household type, race, and Hispanic origin, 2011; numbers in thousands)

	total	Asian	black	Hispanic	non-Hispanic white
TOTAL HOUSEHOLDERS AGED 35 TO 44	**21,251**	**1,162**	**3,008**	**3,367**	**13,560**
Family households	**16,708**	**954**	**2,226**	**2,892**	**10,517**
Married couples	12,087	796	988	1,919	8,269
Female householder, no spouse present	3,480	101	1,039	710	1,641
Male householder, no spouse present	1,141	57	199	263	606
Nonfamily households	**4,542**	**210**	**782**	**475**	**3,043**
Female householder	1,680	79	393	122	1,071
Living alone	1,390	57	353	89	877
Male householder	2,863	131	390	352	1,973
Living alone	2,162	99	335	246	1,464

Percent distribution by race and Hispanic origin

	total	Asian	black	Hispanic	non-Hispanic white
TOTAL HOUSEHOLDERS AGED 35 TO 44	**100.0%**	**5.5%**	**14.2%**	**15.8%**	**63.8%**
Family households	**100.0**	**5.7**	**13.3**	**17.3**	**62.9**
Married couples	100.0	6.6	8.2	15.9	68.4
Female householder, no spouse present	100.0	2.9	29.9	20.4	47.2
Male householder, no spouse present	100.0	5.0	17.4	23.0	53.1
Nonfamily households	**100.0**	**4.6**	**17.2**	**10.5**	**67.0**
Female householder	100.0	4.7	23.4	7.3	63.8
Living alone	100.0	4.1	25.4	6.4	63.1
Male householder	100.0	4.6	13.6	12.3	68.9
Living alone	100.0	4.6	15.5	11.4	67.7

Note: Numbers will not add to total because Asians and blacks are those who identify themselves as being of the race alone and those who identify themselves as being of the race in combination with other races. Hispanics may be of any race. Non-Hispanic whites are those identify themselves as being white alone and not Hispanic.
Source: Bureau of the Census, America's Families and Living Arrangements: 2011, Internet site http://www.census.gov/ population/www/socdemo/hh-fam/cps2011.html; calculations by New Strategist

Table 7.3 Households Headed by People Aged 35 to 44 by Household Type, 2011: Asian Households

(number and percent distribution of total households headed by Asians and households headed by Asians aged 35 to 44, by household type, 2011; numbers in thousands)

		aged 35 to 44		
	total	total	35 to 39	40 to 44
TOTAL ASIAN HOUSEHOLDS	5,040	1,162	649	513
Family households	**3,722**	**954**	**521**	**433**
Married couples	2,939	796	439	357
Female householder, no spouse present	492	101	52	49
Male householder, no spouse present	291	57	30	27
Nonfamily households	**1,318**	**210**	**129**	**81**
Female householder	702	79	42	37
Living alone	558	57	32	25
Male householder	616	131	87	44
Living alone	437	99	70	29
Percent distribution by type				
TOTAL ASIAN HOUSEHOLDS	100.0%	100.0%	100.0%	100.0%
Family households	**73.8**	**82.1**	**80.3**	**84.4**
Married couples	58.3	68.5	67.6	69.6
Female householder, no spouse present	9.8	8.7	8.0	9.6
Male householder, no spouse present	5.8	4.9	4.6	5.3
Nonfamily households	**26.2**	**18.1**	**19.9**	**15.8**
Female householder	13.9	6.8	6.5	7.2
Living alone	11.1	4.9	4.9	4.9
Male householder	12.2	11.3	13.4	8.6
Living alone	8.7	8.5	10.8	5.7
Percent distribution by age				
TOTAL ASIAN HOUSEHOLDS	100.0%	23.1%	12.9%	10.2%
Family households	**100.0**	**25.6**	**14.0**	**11.6**
Married couples	100.0	27.1	14.9	12.1
Female householder, no spouse present	100.0	20.5	10.6	10.0
Male householder, no spouse present	100.0	19.6	10.3	9.3
Nonfamily households	**100.0**	**15.9**	**9.8**	**6.1**
Female householder	100.0	11.3	6.0	5.3
Living alone	100.0	10.2	5.7	4.5
Male householder	100.0	21.3	14.1	7.1
Living alone	100.0	22.7	16.0	6.6

Note: Asians are those who identify themselves as being of the race alone and those who identify themselves as being of the race in combination with other races.
Source: Bureau of the Census, America's Families and Living Arrangements: 2011, Internet site http://www.census.gov/population/www/socdemo/hh-fam/cps2011.html; calculations by New Strategist

Table 7.4 Households Headed by People Aged 35 to 44 by Household Type, 2011: Black Households

(number and percent distribution of total households headed by blacks and households headed by blacks aged 35 to 44, by household type, 2011; numbers in thousands)

	total	aged 35 to 44		
		total	35 to 39	40 to 44
TOTAL BLACK HOUSEHOLDS	**15,613**	**3,008**	**1,514**	**1,494**
Family households	**9,766**	**2,226**	**1,143**	**1,083**
Married couples	4,353	988	480	508
Female householder, no spouse present	4,459	1,039	560	479
Male householder, no spouse present	954	199	103	96
Nonfamily households	**5,847**	**782**	**371**	**411**
Female householder	3,238	393	185	208
Living alone	2,933	353	162	191
Male householder	2,609	390	186	204
Living alone	2,189	335	151	184
Percent distribution by type				
TOTAL BLACK HOUSEHOLDS	**100.0%**	**100.0%**	**100.0%**	**100.0%**
Family households	**62.6**	**74.0**	**75.5**	**72.5**
Married couples	27.9	32.8	31.7	34.0
Female householder, no spouse present	28.6	34.5	37.0	32.1
Male householder, no spouse present	6.1	6.6	6.8	6.4
Nonfamily households	**37.4**	**26.0**	**24.5**	**27.5**
Female householder	20.7	13.1	12.2	13.9
Living alone	18.8	11.7	10.7	12.8
Male householder	16.7	13.0	12.3	13.7
Living alone	14.0	11.1	10.0	12.3
Percent distribution by age				
TOTAL BLACK HOUSEHOLDS	**100.0%**	**19.3%**	**9.7%**	**9.6%**
Family households	**100.0**	**22.8**	**11.7**	**11.1**
Married couples	100.0	22.7	11.0	11.7
Female householder, no spouse present	100.0	23.3	12.6	10.7
Male householder, no spouse present	100.0	20.9	10.8	10.1
Nonfamily households	**100.0**	**13.4**	**6.3**	**7.0**
Female householder	100.0	12.1	5.7	6.4
Living alone	100.0	12.0	5.5	6.5
Male householder	100.0	14.9	7.1	7.8
Living alone	100.0	15.3	6.9	8.4

Note: Blacks are those who identify themselves as being of the race alone and those who identify themselves as being of the race in combination with other races.
Source: Bureau of the Census, America's Families and Living Arrangements: 2011, Internet site http://www.census.gov/ population/www/socdemo/hh-fam/cps2011.html; calculations by New Strategist

Table 7.5 Households Headed by People Aged 35 to 44 by Household Type, 2011: Hispanic Households

(number and percent distribution of total households headed by Hispanics and households headed by Hispanics aged 45 to 64, by household type, 2011; numbers in thousands)

		aged 35 to 44		
	total	total	35 to 39	40 to 44
TOTAL HISPANIC HOUSEHOLDS	13,665	3,367	1,739	1,628
Family households	10,659	2,892	1,503	1,389
Married couples	6,725	1,919	981	938
Female householder, no spouse present	2,754	710	372	338
Male householder, no spouse present	1,180	263	150	113
Nonfamily households	3,006	475	236	239
Female householder	1,371	122	47	75
Living alone	1,098	89	31	58
Male householder	1,635	352	189	163
Living alone	1,100	246	129	117
Percent distribution by type				
TOTAL HISPANIC HOUSEHOLDS	100.0%	100.0%	100.0%	100.0%
Family households	78.0	85.9	86.4	85.3
Married couples	49.2	57.0	56.4	57.6
Female householder, no spouse present	20.2	21.1	21.4	20.8
Male householder, no spouse present	8.6	7.8	8.6	6.9
Nonfamily households	22.0	14.1	13.6	14.7
Female householder	10.0	3.6	2.7	4.6
Living alone	8.0	2.6	1.8	3.6
Male householder	12.0	10.5	10.9	10.0
Living alone	8.0	7.3	7.4	7.2
Percent distribution by age				
TOTAL HISPANIC HOUSEHOLDS	100.0%	24.6%	12.7%	11.9%
Family households	100.0	27.1	14.1	13.0
Married couples	100.0	28.5	14.6	13.9
Female householder, no spouse present	100.0	25.8	13.5	12.3
Male householder, no spouse present	100.0	22.3	12.7	9.6
Nonfamily households	100.0	15.8	7.9	8.0
Female householder	100.0	8.9	3.4	5.5
Living alone	100.0	8.1	2.8	5.3
Male householder	100.0	21.5	11.6	10.0
Living alone	100.0	22.4	11.7	10.6

Source: Bureau of the Census, America's Families and Living Arrangements: 2011, Internet site http://www.census.gov/ population/www/socdemo/hh-fam/cps2011.html; calculations by New Strategist

Table 7.6 Households Headed by People Aged 35 to 44 by Household Type, 2011: Non-Hispanic White Households

(number and percent distribution of total households headed by non-Hispanic whites and households headed by non-Hispanic whites aged 35 to 44, by household type, 2011; numbers in thousands)

	total	aged 35 to 44		
		total	35 to 39	40 to 44
TOTAL NON-HISPANIC WHITE HOUSEHOLDS	**83,471**	**13,560**	**6,340**	**7,220**
Family households	**53,859**	**10,517**	**4,931**	**5,586**
Married couples	43,554	8,269	3,845	4,424
Female householder, no spouse present	7,277	1,641	803	838
Male householder, no spouse present	3,078	606	283	323
Nonfamily households	**29,562**	**3,043**	**1,409**	**1,634**
Female householder	15,749	1,071	495	576
Living alone	13,456	877	418	459
Male householder	13,813	1,973	914	1,059
Living alone	10,675	1,464	673	791
Percent distribution by type				
TOTAL NON-HISPANIC WHITE HOUSEHOLDS	**100.0%**	**100.0%**	**100.0%**	**100.0%**
Family households	**64.5**	**77.6**	**77.8**	**77.4**
Married couples	52.2	61.0	60.6	61.3
Female householder, no spouse present	8.7	12.1	12.7	11.6
Male householder, no spouse present	3.7	4.5	4.5	4.5
Nonfamily households	**35.4**	**22.4**	**22.2**	**22.6**
Female householder	18.9	7.9	7.8	8.0
Living alone	16.1	6.5	6.6	6.4
Male householder	16.5	14.6	14.4	14.7
Living alone	12.8	10.8	10.6	11.0
Percent distribution by age				
TOTAL NON-HISPANIC WHITE HOUSEHOLDS	**100.0%**	**16.2%**	**7.6%**	**8.6%**
Family households	**100.0**	**19.5**	**9.2**	**10.4**
Married couples	100.0	19.0	8.8	10.2
Female householder, no spouse present	100.0	22.6	11.0	11.5
Male householder, no spouse present	100.0	19.7	9.2	10.5
Nonfamily households	**100.0**	**10.3**	**4.8**	**5.5**
Female householder	100.0	6.8	3.1	3.7
Living alone	100.0	6.5	3.1	3.4
Male householder	100.0	14.3	6.6	7.7
Living alone	100.0	13.7	6.3	7.4

Note: Non-Hispanic whites are those who identify themselves as being white alone and not Hispanic.
Source: Bureau of the Census, America's Families and Living Arrangements: 2011, Internet site http://www.census.gov/population/www/socdemo/hh-fam/cps2011.html; calculations by New Strategist

Gen X Households Are Crowded

Household size peaks in the 35-to-39 age group.

The average American household was home to 2.58 people in 2011. Household size peaks among householders aged 35 to 39, at 3.36 people. As householders age into their forties and fifties, the nest empties. Average household size falls below two in the 65-to-74 age group.

Householders aged 35 to 44 average more than one child per household, with the figure peaking at 1.45 children in households headed by 35-to-39-year-olds. As people enter their late forties, the nest empties, and the average number of children per household falls below one.

■ The nest is emptying more slowly for Gen Xers because of the Great Recession.

The nest is full for householders aged 35 to 44

(average household size by age of householder, 2011)

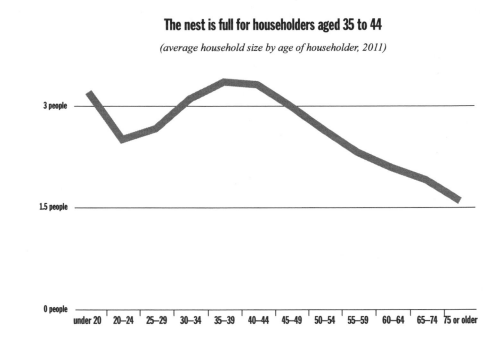

Table 7.7 Average Size of Household by Age of Householder, 2011

(number of households, average number of people per household, and average number of people under age 18 per household, by age of householder, 2011; number of households in thousands)

	number	average number of people	average number of people under age 18
TOTAL HOUSEHOLDS	**118,682**	**2.58**	**0.63**
Under age 20	771	3.21	1.01
Aged 20 to 24	5,369	2.51	0.54
Aged 25 to 29	9,331	2.67	0.83
Aged 30 to 34	10,241	3.11	1.28
Aged 35 to 39	10,334	3.36	1.45
Aged 40 to 44	10,917	3.32	1.27
Aged 45 to 49	12,220	3.00	0.83
Aged 50 to 54	12,310	2.65	0.45
Aged 55 to 59	11,445	2.32	0.22
Aged 60 to 64	10,383	2.09	0.15
Aged 65 to 74	13,348	1.91	0.09
Aged 75 or older	12,015	1.60	0.04

Source: Bureau of the Census, America's Families and Living Arrangements: 2011, Internet site http://www.census.gov/ population/www/socdemo/hh-fam/cps2011.html; calculations by New Strategist

The Majority of Gen Xers Have Children at Home

Female-headed families are most likely to have children.

At least 60 percent of households headed by people aged 35 to 44 (Generation X was aged 35 to 46 in 2011) include children under age 18. The figure rises to more than two-thirds when children of any age are counted.

Among married couples with a householder aged 35 to 39, nearly 83 percent have children under age 18 at home. Families headed by women in the age group are even more likely to have children under age 18, at 91 percent. Among families headed by men, 70 percent include children under age 18.

■ The spending of householders aged 35 to 44 is determined by children's wants and needs.

Male-headed families are least likely to include children under age 18, but most do

(percent of households headed by people aged 35 to 39 with children under age 18 at home, by household type, 2011)

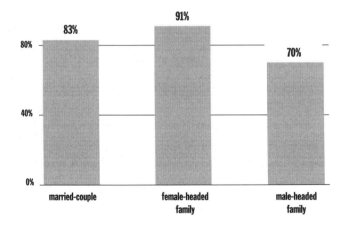

Table 7.8 Households by Type, Age of Householder, and Presence of Children, 2011: Total Households

(total number of households and number and percent with own children under age 18 or of any age at home, by household type and age of householder, 2011; numbers in thousands)

	total	with own children under 18		with own children, any age	
		number	percent	number	percent
TOTAL HOUSEHOLDS	**118,682**	**34,760**	**29.3%**	**47,150**	**39.7%**
Under age 25	6,140	1,738	28.3	1,779	29.0
Aged 25 to 29	9,331	3,883	41.6	3,902	41.8
Aged 30 to 34	10,241	5,971	58.3	6,033	58.9
Aged 35 to 39	10,334	6,824	66.0	6,997	67.7
Aged 40 to 44	10,917	6,576	60.2	7,251	66.4
Aged 45 to 49	12,220	5,251	43.0	7,070	57.9
Aged 50 to 54	12,310	2,957	24.0	5,483	44.5
Aged 55 to 64	21,828	1,371	6.3	5,442	24.9
Aged 65 to 74	13,348	127	1.0	1,830	13.7
Aged 75 or older	12,015	62	0.5	1,361	11.3
MARRIED COUPLES	**58,036**	**23,938**	**41.2**	**30,928**	**53.3**
Under age 25	1,077	580	53.9	587	54.5
Aged 25 to 29	3,348	2,207	65.9	2,219	66.3
Aged 30 to 34	5,203	4,070	78.2	4,106	78.9
Aged 35 to 39	5,820	4,811	82.7	4,887	84.0
Aged 40 to 44	6,267	4,901	78.2	5,245	83.7
Aged 45 to 49	6,721	3,927	58.4	5,054	75.2
Aged 50 to 54	6,785	2,226	32.8	3,888	57.3
Aged 55 to 64	11,851	1,087	9.2	3,663	30.9
Aged 65 to 74	6,871	91	1.3	926	13.5
Aged 75 or older	4,092	38	0.9	354	8.7
FEMALE-HEADED FAMILIES	**15,019**	**8,597**	**57.2**	**12,794**	**85.2**
Under age 25	1,414	962	68.0	975	69.0
Aged 25 to 29	1,585	1,359	85.7	1,365	86.1
Aged 30 to 34	1,696	1,547	91.2	1,570	92.6
Aged 35 to 39	1,780	1,614	90.7	1,697	95.3
Aged 40 to 44	1,700	1,313	77.2	1,577	92.8
Aged 45 to 49	1,741	1,046	60.1	1,602	92.0
Aged 50 to 54	1,393	536	38.5	1,209	86.8
Aged 55 to 64	1,745	177	10.1	1,301	74.6
Aged 65 to 74	976	19	1.9	680	69.7
Aged 75 or older	988	24	2.4	818	82.8
MALE-HEADED FAMILIES	**5,559**	**2,225**	**40.0**	**3,428**	**61.7**
Under age 25	825	196	23.8	217	26.3
Aged 25 to 29	623	316	50.7	317	50.9
Aged 30 to 34	610	354	58.0	357	58.5
Aged 35 to 39	572	399	69.8	414	72.4
Aged 40 to 44	569	362	63.6	430	75.6
Aged 45 to 49	585	277	47.4	414	70.8
Aged 50 to 54	565	195	34.5	386	68.3
Aged 55 to 64	672	108	16.1	478	71.1
Aged 65 to 74	300	18	6.0	225	75.0
Aged 75 or older	237	0	0.0	189	79.7

Source: Bureau of the Census, America's Families and Living Arrangements: 2011, Internet site http://www.census.gov/ population/www/socdemo/hh-fam/cps2011.html; calculations by New Strategist

Regardless of Race or Hispanic Origin, Gen Xers Are Busy with Children

Most have children under age 18 at home.

The majority of Gen X households, regardless of race or Hispanic origin, include children under age 18. The figure ranges from a low of 54 percent among black householders aged 40 to 44 to a high of 73 percent among Hispanic householders aged 35 to 39.

By family type, most married couples and female-headed families headed by a householder aged 35 to 44 are raising children. Only among Asian male-headed families with a householder aged 35 to 39 and Hispanic male-headed families with a householder aged 40 to 44 does the proportion fall below 50 percent.

■ Children dominate Gen X households, controlling their time and money.

Most Gen X households include children

(percent of households headed by people aged 35 to 39 with children under age 18 at home, by race and Hispanic origin, 2011)

Asian	black	Hispanic	non-Hispanic white
64%	65%	73%	64%

Table 7.9 Households by Type, Age of Householder, and Presence of Children, 2011: Asian Households

(total number of Asian households and number and percent with own children under age 18 or of any age at home, by household type and age of householder, 2011; numbers in thousands)

	total	with own children under 18		with own children, any age	
		number	percent	number	percent
TOTAL ASIAN HOUSEHOLDS	**5,040**	**1,774**	**35.2%**	**2,417**	**48.0%**
Under age 25	295	37	12.5	38	12.9
Aged 25 to 29	495	113	22.8	113	22.8
Aged 30 to 34	576	260	45.1	263	45.7
Aged 35 to 39	649	417	64.3	426	65.6
Aged 40 to 44	513	358	69.8	367	71.5
Aged 45 to 49	581	344	59.2	415	71.4
Aged 50 to 54	470	160	34.0	304	64.7
Aged 55 to 64	763	77	10.1	323	42.3
Aged 65 to 74	428	6	1.4	122	28.5
Aged 75 or older	270	3	1.1	46	17.0
MARRIED COUPLES	**2,939**	**1,513**	**51.5**	**1,993**	**67.8**
Under age 25	27	18	66.7	18	66.7
Aged 25 to 29	162	79	48.8	79	48.8
Aged 30 to 34	343	224	65.3	226	65.9
Aged 35 to 39	439	365	83.1	369	84.1
Aged 40 to 44	357	301	84.3	310	86.8
Aged 45 to 49	407	309	75.9	360	88.5
Aged 50 to 54	332	140	42.2	256	77.1
Aged 55 to 64	502	68	13.5	258	51.4
Aged 65 to 74	256	5	2.0	96	37.5
Aged 75 or older	115	3	2.6	20	17.4
FEMALE-HEADED FAMILIES	**492**	**214**	**43.5**	**343**	**69.7**
Under age 25	50	18	36.0	18	36.0
Aged 25 to 29	57	27	47.4	27	47.4
Aged 30 to 34	55	34	61.8	34	61.8
Aged 35 to 39	52	45	86.5	48	92.3
Aged 40 to 44	49	43	87.8	44	89.8
Aged 45 to 49	52	24	46.2	43	82.7
Aged 50 to 54	57	16	28.1	41	71.9
Aged 55 to 64	64	6	9.4	47	73.4
Aged 65 to 74	33	0	0.0	23	69.7
Aged 75 or older	24	0	0.0	18	75.0
MALE-HEADED FAMILIES	**291**	**47**	**16.2**	**81**	**27.8**
Under age 25	67	1	1.5	2	3.0
Aged 25 to 29	42	6	14.3	6	14.3
Aged 30 to 34	38	2	5.3	2	5.3
Aged 35 to 39	30	6	20.0	9	30.0
Aged 40 to 44	27	14	51.9	14	51.9
Aged 45 to 49	29	10	34.5	12	41.4
Aged 50 to 54	15	4	26.7	7	46.7
Aged 55 to 64	26	3	11.5	18	69.2
Aged 65 to 74	7	0	0.0	3	42.9
Aged 75 or older	10	0	0.0	8	80.0

Note: Asians are those who identify themselves as being of the race alone and those who identify themselves as being of the race in combination with other races.
Source: Bureau of the Census, America's Families and Living Arrangements: 2011, Internet site http://www.census.gov/ population/www/socdemo/hh-fam/cps2011.html; calculations by New Strategist

Table 7.10 Households by Type, Age of Householder, and Presence of Children, 2011: Black Households

(total number of black households and number and percent with own children under age 18 or of any age at home, by household type and age of householder, 2011; numbers in thousands)

	total	with own children under 18 number	with own children under 18 percent	with own children, any age number	with own children, any age percent
TOTAL BLACK HOUSEHOLDS	**15,613**	**4,966**	**31.8%**	**6,916**	**44.3%**
Under age 25	1,201	410	34.1	416	34.6
Aged 25 to 29	1,471	786	53.4	793	53.9
Aged 30 to 34	1,526	919	60.2	936	61.3
Aged 35 to 39	1,514	980	64.7	1,035	68.4
Aged 40 to 44	1,494	808	54.1	940	62.9
Aged 45 to 49	1,650	553	33.5	843	51.1
Aged 50 to 54	1,661	307	18.5	670	40.3
Aged 55 to 64	2,682	161	6.0	761	28.4
Aged 65 to 74	1,423	28	2.0	299	21.0
Aged 75 or older	990	13	1.3	222	22.4
MARRIED COUPLES	**4,353**	**1,898**	**43.6**	**2,578**	**59.2**
Under age 25	82	60	73.2	60	73.2
Aged 25 to 29	270	211	78.1	217	80.4
Aged 30 to 34	372	299	80.4	307	82.5
Aged 35 to 39	480	401	83.5	413	86.0
Aged 40 to 44	508	389	76.6	423	83.3
Aged 45 to 49	532	270	50.8	374	70.3
Aged 50 to 54	556	154	27.7	288	51.8
Aged 55 to 64	892	94	10.5	358	40.1
Aged 65 to 74	462	16	3.5	100	21.6
Aged 75 or older	200	4	2.0	36	18.0
FEMALE-HEADED FAMILIES	**4,459**	**2,673**	**59.9**	**3,782**	**84.8**
Under age 25	460	319	69.3	325	70.7
Aged 25 to 29	559	496	88.7	497	88.9
Aged 30 to 34	614	563	91.7	572	93.2
Aged 35 to 39	560	503	89.8	543	97.0
Aged 40 to 44	479	362	75.6	445	92.9
Aged 45 to 49	451	239	53.0	412	91.4
Aged 50 to 54	406	130	32.0	341	84.0
Aged 55 to 64	475	45	9.5	321	67.6
Aged 65 to 74	239	6	2.5	166	69.5
Aged 75 or older	216	9	4.2	160	74.1
MALE-HEADED FAMILIES	**954**	**396**	**41.5**	**556**	**58.3**
Under age 25	150	30	20.0	31	20.7
Aged 25 to 29	141	79	56.0	79	56.0
Aged 30 to 34	91	58	63.7	58	63.7
Aged 35 to 39	103	77	74.8	79	76.7
Aged 40 to 44	96	57	59.4	72	75.0
Aged 45 to 49	89	45	50.6	57	64.0
Aged 50 to 54	83	23	27.7	41	49.4
Aged 55 to 64	114	22	19.3	82	71.9
Aged 65 to 74	55	6	10.9	33	60.0
Aged 75 or older	32	0	0.0	25	78.1

Note: Blacks are those who identify themselves as being of the race alone and those who identify themselves as being of the race in combination with other races.
Source: Bureau of the Census, America's Families and Living Arrangements: 2011, Internet site http://www.census.gov/population/www/socdemo/hh-fam/cps2011.html; calculations by New Strategist

Table 7.11 Households by Type, Age of Householder, and Presence of Children, 2011: Hispanic Households

(total number of Hispanic households and number and percent with own children under age 18 or of any age at home, by household type and age of householder, 2011; numbers in thousands)

	total	with own children under 18		with own children, any age	
		number	percent	number	percent
TOTAL HISPANIC HOUSEHOLDS	**13,665**	**6,373**	**46.6%**	**7,992**	**58.5%**
Under age 25	1,135	468	41.2	471	41.5
Aged 25 to 29	1,476	874	59.2	877	59.4
Aged 30 to 34	1,737	1,231	70.9	1,237	71.2
Aged 35 to 39	1,739	1,276	73.4	1,307	75.2
Aged 40 to 44	1,628	1,124	69.0	1,227	75.4
Aged 45 to 49	1,484	775	52.2	1,036	69.8
Aged 50 to 54	1,245	404	32.4	748	60.1
Aged 55 to 64	1,729	177	10.2	735	42.5
Aged 65 to 74	917	33	3.6	236	25.7
Aged 75 or older	574	11	1.9	118	20.6
MARRIED COUPLES	**6,725**	**4,106**	**61.1**	**5,034**	**74.9**
Under age 25	269	187	69.5	187	69.5
Aged 25 to 29	600	473	78.8	473	78.8
Aged 30 to 34	926	829	89.5	830	89.6
Aged 35 to 39	981	840	85.6	854	87.1
Aged 40 to 44	938	794	84.6	840	89.6
Aged 45 to 49	843	547	64.9	707	83.9
Aged 50 to 54	677	268	39.6	493	72.8
Aged 55 to 64	878	135	15.4	477	54.3
Aged 65 to 74	416	25	6.0	122	29.3
Aged 75 or older	196	8	4.1	51	26.0
FEMALE-HEADED FAMILIES	**2,754**	**1,803**	**65.5**	**2,345**	**85.1**
Under age 25	335	221	66.0	223	66.6
Aged 25 to 29	370	318	85.9	319	86.2
Aged 30 to 34	350	324	92.6	328	93.7
Aged 35 to 39	372	345	92.7	357	96.0
Aged 40 to 44	338	278	82.2	319	94.4
Aged 45 to 49	281	179	63.7	255	90.7
Aged 50 to 54	235	110	46.8	199	84.7
Aged 55 to 64	266	22	8.3	200	75.2
Aged 65 to 74	135	5	3.7	91	67.4
Aged 75 or older	73	3	4.1	55	75.3
MALE-HEADED FAMILIES	**1,180**	**465**	**39.4**	**613**	**51.9**
Under age 25	266	61	22.9	62	23.3
Aged 25 to 29	169	84	49.7	85	50.3
Aged 30 to 34	153	79	51.6	79	51.6
Aged 35 to 39	150	91	60.7	95	63.3
Aged 40 to 44	113	52	46.0	68	60.2
Aged 45 to 49	101	49	48.5	74	73.3
Aged 50 to 54	90	26	28.9	57	63.3
Aged 55 to 64	89	20	22.5	58	65.2
Aged 65 to 74	28	3	10.7	24	85.7
Aged 75 or older	19	0	0.0	12	63.2

Source: Bureau of the Census, America's Families and Living Arrangements: 2011, Internet site http://www.census.gov/population/www/socdemo/hh-fam/cps2011.html; calculations by New Strategist

Table 7.12 Households by Type, Age of Householder, and Presence of Children, 2011: Non-Hispanic White Households

(total number of non-Hispanic white households and number and percent with own children under age 18 or of any age at home, by household type and age of householder, 2011; numbers in thousands)

	total	with own children under 18		with own children, any age	
		number	percent	number	percent
TOTAL NON-HISPANIC WHITE HOUSEHOLDS	**83,471**	**21,457**	**25.7%**	**29,529**	**35.4%**
Under age 25	3,481	830	23.8	859	24.7
Aged 25 to 29	5,845	2,103	36.0	2,113	36.2
Aged 30 to 34	6,344	3,531	55.7	3,568	56.2
Aged 35 to 39	6,340	4,085	64.4	4,162	65.6
Aged 40 to 44	7,220	4,262	59.0	4,684	64.9
Aged 45 to 49	8,394	3,532	42.1	4,732	56.4
Aged 50 to 54	8,842	2,068	23.4	3,731	42.2
Aged 55 to 64	16,439	949	5.8	3,573	21.7
Aged 65 to 74	10,473	62	0.6	1,145	10.9
Aged 75 or older	10,093	33	0.3	961	9.5
MARRIED COUPLES	**43,554**	**16,267**	**37.3**	**21,110**	**48.5**
Under age 25	694	323	46.5	332	47.8
Aged 25 to 29	2,303	1,436	62.4	1,443	62.7
Aged 30 to 34	3,544	2,709	76.4	2,732	77.1
Aged 35 to 39	3,845	3,139	81.6	3,181	82.7
Aged 40 to 44	4,424	3,391	76.7	3,642	82.3
Aged 45 to 49	4,878	2,763	56.6	3,569	73.2
Aged 50 to 54	5,171	1,654	32.0	2,830	54.7
Aged 55 to 64	9,467	785	8.3	2,541	26.8
Aged 65 to 74	5,672	45	0.8	595	10.5
Aged 75 or older	3,557	23	0.6	246	6.9
FEMALE-HEADED FAMILIES	**7,277**	**3,903**	**53.6**	**6,292**	**86.5**
Under age 25	574	406	70.7	412	71.8
Aged 25 to 29	604	524	86.8	527	87.3
Aged 30 to 34	666	614	92.2	624	93.7
Aged 35 to 39	803	727	90.5	757	94.3
Aged 40 to 44	838	639	76.3	774	92.4
Aged 45 to 49	952	593	62.3	887	93.2
Aged 50 to 54	701	280	39.9	629	89.7
Aged 55 to 64	917	104	11.3	717	78.2
Aged 65 to 74	556	8	1.4	388	69.8
Aged 75 or older	665	10	1.5	576	86.6
MALE-HEADED FAMILIES	**3,078**	**1,286**	**41.8**	**2,127**	**69.1**
Under age 25	338	101	29.9	116	34.3
Aged 25 to 29	269	144	53.5	144	53.5
Aged 30 to 34	317	209	65.9	212	66.9
Aged 35 to 39	283	220	77.7	224	79.2
Aged 40 to 44	323	233	72.1	268	83.0
Aged 45 to 49	368	176	47.8	276	75.0
Aged 50 to 54	366	135	36.9	271	74.0
Aged 55 to 64	435	60	13.8	315	72.4
Aged 65 to 74	206	9	4.4	162	78.6
Aged 75 or older	172	0	0.0	139	80.8

Note: Non-Hispanic whites are those who identify themselves as being white alone and not Hispanic.
Source: Bureau of the Census, America's Families and Living Arrangements: 2011, Internet site http://www.census.gov/ population/www/socdemo/hh-fam/cps2011.html; calculations by New Strategist

Many Households Headed by Gen Xers Include Preschoolers

Gen Xers head one-fourth of all households with infants.

During their twenties and early thirties, most people become parents. Among householders under age 35, a 45 percent minority are raising children. The figure rises to the 63 percent majority in the 35-to-44 age group.

Nearly half of the householders aged 35 to 44 have children under age 12 in their home, and 25 percent have preschoolers. One-third of householders aged 35 to 44 has teenagers (aged 12 to 17) at home. This age group accounts for 43 percent of the nation's parents of teenagers.

■ As people have children, their priorities shift from pursuing their own wants and needs to meeting the needs of their children.

Children are the norm for householders aged 35 to 44

(percent of households headed by people aged 35 to 44 with children at home, by age of child, 2011)

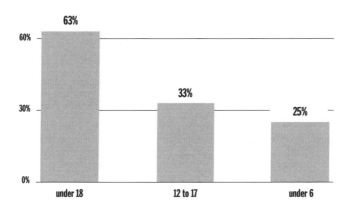

Table 7.13 Households by Presence and Age of Children and Age of Householder, 2011

(number and percent distribution of households by presence of own children at home, by age of children and age of householder, 2011; numbers in thousands)

	total	under 35	aged 35 to 44 total	35 to 39	40 to 44	45 to 54	55 to 64	65 or older
TOTAL HOUSEHOLDS	**118,682**	**25,712**	**21,251**	**10,334**	**10,917**	**46,358**	**21,828**	**25,363**
With children of any age	**47,150**	**11,714**	**14,248**	**6,997**	**7,251**	**17,995**	**5,442**	**3,191**
Under age 25	41,108	11,683	14,204	6,990	7,214	14,836	3,184	385
Under age 18	34,760	11,592	13,400	6,824	6,576	9,579	1,371	189
Under age 12	25,392	11,172	10,242	5,719	4,523	3,880	415	98
Under age 6	15,314	9,044	5,213	3,344	1,869	1,009	106	49
Under age 1	2,942	2,124	726	540	186	82	4	10
Aged 12 to 17	16,247	1,796	6,945	2,975	3,970	7,395	1,101	111

Percemt distribution by age of child

	total	under 35	aged 35 to 44 total	35 to 39	40 to 44	45 to 54	55 to 64	65 or older
TOTAL HOUSEHOLDS	**100.0%**	**100.0%**	**100.0%**	**100.0%**	**100.0%**	**100.0%**	**100.0%**	**100.0%**
With children of any age	**39.7**	**45.6**	**67.0**	**67.7**	**66.4**	**38.8**	**24.9**	**12.6**
Under age 25	34.6	45.4	66.8	67.6	66.1	32.0	14.6	1.5
Under age 18	29.3	45.1	63.1	66.0	60.2	20.7	6.3	0.7
Under age 12	21.4	43.5	48.2	55.3	41.4	8.4	1.9	0.4
Under age 6	12.9	35.2	24.5	32.4	17.1	2.2	0.5	0.2
Under age 1	2.5	8.3	3.4	5.2	1.7	0.2	0.0	0.0
Aged 12 to 17	13.7	7.0	32.7	28.8	36.4	16.0	5.0	0.4

Percemt distribution by age of householder

	total	under 35	aged 35 to 44 total	35 to 39	40 to 44	45 to 54	55 to 64	65 or older
TOTAL HOUSEHOLDS	**100.0%**	**21.7%**	**17.9%**	**8.7%**	**9.2%**	**39.1%**	**18.4%**	**21.4%**
With children of any age	**100.0**	**24.8**	**30.2**	**14.8**	**15.4**	**38.2**	**11.5**	**6.8**
Under age 25	100.0	28.4	34.6	17.0	17.5	36.1	7.7	0.9
Under age 18	100.0	33.3	38.6	19.6	18.9	27.6	3.9	0.5
Under age 12	100.0	44.0	40.3	22.5	17.8	15.3	1.6	0.4
Under age 6	100.0	59.1	34.0	21.8	12.2	6.6	0.7	0.3
Under age 1	100.0	72.2	24.7	18.4	6.3	2.8	0.1	0.3
Aged 12 to 17	100.0	11.1	42.7	18.3	24.4	45.5	6.8	0.7

Source: Bureau of the Census, America's Families and Living Arrangements: 2011, Internet site http://www.census.gov/ population/www/socdemo/hh-fam/cps2011.html; calculations by New Strategist

Two-Child Families Are Most Common

Many Gen X couples have more than two children, however.

Most Americans consider two children to be the ideal number. But many Gen X couples with children have three or more.

Among all married couples aged 35 to 44 with children at home, 45 percent have two children under age 18. Another 29 percent have only one child at home (frequently for these families, an older child has left home), and a sizeable 26 percent has three or more children under age 18 in their home.

Among both female- and male-headed Gen X families with children, one child is the most common number. Forty-seven percent of female-headed Gen X families have only one child under age 18. Among their male counterparts, the figure is an even larger 51 percent.

■ The growing Hispanic population has been boosting the proportion of couples with three or more children.

Most Gen X couples have one or two children at home

(percent distribution of married couples aged 35 to 44 with children under age 18 at home, by number of children, 2011)

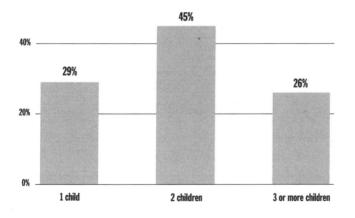

Table 7.14 Married Couples with Children by Number of Children and Age of Householder, 2011

(number and percent distribution of married couples with own children under age 18 at home, by number of children and age of householder, 2011; numbers in thousands)

	total	under 35	aged 35 to 44 total	35 to 39	40 to 44	45 or older
Married couples with children under 18	**23,938**	**6,857**	**9,712**	**4,811**	**4,901**	**7,369**
One	9,300	2,626	2,793	1,274	1,519	3,881
Two	9,527	2,659	4,360	2,177	2,183	2,508
Three	3,618	1,069	1,802	956	846	746
Four or more	1,493	501	757	404	353	234
PERCENT DISTRIBUTION BY NUMBER OF CHILDREN						
Married couples with children under 18	**100.0%**	**100.0%**	**100.0%**	**100.0%**	**100.0%**	**100.0%**
One	38.9	38.3	28.8	26.5	31.0	52.7
Two	39.8	38.8	44.9	45.3	44.5	34.0
Three	15.1	15.6	18.6	19.9	17.3	10.1
Four or more	6.2	7.3	7.8	8.4	7.2	3.2
PERCENT DISTRIBUTION BY AGE OF HOUSEHOLDER						
Married couples with children under 18	**100.0%**	**28.6%**	**40.6%**	**20.1%**	**20.5%**	**30.8%**
One	100.0	28.2	30.0	13.7	16.3	41.7
Two	100.0	27.9	45.8	22.9	22.9	26.3
Three	100.0	29.5	49.8	26.4	23.4	20.6
Four or more	100.0	33.6	50.7	27.1	23.6	15.7

Source: Bureau of the Census, America's Families and Living Arrangements: 2011, Internet site http://www.census.gov/ population/www/socdemo/hh-fam/cps2011.html; calculations by New Strategist

Table 7.15 Female-headed Families with Children by Number of Children and Age of Householder, 2011

(number and percent distribution of female-headed families with own children under age 18 at home, by number of children and age of householder, 2011; numbers in thousands)

	total	under 35	aged 35 to 44 total	35 to 39	40 to 44	45 or older
Female-headed families with children under 18	**8,597**	**3,868**	**2,927**	**1,614**	**1,313**	**1,802**
One	4,375	1,720	1,385	659	726	1,270
Two	2,681	1,295	995	575	420	391
Three	1,100	556	421	283	138	122
Four or more	441	297	125	96	29	19
PERCENT DISTRIBUTION BY NUMBER OF CHILDREN						
Female-headed families with children under 18	**100.0%**	**100.0%**	**100.0%**	**100.0%**	**100.0%**	**100.0%**
One	50.9	44.5	47.3	40.8	55.3	70.5
Two	31.2	33.5	34.0	35.6	32.0	21.7
Three	12.8	14.4	14.4	17.5	10.5	6.8
Four or more	5.1	7.7	4.3	5.9	2.2	1.1
PERCENT DISTRIBUTION BY AGE OF HOUSEHOLDER						
Female-headed families with children under 18	**100.0%**	**45.0%**	**34.0%**	**18.8%**	**15.3%**	**21.0%**
One	100.0	39.3	31.7	15.1	16.6	29.0
Two	100.0	48.3	37.1	21.4	15.7	14.6
Three	100.0	50.5	38.3	25.7	12.5	11.1
Four or more	100.0	67.3	28.3	21.8	6.6	4.3

Source: Bureau of the Census, America's Families and Living Arrangements: 2011, Internet site http://www.census.gov/ population/www/socdemo/hh-fam/cps2011.html; calculations by New Strategist

Table 7.16 Male-headed Families with Children by Number of Children and Age of Householder, 2011

(number and percent distribution of male-headed families with own children under age 18 at home, by number of children and age of householder, 2011; numbers in thousands)

	total	under 35	aged 35 to 44 total	35 to 39	40 to 44	45 or older
Male-headed families with children under 18	**2,225**	**866**	**761**	**399**	**362**	**598**
One	1,337	520	385	186	199	432
Two	627	256	254	140	114	117
Three	199	70	93	55	38	37
Four or more	63	20	31	19	12	11
PERCENT DISTRIBUTION BY NUMBER OF CHILDREN						
Male-headed families with children under 18	**100.0%**	**100.0%**	**100.0%**	**100.0%**	**100.0%**	**100.0%**
One	60.1	60.0	50.6	46.6	55.0	72.2
Two	28.2	29.6	33.4	35.1	31.5	19.6
Three	8.9	8.1	12.2	13.8	10.5	6.2
Four or more	2.8	2.3	4.1	4.8	3.3	1.8
PERCENT DISTRIBUTION BY AGE OF HOUSEHOLDER						
Male-headed families with children under 18	**100.0%**	**38.9%**	**34.2%**	**17.9%**	**16.3%**	**26.9%**
One	100.0	38.9	28.8	13.9	14.9	32.3
Two	100.0	40.8	40.5	22.3	18.2	18.7
Three	100.0	35.2	46.7	27.6	19.1	18.6
Four or more	100.0	31.7	49.2	30.2	19.0	17.5

Source: Bureau of the Census, America's Families and Living Arrangements: 2011, Internet site http://www.census.gov/population/www/socdemo/hh-fam/cps2011.html; calculations by New Strategist

Gen Xers Account for Few People Who Live Alone

Fewer than one in 10 Gen Xers lives alone.

Among the 33 million Americans who live alone, Gen Xers (aged 35 to 46 in 2011) accounted for only 11 percent. Among men who live alone, Gen Xers are a larger 15 percent of the total. Among women who live alone, Gen Xers are a smaller 8 percent.

Gen X men are more likely than Gen X women to live alone. Among men aged 35 to 44, 11 percent live by themselves. The figure is only 7 percent for women in the age group. As they age, the pattern will reverse, and living alone will become more common for Gen X women than Gen X men.

■ Because of the higher mortality rate of men, a growing share of Gen X women will become widows and live by themselves in the decades ahead.

Gen X men are more likely than Gen X women to live alone

(percent of people aged 35 to 44 who live alone, by age and sex, 2011)

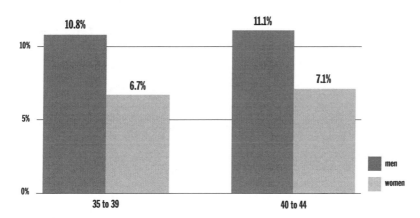

Table 7.17 People Who Live Alone by Age, 2011

(number of people aged 15 or older and number, percent, and percent distribution of people who live alone by sex and age, 2011; numbers in thousands)

| | | living alone | | |
	total	number	percent	percent distribution
Total people	**243,955**	**32,723**	**13.4%**	**100.0%**
Under age 35	83,996	5,602	6.7	17.1
Aged 35 to 44	39,842	3,552	8.9	10.9
Aged 35 to 39	19,255	1,682	8.7	5.1
Aged 40 to 44	20,587	1,870	9.1	5.7
Aged 45 to 64	80,938	12,266	15.2	37.5
Aged 65 or older	39,179	11,304	28.9	34.5
Total men	**118,871**	**14,539**	**12.2**	**100.0**
Under age 35	42,636	3,052	7.2	21.0
Aged 35 to 44	19,714	2,162	11.0	14.9
Aged 35 to 39	9,542	1,028	10.8	7.1
Aged 40 to 44	10,172	1,134	11.1	7.8
Aged 45 to 64	39,441	6,115	15.5	42.1
Aged 65 or older	17,081	3,210	18.8	22.1
Total women	**125,084**	**18,184**	**14.5**	**100.0**
Under age 35	41,360	2,550	6.2	14.0
Aged 35 to 44	20,128	1,390	6.9	7.6
Aged 35 to 39	9,713	654	6.7	3.6
Aged 40 to 44	10,415	736	7.1	4.0
Aged 45 to 64	41,497	6,151	14.8	33.8
Aged 65 or older	22,098	8,094	36.6	44.5

Source: Bureau of the Census, 2011 Current Population Survey, Internet site http://www.census.gov/hhes/www/income/data/ incpovhlth/2010/dtables.html; calculations by New Strategist

Most Gen Xers Are Married

Among 40-to-44-year-olds, however, more than one in 10 is divorced.

Overall, 63 to 64 percent of men and women aged 35 to 44 were married and living with their spouse in 2011 (Gen Xers were aged 35 to 46 in that year). A substantial 22 percent of Gen X men are not yet married. Among Gen X women, a smaller 17 percent have not married yet.

Divorce becomes a significant factor in the Gen X age group. Twelve percent of men aged 40 to 44 are currently divorced. Among women, 12 percent in the 35-to-39 age group and 14 percent in the 40-to-44 age group are currently divorced.

■ As Gen Xers age, a growing share of women will become widows.

Divorce climbs in the Gen X age group

(percent of people aged 35 to 44 who are currently divorced, by sex, 2011)

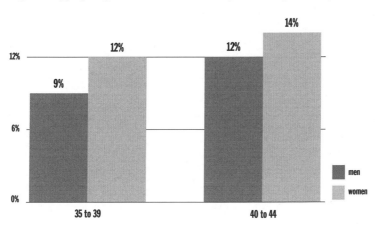

Table 7.18 Marital Status by Sex and Age, 2011: Total People

(number and percent distribution of people aged 15 or older by sex, age, and current marital status, 2011; numbers in thousands)

	total	never married	married spouse present	married spouse absent	separated	divorced	widowed
NUMBER							
Total men	**118,828**	**38,685**	**60,129**	**1,944**	**2,144**	**9,782**	**2,916**
Under age 35	42,620	28,949	9,198	679	374	168	23
Aged 35 to 44	19,709	4,266	12,341	361	623	2,023	95
Aged 35 to 39	9,540	2,293	5,902	165	314	821	46
Aged 40 to 44	10,169	1,973	6,439	196	309	1,202	49
Aged 45 to 54	21,486	3,105	14,070	379	556	3,150	227
Aged 55 to 64	17,937	1,605	12,476	267	363	2,804	422
Aged 65 or older	17,076	760	12,044	258	228	1,637	2,149
Total women	**125,030**	**34,963**	**60,155**	**1,754**	**3,091**	**13,762**	**11,306**
Under age 35	41,351	26,521	11,748	571	933	1,468	108
Aged 35 to 44	20,122	3,356	12,811	302	772	2,669	212
Aged 35 to 39	9,708	1,824	6,070	143	391	1,197	83
Aged 40 to 44	10,414	1,532	6,741	159	381	1,472	129
Aged 45 to 54	22,450	2,594	14,188	360	761	3,733	815
Aged 55 to 64	19,032	1,544	11,760	286	413	3,384	1,645
Aged 65 or older	22,075	948	9,648	235	212	2,508	8,526
PERCENT DISTRIBUTION							
Total men	**100.0%**	**32.6%**	**50.6%**	**1.6%**	**1.8%**	**8.2%**	**2.5%**
Under age 35	100.0	67.9	21.6	1.6	0.9	0.4	0.1
Aged 35 to 44	100.0	21.6	62.6	1.8	3.2	10.3	0.5
Aged 35 to 39	100.0	24.0	61.9	1.7	3.3	8.6	0.5
Aged 40 to 44	100.0	19.4	63.3	1.9	3.0	11.8	0.5
Aged 45 to 54	100.0	14.5	65.5	1.8	2.6	14.7	1.1
Aged 55 to 64	100.0	8.9	69.6	1.5	2.0	15.6	2.4
Aged 65 or older	100.0	4.5	70.5	1.5	1.3	9.6	12.6
Total women	**100.0**	**28.0**	**48.1**	**1.4**	**2.5**	**11.0**	**9.0**
Under age 35	100.0	64.1	28.4	1.4	2.3	3.6	0.3
Aged 35 to 44	100.0	16.7	63.7	1.5	3.8	13.3	1.1
Aged 35 to 39	100.0	18.8	62.5	1.5	4.0	12.3	0.9
Aged 40 to 44	100.0	14.7	64.7	1.5	3.7	14.1	1.2
Aged 45 to 54	100.0	11.6	63.2	1.6	3.4	16.6	3.6
Aged 55 to 64	100.0	8.1	61.8	1.5	2.2	17.8	8.6
Aged 65 or older	100.0	4.3	43.7	1.1	1.0	11.4	38.6

Source: Bureau of the Census, America's Families and Living Arrangements: 2011, Internet site http://www.census.gov/population/www/socdemo/hh-fam/cps2011.html; calculations by New Strategist

Black Gen Xers Are Least Likely to Be Married

The single outnumber the married among black women aged 35 to 44.

Among Asians, Hispanics, and non-Hispanic whites aged 35 to 44, the percentage who are currently married and living with their spouse ranges from 56 to 71 percent among men and from 62 to 74 percent among women. Blacks in the age group are far less likely to be currently married—only 36 percent of black women and 45 percent of black men are currently married. More than one-third have not yet married.

Among Gen Xers, Asians and Hispanics are about half as likely to be currently divorced as blacks and non-Hispanic whites. Only 5 to 6 percent of Hispanic and Asian men aged 35 to 44 are currently divorced compared with 11 to 12 percent of non-Hispanic white and black men in the age group. Among Hispanic and Asian women aged 35 to 44, only 6 to 7 percent are currently divorced compared with 14 to 16 percent of non-Hispanic white and black women.

■ As the nation has become more diverse racially and ethnically, it has also become more diverse in its living arrangements.

Among 35-to-44-year-olds, Asian women are most likely to be married

(percent of people aged 35 to 44 who are currently married and living with their spouse by race, Hispanic origin, and sex, 2011)

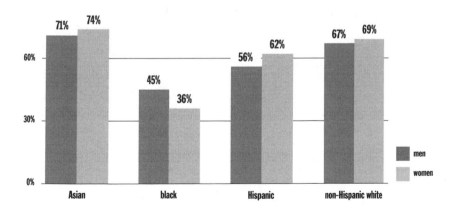

Table 7.19 Marital Status by Sex and Age, 2011: Asians

(number and percent distribution of Asians aged 15 or older by sex, age, and current marital status, 2011; numbers in thousands)

	total	never married	married spouse present	married spouse absent	separated	divorced	widowed
NUMBER							
Total Asian men	**5,786**	**2,031**	**3,234**	**168**	**55**	**208**	**89**
Under age 35	2,267	1,654	528	45	16	23	2
Aged 35 to 44	1,191	215	845	41	20	71	0
Aged 35 to 39	618	132	419	18	14	34	0
Aged 40 to 44	573	83	426	23	6	37	0
Aged 45 to 54	988	93	797	38	8	41	9
Aged 55 to 64	708	47	567	25	8	48	13
Aged 65 or older	632	23	498	19	4	25	64
Total Asian women	**6,460**	**1,742**	**3,600**	**177**	**112**	**365**	**464**
Under age 35	2,311	1,367	815	47	28	51	6
Aged 35 to 44	1,336	174	995	34	34	90	9
Aged 35 to 39	701	93	526	18	14	45	6
Aged 40 to 44	635	81	469	16	20	45	3
Aged 45 to 54	1,099	113	786	41	19	105	35
Aged 55 to 64	862	56	589	33	15	75	94
Aged 65 or older	850	33	416	23	16	43	319
PERCENT DISTRIBUTION							
Total Asian men	**100.0%**	**35.1%**	**55.9%**	**2.9%**	**1.0%**	**3.6%**	**1.5%**
Under age 35	100.0	73.0	23.3	2.0	0.7	1.0	0.1
Aged 35 to 44	100.0	18.1	70.9	3.4	1.7	6.0	0.0
Aged 35 to 39	100.0	21.4	67.8	2.9	2.3	5.5	0.0
Aged 40 to 44	100.0	14.5	74.3	4.0	1.0	6.5	0.0
Aged 45 to 54	100.0	9.4	80.7	3.8	0.8	4.1	0.9
Aged 55 to 64	100.0	6.6	80.1	3.5	1.1	6.8	1.8
Aged 65 or older	100.0	3.6	78.8	3.0	0.6	4.0	10.1
Total Asian women	**100.0**	**27.0**	**55.7**	**2.7**	**1.7**	**5.7**	**7.2**
Under age 35	100.0	59.2	35.3	2.0	1.2	2.2	0.3
Aged 35 to 44	100.0	13.0	74.5	2.5	2.5	6.7	0.7
Aged 35 to 39	100.0	13.3	75.0	2.6	2.0	6.4	0.9
Aged 40 to 44	100.0	12.8	73.9	2.5	3.1	7.1	0.5
Aged 45 to 54	100.0	10.3	71.5	3.7	1.7	9.6	3.2
Aged 55 to 64	100.0	6.5	68.3	3.8	1.7	8.7	10.9
Aged 65 or older	100.0	3.9	48.9	2.7	1.9	5.1	37.5

Note: Asians are those who identify themselves as being of the race alone and those who identify themselves as being of the race in combination with other races.
Source: Bureau of the Census, America's Families and Living Arrangements: 2011, Internet site http://www.census.gov/ population/www/socdemo/hh-fam/cps2011.html; calculations by New Strategist

Table 7.20 Marital Status by Sex and Age, 2011: Blacks

(number and percent distribution of blacks aged 15 or older by sex, age, and current marital status, 2011; numbers in thousands)

	total	never married	married spouse present	married spouse absent	separated	divorced	widowed
NUMBER							
Total black men	**14,096**	**6,970**	**4,627**	**273**	**540**	**1,352**	**334**
Under age 35	6,121	5,046	724	77	142	124	8
Aged 35 to 44	2,334	828	1,040	53	132	272	10
Aged 35 to 39	1,141	444	507	24	57	105	5
Aged 40 to 44	1,193	384	533	29	75	167	5
Aged 45 to 54	2,459	666	1,161	65	114	422	29
Aged 55 to 64	1,812	340	918	43	91	337	82
Aged 65 or older	1,369	89	784	35	60	196	205
Total black women	**16,875**	**7,803**	**4,383**	**375**	**802**	**2,105**	**1,406**
Under age 35	6,645	5,249	873	104	177	208	32
Aged 35 to 44	2,883	1,082	1,043	78	192	447	40
Aged 35 to 39	1,419	613	480	31	81	197	17
Aged 40 to 44	1,464	469	563	47	111	250	23
Aged 45 to 54	3,001	861	1,093	89	251	568	137
Aged 55 to 64	2,218	431	829	71	117	541	229
Aged 65 or older	2,128	180	544	33	64	340	967
PERCENT DISTRIBUTION							
Total black men	**100.0%**	**49.4%**	**32.8%**	**1.9%**	**3.8%**	**9.6%**	**2.4%**
Under age 35	100.0	82.4	11.8	1.3	2.3	2.0	0.1
Aged 35 to 44	100.0	35.5	44.6	2.3	5.7	11.7	0.4
Aged 35 to 39	100.0	38.9	44.4	2.1	5.0	9.2	0.4
Aged 40 to 44	100.0	32.2	44.7	2.4	6.3	14.0	0.4
Aged 45 to 54	100.0	27.1	47.2	2.6	4.6	17.2	1.2
Aged 55 to 64	100.0	18.8	50.7	2.4	5.0	18.6	4.5
Aged 65 or older	**100.0**	**6.5**	**57.3**	**2.6**	**4.4**	**14.3**	**15.0**
Total black women	**100.0**	**46.2**	**26.0**	**2.2**	**4.8**	**12.5**	**8.3**
Under age 35	100.0	79.0	13.1	1.6	2.7	3.1	0.5
Aged 35 to 44	100.0	37.5	36.2	2.7	6.7	15.5	1.4
Aged 35 to 39	100.0	43.2	33.8	2.2	5.7	13.9	1.2
Aged 40 to 44	100.0	32.0	38.5	3.2	7.6	17.1	1.6
Aged 45 to 54	100.0	28.7	36.4	3.0	8.4	18.9	4.6
Aged 55 to 64	100.0	19.4	37.4	3.2	5.3	24.4	10.3
Aged 65 or older	100.0	8.5	25.6	1.6	3.0	16.0	45.4

Note: Blacks are those who identify themselves as being of the race alone and those who identify themselves as being of the race in combination with other races.
Source: Bureau of the Census, America's Families and Living Arrangements: 2011, Internet site http://www.census.gov/ population/www/socdemo/hh-fam/cps2011.html; calculations by New Strategist

Table 7.21 Marital Status by Sex and Age, 2011: Hispanics

(number and percent distribution of Hispanics aged 15 or older by sex, age, and current marital status, 2011; numbers in thousands)

	total	never married	married spouse present	married spouse absent	separated	divorced	widowed
NUMBER							
Total Hispanic men	**18,097**	**8,118**	**7,382**	**652**	**1,090**	**553**	**302**
Under age 35	8,916	6,474	1,859	230	151	187	12
Aged 35 to 44	3,686	941	2,078	164	308	174	22
Aged 35 to 39	1,949	553	1,062	85	147	89	13
Aged 40 to 44	1,737	388	1,016	79	161	85	9
Aged 45 to 54	2,693	436	1,691	157	288	96	27
Aged 55 to 64	1,572	154	1,020	55	241	57	44
Aged 65 or older	1,230	114	735	46	103	39	195
Total Hispanic women	**16,954**	**5,909**	**7,491**	**374**	**1,495**	**742**	**942**
Under age 35	7,605	4,655	2,290	156	238	241	25
Aged 35 to 44	3,377	608	2,080	73	373	209	35
Aged 35 to 39	1,760	321	1,110	35	176	110	9
Aged 40 to 44	1,617	287	970	38	197	99	26
Aged 45 to 54	2,668	353	1,585	64	398	164	106
Aged 55 to 64	1,679	166	917	47	279	85	185
Aged 65 or older	1,624	126	621	34	208	44	591
PERCENT DISTRIBUTION							
Total Hispanic men	**100.0%**	**44.9%**	**40.8%**	**3.6%**	**6.0%**	**3.1%**	**1.7%**
Under age 35	100.0	72.6	20.9	2.6	1.7	2.1	0.1
Aged 35 to 44	100.0	25.5	56.4	4.4	8.4	4.7	0.6
Aged 35 to 39	100.0	28.4	54.5	4.4	7.5	4.6	0.7
Aged 40 to 44	100.0	22.3	58.5	4.5	9.3	4.9	0.5
Aged 45 to 54	100.0	16.2	62.8	5.8	10.7	3.6	1.0
Aged 55 to 64	100.0	9.8	64.9	3.5	15.3	3.6	2.8
Aged 65 or older	100.0	9.3	59.8	3.7	8.4	3.2	15.9
Total Hispanic women	**100.0**	**34.9**	**44.2**	**2.2**	**8.8**	**4.4**	**5.6**
Under age 35	100.0	61.2	30.1	2.1	3.1	3.2	0.3
Aged 35 to 44	100.0	18.0	61.6	2.2	11.0	6.2	1.0
Aged 35 to 39	100.0	18.2	63.1	2.0	10.0	6.3	0.5
Aged 40 to 44	100.0	17.7	60.0	2.4	12.2	6.1	1.6
Aged 45 to 54	100.0	13.2	59.4	2.4	14.9	6.1	4.0
Aged 55 to 64	100.0	9.9	54.6	2.8	16.6	5.1	11.0
Aged 65 or older	100.0	7.8	38.2	2.1	12.8	2.7	36.4

Source: Bureau of the Census, America's Families and Living Arrangements: 2011, Internet site http://www.census.gov/population/www/socdemo/hh-fam/cps2011.html; calculations by New Strategist

Table 7.22 Marital Status by Sex and Age, 2011: Non-Hispanic whites

(number and percent distribution of non-Hispanic whites aged 15 or older by sex, age, and current marital status, 2011; numbers in thousands)

	total	never married	married spouse present	married spouse absent	separated	divorced	widowed
NUMBER							
Total non-Hispanic white men	**80,079**	**23,589**	**44,413**	**731**	**1,266**	**7,921**	**2,160**
Under age 35	25,202	17,844	6,092	201	299	755	12
Aged 35 to 44	12,352	2,267	8,252	106	309	1,364	53
Aged 35 to 39	5,764	1,158	3,846	43	164	530	22
Aged 40 to 44	6,588	1,109	4,406	63	145	834	31
Aged 45 to 54	15,158	1,880	10,308	125	333	2,357	154
Aged 55 to 64	13,659	1,063	9,841	140	203	2,139	273
Aged 65 or older	13,708	534	9,919	158	124	1,305	1,668
Total non-Hispanic white women	**83,992**	**19,435**	**44,265**	**812**	**1,429**	**9,662**	**8,389**
Under age 35	24,635	15,175	7,731	256	473	951	45
Aged 35 to 44	12,432	1,508	8,599	117	347	1,735	125
Aged 35 to 39	5,766	804	3,906	58	186	760	51
Aged 40 to 44	6,666	704	4,693	59	161	975	74
Aged 45 to 54	15,520	1,257	10,608	165	335	2,623	531
Aged 55 to 64	14,083	881	9,316	134	187	2,451	1,113
Aged 65 or older	17,322	611	8,009	139	87	1,902	6,574
PERCENT DISTRIBUTION							
Total non-Hispanic white men	**100.0%**	**29.5%**	**55.5%**	**0.9%**	**1.6%**	**9.9%**	**2.7%**
Under age 35	100.0	70.8	24.2	0.8	1.2	3.0	0.0
Aged 35 to 44	100.0	18.4	66.8	0.9	2.5	11.0	0.4
Aged 35 to 39	100.0	20.1	66.7	0.7	2.8	9.2	0.4
Aged 40 to 44	100.0	16.8	66.9	1.0	2.2	12.7	0.5
Aged 45 to 54	100.0	12.4	68.0	0.8	2.2	15.5	1.0
Aged 55 to 64	100.0	7.8	72.0	1.0	1.5	15.7	2.0
Aged 65 or older	100.0	3.9	72.4	1.2	0.9	9.5	12.2
Total non-Hispanic white women	**100.0**	**23.1**	**52.7**	**1.0**	**1.7**	**11.5**	**10.0**
Under age 35	100.0	61.6	31.4	1.0	1.9	3.9	0.2
Aged 35 to 44	100.0	12.1	69.2	0.9	2.8	14.0	1.0
Aged 35 to 39	100.0	13.9	67.7	1.0	3.2	13.2	0.9
Aged 40 to 44	100.0	10.6	70.4	0.9	2.4	14.6	1.1
Aged 45 to 54	100.0	8.1	68.4	1.1	2.2	16.9	3.4
Aged 55 to 64	100.0	6.3	66.2	1.0	1.3	17.4	7.9
Aged 65 or older	100.0	3.5	46.2	0.8	0.5	11.0	38.0

Note: Non-Hispanic whites are those who identify themselves as being white alone and not Hispanic.
Source: Bureau of the Census, America's Families and Living Arrangements: 2011, Internet site http://www.census.gov/ population/www/socdemo/hh-fam/cps2011.html; calculations by New Strategist

Divorce Is Highest among Older Men and Women

A substantial share of Gen Xers has experienced divorce, according to a 2009 study.

The experience of divorce is most common among people aged 50 to 69. In this broad age group, more than one-third of men and women have experienced divorce, according to a Census Bureau study. Among people aged 35 to 49, the percentage who have been through a divorce ranges from a low of 18 percent among men aged 35 to 39 to a high of 31 percent among women aged 40 to 49.

Among all Americans aged 15 or older, 40.6 percent of women and 42.5 percent of men have been married once and are still married. The figure tops 50 percent among men aged 30 or older and among women aged 30 to 49.

■ Most Gen Xers have been married once and are still married.

More than one in five adults have experienced divorce

(percent of people aged 15 or older by selected marital history and sex, 2009)

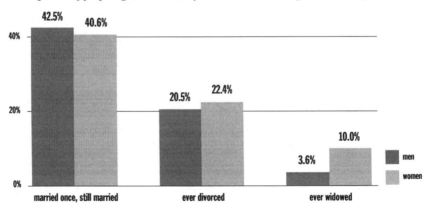

Table 7.23 Marital History of Men by Age, 2009

(number of men aged 15 or older and percent distribution by marital history and age, 2009; numbers in thousands)

	total	15–19	20–24	25–29	30–34	35–39	40–49	50–59	60–69	70+
TOTAL MEN, NUMBER	115,797	10,870	10,152	10,567	9,518	9,995	21,504	19,568	12,774	10,849
TOTAL MEN, PERCENT	100.0%	100.0%	100.0%	100.0%	100.0%	100.0%	100.0%	100.0%	100.0%	100.0%
Never married	33.0	98.0	87.5	59.7	35.6	23.5	16.4	10.8	4.6	3.4
Ever married	67.0	2.0	12.5	40.3	64.4	76.5	83.6	89.2	95.4	96.6
Married once	52.3	1.9	12.5	38.8	59.4	66.9	65.8	63.4	64.8	72.3
Still married	42.5	1.3	11.2	34.2	52.2	56.1	52.2	50.4	53.5	54.0
Married twice	11.6	0.1	0.0	1.5	4.8	8.7	14.8	20.0	22.1	18.9
Still married	9.0	0.1	0.0	1.3	4.0	7.4	11.3	15.5	17.5	13.2
Married three or more times	3.1	0.0	0.0	0.1	0.2	1.0	3.0	5.8	8.5	5.4
Still married	2.3	0.0	0.0	0.1	0.2	0.8	2.2	4.3	6.5	3.8
Ever divorced	20.5	0.3	0.8	5.0	10.5	17.9	28.5	35.7	36.5	23.4
Currently divorced	9.1	0.2	0.7	3.7	6.2	9.5	14.2	15.5	12.4	7.2
Ever widowed	3.6	0.4	0.1	0.3	0.2	0.5	1.3	2.5	6.4	22.6
Currently widowed	2.6	0.3	0.1	0.3	0.1	0.3	0.9	1.6	3.9	17.4

Source: Bureau of the Census, Number, Timing, and Duration of Marriages and Divorces: 2009, Current Population Reports P70-125, 2011, Internet site http://www.census.gov/hhes/socdemo/marriage/data/sipp/index.html; calculations by New Strategist

Table 7.24 Marital History of Women by Age, 2009

(number of women aged 15 or older and percent distribution by marital history and age, 2009; numbers in thousands)

	total	15–19	20–24	25–29	30–34	35–39	40–49	50–59	60–69	70+
TOTAL WOMEN, NUMBER	123,272	10,478	10,158	10,408	9,645	10,267	22,119	20,702	14,288	15,207
TOTAL WOMEN, PERCENT	100.0%	100.0%	100.0%	100.0%	100.0%	100.0%	100.0%	100.0%	100.0%	100.0%
Never married	27.2	97.5	77.3	46.8	26.7	17.3	13.0	9.1	6.0	4.3
Ever married	72.8	2.5	22.7	53.2	73.3	82.7	87.0	90.9	94.0	95.7
Married once	57.5	2.5	22.4	50.8	64.5	69.3	67.4	65.5	67.7	76.1
Still married	40.6	1.9	19.7	43.2	54.5	55.8	51.6	47.5	45.7	30.1
Married twice	12.1	0.1	0.3	2.3	8.0	11.6	15.8	19.5	20.1	15.2
Still married	7.9	0.6	0.2	2.0	6.9	9.1	11.3	13.4	13.2	5.2
Married three or more times	3.2	0.0	0.0	0.0	0.8	1.9	3.8	5.9	6.2	4.4
Still married	1.9	0.0	0.0	0.0	0.7	1.4	2.5	4.1	3.6	1.4
Ever divorced	22.4	0.2	1.8	7.3	15.6	22.7	31.0	37.3	34.5	21.4
Currently divorced	11.3	0.1	1.5	5.3	8.1	11.8	16.4	18.6	16.0	9.9
Ever widowed	10.0	0.3	0.1	0.2	0.6	1.4	2.6	6.5	17.0	51.2
Currently widowed	8.9	0.3	0.1	0.1	0.4	0.8	1.8	4.9	13.9	48.3

Source: Bureau of the Census, Number, Timing, and Duration of Marriages and Divorces: 2009, Current Population Reports P70-125, 2011, Internet site http://www.census.gov/hhes/socdemo/marriage/data/sipp/index.html; calculations by New Strategist

8

Population

■ Generation X numbers 50 million, a figure that includes all those born between 1965 and 1976 (aged 34 to 45 in 2010). Generation Xers account for 16 percent of the population.

■ Sixty-two percent of Generation Xers are non-Hispanic white. Within Generation X, Hispanics outnumber blacks. Eighteen percent of Gen Xers are Hispanic, 13 percent are black, and 7 percent are Asian.

■ Twenty-one percent of 35-to-44-year-olds were born in another country—a much greater share than the 13 percent of all U.S. residents who are foreign-born.

■ Generation X is diverse at the state level. Among Gen Xers aged 35 to 39 in California, Hispanics outnumber non-Hispanic whites.

Generation X Is Sandwiched between Larger Generations

Age groups shrink when Generation X moves in.

Generation X numbers about 50 million, a figure that includes all those born between 1965 and 1976 (aged 34 to 45 in 2010). Generation Xers account for 16 percent of the total population. They are surrounded by the two largest generations: the Boomers (25 percent of the population) and the Millennials (also 25 percent).

As Generation X moves through the age structure, age groups shrink. Between 2000 and 2010, the number of 35-to-39-year-olds fell by 11 percent as Generation Xers replaced Boomers in the age group. The number of 40-to-44-year-olds fell 7 percent during those years.

■ Generation X may be relatively small, but the cohort accounts for a large share of the nation's parents and workers.

Generation X outnumbers only older Americans

(number of people by generation, 2010)

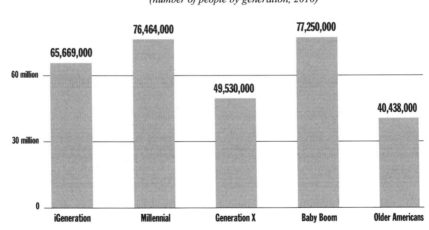

| iGeneration | Millennial | Generation X | Baby Boom | Older Americans |
| 65,669,000 | 76,464,000 | 49,530,000 | 77,250,000 | 40,438,000 |

Table 8.1 Population by Age and Generation, 2010

(number and percent distribution of people by age and generation, 2010; numbers in thousands)

	number	percent distribution
Total people	**309,350**	**100.0%**
Under age 5	20,201	6.5
Aged 5 to 9	20,382	6.6
Aged 10 to 14	20,694	6.7
Aged 15 to 19	21,959	7.1
Aged 20 to 24	21,668	7.0
Aged 25 to 29	21,153	6.8
Aged 30 to 34	20,094	6.5
Aged 35 to 44	40,981	13.2
Aged 35 to 39	20,082	6.5
Aged 40 to 44	20,899	6.8
Aged 45 to 49	22,648	7.3
Aged 50 to 54	22,365	7.2
Aged 55 to 59	19,779	6.4
Aged 60 to 64	16,987	5.5
Aged 65 to 69	12,515	4.0
Aged 70 to 74	9,326	3.0
Aged 75 to 79	7,313	2.4
Aged 80 to 84	5,750	1.9
Aged 85 or older	5,533	1.8
Total people	**309,350**	**100.0**
iGeneration (under 16)	65,669	21.2
Millennial (16 to 33)	76,464	24.7
Generation X (34 to 45)	49,530	16.0
Baby Boom (46 to 64)	77,250	25.0
Older Americans (65 or older)	40,438	13.1

Source: Bureau of the Census, Population Estimates, Internet site http://www.census.gov/popest/data/intercensal/national/nat2010.html; calculations by New Strategist

Table 8.2 Population by Age and Sex, 2010

(number of people by age and sex, and sex ratio by age, 2010; numbers in thousands)

	total	female	male	sex ratio
Total people	**309,350**	**157,242**	**152,108**	**97**
Under age 5	20,201	9,883	10,318	104
Aged 5 to 9	20,382	9,975	10,407	104
Aged 10 to 14	20,694	10,107	10,587	105
Aged 15 to 19	21,959	10,696	11,263	105
Aged 20 to 24	21,668	10,612	11,056	104
Aged 25 to 29	21,153	10,477	10,676	102
Aged 30 to 34	20,094	10,030	10,063	100
Aged 35 to 44	40,981	20,585	20,396	99
Aged 35 to 39	20,082	10,086	9,997	99
Aged 40 to 44	20,899	10,500	10,399	99
Aged 45 to 49	22,648	11,465	11,183	98
Aged 50 to 54	22,365	11,399	10,966	96
Aged 55 to 59	19,779	10,199	9,580	94
Aged 60 to 64	16,987	8,829	8,159	92
Aged 65 to 69	12,515	6,623	5,892	89
Aged 70 to 74	9,326	5,057	4,269	84
Aged 75 to 79	7,313	4,130	3,184	77
Aged 80 to 84	5,750	3,448	2,302	67
Aged 85 or older	5,533	3,726	1,807	49

Note: The sex ratio is the number of males per 100 females.
Source: Bureau of the Census, Population Estimates, Internet site http://www.census.gov/popest/data/intercensal/national/nat2010.html; calculations by New Strategist

Table 8.3 Population by Age, 2000 and 2010

(number of people by age, 2000 and 2010; percent change, 2000–10)

	2010	2000	percent change 2000–10
Total people	**309,350**	**282,162**	**9.6%**
Under age 5	20,201	19,178	5.3
Aged 5 to 9	20,382	20,464	–0.4
Aged 10 to 14	20,694	20,638	0.3
Aged 15 to 19	21,959	20,295	8.2
Aged 20 to 24	21,668	19,117	13.3
Aged 25 to 29	21,153	19,280	9.7
Aged 30 to 34	20,094	20,524	–2.1
Aged 35 to 39	20,082	22,651	–11.3
Aged 40 to 44	20,899	22,518	–7.2
Aged 45 to 49	22,648	20,220	12.0
Aged 50 to 54	22,365	17,779	25.8
Aged 55 to 59	19,779	13,566	45.8
Aged 60 to 64	16,987	10,863	56.4
Aged 65 to 69	12,515	9,524	31.4
Aged 70 to 74	9,326	8,860	5.3
Aged 75 to 79	7,313	7,439	–1.7
Aged 80 to 84	5,750	4,985	15.4
Aged 85 or older	5,533	4,262	29.8
Aged 18 to 24	30,708	27,315	12.4
Aged 18 or older	235,154	209,786	12.1
Aged 65 or older	40,438	35,070	15.3

Source: Bureau of the Census, Population Estimates, Internet site http://www.census.gov/popest/data/intercensal/national/ nat2010.html; calculations by New Strategist

Generation X Is More Diverse than Average

The generation is less diverse than children and young adults, however.

Sixty-two percent of Generation Xers are non-Hispanic white, according to the 2010 census. This figure is smaller than the 64 percent for the population as a whole, but larger than the share among the youngest Americans—only 51 percent of children under age 5 are non-Hispanic white. Older generations of Americans are much less diverse than Generation X. Among Boomers, 72 percent are non-Hispanic white. Among older Americans (aged 65 or older), the proportion is 80 percent.

Within Generation X, Hispanics outnumber blacks. Eighteen percent of Gen Xers are Hispanic, 13 percent are black, and 7 percent are Asian. Generation Xers accounts for 16 to 17 percent of the non-Hispanic white, black, and Hispanic populations. They account for a larger 19 percent of Asians. Among Hispanics, Generation Xers outnumber Boomers.

■ The differing racial and ethnic makeup of older versus younger generations of Americans may create political tension in the years ahead.

Fewer than two-thirds of Generation Xers are non-Hispanic white

(non-Hispanic white share of population by generation, 2010)

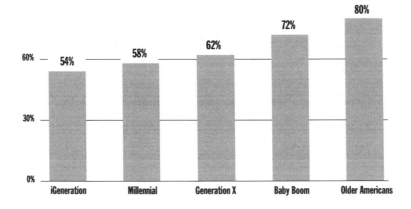

Table 8.4 Number of People by Age, Race Alone, and Hispanic Origin, 2010

(number of people by age, race alone, and Hispanic origin, 2010; numbers in thousands)

	total	Asian	black	Hispanic	non-Hispanic white	two or more races
Total people	**308,746**	**15,160**	**40,251**	**50,478**	**197,319**	**7,026**
Under age 5	20,201	948	3,055	5,114	10,307	1,123
Aged 5 to 9	20,349	972	3,013	4,791	10,885	948
Aged 10 to 14	20,677	922	3,154	4,525	11,449	836
Aged 15 to 19	22,040	999	3,573	4,532	12,387	726
Aged 20 to 24	21,586	1,149	3,240	4,322	12,467	571
Aged 25 to 29	21,102	1,279	2,911	4,310	12,268	491
Aged 30 to 34	19,962	1,284	2,743	4,124	11,534	424
Aged 35 to 44	41,071	2,521	5,458	7,299	25,267	672
Aged 35 to 39	20,180	1,334	2,706	3,856	12,018	357
Aged 40 to 44	20,891	1,188	2,752	3,442	13,250	315
Aged 45 to 49	22,709	1,105	2,901	3,022	15,387	302
Aged 50 to 54	22,298	1,004	2,753	2,441	15,813	269
Aged 55 to 59	19,665	863	2,246	1,841	14,476	209
Aged 60 to 64	16,818	703	1,715	1,372	12,839	157
Aged 65 to 69	12,435	483	1,181	949	9,693	106
Aged 70 to 74	9,278	361	865	700	7,265	73
Aged 75 to 79	7,318	255	625	511	5,867	51
Aged 80 to 84	5,743	171	430	351	4,751	35
Aged 85 or older	5,493	140	386	271	4,664	30
PERCENT DISTRIBUTION						
Total people	**100.0%**	**4.9%**	**13.0%**	**16.3%**	**63.9%**	**2.3%**
Under age 5	100.0	4.7	15.1	25.3	51.0	5.6
Aged 5 to 9	100.0	4.8	14.8	23.5	53.5	4.7
Aged 10 to 14	100.0	4.5	15.3	21.9	55.4	4.0
Aged 15 to 19	100.0	4.5	16.2	20.6	56.2	3.3
Aged 20 to 24	100.0	5.3	15.0	20.0	57.8	2.6
Aged 25 to 29	100.0	6.1	13.8	20.4	58.1	2.3
Aged 30 to 34	100.0	6.4	13.7	20.7	57.8	2.1
Aged 35 to 44	100.0	6.1	13.3	17.8	61.5	1.6
Aged 35 to 39	100.0	6.6	13.4	19.1	59.6	1.8
Aged 40 to 44	100.0	5.7	13.2	16.5	63.4	1.5
Aged 45 to 49	100.0	4.9	12.8	13.3	67.8	1.3
Aged 50 to 54	100.0	4.5	12.3	10.9	70.9	1.2
Aged 55 to 59	100.0	4.4	11.4	9.4	73.6	1.1
Aged 60 to 64	100.0	4.2	10.2	8.2	76.3	0.9
Aged 65 to 69	100.0	3.9	9.5	7.6	78.0	0.9
Aged 70 to 74	100.0	3.9	9.3	7.5	78.3	0.8
Aged 75 to 79	100.0	3.5	8.5	7.0	80.2	0.7
Aged 80 to 84	100.0	3.0	7.5	6.1	82.7	0.6
Aged 85 or older	100.0	2.5	7.0	4.9	84.9	0.6

Note: Asians and blacks are those who identify themselves as being of the race alone. Numbers do not add to total because not all races are shown and Hispanics may be of any race. Non-Hispanic whites are those who identify themselves as being white alone and not Hispanic.
Source: Bureau of the Census, 2010 Census, American Factfinder, Population Estimates, Internet site http:// factfinder2.census.gov/faces/nav/jsf/pages/index.xhtml; calculations by New Strategist

Table 8.5 Number of People by Age, Race Alone or in Combination, and Hispanic Origin, 2010

(number of people by age, race alone or in combination, and Hispanic origin, 2010; numbers in thousands)

	total	Asian	black	Hispanic	non-Hispanic white
Total people	**308,746**	**17,321**	**42,021**	**50,478**	**197,319**
Under age 5	20,201	1,317	3,538	5,114	10,307
Aged 5 to 9	20,349	1,285	3,389	4,791	10,885
Aged 10 to 14	20,677	1,184	3,468	4,525	11,449
Aged 15 to 19	22,040	1,229	3,796	4,532	12,387
Aged 20 to 24	21,586	1,333	3,350	4,322	12,467
Aged 25 to 29	21,102	1,433	2,971	4,310	12,268
Aged 30 to 34	19,962	1,412	2,780	4,124	11,534
Aged 35 to 44	41,071	2,724	5,511	7,299	25,267
Aged 35 to 39	20,180	1,445	2,738	3,856	12,018
Aged 40 to 44	20,891	1,279	2,773	3,442	13,250
Aged 45 to 49	22,709	1,188	2,922	3,022	15,387
Aged 50 to 54	22,298	1,076	2,775	2,441	15,813
Aged 55 to 59	19,665	916	2,267	1,841	14,476
Aged 60 to 64	16,818	740	1,732	1,372	12,839
Aged 65 to 69	12,435	508	1,192	949	9,693
Aged 70 to 74	9,278	379	873	700	7,265
Aged 75 to 79	7,318	269	631	511	5,867
Aged 80 to 84	5,743	180	435	351	4,751
Aged 85 or older	5,493	147	392	271	4,664
PERCENT DISTRIBUTION					
Total people	**100.0%**	**5.6%**	**13.6%**	**16.3%**	**63.9%**
Under age 5	100.0	6.5	17.5	25.3	51.0
Aged 5 to 9	100.0	6.3	16.7	23.5	53.5
Aged 10 to 14	100.0	5.7	16.8	21.9	55.4
Aged 15 to 19	100.0	5.6	17.2	20.6	56.2
Aged 20 to 24	100.0	6.2	15.5	20.0	57.8
Aged 25 to 29	100.0	6.8	14.1	20.4	58.1
Aged 30 to 34	100.0	7.1	13.9	20.7	57.8
Aged 35 to 44	100.0	6.6	13.4	17.8	61.5
Aged 35 to 39	100.0	7.2	13.6	19.1	59.6
Aged 40 to 44	100.0	6.1	13.3	16.5	63.4
Aged 45 to 49	100.0	5.2	12.9	13.3	67.8
Aged 50 to 54	100.0	4.8	12.4	10.9	70.9
Aged 55 to 59	100.0	4.7	11.5	9.4	73.6
Aged 60 to 64	100.0	4.4	10.3	8.2	76.3
Aged 65 to 69	100.0	4.1	9.6	7.6	78.0
Aged 70 to 74	100.0	4.1	9.4	7.5	78.3
Aged 75 to 79	100.0	3.7	8.6	7.0	80.2
Aged 80 to 84	100.0	3.1	7.6	6.1	82.7
Aged 85 or older	100.0	2.7	7.1	4.9	84.9

Note: Asians and blacks are those who identify themselves as being of the race alone and those who identify themselves as being of the race in combination with other races. Numbers do not add to total because not all races are shown, some mixed-race individuals are counted more than once, and Hispanics may be of any race. Non-Hispanic whites are those who identify themselves as being white alone and not Hispanic.
Source: Bureau of the Census, 2010 Census, American Factfinder, Population Estimates, Internet site http://factfinder2.census.gov/faces/nav/jsf/pages/index.xhtml; calculations by New Strategist

Table 8.6 Population by Generation, Race Alone or in Combination, and Hispanic Origin, 2010

(number and percent distribution of people by generation, race alone or in combination, and Hispanic origin, 2010; numbers in thousands)

	total	Asian	black	Hispanic	non-Hispanic white
Total people	**308,746**	**17,321**	**42,021**	**50,478**	**197,319**
iGeneration (under age 16)	65,635	4,031	11,154	15,337	35,119
Millennial (16 to 33)	76,290	4,879	11,582	15,558	43,871
Generation X (34 to 45)	49,605	3,244	6,651	8,728	30,651
Baby Boom (46 to 64)	76,948	3,683	9,111	8,073	55,437
Older Americans (65 or older)	40,268	1,483	3,522	2,782	32,241

PERCENT DISTRIBUTION BY RACE AND HISPANIC ORIGIN

Total people	**100.0%**	**5.6%**	**13.6%**	**16.3%**	**63.9%**
iGeneration (under age 16)	100.0	6.1	17.0	23.4	53.5
Millennial (16 to 33)	100.0	6.4	15.2	20.4	57.5
Generation X (34 to 45)	100.0	6.5	13.4	17.6	61.8
Baby Boom (46 to 64)	100.0	4.8	11.8	10.5	72.0
Older Americans (65 or older)	100.0	3.7	8.7	6.9	80.1

PERCENT DISTRIBUTION BY GENERATION

Total people	**100.0%**	**100.0%**	**100.0%**	**100.0%**	**100.0%**
iGeneration (under age 16)	21.3	23.3	26.5	30.4	17.8
Millennial (16 to 33)	24.7	28.2	27.6	30.8	22.2
Generation X (34 to 45)	16.1	18.7	15.8	17.3	15.5
Baby Boom (46 to 64)	24.9	21.3	21.7	16.0	28.1
Older Americans (65 or older)	13.0	8.6	8.4	5.5	16.3

Note: Asians and blacks are those who identify themselves as being of the race alone and those who identify themselves as being of the race in combination with other races. Numbers do not add to total because not all races are shown, some mixed-race individuals are counted more than once, and Hispanics may be of any race. Non-Hispanic whites are those who identify themselves as being white alone and not Hispanic.
Source: Bureau of the Census, 2010 Census, American Factfinder, Population Estimates, Internet site http:// factfinder2.census.gov/faces/nav/jsf/pages/index.xhtml; calculations by New Strategist

Many Gen Xers Live in Their State of Birth

One in five is foreign-born.

According to the 2010 American Community Survey, 48 percent of people aged 35 to 44 (Gen Xers were aged 34 to 45 in that year) were born in their state of residence—a figure that is nearly identical to that among older U.S. residents. Twenty-nine percent of Gen Xers were born in the United States, but in a different state. A substantial 21 percent were born in another country—a much greater share than the 13 percent of all U.S. residents who are foreign-born.

Among the foreign-born, the broad 25-to-44 age group accounts for a large share of the total. Half of the foreign-born from Mexico are aged 25 to 44, as are 40 percent of the Asian foreign-born. Among the European foreign-born, however, only 27 percent are aged 25 to 44.

■ The foreign-born population adds to the multicultural mix, which is now a significant factor in American business and politics.

Among the foreign-born, those from Mexico are the youngest

(median age of the foreign-born by world region of birth, 2010)

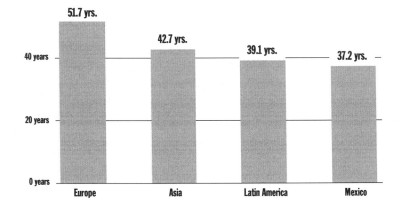

Table 8.7 Population by Age and Place of Birth, 2010

(number and percent distribution of people by age and place of birth, 2010; numbers in thousands)

| | | born in the United States | | | |
	total	in state of current residence	outside state of current residence	citizen born outside U.S.	foreign-born
Total people	**309,350**	**181,748**	**83,418**	**4,228**	**39,956**
Under age 5	20,134	17,981	1,768	121	263
Aged 5 to 17	54,031	42,287	8,580	597	2,568
Aged 18 to 24	30,895	19,665	7,263	468	3,499
Aged 25 to 34	40,972	21,661	10,755	662	7,894
Aged 35 to 44	41,192	19,842	11,949	701	8,701
Aged 45 to 54	44,929	22,521	14,474	738	7,196
Aged 55 to 59	19,683	9,944	6,803	270	2,666
Aged 60 to 61	7,222	3,583	2,595	94	951
Aged 62 to 64	9,857	4,752	3,714	135	1,256
Aged 65 to 74	21,854	10,324	8,430	255	2,845
Aged 75 or older	18,579	9,187	7,087	188	2,118

PERCENT DISTRIBUTION BY PLACE OF BIRTH

Total people	**100.0%**	**58.8%**	**27.0%**	**1.4%**	**12.9%**
Under age 5	100.0	89.3	8.8	0.6	1.3
Aged 5 to 17	100.0	78.3	15.9	1.1	4.8
Aged 18 to 24	100.0	63.7	23.5	1.5	11.3
Aged 25 to 34	100.0	52.9	26.2	1.6	19.3
Aged 35 to 44	100.0	48.2	29.0	1.7	21.1
Aged 45 to 54	100.0	50.1	32.2	1.6	16.0
Aged 55 to 59	100.0	50.5	34.6	1.4	13.5
Aged 60 to 61	100.0	49.6	35.9	1.3	13.2
Aged 62 to 64	100.0	48.2	37.7	1.4	12.7
Aged 65 to 74	100.0	47.2	38.6	1.2	13.0
Aged 75 or older	100.0	49.4	38.1	1.0	11.4

PERCENT DISTRIBUTION BY AGE

Total people	**100.0%**	**100.0%**	**100.0%**	**100.0%**	**100.0%**
Under age 5	6.5	9.9	2.1	2.9	0.7
Aged 5 to 17	17.5	23.3	10.3	14.1	6.4
Aged 18 to 24	10.0	10.8	8.7	11.1	8.8
Aged 25 to 34	13.2	11.9	12.9	15.7	19.8
Aged 35 to 44	13.3	10.9	14.3	16.6	21.8
Aged 45 to 54	14.5	12.4	17.4	17.5	18.0
Aged 55 to 59	6.4	5.5	8.2	6.4	6.7
Aged 60 to 61	2.3	2.0	3.1	2.2	2.4
Aged 62 to 64	3.2	2.6	4.5	3.2	3.1
Aged 65 to 74	7.1	5.7	10.1	6.0	7.1
Aged 75 or older	6.0	5.1	8.5	4.5	5.3

Source: Bureau of the Census, 2010 American Community Survey, Internet site http://factfinder2.census.gov/faces/nav/jsf/pages/index.xhtml; calculations by New Strategist

Table 8.8 Foreign-Born Population by Age and World Region of Birth, 2010

(number and percent distribution of foreign-born by age and world region of birth, 2010; numbers in thousands)

	total	Asian	Europe	Latin America total	Mexico
Total foreign-born, number	39,956	11,284	4,817	21,224	11,711
Total foreign-born, percent	100.0%	100.0%	100.0%	100.0%	100.0%
Under age 5	0.7	0.9	0.5	0.5	0.5
Aged 5 to 17	6.4	6.0	5.1	6.7	7.4
Aged 18 to 24	8.8	7.7	5.5	10.1	11.1
Aged 25 to 44	41.5	39.9	27.4	46.0	50.1
Aged 45 to 54	18.0	18.7	16.7	17.9	16.2
Aged 55 to 64	12.2	14.1	16.3	10.2	8.4
Aged 65 to 74	7.1	7.8	13.8	5.3	0.4
Aged 75 to 84	3.9	3.7	10.0	2.6	1.7
Aged 85 or older	1.4	1.1	4.6	0.8	0.6
Median age	41.4	42.7	51.7	39.1	37.2

Note: Number of foreign-born by region do not add to total because "other region" is not shown.
Source: Bureau of the Census, 2010 American Community Survey, Internet site http://factfinder2.census.gov/faces/nav/jsf/pages/index.xhtml; calculations by New Strategist

Many 2011 Immigrants Were Generation Xers

Nearly one in five immigrants in 2011 was aged 35 to 44.

The number of legal immigrants admitted to the United States in 2011 surpassed 1 million. Nearly 200,000 were aged 35 to 44, accounting for 19 percent of the total.

The Millennial generation accounts for a larger share of immigrants than any other. More than 40 percent of legal immigrants in 2011 were in the Millennial age group (between the ages of 15 and 34). The Baby-Boom age group (45 to 64) accounts for the same share of immigrants as Generation X—19 percent. Only 5 percent of immigrants were aged 65 or older.

■ Because most immigrants are young adults, immigration has a much greater impact on the diversity of younger Americans than on the middle-aged or older population.

Immigrants aged 35 to 44 account for 19 percent of the 2011 total

(percent distribution of 2011 immigrants by age)

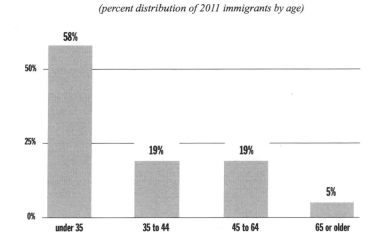

Table 8.9 Immigrants by Age, 2011

(number and percent distribution of immigrants by age, 2011)

	number	percent distribution
Total immigrants	**1,062,040**	**100.0%**
Under age 1	4,361	0.4
Aged 1 to 4	34,017	3.2
Aged 5 to 9	52,828	5.0
Aged 10 to 14	70,295	6.6
Aged 15 to 19	88,970	8.4
Aged 20 to 24	110,144	10.4
Aged 25 to 29	122,128	11.5
Aged 30 to 34	130,789	12.3
Aged 35 to 44	197,377	18.6
Aged 35 to 39	112,983	10.6
Aged 40 to 44	84,394	7.9
Aged 45 to 49	68,174	6.4
Aged 50 to 54	52,623	5.0
Aged 55 to 59	42,941	4.0
Aged 60 to 64	34,257	3.2
Aged 65 to 74	39,386	3.7
Aged 75 or older	13,740	1.3

Note: Immigrants are those granted legal permanent residence in the United States. They either arrive in the United States with immigrant visas issued abroad or adjust their status in the United States from temporary to permanent residence. Numbers may not sum to total because "age not stated" is not shown.
Source: Department of Homeland Security, 2011 Yearbook of Immigration Statistics, Internet site http://www.dhs.gov/files/statistics/publications/yearbook.shtm

Many Working-Age Adults Do Not Speak English at Home

Most are Spanish speakers, and half have trouble speaking English.

Sixty million residents of the United States speak a language other than English at home, according to the Census Bureau's 2010 American Community Survey—21 percent of the population aged 5 or older. The 62 percent majority of those who do not speak English at home are Spanish speakers.

Among working-age adults (aged 18 to 64), 22 percent do not speak English at home, and 62 percent of those who do not speak English at home are Spanish speakers. Among the Spanish speakers, 50 percent say they speak English less than very well.

■ The language barrier is a problem for many working-age adults.

Half of adults who speak Spanish at home cannot speak English very well

(percent of people aged 18 to 64 who speak a language other than English at home who speak English less than very well, by language spoken at home, 2010)

Table 8.10 Language Spoken at Home by People Aged 18 to 64, 2010

(number and percent distribution of people aged 5 or older and aged 18 to 64 who speak a language other than English at home by language spoken at home and ability to speak English very well, 2010; numbers in thousands)

	total		aged 18 to 64	
	number	percent distribution	number	percent distribution
Total, aged 5 or older	**289,216**	**100.0%**	**194,751**	**100.0%**
Speak only English at home	229,673	79.4	152,732	78.4
Speak a language other than English at home	59,542	20.6	42,018	21.6
Speak English less than very well	21,853	7.6	19,149	9.8
Total who speak a language other than English at home	**59,542**	**100.0**	**42,018**	**100.0**
Speak Spanish at home	36,996	62.1	25,934	61.7
Speak other Indo-European language at home	10,666	17.9	7,268	17.3
Speak Asian or Pacific Island language at home	9,340	15.7	6,943	16.5
Speak other language at home	2,540	4.3	1,873	4.5
Speak Spanish at home	36,996	100.0	25,934	100.0
Speak English less than very well	16,523	44.7	12,882	49.7
Speak other Indo-European language at home	10,666	100.0	7,268	100.0
Speak English less than very well	3,440	32.3	2,333	32.1
Speak Asian or Pacific Island language at home	9,340	100.0	6,943	100.0
Speak English less than very well	4,471	47.9	3,348	48.2
Speak other language at home	2,540	100.0	1,873	100.0
Speak English less than very well	786	30.9	586	31.3

Source: Bureau of the Census, 2010 American Community Survey, Internet site http://factfinder2.census.gov/faces/nav/jsf/pages/index.xhtml; calculations by New Strategist

Largest Share of Generation Xers Lives in the South

Among Gen Xers aged 35 to 39 in California, Hispanics outnumber non-Hispanic whites.

The South is home to the largest share of the population, and consequently to the largest share of Generation X. Thirty-seven percent of Gen Xers live in the South, where the generation accounts for 16 percent of the population.

Generation X is diverse, especially at the state level. While nation-wide 18 percent of Gen Xers are Hispanic, in California the Hispanic share of 35-to-44-year-olds is a much larger 38 to 41 percent. In the 35-to-39 age group, Hispanics outnumber non-Hispanic whites.

■ In most states, Gen Xers outnumber older Americans.

The Northeast is home to just 18 percent of Gen Xers

(percent distribution of the Generation X by region, 2010)

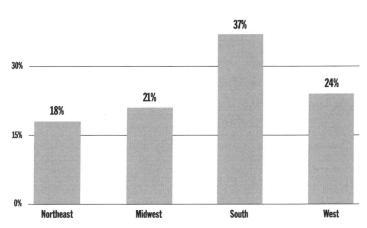

Table 8.11 Population by Age and Region, 2010

(number of people by age and region, 2010; numbers in thousands)

	total	Northeast	Midwest	South	West
Total people	**309,350**	**55,361**	**66,976**	**114,866**	**72,147**
Under age 5	20,201	3,219	4,329	7,680	4,973
Aged 5 to 9	20,382	3,339	4,432	7,691	4,921
Aged 10 to 14	20,694	3,498	4,520	7,711	4,965
Aged 15 to 19	21,959	3,873	4,781	8,062	5,243
Aged 20 to 24	21,668	3,830	4,595	8,038	5,205
Aged 25 to 29	21,153	3,623	4,427	7,861	5,243
Aged 30 to 34	20,094	3,433	4,203	7,506	4,952
Aged 35 to 44	40,981	7,375	8,546	15,348	9,712
Aged 35 to 39	20,082	3,487	4,159	7,596	4,840
Aged 40 to 44	20,899	3,888	4,387	7,751	4,872
Aged 45 to 49	22,648	4,261	4,931	8,359	5,096
Aged 50 to 54	22,365	4,225	5,013	8,122	5,005
Aged 55 to 59	19,779	3,691	4,449	7,186	4,453
Aged 60 to 64	16,987	3,165	3,702	6,335	3,785
Aged 65 to 69	12,515	2,298	2,702	4,789	2,726
Aged 70 to 74	9,326	1,718	2,046	3,571	1,992
Aged 75 to 79	7,313	1,416	1,638	2,730	1,530
Aged 80 to 84	5,750	1,191	1,335	2,039	1,184
Aged 85 or older	5,533	1,206	1,328	1,836	1,162

Source: Bureau of the Census, State Population Estimates, Internet site http://www.census.gov/popest/data/intercensal/state/state2010.html; calculations by New Strategist

Table 8.12 Regional Distribution of Population by Age, 2010

(regional distribution of people by age, 2010)

	total	Northeast	Midwest	South	West
Total people	**100.0%**	**17.9%**	**21.7%**	**37.1%**	**23.3%**
Under age 5	100.0	15.9	21.4	38.0	24.6
Aged 5 to 9	100.0	16.4	21.7	37.7	24.1
Aged 10 to 14	100.0	16.9	21.8	37.3	24.0
Aged 15 to 19	100.0	17.6	21.8	36.7	23.9
Aged 20 to 24	100.0	17.7	21.2	37.1	24.0
Aged 25 to 29	100.0	17.1	20.9	37.2	24.8
Aged 30 to 34	100.0	17.1	20.9	37.4	24.6
Aged 35 to 44	100.0	18.0	20.9	37.5	23.7
Aged 35 to 39	100.0	17.4	20.7	37.8	24.1
Aged 40 to 44	100.0	18.6	21.0	37.1	23.3
Aged 45 to 49	100.0	18.8	21.8	36.9	22.5
Aged 50 to 54	100.0	18.9	22.4	36.3	22.4
Aged 55 to 59	100.0	18.7	22.5	36.3	22.5
Aged 60 to 64	100.0	18.6	21.8	37.3	22.3
Aged 65 to 69	100.0	18.4	21.6	38.3	21.8
Aged 70 to 74	100.0	18.4	21.9	38.3	21.4
Aged 75 to 79	100.0	19.4	22.4	37.3	20.9
Aged 80 to 84	100.0	20.7	23.2	35.5	20.6
Aged 85 or older	100.0	21.8	24.0	33.2	21.0

Source: Bureau of the Census, State Population Estimates, Internet site http://www.census.gov/popest/data/intercensal/state/state2010.html; calculations by New Strategist

Table 8.13 Age Distribution of Population by Region, 2010

(age distribution of people by region, 2010)

	total	Northeast	Midwest	South	West
Total people	**100.0%**	**100.0%**	**100.0%**	**100.0%**	**100.0%**
Under age 5	6.5	5.8	6.5	6.7	6.9
Aged 5 to 9	6.6	6.0	6.6	6.7	6.8
Aged 10 to 14	6.7	6.3	6.7	6.7	6.9
Aged 15 to 19	7.1	7.0	7.1	7.0	7.3
Aged 20 to 24	7.0	6.9	6.9	7.0	7.2
Aged 25 to 29	6.8	6.5	6.6	6.8	7.3
Aged 30 to 34	6.5	6.2	6.3	6.5	6.9
Aged 35 to 44	13.2	13.3	12.8	13.4	13.5
Aged 35 to 39	6.5	6.3	6.2	6.6	6.7
Aged 40 to 44	6.8	7.0	6.6	6.7	6.8
Aged 45 to 49	7.3	7.7	7.4	7.3	7.1
Aged 50 to 54	7.2	7.6	7.5	7.1	6.9
Aged 55 to 59	6.4	6.7	6.6	6.3	6.2
Aged 60 to 64	5.5	5.7	5.5	5.5	5.2
Aged 65 to 69	4.0	4.2	4.0	4.2	3.8
Aged 70 to 74	3.0	3.1	3.1	3.1	2.8
Aged 75 to 79	2.4	2.6	2.4	2.4	2.1
Aged 80 to 84	1.9	2.2	2.0	1.8	1.6
Aged 85 or older	1.8	2.2	2.0	1.6	1.6

Source: Bureau of the Census, State Population Estimates, Internet site http://www.census.gov/popest/data/intercensal/state/state2010.html; calculations by New Strategist

Table 8.14 Population by Generation and Region, 2010

(number and percent distribution of people by generation and region, 2010; numbers in thousands)

	total	Northeast	Midwest	South	West
Total people	**309,350**	**55,361**	**66,976**	**114,866**	**72,147**
iGeneration (under 16)	65,669	10,831	14,236	24,695	15,907
Millennial (16 to 33)	76,464	13,297	16,209	28,353	18,604
Generation X (34 to 45)	49,530	8,914	10,373	18,521	11,722
Baby Boom (46 to 64)	77,250	14,489	17,109	28,332	17,320
Older Americans (65 or older)	40,438	7,829	9,049	14,965	8,595
PERCENT DISTRIBUTION BY GENERATION					
Total people	**100.0%**	**100.0%**	**100.0%**	**100.0%**	**100.0%**
iGeneration (under 16)	21.2	19.6	21.3	21.5	22.0
Millennial (16 to 33)	24.7	24.0	24.2	24.7	25.8
Generation X (34 to 45)	16.0	16.1	15.5	16.1	16.2
Baby Boom (46 to 64)	25.0	26.2	25.5	24.7	24.0
Older Americans (65 or older)	13.1	14.1	13.5	13.0	11.9
PERCENT DISTRIBUTION BY REGION					
Total people	**100.0%**	**17.9%**	**21.7%**	**37.1%**	**23.3%**
iGeneration (under 16)	100.0	16.5	21.7	37.6	24.2
Millennial (16 to 33)	100.0	17.4	21.2	37.1	24.3
Generation X (34 to 45)	100.0	18.0	20.9	37.4	23.7
Baby Boom (46 to 64)	100.0	18.8	22.1	36.7	22.4
Older Americans (65 or older)	100.0	19.4	22.4	37.0	21.3

Source: Bureau of the Census, State Population Estimates, Internet site http://www.census.gov/popest/data/intercensal/state/state2010.html; calculations by New Strategist

Table 8.15 State Populations by Age, 2010

(total number of people and number aged 35 to 44 by state, 2010; numbers in thousands)

| | total population | aged 35 to 44 | | |
		total	35 to 39	40 to 44
United States	**309,350**	**40,981**	**20,082**	**20,899**
Alabama	4,785	617	306	311
Alaska	714	93	46	47
Arizona	6,414	822	414	408
Arkansas	2,922	365	183	183
California	37,349	5,182	2,567	2,614
Colorado	5,049	699	352	347
Connecticut	3,577	483	221	262
Delaware	900	116	55	61
District of Columbia	604	81	43	38
Florida	18,843	2,427	1,173	1,253
Georgia	9,713	1,395	695	700
Hawaii	1,364	176	86	90
Idaho	1,571	191	96	95
Illinois	12,843	1,721	851	870
Indiana	6,491	838	414	424
Iowa	3,050	363	176	187
Kansas	2,859	346	171	174
Kentucky	4,346	575	284	291
Louisiana	4,544	563	275	288
Maine	1,328	170	79	91
Maryland	5,786	794	376	418
Massachusetts	6,557	885	416	469
Michigan	9,878	1,271	607	664
Minnesota	5,311	679	326	353
Mississippi	2,970	374	186	187
Missouri	5,996	746	366	380
Montana	991	112	55	57
Nebraska	1,830	220	110	111
Nevada	2,705	382	191	191
New Hampshire	1,317	178	82	97
New Jersey	8,802	1,235	585	650
New Mexico	2,066	249	123	125
New York	19,392	2,602	1,247	1,355
North Carolina	9,562	1,324	657	668
North Dakota	674	75	37	38
Ohio	11,536	1,472	712	760
Oklahoma	3,762	460	232	228
Oregon	3,839	498	250	249
Pennsylvania	12,710	1,609	758	850
Rhode Island	1,053	136	63	73
South Carolina	4,636	600	295	305

	total population	aged 35 to 44		
		total	35 to 39	40 to 44
South Dakota	816	93	45	47
Tennessee	6,357	851	421	430
Texas	25,257	3,462	1,762	1,700
Utah	2,776	333	178	155
Vermont	626	78	36	42
Virginia	8,025	1,107	538	570
Washington	6,744	907	447	460
West Virginia	1,854	236	116	120
Wisconsin	5,691	723	343	380
Wyoming	564	67	34	33

Source: Bureau of the Census, State Population Estimates, Internet site http://www.census.gov/popest/data/intercensal/state/ state2010.html; calculations by New Strategist

Table 8.16 Distribution of State Populations By Age, 2010

(percent distribution of people by state and age, 2010)

	total population	aged 35 to 44 total	35 to 39	40 to 44
United States	**100.0%**	**13.2%**	**6.5%**	**6.8%**
Alabama	100.0	12.9	6.4	6.5
Alaska	100.0	13.1	6.4	6.6
Arizona	100.0	12.8	6.5	6.4
Arkansas	100.0	12.5	6.2	6.3
California	100.0	13.9	6.9	7.0
Colorado	100.0	13.9	7.0	6.9
Connecticut	100.0	13.5	6.2	7.3
Delaware	100.0	12.9	6.1	6.8
District of Columbia	100.0	13.4	7.1	6.3
Florida	100.0	12.9	6.2	6.7
Georgia	100.0	14.4	7.2	7.2
Hawaii	100.0	12.9	6.3	6.6
Idaho	100.0	12.2	6.1	6.0
Illinois	100.0	13.4	6.6	6.8
Indiana	100.0	12.9	6.4	6.5
Iowa	100.0	11.9	5.8	6.1
Kansas	100.0	12.1	6.0	6.1
Kentucky	100.0	13.2	6.5	6.7
Louisiana	100.0	12.4	6.1	6.3
Maine	100.0	12.8	6.0	6.9
Maryland	100.0	13.7	6.5	7.2
Massachusetts	100.0	13.5	6.3	7.2
Michigan	100.0	12.9	6.1	6.7
Minnesota	100.0	12.8	6.1	6.6
Mississippi	100.0	12.6	6.3	6.3
Missouri	100.0	12.4	6.1	6.3
Montana	100.0	11.4	5.6	5.8
Nebraska	100.0	12.0	6.0	6.0
Nevada	100.0	14.1	7.1	7.1
New Hampshire	100.0	13.5	6.2	7.4
New Jersey	100.0	14.0	6.7	7.4
New Mexico	100.0	12.0	6.0	6.1
New York	100.0	13.4	6.4	7.0
North Carolina	100.0	13.9	6.9	7.0
North Dakota	100.0	11.1	5.5	5.7
Ohio	100.0	12.8	6.2	6.6
Oklahoma	100.0	12.2	6.2	6.1
Oregon	100.0	13.0	6.5	6.5
Pennsylvania	100.0	12.7	6.0	6.7
Rhode Island	100.0	12.9	6.0	6.9
South Carolina	100.0	12.9	6.4	6.6

		aged 35 to 44		
	total population	total	35 to 39	40 to 44
South Dakota	100.0%	11.4%	5.6%	5.8%
Tennessee	100.0	13.4	6.6	6.8
Texas	100.0	13.7	7.0	6.7
Utah	100.0	12.0	6.4	5.6
Vermont	100.0	12.4	5.7	6.7
Virginia	100.0	13.8	6.7	7.1
Washington	100.0	13.4	6.6	6.8
West Virginia	100.0	12.7	6.3	6.5
Wisconsin	100.0	12.7	6.0	6.7
Wyoming	100.0	11.8	5.9	5.8

Source: Bureau of the Census, State Population Estimates, Internet site http://www.census.gov/popest/data/intercensal/state/state2010.html; calculations by New Strategist

Table 8.17 State Populations by Generation, 2010

(number of people by state and generation, 2010; numbers in thousands)

	total population	iGeneration (under 16)	Millennial (16 to 33)	Generation X (34 to 45)	Baby Boom (46 to 64)	Older Americans (65 or older)
United States	**309,350**	**65,669**	**76,464**	**49,530**	**77,250**	**40,438**
Alabama	4,785	1,001	1,162	746	1,217	660
Alaska	714	167	191	114	187	55
Arizona	6,414	1,454	1,590	991	1,491	887
Arkansas	2,922	633	704	443	720	421
California	37,349	8,208	9,845	6,236	8,790	4,270
Colorado	5,049	1,096	1,281	845	1,273	553
Connecticut	3,577	715	809	582	963	508
Delaware	900	182	216	140	232	130
District of Columbia	604	92	211	100	133	69
Florida	18,843	3,531	4,288	2,930	4,820	3,274
Georgia	9,713	2,216	2,459	1,673	2,327	1,037
Hawaii	1,364	269	332	213	352	198
Idaho	1,571	383	390	233	370	195
Illinois	12,843	2,757	3,224	2,082	3,165	1,615
Indiana	6,491	1,425	1,581	1,014	1,626	844
Iowa	3,050	647	734	444	771	454
Kansas	2,859	648	711	422	700	377
Kentucky	4,346	908	1,040	696	1,121	580
Louisiana	4,544	993	1,173	688	1,130	560
Maine	1,328	240	281	206	389	211
Maryland	5,786	1,192	1,411	960	1,512	711
Massachusetts	6,557	1,251	1,614	1,069	1,719	906
Michigan	9,878	2,052	2,310	1,535	2,617	1,364
Minnesota	5,311	1,136	1,300	829	1,360	685
Mississippi	2,970	669	742	453	725	381
Missouri	5,996	1,261	1,456	909	1,528	841
Montana	991	198	232	138	275	147
Nebraska	1,830	410	456	269	448	248
Nevada	2,705	590	674	459	656	326
New Hampshire	1,317	251	290	215	382	179
New Jersey	8,802	1,812	2,020	1,487	2,292	1,190
New Mexico	2,066	461	505	303	523	274
New York	19,392	3,801	4,911	3,149	4,904	2,627
North Carolina	9,562	2,033	2,320	1,589	2,379	1,240
North Dakota	674	134	180	92	170	98
Ohio	11,536	2,403	2,696	1,781	3,030	1,626
Oklahoma	3,762	831	942	561	918	509
Oregon	3,839	769	932	603	1,000	536
Pennsylvania	12,710	2,452	2,967	1,946	3,380	1,965
Rhode Island	1,053	198	261	165	277	152
South Carolina	4,636	962	1,134	724	1,182	635

	total population	iGeneration (under 16)	Millennial (16 to 33)	Generation X (34 to 45)	Baby Boom (46 to 64)	Older Americans (65 or older)
South Dakota	816	181	200	114	204	117
Tennessee	6,357	1,326	1,523	1,026	1,625	857
Texas	25,257	6,138	6,612	4,169	5,718	2,620
Utah	2,776	788	810	407	520	251
Vermont	626	113	144	95	183	91
Virginia	8,025	1,645	2,005	1,337	2,055	982
Washington	6,744	1,402	1,680	1,097	1,733	833
West Virginia	1,854	343	412	285	515	298
Wisconsin	5,691	1,182	1,360	880	1,490	779
Wyoming	564	121	142	82	149	70

Source: Bureau of the Census, State Population Estimates, Internet site http://www.census.gov/popest/data/intercensal/state/ state2010.html; calculations by New Strategist

Table 8.18 Distribution of State Populations by Generation, 2010

(percent distribution of people by state and generation, 2010)

	total population	iGeneration (under 16)	Millennial (16 to 33)	Generation X (34 to 45)	Baby Boom (46 to 64)	Older Americans (65 or older)
United States	**100.0%**	**21.2%**	**24.7%**	**16.0%**	**25.0%**	**13.1%**
Alabama	100.0	20.9	24.3	15.6	25.4	13.8
Alaska	100.0	23.4	26.7	15.9	26.2	7.7
Arizona	100.0	22.7	24.8	15.5	23.3	13.8
Arkansas	100.0	21.7	24.1	15.2	24.6	14.4
California	100.0	22.0	26.4	16.7	23.5	11.4
Colorado	100.0	21.7	25.4	16.7	25.2	11.0
Connecticut	100.0	20.0	22.6	16.3	26.9	14.2
Delaware	100.0	20.3	24.0	15.6	25.7	14.4
District of Columbia	100.0	15.3	34.9	16.5	21.9	11.4
Florida	100.0	18.7	22.8	15.5	25.6	17.4
Georgia	100.0	22.8	25.3	17.2	24.0	10.7
Hawaii	100.0	19.7	24.3	15.6	25.8	14.5
Idaho	100.0	24.4	24.8	14.8	23.5	12.4
Illinois	100.0	21.5	25.1	16.2	24.6	12.6
Indiana	100.0	22.0	24.4	15.6	25.1	13.0
Iowa	100.0	21.2	24.1	14.5	25.3	14.9
Kansas	100.0	22.7	24.9	14.8	24.5	13.2
Kentucky	100.0	20.9	23.9	16.0	25.8	13.4
Louisiana	100.0	21.9	25.8	15.1	24.9	12.3
Maine	100.0	18.1	21.2	15.5	29.3	15.9
Maryland	100.0	20.6	24.4	16.6	26.1	12.3
Massachusetts	100.0	19.1	24.6	16.3	26.2	13.8
Michigan	100.0	20.8	23.4	15.5	26.5	13.8
Minnesota	100.0	21.4	24.5	15.6	25.6	12.9
Mississippi	100.0	22.5	25.0	15.3	24.4	12.8
Missouri	100.0	21.0	24.3	15.2	25.5	14.0
Montana	100.0	19.9	23.5	14.0	27.8	14.9
Nebraska	100.0	22.4	24.9	14.7	24.5	13.5
Nevada	100.0	21.8	24.9	17.0	24.2	12.1
New Hampshire	100.0	19.0	22.0	16.4	29.0	13.6
New Jersey	100.0	20.6	23.0	16.9	26.0	13.5
New Mexico	100.0	22.3	24.5	14.7	25.3	13.2
New York	100.0	19.6	25.3	16.2	25.3	13.5
North Carolina	100.0	21.3	24.3	16.6	24.9	13.0
North Dakota	100.0	19.9	26.7	13.7	25.2	14.5
Ohio	100.0	20.8	23.4	15.4	26.3	14.1
Oklahoma	100.0	22.1	25.1	14.9	24.4	13.5
Oregon	100.0	20.0	24.3	15.7	26.1	14.0
Pennsylvania	100.0	19.3	23.3	15.3	26.6	15.5
Rhode Island	100.0	18.8	24.8	15.7	26.3	14.4
South Carolina	100.0	20.7	24.5	15.6	25.5	13.7

	total population	iGeneration (under 16)	Millennial (16 to 33)	Generation X (34 to 45)	Baby Boom (46 to 64)	Older Americans (65 or older)
South Dakota	100.0%	22.2%	24.5%	14.0%	25.0%	14.3%
Tennessee	100.0	20.9	24.0	16.1	25.6	13.5
Texas	100.0	24.3	26.2	16.5	22.6	10.4
Utah	100.0	28.4	29.2	14.7	18.7	9.0
Vermont	100.0	18.1	23.0	15.1	29.2	14.6
Virginia	100.0	20.5	25.0	16.7	25.6	12.2
Washington	100.0	20.8	24.9	16.3	25.7	12.3
West Virginia	100.0	18.5	22.2	15.4	27.8	16.1
Wisconsin	100.0	20.8	23.9	15.5	26.2	13.7
Wyoming	100.0	21.5	25.1	14.5	26.5	12.4

Source: Bureau of the Census, State Population Estimates, Internet site http://www.census.gov/popest/data/intercensal/state/state2010.html; calculations by New Strategist

Table 8.19 State Populations by Age, Race Alone or in Combination, and Hispanic Origin, 2010

(total number of people and percent distribution by age, race alone or in combination, and Hispanic origin, by state, 2010; numbers in thousands)

	total number	total percent	Asian	black	Hispanic	non-Hispanic white
Total population	**308,746**	**100.0%**	**5.6%**	**13.6%**	**16.3%**	**63.9%**
Under age 5	20,201	100.0	6.5	17.5	25.3	51.0
Aged 5 to 9	20,349	100.0	6.3	16.7	23.5	53.5
Aged 10 to 14	20,677	100.0	5.7	16.8	21.9	55.4
Aged 15 to 19	22,040	100.0	5.6	17.2	20.6	56.2
Aged 20 to 24	21,586	100.0	6.2	15.5	20.0	57.8
Aged 25 to 29	21,102	100.0	6.8	14.1	20.4	58.1
Aged 30 to 34	19,962	100.0	7.1	13.9	20.7	57.8
Aged 35 to 39	20,180	100.0	7.2	13.6	19.1	59.6
Aged 40 to 44	20,891	100.0	6.1	13.3	16.5	63.4
Aged 45 to 49	22,709	100.0	5.2	12.9	13.3	67.8
Aged 50 to 54	22,298	100.0	4.8	12.4	10.9	70.9
Aged 55 to 59	19,665	100.0	4.7	11.5	9.4	73.6
Aged 60 to 64	16,818	100.0	4.4	10.3	8.2	76.3
Aged 65 to 69	12,435	100.0	4.1	9.6	7.6	78.0
Aged 70 to 74	9,278	100.0	4.1	9.4	7.5	78.3
Aged 75 to 79	7,318	100.0	3.7	8.6	7.0	80.2
Aged 80 to 84	5,743	100.0	3.1	7.6	6.1	82.7
Aged 85 or older	5,493	100.0	2.7	7.1	4.9	84.9
Alabama	**4,780**	**100.0**	**1.4**	**26.8**	**3.9**	**67.0**
Under age 5	305	100.0	1.9	32.4	8.2	56.9
Aged 5 to 9	308	100.0	1.8	31.3	6.3	59.8
Aged 10 to 14	320	100.0	1.6	32.0	4.6	60.9
Aged 15 to 19	343	100.0	1.4	33.1	4.2	60.4
Aged 20 to 24	335	100.0	1.7	31.0	6.1	60.5
Aged 25 to 29	311	100.0	2.0	29.0	7.0	61.2
Aged 30 to 34	298	100.0	2.0	28.5	6.3	62.4
Aged 35 to 39	308	100.0	1.9	26.6	4.7	65.9
Aged 40 to 44	311	100.0	1.6	25.5	3.4	68.5
Aged 45 to 49	346	100.0	1.3	25.3	2.3	70.0
Aged 50 to 54	347	100.0	1.1	25.7	1.7	70.3
Aged 55 to 59	312	100.0	1.0	24.7	1.3	72.0
Aged 60 to 64	276	100.0	0.9	20.9	1.0	76.3
Aged 65 to 69	210	100.0	0.7	18.3	0.9	79.2
Aged 70 to 74	161	100.0	0.6	18.0	0.8	79.9
Aged 75 to 79	123	100.0	0.5	17.2	0.7	80.9
Aged 80 to 84	89	100.0	0.4	17.0	0.7	81.4
Aged 85 or older	76	100.0	0.3	18.6	0.6	80.1

	total		Asian	black	Hispanic	non-Hispanic white
	number	percent				
Alaska	**710**	**100.0%**	**7.1%**	**4.7%**	**5.5%**	**64.1%**
Under age 5	54	100.0	8.6	7.5	8.7	51.0
Aged 5 to 9	51	100.0	9.0	7.1	8.1	51.8
Aged 10 to 14	51	100.0	8.8	6.6	7.5	53.1
Aged 15 to 19	52	100.0	8.3	5.8	6.9	54.6
Aged 20 to 24	54	100.0	7.2	5.6	7.1	58.5
Aged 25 to 29	55	100.0	6.7	5.1	6.4	63.4
Aged 30 to 34	48	100.0	6.8	4.7	6.0	65.2
Aged 35 to 39	46	100.0	7.4	4.4	5.6	66.3
Aged 40 to 44	47	100.0	7.1	3.8	5.1	67.5
Aged 45 to 49	55	100.0	6.3	3.5	4.2	69.8
Aged 50 to 54	56	100.0	5.8	3.1	3.5	73.6
Aged 55 to 59	50	100.0	5.5	2.9	2.9	75.5
Aged 60 to 64	36	100.0	5.7	2.3	2.6	76.5
Aged 65 to 69	22	100.0	5.5	2.1	2.4	75.6
Aged 70 to 74	13	100.0	6.3	2.6	2.4	73.0
Aged 75 to 79	9	100.0	6.2	2.2	2.1	71.9
Aged 80 to 84	6	100.0	6.2	2.1	1.6	73.3
Aged 85 or older	5	100.0	4.9	2.1	1.7	77.8
Arizona	**6,392**	**100.0**	**3.6**	**5.0**	**29.6**	**57.8**
Under age 5	456	100.0	4.5	7.3	44.9	39.6
Aged 5 to 9	454	100.0	4.3	6.8	43.9	41.1
Aged 10 to 14	449	100.0	3.9	6.8	42.2	42.8
Aged 15 to 19	462	100.0	3.7	6.7	39.8	44.8
Aged 20 to 24	443	100.0	4.0	6.1	35.9	48.9
Aged 25 to 29	440	100.0	4.5	5.6	34.2	51.1
Aged 30 to 34	417	100.0	4.8	5.3	35.0	50.5
Aged 35 to 39	416	100.0	5.0	5.1	33.0	52.9
Aged 40 to 44	407	100.0	4.2	4.9	29.7	57.2
Aged 45 to 49	427	100.0	3.5	4.6	24.9	62.9
Aged 50 to 54	416	100.0	3.0	4.2	20.9	68.0
Aged 55 to 59	375	100.0	2.8	3.5	17.6	72.6
Aged 60 to 64	351	100.0	2.4	2.8	14.1	77.7
Aged 65 to 69	283	100.0	2.0	2.4	12.1	80.7
Aged 70 to 74	215	100.0	2.0	2.2	11.4	81.7
Aged 75 to 79	162	100.0	1.8	2.0	10.7	83.2
Aged 80 to 84	118	100.0	1.3	1.6	9.9	85.1
Aged 85 or older	103	100.0	1.1	1.5	8.2	87.3

| | total | | | | | non-Hispanic |
	number	percent	Asian	black	Hispanic	white
Arkansas	**2,916**	**100.0%**	**1.5%**	**16.1%**	**6.4%**	**74.5%**
Under age 5	198	100.0	2.1	21.4	12.5	62.7
Aged 5 to 9	197	100.0	2.0	20.2	11.1	65.1
Aged 10 to 14	198	100.0	1.7	20.6	9.3	66.9
Aged 15 to 19	204	100.0	1.7	20.6	8.2	67.8
Aged 20 to 24	200	100.0	2.1	18.9	8.4	69.0
Aged 25 to 29	192	100.0	2.3	17.6	9.2	69.4
Aged 30 to 34	184	100.0	2.2	17.2	9.1	69.9
Aged 35 to 39	184	100.0	2.0	15.5	7.9	73.1
Aged 40 to 44	183	100.0	1.7	15.1	6.3	75.4
Aged 45 to 49	206	100.0	1.3	15.0	4.3	77.8
Aged 50 to 54	202	100.0	1.2	15.2	3.3	78.7
Aged 55 to 59	184	100.0	1.1	14.4	2.4	80.7
Aged 60 to 64	167	100.0	0.9	11.4	1.8	84.6
Aged 65 to 69	133	100.0	0.7	9.2	1.3	87.5
Aged 70 to 74	101	100.0	0.6	8.9	1.2	88.3
Aged 75 to 79	78	100.0	0.5	8.5	0.9	89.1
Aged 80 to 84	56	100.0	0.4	8.8	0.8	89.1
Aged 85 or older	51	100.0	0.3	9.8	0.6	88.6
California	**37,254**	**100.0**	**14.9**	**7.2**	**37.6**	**40.1**
Under age 5	2,531	100.0	14.7	8.5	53.3	25.5
Aged 5 to 9	2,506	100.0	14.6	8.2	51.6	27.0
Aged 10 to 14	2,591	100.0	13.9	8.5	50.3	28.3
Aged 15 to 19	2,824	100.0	13.9	8.7	47.9	30.0
Aged 20 to 24	2,766	100.0	14.7	7.9	44.0	33.4
Aged 25 to 29	2,744	100.0	15.4	6.9	42.6	34.8
Aged 30 to 34	2,573	100.0	16.1	6.7	42.9	33.9
Aged 35 to 39	2,574	100.0	17.1	6.5	41.3	34.7
Aged 40 to 44	2,609	100.0	15.7	6.9	37.6	39.2
Aged 45 to 49	2,690	100.0	14.9	7.2	31.6	45.3
Aged 50 to 54	2,563	100.0	14.8	7.1	27.1	49.9
Aged 55 to 59	2,204	100.0	15.0	6.6	23.5	53.9
Aged 60 to 64	1,832	100.0	14.6	6.1	20.3	57.9
Aged 65 to 69	1,304	100.0	14.1	6.0	19.4	59.5
Aged 70 to 74	972	100.0	15.1	6.2	19.0	58.9
Aged 75 to 79	767	100.0	14.6	5.5	18.0	61.2
Aged 80 to 84	603	100.0	13.1	4.6	16.1	65.4
Aged 85 or older	601	100.0	11.2	4.5	12.6	71.2

	total		Asian	black	Hispanic	non-Hispanic white
	number	percent				
Colorado	**5,029**	**100.0%**	**3.7%**	**5.0%**	**20.7%**	**70.0%**
Under age 5	344	100.0	4.9	7.4	32.8	55.5
Aged 5 to 9	349	100.0	4.9	6.8	31.3	57.1
Aged 10 to 14	333	100.0	4.5	6.7	29.3	59.4
Aged 15 to 19	339	100.0	4.0	6.6	26.8	62.0
Aged 20 to 24	349	100.0	4.1	5.7	24.1	65.2
Aged 25 to 29	372	100.0	4.2	5.0	23.3	66.5
Aged 30 to 34	354	100.0	4.3	4.9	23.9	66.1
Aged 35 to 39	354	100.0	4.6	4.7	22.2	67.6
Aged 40 to 44	346	100.0	3.9	4.6	19.3	71.1
Aged 45 to 49	372	100.0	3.2	4.5	15.9	75.3
Aged 50 to 54	371	100.0	2.7	4.1	13.1	79.0
Aged 55 to 59	328	100.0	2.4	3.6	11.4	81.5
Aged 60 to 64	269	100.0	2.3	3.0	10.6	83.2
Aged 65 to 69	182	100.0	2.3	3.0	10.3	83.5
Aged 70 to 74	127	100.0	2.3	3.1	10.9	82.8
Aged 75 to 79	97	100.0	2.3	3.0	10.1	83.9
Aged 80 to 84	73	100.0	2.0	2.4	8.9	86.2
Aged 85 or older	70	100.0	1.6	1.9	7.1	89.0
Connecticut	**3,574**	**100.0**	**4.4**	**11.3**	**13.4**	**71.2**
Under age 5	202	100.0	7.1	16.5	23.2	55.5
Aged 5 to 9	223	100.0	6.1	14.9	19.7	60.9
Aged 10 to 14	240	100.0	4.7	14.7	18.1	63.7
Aged 15 to 19	251	100.0	4.1	15.2	17.6	64.1
Aged 20 to 24	228	100.0	4.9	14.4	18.3	63.0
Aged 25 to 29	214	100.0	6.9	13.3	19.4	60.8
Aged 30 to 34	206	100.0	7.3	13.1	19.7	60.1
Aged 35 to 39	222	100.0	6.6	12.0	16.5	65.0
Aged 40 to 44	262	100.0	4.7	11.1	13.3	70.9
Aged 45 to 49	291	100.0	3.6	10.0	10.4	75.8
Aged 50 to 54	284	100.0	3.0	9.0	8.3	79.5
Aged 55 to 59	240	100.0	2.8	8.0	7.0	82.1
Aged 60 to 64	203	100.0	2.5	7.7	6.2	83.4
Aged 65 to 69	149	100.0	2.3	7.5	5.6	84.5
Aged 70 to 74	106	100.0	2.2	7.6	5.4	84.6
Aged 75 to 79	89	100.0	1.7	6.2	4.2	87.8
Aged 80 to 84	77	100.0	1.1	4.8	3.1	90.9
Aged 85 or older	85	100.0	0.6	3.9	2.2	93.1

	total					non-Hispanic
	number	percent	Asian	black	Hispanic	white
Delaware	**898**	**100.0%**	**3.8%**	**22.9%**	**8.2%**	**65.3%**
Under age 5	56	100.0	5.2	31.1	16.2	49.3
Aged 5 to 9	56	100.0	4.9	30.4	14.0	52.0
Aged 10 to 14	57	100.0	3.9	30.6	11.4	55.1
Aged 15 to 19	65	100.0	3.7	29.3	10.0	57.7
Aged 20 to 24	63	100.0	3.9	25.1	11.2	60.1
Aged 25 to 29	58	100.0	5.6	23.4	12.8	58.5
Aged 30 to 34	54	100.0	6.0	23.9	12.3	58.0
Aged 35 to 39	55	100.0	5.5	23.9	10.3	60.3
Aged 40 to 44	61	100.0	4.1	24.1	7.8	64.0
Aged 45 to 49	68	100.0	3.3	22.2	5.4	68.8
Aged 50 to 54	66	100.0	2.7	20.6	4.0	72.3
Aged 55 to 59	58	100.0	2.5	18.7	3.3	75.2
Aged 60 to 64	53	100.0	2.3	16.4	2.6	78.3
Aged 65 to 69	42	100.0	2.3	14.5	2.1	80.7
Aged 70 to 74	31	100.0	2.3	14.0	2.1	81.2
Aged 75 to 79	24	100.0	1.6	12.6	1.7	83.7
Aged 80 to 84	17	100.0	1.2	10.7	1.7	86.0
Aged 85 or older	16	100.0	1.0	10.8	1.4	86.5
District of Columbia	**602**	**100.0**	**4.5**	**52.2**	**9.1**	**34.8**
Under age 5	33	100.0	4.5	59.6	13.8	23.8
Aged 5 to 9	26	100.0	3.2	67.5	12.6	18.3
Aged 10 to 14	25	100.0	2.4	75.5	10.4	12.9
Aged 15 to 19	40	100.0	4.0	63.0	9.0	25.2
Aged 20 to 24	64	100.0	6.3	38.7	9.5	46.1
Aged 25 to 29	70	100.0	6.7	31.4	10.3	51.9
Aged 30 to 34	55	100.0	7.2	35.5	11.5	46.4
Aged 35 to 39	43	100.0	6.2	43.0	11.7	39.7
Aged 40 to 44	38	100.0	4.1	51.5	10.2	34.7
Aged 45 to 49	39	100.0	3.0	60.5	8.5	28.4
Aged 50 to 54	37	100.0	2.7	64.1	7.2	26.5
Aged 55 to 59	34	100.0	2.6	62.2	5.8	29.6
Aged 60 to 64	30	100.0	2.7	58.0	5.3	34.2
Aged 65 to 69	21	100.0	2.3	57.7	4.8	35.3
Aged 70 to 74	15	100.0	2.5	64.1	4.7	29.0
Aged 75 to 79	12	100.0	2.2	67.6	3.6	26.6
Aged 80 to 84	10	100.0	1.8	67.9	3.5	27.0
Aged 85 or older	10	100.0	1.9	63.4	2.5	32.2

| | total | | | | | non-Hispanic |
	number	percent	Asian	black	Hispanic	white
Florida	**18,801**	**100.0%**	**3.0%**	**17.0%**	**22.5%**	**57.9%**
Under age 5	1,074	100.0	4.0	25.4	29.1	43.2
Aged 5 to 9	1,080	100.0	4.0	24.1	27.7	45.4
Aged 10 to 14	1,131	100.0	3.5	23.4	26.9	47.0
Aged 15 to 19	1,228	100.0	3.3	23.7	26.1	47.7
Aged 20 to 24	1,229	100.0	3.5	21.8	26.4	48.9
Aged 25 to 29	1,179	100.0	3.8	20.3	27.0	49.5
Aged 30 to 34	1,110	100.0	4.1	19.3	28.8	48.3
Aged 35 to 39	1,178	100.0	4.1	17.9	28.3	50.1
Aged 40 to 44	1,253	100.0	3.6	16.6	25.8	54.3
Aged 45 to 49	1,401	100.0	2.9	15.6	22.8	58.9
Aged 50 to 54	1,340	100.0	2.7	15.2	18.6	63.4
Aged 55 to 59	1,202	100.0	2.6	13.6	16.6	67.1
Aged 60 to 64	1,135	100.0	2.2	10.9	14.3	72.5
Aged 65 to 69	959	100.0	1.9	9.3	13.7	75.2
Aged 70 to 74	769	100.0	1.7	8.9	14.4	75.1
Aged 75 to 79	616	100.0	1.3	7.7	13.8	77.3
Aged 80 to 84	482	100.0	0.9	6.5	12.6	80.1
Aged 85 or older	434	100.0	0.7	6.0	11.2	82.2
Georgia	**9,688**	**100.0**	**3.8**	**31.5**	**8.8**	**55.9**
Under age 5	687	100.0	4.4	36.5	15.5	44.3
Aged 5 to 9	695	100.0	4.4	35.6	13.4	47.1
Aged 10 to 14	690	100.0	3.9	36.8	10.8	48.7
Aged 15 to 19	710	100.0	3.7	38.3	9.7	48.4
Aged 20 to 24	680	100.0	4.0	34.7	11.6	49.9
Aged 25 to 29	674	100.0	4.6	32.6	13.4	49.7
Aged 30 to 34	662	100.0	4.8	32.7	13.2	49.4
Aged 35 to 39	698	100.0	5.1	31.8	10.6	52.6
Aged 40 to 44	699	100.0	4.2	31.3	8.2	56.1
Aged 45 to 49	723	100.0	3.5	30.7	5.9	59.6
Aged 50 to 54	669	100.0	3.2	29.6	4.4	62.4
Aged 55 to 59	574	100.0	2.9	28.1	3.3	65.3
Aged 60 to 64	496	100.0	2.6	24.5	2.5	70.0
Aged 65 to 69	356	100.0	2.5	22.2	2.2	72.7
Aged 70 to 74	250	100.0	2.3	21.5	2.1	73.7
Aged 75 to 79	183	100.0	1.9	19.9	1.8	76.1
Aged 80 to 84	129	100.0	1.4	18.7	1.7	77.9
Aged 85 or older	114	100.0	1.0	19.3	1.4	78.1

| | total | | | | | non-Hispanic |
	number	percent	Asian	black	Hispanic	white
Hawaii	**1,360**	**100.0%**	**57.4%**	**2.9%**	**8.9%**	**22.7%**
Under age 5	87	100.0	58.4	5.4	16.9	14.7
Aged 5 to 9	83	100.0	61.4	4.9	15.3	13.0
Aged 10 to 14	82	100.0	63.0	4.4	13.6	12.4
Aged 15 to 19	86	100.0	61.9	3.8	12.6	13.7
Aged 20 to 24	96	100.0	49.0	4.3	11.5	25.7
Aged 25 to 29	97	100.0	49.3	4.0	10.7	26.5
Aged 30 to 34	88	100.0	52.2	3.6	10.2	24.3
Aged 35 to 39	87	100.0	55.8	3.1	9.0	22.5
Aged 40 to 44	90	100.0	57.4	2.6	7.7	22.9
Aged 45 to 49	96	100.0	57.1	2.0	6.8	24.2
Aged 50 to 54	98	100.0	56.6	1.7	5.8	26.7
Aged 55 to 59	93	100.0	55.3	1.4	4.7	30.2
Aged 60 to 64	82	100.0	54.7	1.1	3.9	32.3
Aged 65 to 69	59	100.0	57.4	0.9	3.9	29.7
Aged 70 to 74	41	100.0	62.5	0.7	3.7	25.5
Aged 75 to 79	35	100.0	67.6	0.6	3.3	21.8
Aged 80 to 84	30	100.0	71.8	0.5	2.5	20.1
Aged 85 or older	30	100.0	73.4	0.4	2.1	20.6
Idaho	**1,568**	**100.0**	**1.9**	**1.0**	**11.2**	**84.0**
Under age 5	122	100.0	2.4	2.0	18.8	75.1
Aged 5 to 9	121	100.0	2.4	1.8	17.1	76.7
Aged 10 to 14	117	100.0	2.3	1.7	16.1	77.9
Aged 15 to 19	115	100.0	2.2	1.6	15.2	78.7
Aged 20 to 24	108	100.0	2.3	1.4	14.2	79.9
Aged 25 to 29	107	100.0	2.4	1.1	14.1	80.4
Aged 30 to 34	102	100.0	2.3	1.0	13.2	81.6
Aged 35 to 39	97	100.0	2.4	0.9	12.6	82.1
Aged 40 to 44	95	100.0	2.0	0.8	10.8	84.4
Aged 45 to 49	104	100.0	1.7	0.6	8.5	87.2
Aged 50 to 54	105	100.0	1.4	0.5	6.4	89.6
Aged 55 to 59	97	100.0	1.3	0.4	5.0	91.4
Aged 60 to 64	83	100.0	1.1	0.3	4.0	92.9
Aged 65 to 69	63	100.0	1.0	0.2	3.5	93.7
Aged 70 to 74	46	100.0	0.8	0.2	3.1	94.4
Aged 75 to 79	34	100.0	0.9	0.1	2.8	94.9
Aged 80 to 84	26	100.0	0.9	0.2	2.1	95.8
Aged 85 or older	25	100.0	0.9	0.2	1.7	96.5

	total		Asian	black	Hispanic	non-Hispanic white
	number	percent				
Illinois	**12,831**	**100.0%**	**5.2%**	**15.4%**	**15.8%**	**63.7%**
Under age 5	836	100.0	6.3	18.7	25.5	50.4
Aged 5 to 9	859	100.0	5.9	18.2	24.1	52.4
Aged 10 to 14	879	100.0	5.0	19.2	21.9	54.4
Aged 15 to 19	922	100.0	4.6	20.3	19.7	55.7
Aged 20 to 24	879	100.0	5.8	17.1	19.2	58.1
Aged 25 to 29	910	100.0	6.7	14.6	19.6	59.1
Aged 30 to 34	866	100.0	7.0	14.5	20.7	57.8
Aged 35 to 39	856	100.0	6.9	14.9	19.5	58.7
Aged 40 to 44	870	100.0	5.6	14.4	16.0	63.9
Aged 45 to 49	940	100.0	4.4	14.3	11.9	69.1
Aged 50 to 54	931	100.0	4.1	14.3	9.8	71.6
Aged 55 to 59	808	100.0	4.4	13.4	8.3	73.6
Aged 60 to 64	665	100.0	4.5	12.6	7.1	75.5
Aged 65 to 69	485	100.0	4.4	12.5	6.3	76.6
Aged 70 to 74	364	100.0	3.9	12.7	5.8	77.4
Aged 75 to 79	289	100.0	3.0	11.7	5.2	79.9
Aged 80 to 84	235	100.0	2.3	9.8	4.0	83.6
Aged 85 or older	235	100.0	1.8	8.5	2.8	86.8
Indiana	**6,484**	**100.0**	**2.0**	**10.1**	**6.0**	**81.5**
Under age 5	434	100.0	2.7	15.0	11.6	70.6
Aged 5 to 9	445	100.0	2.5	13.8	10.2	73.3
Aged 10 to 14	452	100.0	2.1	13.4	8.3	75.8
Aged 15 to 19	476	100.0	2.2	12.8	7.2	77.4
Aged 20 to 24	452	100.0	3.1	11.0	7.3	78.2
Aged 25 to 29	420	100.0	2.9	10.8	8.4	77.6
Aged 30 to 34	408	100.0	2.7	10.7	8.7	77.6
Aged 35 to 39	417	100.0	2.6	10.0	7.2	79.7
Aged 40 to 44	424	100.0	2.1	9.2	5.5	82.7
Aged 45 to 49	474	100.0	1.5	8.6	3.9	85.3
Aged 50 to 54	473	100.0	1.2	8.5	3.2	86.5
Aged 55 to 59	419	100.0	1.1	7.7	2.5	88.0
Aged 60 to 64	351	100.0	1.1	6.7	2.1	89.6
Aged 65 to 69	259	100.0	0.9	6.5	1.7	90.3
Aged 70 to 74	193	100.0	0.8	6.2	1.6	91.0
Aged 75 to 79	152	100.0	0.7	6.0	1.6	91.3
Aged 80 to 84	122	100.0	0.5	5.2	1.4	92.5
Aged 85 or older	115	100.0	0.3	4.8	1.0	93.5

	total		Asian	black	Hispanic	non-Hispanic white
	number	percent				
Iowa	**3,046**	**100.0%**	**2.1%**	**3.7%**	**5.0%**	**88.7%**
Under age 5	202	100.0	2.9	7.6	10.3	78.8
Aged 5 to 9	201	100.0	2.9	6.8	9.1	80.8
Aged 10 to 14	201	100.0	2.5	6.1	7.8	83.0
Aged 15 to 19	217	100.0	2.6	5.6	6.8	84.4
Aged 20 to 24	213	100.0	3.7	4.8	6.6	84.3
Aged 25 to 29	198	100.0	3.3	4.2	6.7	85.2
Aged 30 to 34	185	100.0	3.0	4.0	6.6	85.7
Aged 35 to 39	177	100.0	3.0	3.7	6.1	86.6
Aged 40 to 44	187	100.0	2.3	3.0	4.9	89.2
Aged 45 to 49	216	100.0	1.6	2.6	3.3	92.0
Aged 50 to 54	223	100.0	1.2	2.2	2.4	93.7
Aged 55 to 59	204	100.0	1.1	1.8	1.8	94.8
Aged 60 to 64	168	100.0	1.0	1.5	1.5	95.6
Aged 65 to 69	124	100.0	0.9	1.3	1.2	96.2
Aged 70 to 74	100	100.0	0.8	1.2	1.0	96.7
Aged 75 to 79	83	100.0	0.6	1.0	0.8	97.3
Aged 80 to 84	70	100.0	0.4	0.9	0.7	97.8
Aged 85 or older	75	100.0	0.2	0.7	0.6	98.4
Kansas	**2,853**	**100.0**	**2.9**	**7.1**	**10.5**	**78.2**
Under age 5	205	100.0	4.0	11.1	19.1	65.3
Aged 5 to 9	202	100.0	3.9	9.9	17.5	67.9
Aged 10 to 14	199	100.0	3.3	9.5	15.4	70.5
Aged 15 to 19	204	100.0	3.1	9.4	13.6	72.4
Aged 20 to 24	204	100.0	3.9	8.4	12.7	73.5
Aged 25 to 29	198	100.0	3.9	7.6	13.2	73.9
Aged 30 to 34	180	100.0	3.9	7.2	13.7	73.8
Aged 35 to 39	172	100.0	4.2	6.6	12.7	74.9
Aged 40 to 44	174	100.0	3.3	6.3	10.5	78.2
Aged 45 to 49	202	100.0	2.3	6.2	7.3	82.7
Aged 50 to 54	204	100.0	2.0	5.9	5.6	85.1
Aged 55 to 59	183	100.0	1.9	4.9	4.4	87.4
Aged 60 to 64	149	100.0	1.8	4.5	3.7	88.7
Aged 65 to 69	108	100.0	1.7	4.2	3.3	89.7
Aged 70 to 74	83	100.0	1.4	4.2	3.0	90.3
Aged 75 to 79	69	100.0	1.0	3.6	2.7	91.8
Aged 80 to 84	57	100.0	0.7	3.1	2.4	93.1
Aged 85 or older	59	100.0	0.5	2.6	1.7	94.6

	total		Asian	black	Hispanic	non-Hispanic white
	number	percent				
Kentucky	**4,339**	**100.0%**	**1.4%**	**8.7%**	**3.1%**	**86.3%**
Under age 5	282	100.0	2.2	13.0	6.6	78.0
Aged 5 to 9	283	100.0	2.2	11.8	5.2	80.4
Aged 10 to 14	284	100.0	1.7	11.3	3.8	82.7
Aged 15 to 19	297	100.0	1.4	11.5	3.5	83.1
Aged 20 to 24	290	100.0	1.7	10.5	4.5	82.8
Aged 25 to 29	285	100.0	2.0	9.2	5.0	83.3
Aged 30 to 34	281	100.0	2.1	9.1	4.5	83.9
Aged 35 to 39	285	100.0	2.0	8.2	3.8	85.5
Aged 40 to 44	291	100.0	1.6	7.8	2.7	87.4
Aged 45 to 49	324	100.0	1.1	7.6	2.0	88.6
Aged 50 to 54	319	100.0	0.9	7.6	1.3	89.4
Aged 55 to 59	288	100.0	0.8	6.9	1.0	90.7
Aged 60 to 64	251	100.0	0.8	5.7	0.8	92.1
Aged 65 to 69	186	100.0	0.7	5.0	0.8	92.9
Aged 70 to 74	140	100.0	0.6	4.9	0.7	93.2
Aged 75 to 79	105	100.0	0.5	4.9	0.7	93.4
Aged 80 to 84	78	100.0	0.4	4.8	0.6	93.7
Aged 85 or older	69	100.0	0.3	5.1	0.5	93.7
Louisiana	**4,533**	**100.0**	**1.9**	**32.8**	**4.2**	**60.3**
Under age 5	314	100.0	2.1	40.4	6.2	50.8
Aged 5 to 9	306	100.0	2.1	39.8	4.8	52.6
Aged 10 to 14	307	100.0	1.8	39.2	4.1	53.9
Aged 15 to 19	327	100.0	1.8	40.3	4.2	52.8
Aged 20 to 24	338	100.0	2.3	36.6	5.7	54.7
Aged 25 to 29	333	100.0	2.5	33.8	6.3	56.8
Aged 30 to 34	296	100.0	2.4	33.4	6.1	57.4
Aged 35 to 39	276	100.0	2.5	30.9	5.4	60.4
Aged 40 to 44	288	100.0	2.0	31.0	4.3	61.7
Aged 45 to 49	325	100.0	1.6	30.6	3.5	63.3
Aged 50 to 54	329	100.0	1.6	30.3	2.9	64.4
Aged 55 to 59	293	100.0	1.6	29.3	2.6	65.8
Aged 60 to 64	243	100.0	1.4	26.5	2.3	69.0
Aged 65 to 69	178	100.0	1.2	24.4	2.2	71.5
Aged 70 to 74	134	100.0	1.1	23.7	2.3	72.3
Aged 75 to 79	103	100.0	0.9	21.9	2.1	74.4
Aged 80 to 84	77	100.0	0.7	20.0	2.0	76.7
Aged 85 or older	66	100.0	0.6	20.9	1.8	76.2

	total		Asian	black	Hispanic	non-Hispanic white
	number	percent				
Maine	**1,328**	**100.0%**	**1.4%**	**1.6%**	**1.3%**	**94.4%**
Under age 5	70	100.0	2.4	5.0	2.9	88.1
Aged 5 to 9	74	100.0	2.3	3.8	2.4	89.9
Aged 10 to 14	79	100.0	2.1	3.3	2.0	91.1
Aged 15 to 19	88	100.0	2.3	2.9	2.1	91.1
Aged 20 to 24	80	100.0	1.9	2.5	2.0	92.0
Aged 25 to 29	73	100.0	1.9	1.9	1.8	92.8
Aged 30 to 34	72	100.0	1.8	1.7	1.7	93.4
Aged 35 to 39	80	100.0	1.8	1.6	1.2	94.1
Aged 40 to 44	91	100.0	1.4	1.2	1.1	94.9
Aged 45 to 49	108	100.0	1.0	0.9	0.9	95.9
Aged 50 to 54	111	100.0	0.9	0.7	0.7	96.4
Aged 55 to 59	102	100.0	0.8	0.6	0.6	96.9
Aged 60 to 64	90	100.0	0.6	0.4	0.5	97.4
Aged 65 to 69	65	100.0	0.5	0.4	0.4	97.7
Aged 70 to 74	48	100.0	0.6	0.4	0.4	97.8
Aged 75 to 79	39	100.0	0.4	0.3	0.4	98.3
Aged 80 to 84	30	100.0	0.3	0.2	0.3	98.6
Aged 85 or older	29	100.0	0.2	0.3	0.3	98.8
Maryland	**5,774**	**100.0**	**6.4**	**30.9**	**8.2**	**54.7**
Under age 5	364	100.0	8.0	36.6	13.8	42.8
Aged 5 to 9	367	100.0	7.6	35.7	11.2	46.3
Aged 10 to 14	379	100.0	6.6	36.1	9.5	48.4
Aged 15 to 19	406	100.0	6.1	36.5	8.9	48.9
Aged 20 to 24	394	100.0	6.4	33.5	11.1	49.3
Aged 25 to 29	394	100.0	7.3	31.3	12.8	48.8
Aged 30 to 34	368	100.0	8.4	31.8	13.2	46.8
Aged 35 to 39	377	100.0	8.5	32.1	10.8	48.7
Aged 40 to 44	418	100.0	6.9	31.9	8.2	53.0
Aged 45 to 49	462	100.0	5.8	30.4	6.0	57.5
Aged 50 to 54	441	100.0	5.5	28.9	4.7	60.7
Aged 55 to 59	378	100.0	5.2	27.3	3.8	63.5
Aged 60 to 64	318	100.0	5.1	25.8	3.0	65.7
Aged 65 to 69	227	100.0	5.0	24.3	2.7	67.7
Aged 70 to 74	160	100.0	5.3	24.0	2.6	67.9
Aged 75 to 79	125	100.0	4.3	21.9	2.4	71.2
Aged 80 to 84	99	100.0	3.2	18.2	2.0	76.4
Aged 85 or older	98	100.0	2.3	16.3	1.5	79.7

	total		Asian	black	Hispanic	non-Hispanic white
	number	percent				
Massachusetts	**6,548**	**100.0%**	**6.0%**	**7.8%**	**9.6%**	**76.1%**
Under age 5	367	100.0	8.5	11.8	17.2	62.6
Aged 5 to 9	386	100.0	7.8	10.7	14.7	67.2
Aged 10 to 14	406	100.0	6.2	10.3	13.7	69.9
Aged 15 to 19	463	100.0	6.5	10.6	13.6	69.3
Aged 20 to 24	476	100.0	7.9	9.5	12.8	69.4
Aged 25 to 29	442	100.0	8.8	8.5	12.6	69.0
Aged 30 to 34	404	100.0	8.9	8.7	13.0	68.2
Aged 35 to 39	418	100.0	8.5	8.1	11.0	71.5
Aged 40 to 44	469	100.0	6.1	7.4	9.1	76.5
Aged 45 to 49	515	100.0	4.9	6.7	7.3	80.3
Aged 50 to 54	497	100.0	4.2	6.3	5.9	82.9
Aged 55 to 59	433	100.0	3.9	5.6	5.0	85.0
Aged 60 to 64	371	100.0	3.4	5.0	4.3	86.8
Aged 65 to 69	264	100.0	3.3	4.9	3.9	87.5
Aged 70 to 74	192	100.0	3.6	4.8	3.7	87.5
Aged 75 to 79	163	100.0	2.9	4.1	2.9	89.5
Aged 80 to 84	138	100.0	2.1	3.3	2.1	92.0
Aged 85 or older	145	100.0	1.5	2.9	1.5	93.7
Michigan	**9,884**	**100.0**	**2.9**	**15.2**	**4.4**	**76.6**
Under age 5	596	100.0	4.2	20.8	8.8	65.8
Aged 5 to 9	638	100.0	4.1	18.9	7.8	68.6
Aged 10 to 14	675	100.0	3.4	18.9	6.6	70.2
Aged 15 to 19	740	100.0	3.1	20.1	5.7	70.3
Aged 20 to 24	669	100.0	3.8	17.5	5.4	72.4
Aged 25 to 29	590	100.0	4.0	15.8	5.8	73.5
Aged 30 to 34	575	100.0	4.3	16.0	5.9	72.9
Aged 35 to 39	612	100.0	4.1	16.5	5.1	73.3
Aged 40 to 44	665	100.0	3.2	14.6	3.9	77.3
Aged 45 to 49	745	100.0	2.4	12.9	3.0	80.6
Aged 50 to 54	765	100.0	1.9	13.0	2.4	81.8
Aged 55 to 59	683	100.0	1.7	12.5	2.1	82.8
Aged 60 to 64	569	100.0	1.8	12.0	1.9	83.5
Aged 65 to 69	419	100.0	1.7	10.7	1.6	85.2
Aged 70 to 74	306	100.0	1.6	10.1	1.5	86.1
Aged 75 to 79	244	100.0	1.2	10.2	1.5	86.6
Aged 80 to 84	201	100.0	0.9	9.2	1.3	88.2
Aged 85 or older	192	100.0	0.6	8.8	1.0	89.1

	total		Asian	black	Hispanic	non-Hispanic white
	number	percent				
Minnesota	**5,304**	**100.0%**	**4.7%**	**6.2%**	**4.7%**	**83.1%**
Under age 5	356	100.0	7.5	12.0	9.5	69.3
Aged 5 to 9	356	100.0	7.0	10.5	8.4	72.5
Aged 10 to 14	352	100.0	6.2	9.2	6.9	75.9
Aged 15 to 19	368	100.0	6.3	8.7	6.1	77.1
Aged 20 to 24	356	100.0	6.7	7.9	6.1	77.5
Aged 25 to 29	373	100.0	6.5	7.3	6.5	78.2
Aged 30 to 34	343	100.0	6.1	6.9	6.9	78.7
Aged 35 to 39	328	100.0	6.1	6.8	6.0	79.8
Aged 40 to 44	353	100.0	4.4	5.7	4.3	84.2
Aged 45 to 49	406	100.0	3.0	4.3	2.9	88.4
Aged 50 to 54	402	100.0	2.4	3.8	2.1	90.4
Aged 55 to 59	350	100.0	2.2	3.1	1.7	91.9
Aged 60 to 64	280	100.0	2.1	2.5	1.3	92.9
Aged 65 to 69	203	100.0	2.0	2.2	1.1	93.8
Aged 70 to 74	152	100.0	1.8	1.9	1.0	94.5
Aged 75 to 79	122	100.0	1.5	1.6	0.9	95.4
Aged 80 to 84	100	100.0	1.2	1.2	0.6	96.6
Aged 85 or older	107	100.0	0.9	0.9	0.5	97.4
Mississippi	**2,967**	**100.0**	**1.1**	**37.6**	**2.7**	**58.0**
Under age 5	211	100.0	1.2	45.8	4.7	47.8
Aged 5 to 9	206	100.0	1.3	44.3	3.6	50.2
Aged 10 to 14	208	100.0	1.1	44.9	2.8	50.7
Aged 15 to 19	225	100.0	1.1	45.8	2.8	49.8
Aged 20 to 24	211	100.0	1.3	41.9	4.2	52.1
Aged 25 to 29	199	100.0	1.5	40.5	4.8	52.8
Aged 30 to 34	188	100.0	1.4	40.0	4.4	53.6
Aged 35 to 39	187	100.0	1.5	37.4	3.5	57.1
Aged 40 to 44	188	100.0	1.3	36.3	2.7	59.2
Aged 45 to 49	208	100.0	1.0	35.3	2.0	61.1
Aged 50 to 54	209	100.0	0.9	35.5	1.5	61.4
Aged 55 to 59	187	100.0	0.9	33.7	1.1	63.8
Aged 60 to 64	161	100.0	0.7	28.6	0.9	69.3
Aged 65 to 69	121	100.0	0.6	25.5	0.9	72.6
Aged 70 to 74	94	100.0	0.5	24.8	0.7	73.5
Aged 75 to 79	70	100.0	0.5	22.9	0.7	75.6
Aged 80 to 84	52	100.0	0.4	22.5	0.6	76.1
Aged 85 or older	44	100.0	0.3	25.1	0.5	73.8

	total		Asian	black	Hispanic	non-Hispanic white
	number	percent				
Missouri	**5,989**	**100.0%**	**2.1%**	**12.5%**	**3.5%**	**81.0%**
Under age 5	390	100.0	2.8	17.2	6.9	72.4
Aged 5 to 9	390	100.0	2.7	16.2	6.0	74.4
Aged 10 to 14	397	100.0	2.3	16.0	4.9	75.9
Aged 15 to 19	424	100.0	2.2	16.8	4.5	75.4
Aged 20 to 24	413	100.0	2.9	14.5	4.8	76.9
Aged 25 to 29	403	100.0	2.9	13.0	4.8	78.4
Aged 30 to 34	372	100.0	3.0	12.9	4.8	78.5
Aged 35 to 39	368	100.0	2.9	12.8	4.2	79.1
Aged 40 to 44	381	100.0	2.3	12.1	3.3	81.3
Aged 45 to 49	445	100.0	1.6	11.2	2.4	83.7
Aged 50 to 54	444	100.0	1.3	11.0	1.9	84.6
Aged 55 to 59	390	100.0	1.3	10.0	1.6	86.1
Aged 60 to 64	333	100.0	1.2	8.8	1.3	87.7
Aged 65 to 69	257	100.0	1.1	8.1	1.1	88.8
Aged 70 to 74	193	100.0	1.0	7.8	1.1	89.3
Aged 75 to 79	155	100.0	0.8	7.4	1.0	90.2
Aged 80 to 84	119	100.0	0.6	6.7	0.9	91.3
Aged 85 or older	114	100.0	0.4	6.1	0.8	92.2
Montana	**989**	**100.0**	**1.1**	**0.8**	**2.9**	**87.8**
Under age 5	62	100.0	1.6	2.0	5.5	78.2
Aged 5 to 9	61	100.0	1.5	1.8	5.1	79.7
Aged 10 to 14	61	100.0	1.5	1.5	4.7	81.8
Aged 15 to 19	67	100.0	1.6	1.4	4.4	82.4
Aged 20 to 24	67	100.0	1.7	1.3	4.1	83.7
Aged 25 to 29	64	100.0	1.3	0.9	3.5	85.9
Aged 30 to 34	59	100.0	1.3	0.8	3.2	86.8
Aged 35 to 39	56	100.0	1.2	0.6	3.0	87.5
Aged 40 to 44	57	100.0	1.1	0.5	2.6	88.7
Aged 45 to 49	71	100.0	0.8	0.4	2.2	89.9
Aged 50 to 54	79	100.0	0.7	0.4	1.7	91.2
Aged 55 to 59	76	100.0	0.6	0.3	1.5	92.8
Aged 60 to 64	63	100.0	0.6	0.2	1.3	93.6
Aged 65 to 69	47	100.0	0.4	0.2	1.1	94.3
Aged 70 to 74	34	100.0	0.4	0.2	1.1	94.2
Aged 75 to 79	26	100.0	0.4	0.2	1.0	95.0
Aged 80 to 84	20	100.0	0.3	0.1	0.8	96.5
Aged 85 or older	20	100.0	0.3	0.1	0.7	97.3

	total		Asian	black	Hispanic	non-Hispanic white
	number	percent				
Nebraska	**1,826**	**100.0%**	**2.2%**	**5.4%**	**9.2%**	**82.1%**
Under age 5	132	100.0	3.1	9.2	17.2	69.2
Aged 5 to 9	129	100.0	3.0	8.2	15.6	71.8
Aged 10 to 14	123	100.0	2.6	7.7	13.9	74.4
Aged 15 to 19	129	100.0	2.5	7.3	12.1	76.7
Aged 20 to 24	129	100.0	3.2	6.4	11.3	77.9
Aged 25 to 29	129	100.0	3.2	6.0	11.6	78.1
Aged 30 to 34	116	100.0	3.0	5.7	12.0	78.1
Aged 35 to 39	110	100.0	3.1	5.4	11.2	79.3
Aged 40 to 44	110	100.0	2.5	4.9	9.3	82.1
Aged 45 to 49	128	100.0	1.6	4.5	6.1	86.7
Aged 50 to 54	130	100.0	1.3	4.0	4.7	89.0
Aged 55 to 59	118	100.0	1.2	3.4	3.6	90.8
Aged 60 to 64	95	100.0	1.2	3.0	3.0	92.0
Aged 65 to 69	69	100.0	1.1	2.7	2.5	93.0
Aged 70 to 74	54	100.0	0.9	2.6	2.1	93.7
Aged 75 to 79	46	100.0	0.6	2.3	1.8	94.8
Aged 80 to 84	38	100.0	0.5	1.8	1.4	96.0
Aged 85 or older	39	100.0	0.3	1.3	1.0	97.0
Nevada	**2,701**	**100.0**	**9.0**	**9.4**	**26.5**	**54.1**
Under age 5	187	100.0	9.2	12.6	41.5	37.8
Aged 5 to 9	183	100.0	9.3	12.0	40.3	38.9
Aged 10 to 14	183	100.0	9.3	11.8	38.4	40.4
Aged 15 to 19	183	100.0	9.0	12.5	35.7	42.3
Aged 20 to 24	178	100.0	9.4	10.9	33.0	45.7
Aged 25 to 29	197	100.0	9.4	9.7	31.3	48.4
Aged 30 to 34	191	100.0	9.7	9.4	31.8	48.0
Aged 35 to 39	192	100.0	10.2	9.2	30.4	49.2
Aged 40 to 44	191	100.0	9.5	9.0	26.6	53.6
Aged 45 to 49	194	100.0	8.9	8.8	21.3	59.4
Aged 50 to 54	183	100.0	8.8	8.1	17.0	64.5
Aged 55 to 59	165	100.0	8.8	7.3	13.8	68.5
Aged 60 to 64	151	100.0	8.4	6.5	10.7	72.9
Aged 65 to 69	116	100.0	7.9	6.4	9.7	74.5
Aged 70 to 74	82	100.0	7.9	6.7	9.2	74.9
Aged 75 to 79	58	100.0	7.3	6.0	8.6	77.0
Aged 80 to 84	39	100.0	5.8	5.1	7.6	80.4
Aged 85 or older	30	100.0	4.1	4.8	6.5	83.6

	total		Asian	black	Hispanic	non-Hispanic white
	number	percent				
New Hampshire	**1,316**	**100.0%**	**2.6%**	**1.7%**	**2.8%**	**92.3%**
Under age 5	70	100.0	4.9	3.9	6.0	84.8
Aged 5 to 9	78	100.0	4.2	3.3	5.0	87.0
Aged 10 to 14	85	100.0	3.2	2.8	4.1	89.2
Aged 15 to 19	94	100.0	2.7	2.4	4.0	90.2
Aged 20 to 24	85	100.0	3.1	2.4	3.8	90.0
Aged 25 to 29	73	100.0	3.9	2.0	4.1	89.4
Aged 30 to 34	71	100.0	4.5	2.0	3.9	88.8
Aged 35 to 39	82	100.0	4.1	1.7	3.2	90.3
Aged 40 to 44	97	100.0	2.7	1.4	2.6	92.6
Aged 45 to 49	114	100.0	1.9	1.2	2.0	94.2
Aged 50 to 54	112	100.0	1.5	0.9	1.5	95.4
Aged 55 to 59	96	100.0	1.5	0.7	1.2	96.0
Aged 60 to 64	82	100.0	1.3	0.6	1.0	96.6
Aged 65 to 69	57	100.0	1.2	0.6	0.9	96.9
Aged 70 to 74	40	100.0	0.9	0.5	0.9	97.3
Aged 75 to 79	32	100.0	0.9	0.4	0.8	97.5
Aged 80 to 84	25	100.0	0.6	0.4	0.6	98.0
Aged 85 or older	25	100.0	0.4	0.2	0.5	98.5
New Jersey	**8,792**	**100.0**	**9.0**	**14.8**	**17.7**	**59.3**
Under age 5	541	100.0	11.5	18.0	25.6	47.1
Aged 5 to 9	565	100.0	10.7	17.3	22.5	51.4
Aged 10 to 14	587	100.0	9.3	17.6	20.5	54.1
Aged 15 to 19	598	100.0	8.1	18.8	21.1	53.3
Aged 20 to 24	541	100.0	8.5	17.9	24.1	50.7
Aged 25 to 29	553	100.0	11.6	15.8	24.6	49.0
Aged 30 to 34	557	100.0	13.2	15.5	24.1	48.1
Aged 35 to 39	588	100.0	12.6	15.2	21.3	51.7
Aged 40 to 44	650	100.0	9.9	14.8	18.1	57.8
Aged 45 to 49	705	100.0	8.4	14.1	15.2	62.8
Aged 50 to 54	675	100.0	7.8	13.2	12.8	66.6
Aged 55 to 59	566	100.0	7.4	12.2	11.3	69.4
Aged 60 to 64	481	100.0	7.1	11.6	10.0	71.4
Aged 65 to 69	351	100.0	6.8	11.6	9.5	72.3
Aged 70 to 74	260	100.0	6.4	11.8	9.4	72.6
Aged 75 to 79	216	100.0	4.6	10.2	7.9	77.5
Aged 80 to 84	179	100.0	3.1	8.1	6.1	82.7
Aged 85 or older	180	100.0	2.2	6.8	4.5	86.4

	total		Asian	black	Hispanic	non-Hispanic white
	number	percent				
New Mexico	**2,059**	**100.0%**	**2.0%**	**2.8%**	**46.3%**	**40.5%**
Under age 5	145	100.0	2.4	4.3	59.6	24.8
Aged 5 to 9	143	100.0	2.3	3.8	58.9	25.6
Aged 10 to 14	142	100.0	2.2	3.7	57.8	26.9
Aged 15 to 19	150	100.0	2.0	3.6	55.0	28.6
Aged 20 to 24	142	100.0	2.2	3.5	51.4	32.2
Aged 25 to 29	140	100.0	2.4	3.1	50.5	34.3
Aged 30 to 34	128	100.0	2.6	2.8	50.1	35.0
Aged 35 to 39	123	100.0	2.5	2.7	49.4	36.3
Aged 40 to 44	125	100.0	2.3	2.5	47.1	39.3
Aged 45 to 49	145	100.0	1.9	2.4	43.3	43.9
Aged 50 to 54	147	100.0	1.7	2.2	39.0	49.5
Aged 55 to 59	137	100.0	1.5	2.0	34.3	55.3
Aged 60 to 64	120	100.0	1.4	1.6	32.3	58.6
Aged 65 to 69	88	100.0	1.2	1.5	31.1	60.2
Aged 70 to 74	66	100.0	1.1	1.5	32.8	58.6
Aged 75 to 79	50	100.0	1.0	1.5	31.9	60.1
Aged 80 to 84	36	100.0	1.0	1.4	30.9	62.0
Aged 85 or older	32	100.0	0.7	1.3	27.1	66.4
New York	**19,378**	**100.0**	**8.2**	**17.2**	**17.6**	**58.3**
Under age 5	1,156	100.0	8.7	20.7	24.6	48.8
Aged 5 to 9	1,164	100.0	8.4	20.2	22.5	51.1
Aged 10 to 14	1,211	100.0	7.8	20.5	21.2	52.4
Aged 15 to 19	1,366	100.0	7.7	21.0	21.3	51.8
Aged 20 to 24	1,411	100.0	9.3	19.1	21.3	52.0
Aged 25 to 29	1,380	100.0	10.4	17.3	21.5	52.3
Aged 30 to 34	1,279	100.0	10.7	17.3	22.0	51.4
Aged 35 to 39	1,254	100.0	10.2	17.0	20.6	53.4
Aged 40 to 44	1,356	100.0	8.7	17.2	18.2	56.9
Aged 45 to 49	1,459	100.0	8.0	17.0	15.5	60.4
Aged 50 to 54	1,420	100.0	7.7	16.1	13.4	63.6
Aged 55 to 59	1,237	100.0	7.3	14.9	12.2	66.4
Aged 60 to 64	1,066	100.0	6.8	14.1	11.3	68.5
Aged 65 to 69	773	100.0	6.2	14.6	11.0	68.9
Aged 70 to 74	587	100.0	6.2	14.3	11.0	69.3
Aged 75 to 79	475	100.0	5.2	12.3	9.6	73.5
Aged 80 to 84	392	100.0	3.9	10.6	7.7	78.2
Aged 85 or older	391	100.0	3.1	9.8	6.2	81.3

	total		Asian	black	Hispanic	non-Hispanic white
	number	percent				
North Carolina	**9,535**	**100.0%**	**2.6%**	**22.6%**	**8.4%**	**65.3%**
Under age 5	632	100.0	3.7	26.8	16.9	51.9
Aged 5 to 9	636	100.0	3.6	25.9	14.4	55.3
Aged 10 to 14	631	100.0	3.1	27.1	11.4	57.1
Aged 15 to 19	660	100.0	2.8	28.6	9.7	57.6
Aged 20 to 24	662	100.0	3.1	25.1	11.2	59.6
Aged 25 to 29	627	100.0	3.7	22.4	13.3	59.6
Aged 30 to 34	620	100.0	3.7	22.4	13.4	59.4
Aged 35 to 39	660	100.0	3.5	21.9	10.4	62.9
Aged 40 to 44	667	100.0	2.9	22.1	7.6	66.2
Aged 45 to 49	699	100.0	2.2	22.0	5.3	69.2
Aged 50 to 54	670	100.0	1.9	21.9	3.8	71.1
Aged 55 to 59	601	100.0	1.7	21.0	2.6	73.4
Aged 60 to 64	538	100.0	1.4	18.3	1.9	77.1
Aged 65 to 69	403	100.0	1.3	16.5	1.7	79.4
Aged 70 to 74	295	100.0	1.2	16.2	1.5	80.0
Aged 75 to 79	224	100.0	1.0	15.4	1.3	81.4
Aged 80 to 84	165	100.0	0.7	14.7	1.1	82.8
Aged 85 or older	147	100.0	0.5	15.2	0.9	82.8
North Dakota	**673**	**100.0**	**1.4**	**1.6**	**2.0**	**88.9**
Under age 5	45	100.0	1.8	4.2	4.5	79.0
Aged 5 to 9	40	100.0	1.7	3.2	3.8	80.9
Aged 10 to 14	40	100.0	1.4	2.7	3.1	83.4
Aged 15 to 19	47	100.0	1.6	2.3	2.9	84.8
Aged 20 to 24	59	100.0	2.9	2.8	2.8	85.1
Aged 25 to 29	50	100.0	2.2	2.3	2.7	86.4
Aged 30 to 34	41	100.0	1.9	2.0	2.5	86.8
Aged 35 to 39	37	100.0	1.9	1.5	2.0	88.1
Aged 40 to 44	38	100.0	1.4	1.1	1.6	89.6
Aged 45 to 49	46	100.0	0.9	0.7	1.2	91.7
Aged 50 to 54	50	100.0	0.6	0.6	1.0	93.4
Aged 55 to 59	46	100.0	0.5	0.5	0.7	94.7
Aged 60 to 64	36	100.0	0.7	0.4	0.6	95.0
Aged 65 to 69	26	100.0	0.6	0.3	0.5	95.5
Aged 70 to 74	21	100.0	0.4	0.2	0.4	96.3
Aged 75 to 79	18	100.0	0.3	0.1	0.4	97.0
Aged 80 to 84	16	100.0	0.3	0.1	0.3	97.9
Aged 85 or older	17	100.0	0.1	0.1	0.3	98.7

| | total | | | | | non-Hispanic |
	number	percent	Asian	black	Hispanic	white
Ohio	**11,537**	**100.0%**	**2.1%**	**13.4%**	**3.1%**	**81.1%**
Under age 5	721	100.0	3.0	19.7	6.2	71.3
Aged 5 to 9	748	100.0	2.8	17.7	5.2	74.2
Aged 10 to 14	775	100.0	2.2	17.1	4.3	76.1
Aged 15 to 19	824	100.0	2.1	17.4	3.9	76.2
Aged 20 to 24	763	100.0	2.7	15.4	4.1	77.5
Aged 25 to 29	719	100.0	3.1	14.1	4.3	78.2
Aged 30 to 34	691	100.0	3.1	13.7	4.1	78.7
Aged 35 to 39	718	100.0	2.9	13.2	3.4	80.0
Aged 40 to 44	761	100.0	2.2	12.1	2.7	82.4
Aged 45 to 49	855	100.0	1.7	11.7	2.1	83.9
Aged 50 to 54	887	100.0	1.3	11.5	1.7	84.8
Aged 55 to 59	787	100.0	1.3	10.7	1.4	86.1
Aged 60 to 64	665	100.0	1.2	9.6	1.3	87.4
Aged 65 to 69	479	100.0	1.2	9.1	1.1	88.1
Aged 70 to 74	371	100.0	1.1	9.2	1.0	88.3
Aged 75 to 79	298	100.0	0.8	9.0	1.0	88.8
Aged 80 to 84	244	100.0	0.6	8.0	0.8	90.2
Aged 85 or older	230	100.0	0.4	7.2	0.7	91.5
Oklahoma	**3,751**	**100.0**	**2.2**	**8.7**	**8.9**	**68.7**
Under age 5	264	100.0	2.9	12.8	16.8	53.0
Aged 5 to 9	259	100.0	2.7	11.9	15.0	55.3
Aged 10 to 14	254	100.0	2.5	11.6	12.6	57.6
Aged 15 to 19	264	100.0	2.6	11.5	11.3	59.8
Aged 20 to 24	269	100.0	3.0	10.3	11.8	62.9
Aged 25 to 29	266	100.0	3.0	9.2	12.0	64.0
Aged 30 to 34	241	100.0	2.8	9.0	11.8	64.6
Aged 35 to 39	233	100.0	2.9	8.4	10.2	66.9
Aged 40 to 44	228	100.0	2.5	8.0	8.5	70.0
Aged 45 to 49	261	100.0	1.9	7.7	6.2	73.5
Aged 50 to 54	264	100.0	1.7	7.6	4.6	76.1
Aged 55 to 59	236	100.0	1.6	6.8	3.6	78.6
Aged 60 to 64	205	100.0	1.4	5.8	2.8	81.1
Aged 65 to 69	159	100.0	1.2	5.1	2.3	83.0
Aged 70 to 74	121	100.0	1.1	4.7	2.0	84.4
Aged 75 to 79	95	100.0	0.9	4.4	1.7	86.1
Aged 80 to 84	69	100.0	0.7	4.0	1.5	88.0
Aged 85 or older	62	100.0	0.5	4.0	1.3	89.1

	total		Asian	black	Hispanic	non-Hispanic white
	number	percent				
Oregon	**3,831**	**100.0%**	**4.9%**	**2.6%**	**11.7%**	**78.5%**
Under age 5	238	100.0	6.6	4.7	23.3	63.2
Aged 5 to 9	237	100.0	6.6	4.2	21.8	65.0
Aged 10 to 14	243	100.0	6.0	4.1	19.5	67.7
Aged 15 to 19	255	100.0	5.9	3.8	16.9	70.4
Aged 20 to 24	253	100.0	6.0	3.2	15.1	72.8
Aged 25 to 29	265	100.0	5.5	2.8	15.0	74.1
Aged 30 to 34	259	100.0	5.8	2.7	15.3	73.8
Aged 35 to 39	251	100.0	6.4	2.5	14.3	74.4
Aged 40 to 44	248	100.0	5.4	2.3	11.5	78.2
Aged 45 to 49	263	100.0	4.6	2.1	8.3	82.4
Aged 50 to 54	276	100.0	3.8	1.9	5.9	85.9
Aged 55 to 59	273	100.0	3.2	1.5	4.3	88.8
Aged 60 to 64	236	100.0	2.8	1.3	3.4	90.4
Aged 65 to 69	170	100.0	2.6	1.1	2.9	91.5
Aged 70 to 74	120	100.0	2.7	1.1	2.7	91.8
Aged 75 to 79	92	100.0	2.5	0.9	2.2	92.9
Aged 80 to 84	74	100.0	2.3	0.8	1.9	94.0
Aged 85 or older	78	100.0	1.7	0.7	1.5	95.3
Pennsylvania	**12,702**	**100.0**	**3.2**	**11.9**	**5.7**	**79.5**
Under age 5	730	100.0	4.5	17.9	10.9	67.9
Aged 5 to 9	754	100.0	4.2	16.3	9.6	70.8
Aged 10 to 14	791	100.0	3.5	15.8	8.5	72.8
Aged 15 to 19	905	100.0	3.4	16.1	7.9	73.1
Aged 20 to 24	874	100.0	4.3	14.5	7.7	73.9
Aged 25 to 29	782	100.0	4.8	12.9	7.8	74.7
Aged 30 to 34	730	100.0	4.8	12.9	7.9	74.7
Aged 35 to 39	764	100.0	4.5	12.0	6.7	76.9
Aged 40 to 44	851	100.0	3.4	11.4	5.6	79.7
Aged 45 to 49	956	100.0	2.7	10.6	4.3	82.3
Aged 50 to 54	985	100.0	2.2	9.9	3.3	84.4
Aged 55 to 59	879	100.0	2.1	9.0	2.7	86.0
Aged 60 to 64	743	100.0	2.0	8.2	2.4	87.3
Aged 65 to 69	553	100.0	1.8	7.7	2.1	88.2
Aged 70 to 74	427	100.0	1.7	7.5	1.8	88.9
Aged 75 to 79	362	100.0	1.3	7.0	1.4	90.1
Aged 80 to 84	312	100.0	0.8	5.9	1.1	92.0
Aged 85 or older	306	100.0	0.6	5.6	0.8	92.9

| | total | | | | | non-Hispanic |
	number	percent	Asian	black	Hispanic	white
Rhode Island	**1,053**	**100.0%**	**3.5%**	**7.4%**	**12.4%**	**76.4%**
Under age 5	57	100.0	5.2	13.4	23.2	59.2
Aged 5 to 9	60	100.0	4.6	11.7	20.7	63.4
Aged 10 to 14	64	100.0	3.9	10.8	19.1	66.3
Aged 15 to 19	80	100.0	4.6	10.3	17.3	67.8
Aged 20 to 24	82	100.0	5.6	9.1	15.3	69.7
Aged 25 to 29	66	100.0	5.7	8.7	16.9	68.3
Aged 30 to 34	61	100.0	4.9	8.5	16.7	69.3
Aged 35 to 39	64	100.0	4.0	7.7	14.7	73.1
Aged 40 to 44	73	100.0	3.1	6.7	12.3	77.2
Aged 45 to 49	81	100.0	2.6	5.9	9.4	81.4
Aged 50 to 54	81	100.0	2.3	5.6	7.5	83.9
Aged 55 to 59	71	100.0	2.1	4.8	6.2	86.3
Aged 60 to 64	60	100.0	1.9	3.8	5.2	88.5
Aged 65 to 69	43	100.0	1.7	3.4	4.8	89.4
Aged 70 to 74	31	100.0	1.8	3.7	4.4	89.3
Aged 75 to 79	27	100.0	1.2	3.3	3.4	91.3
Aged 80 to 84	25	100.0	0.9	2.6	2.3	93.5
Aged 85 or older	27	100.0	0.6	1.8	1.6	95.2
South Carolina	**4,625**	**100.0**	**1.6**	**28.8**	**5.1**	**64.1**
Under age 5	302	100.0	2.2	35.7	9.9	52.2
Aged 5 to 9	296	100.0	2.2	34.0	8.0	55.7
Aged 10 to 14	297	100.0	1.9	34.4	6.0	57.4
Aged 15 to 19	329	100.0	1.7	35.6	5.6	56.7
Aged 20 to 24	332	100.0	1.8	32.2	7.5	58.2
Aged 25 to 29	304	100.0	2.2	29.8	9.0	58.7
Aged 30 to 34	288	100.0	2.2	29.2	8.4	59.8
Aged 35 to 39	297	100.0	2.2	27.5	6.5	63.3
Aged 40 to 44	305	100.0	1.8	27.8	4.9	64.9
Aged 45 to 49	333	100.0	1.5	27.8	3.3	66.7
Aged 50 to 54	327	100.0	1.3	27.9	2.5	67.6
Aged 55 to 59	303	100.0	1.2	26.8	1.8	69.6
Aged 60 to 64	281	100.0	1.0	23.1	1.4	74.0
Aged 65 to 69	216	100.0	0.9	20.6	1.2	76.8
Aged 70 to 74	153	100.0	0.9	20.3	1.1	77.4
Aged 75 to 79	113	100.0	0.7	19.4	1.0	78.6
Aged 80 to 84	79	100.0	0.5	18.9	0.9	79.4
Aged 85 or older	71	100.0	0.4	20.0	0.8	78.6

	total		Asian	black	Hispanic	non-Hispanic white
	number	percent				
South Dakota	**814**	**100.0%**	**1.3%**	**1.8%**	**2.7%**	**84.7%**
Under age 5	60	100.0	1.8	4.2	5.4	72.7
Aged 5 to 9	56	100.0	1.7	3.5	4.7	74.5
Aged 10 to 14	54	100.0	1.7	2.9	4.0	76.8
Aged 15 to 19	58	100.0	1.6	2.4	3.6	78.6
Aged 20 to 24	58	100.0	2.1	2.4	3.7	80.3
Aged 25 to 29	56	100.0	1.7	2.5	3.7	81.4
Aged 30 to 34	50	100.0	1.7	2.0	3.7	82.7
Aged 35 to 39	46	100.0	1.7	1.9	3.0	83.8
Aged 40 to 44	47	100.0	1.3	1.5	2.6	85.4
Aged 45 to 49	58	100.0	1.0	1.1	1.9	88.4
Aged 50 to 54	59	100.0	0.8	0.8	1.3	90.6
Aged 55 to 59	54	100.0	0.6	0.6	0.9	92.3
Aged 60 to 64	44	100.0	0.6	0.4	0.8	92.9
Aged 65 to 69	32	100.0	0.4	0.3	0.7	93.9
Aged 70 to 74	26	100.0	0.4	0.3	0.6	94.4
Aged 75 to 79	22	100.0	0.3	0.2	0.5	95.8
Aged 80 to 84	18	100.0	0.2	0.2	0.4	96.8
Aged 85 or older	19	100.0	0.1	0.2	0.5	97.6
Tennessee	**6,346**	**100.0**	**1.8**	**17.4**	**4.6**	**75.6**
Under age 5	408	100.0	2.5	23.1	9.6	64.6
Aged 5 to 9	412	100.0	2.5	21.7	7.7	67.8
Aged 10 to 14	419	100.0	2.0	22.2	5.8	69.5
Aged 15 to 19	437	100.0	1.9	23.0	5.2	69.4
Aged 20 to 24	426	100.0	2.0	21.0	6.8	69.7
Aged 25 to 29	418	100.0	2.4	18.9	7.8	70.4
Aged 30 to 34	406	100.0	2.5	18.2	7.3	71.5
Aged 35 to 39	424	100.0	2.4	17.2	5.5	74.3
Aged 40 to 44	431	100.0	2.0	16.6	4.0	76.7
Aged 45 to 49	467	100.0	1.5	16.2	2.8	78.7
Aged 50 to 54	459	100.0	1.3	16.2	2.1	79.7
Aged 55 to 59	415	100.0	1.2	15.1	1.5	81.4
Aged 60 to 64	371	100.0	1.0	12.2	1.2	84.8
Aged 65 to 69	281	100.0	0.9	10.3	1.0	87.1
Aged 70 to 74	207	100.0	0.8	10.1	0.9	87.7
Aged 75 to 79	155	100.0	0.7	9.9	0.8	88.1
Aged 80 to 84	112	100.0	0.5	9.4	0.7	88.9
Aged 85 or older	100	100.0	0.3	9.6	0.6	89.1

	total		Asian	black	Hispanic	non-Hispanic white
	number	percent				
Texas	**25,146**	**100.0%**	**4.4%**	**12.6%**	**37.6%**	**45.3%**
Under age 5	1,928	100.0	4.7	14.2	50.6	31.7
Aged 5 to 9	1,928	100.0	4.7	13.8	49.1	33.2
Aged 10 to 14	1,882	100.0	4.2	14.1	46.9	35.2
Aged 15 to 19	1,883	100.0	4.0	14.6	44.9	36.7
Aged 20 to 24	1,817	100.0	4.5	13.5	42.8	39.2
Aged 25 to 29	1,853	100.0	5.1	12.7	41.8	40.3
Aged 30 to 34	1,760	100.0	5.5	12.8	42.1	39.6
Aged 35 to 39	1,764	100.0	5.9	12.6	40.1	41.2
Aged 40 to 44	1,695	100.0	5.2	12.7	36.7	45.0
Aged 45 to 49	1,760	100.0	4.3	12.7	31.7	50.7
Aged 50 to 54	1,675	100.0	3.9	12.4	27.8	55.3
Aged 55 to 59	1,423	100.0	3.9	11.6	25.2	58.7
Aged 60 to 64	1,175	100.0	3.6	10.2	23.2	62.3
Aged 65 to 69	853	100.0	3.3	9.2	21.6	65.2
Aged 70 to 74	619	100.0	3.1	8.8	21.5	66.0
Aged 75 to 79	477	100.0	2.5	8.5	20.5	68.1
Aged 80 to 84	347	100.0	2.0	7.7	19.4	70.4
Aged 85 or older	305	100.0	1.5	7.8	16.4	73.9
Utah	**2,764**	**100.0**	**2.8**	**1.6**	**13.0**	**80.4**
Under age 5	264	100.0	2.9	2.5	17.2	74.9
Aged 5 to 9	250	100.0	2.9	2.4	16.6	75.6
Aged 10 to 14	228	100.0	2.9	2.3	16.1	76.0
Aged 15 to 19	221	100.0	3.1	2.1	15.3	76.5
Aged 20 to 24	227	100.0	3.4	1.8	14.1	78.1
Aged 25 to 29	230	100.0	3.2	1.4	13.7	79.2
Aged 30 to 34	216	100.0	2.9	1.3	14.3	79.4
Aged 35 to 39	178	100.0	3.2	1.3	15.4	77.9
Aged 40 to 44	154	100.0	3.2	1.3	14.3	79.0
Aged 45 to 49	155	100.0	2.8	1.2	11.2	82.6
Aged 50 to 54	152	100.0	2.4	1.0	8.7	85.9
Aged 55 to 59	133	100.0	2.3	0.8	7.0	88.1
Aged 60 to 64	107	100.0	2.2	0.7	6.0	89.6
Aged 65 to 69	79	100.0	1.8	0.5	5.2	91.0
Aged 70 to 74	59	100.0	1.7	0.5	4.8	91.8
Aged 75 to 79	46	100.0	1.6	0.4	4.2	92.9
Aged 80 to 84	34	100.0	1.6	0.4	3.6	93.6
Aged 85 or older	31	100.0	1.6	0.5	2.9	94.2

	total		Asian	black	Hispanic	non-Hispanic white
	number	percent				
Vermont	**626**	**100.0%**	**1.7%**	**1.5%**	**1.5%**	**94.3%**
Under age 5	32	100.0	2.7	3.9	2.5	89.9
Aged 5 to 9	35	100.0	2.7	3.3	2.3	90.7
Aged 10 to 14	38	100.0	2.4	2.8	2.0	91.6
Aged 15 to 19	46	100.0	2.7	2.6	2.6	91.2
Aged 20 to 24	44	100.0	2.6	2.2	2.6	91.6
Aged 25 to 29	35	100.0	2.4	2.0	2.0	92.5
Aged 30 to 34	34	100.0	2.3	1.7	1.8	93.1
Aged 35 to 39	36	100.0	2.4	1.3	1.5	93.7
Aged 40 to 44	42	100.0	1.7	1.0	1.2	95.0
Aged 45 to 49	50	100.0	1.2	0.8	1.1	95.7
Aged 50 to 54	52	100.0	0.9	0.7	0.8	96.3
Aged 55 to 59	49	100.0	0.8	0.6	0.7	96.7
Aged 60 to 64	41	100.0	0.7	0.4	0.7	97.1
Aged 65 to 69	29	100.0	0.5	0.4	0.6	97.5
Aged 70 to 74	20	100.0	0.6	0.3	0.5	97.9
Aged 75 to 79	16	100.0	0.5	0.3	0.7	97.8
Aged 80 to 84	13	100.0	0.4	0.2	0.6	98.1
Aged 85 or older	13	100.0	0.3	0.3	0.7	98.4
Virginia	**8,001**	**100.0**	**6.5**	**20.7**	**7.9**	**64.8**
Under age 5	510	100.0	8.6	24.9	13.4	53.9
Aged 5 to 9	512	100.0	8.3	24.4	11.3	56.6
Aged 10 to 14	511	100.0	7.1	24.7	9.8	58.7
Aged 15 to 19	551	100.0	6.3	25.8	9.0	59.0
Aged 20 to 24	572	100.0	6.5	22.9	10.5	60.1
Aged 25 to 29	564	100.0	7.8	20.8	11.7	59.7
Aged 30 to 34	526	100.0	8.8	20.2	12.1	58.8
Aged 35 to 39	540	100.0	9.1	19.5	10.1	61.2
Aged 40 to 44	569	100.0	7.3	20.1	8.0	64.3
Aged 45 to 49	621	100.0	5.9	20.2	6.0	67.5
Aged 50 to 54	593	100.0	5.2	19.8	4.7	69.8
Aged 55 to 59	513	100.0	4.8	18.6	3.6	72.5
Aged 60 to 64	442	100.0	4.5	16.1	2.8	76.1
Aged 65 to 69	320	100.0	4.3	15.4	2.4	77.4
Aged 70 to 74	230	100.0	4.2	15.9	2.2	77.4
Aged 75 to 79	174	100.0	3.5	15.5	1.9	78.8
Aged 80 to 84	131	100.0	2.6	14.3	1.6	81.2
Aged 85 or older	122	100.0	1.8	14.2	1.4	82.3

	total		Asian	black	Hispanic	non-Hispanic white
	number	percent				
Washington	**6,725**	**100.0%**	**9.0%**	**4.8%**	**11.2%**	**72.5%**
Under age 5	440	100.0	11.3	8.2	21.7	57.0
Aged 5 to 9	430	100.0	10.9	7.5	19.6	59.8
Aged 10 to 14	438	100.0	9.8	7.1	17.4	62.9
Aged 15 to 19	462	100.0	10.0	6.5	15.5	65.0
Aged 20 to 24	462	100.0	10.2	5.8	14.9	66.3
Aged 25 to 29	480	100.0	10.5	5.3	14.5	67.0
Aged 30 to 34	453	100.0	10.9	5.0	14.4	67.0
Aged 35 to 39	449	100.0	11.2	4.7	12.9	68.6
Aged 40 to 44	460	100.0	9.5	4.5	10.2	73.3
Aged 45 to 49	493	100.0	8.1	4.1	7.4	77.7
Aged 50 to 54	495	100.0	7.3	3.8	5.7	80.7
Aged 55 to 59	453	100.0	6.8	3.1	4.3	83.4
Aged 60 to 64	382	100.0	6.3	2.6	3.6	85.5
Aged 65 to 69	270	100.0	6.0	2.2	3.2	86.7
Aged 70 to 74	187	100.0	6.5	2.1	2.9	86.6
Aged 75 to 79	142	100.0	6.1	1.9	2.5	87.9
Aged 80 to 84	111	100.0	5.2	1.7	2.1	89.9
Aged 85 or older	117	100.0	4.0	1.5	1.5	92.3
West Virginia	**1,853**	**100.0**	**0.9**	**4.2**	**1.2**	**93.2**
Under age 5	104	100.0	1.3	7.2	2.4	88.8
Aged 5 to 9	106	100.0	1.2	6.2	2.0	90.2
Aged 10 to 14	109	100.0	1.0	5.8	1.7	90.9
Aged 15 to 19	120	100.0	1.0	5.9	1.7	90.8
Aged 20 to 24	117	100.0	1.4	5.6	1.8	90.7
Aged 25 to 29	108	100.0	1.4	4.7	1.7	91.5
Aged 30 to 34	112	100.0	1.2	4.5	1.6	92.2
Aged 35 to 39	117	100.0	1.1	3.8	1.3	93.2
Aged 40 to 44	120	100.0	0.9	3.5	1.1	93.9
Aged 45 to 49	133	100.0	0.7	3.5	0.9	94.1
Aged 50 to 54	143	100.0	0.6	3.5	0.7	94.4
Aged 55 to 59	139	100.0	0.6	3.2	0.6	94.9
Aged 60 to 64	125	100.0	0.6	2.6	0.5	95.6
Aged 65 to 69	92	100.0	0.6	2.2	0.5	95.9
Aged 70 to 74	72	100.0	0.5	2.1	0.5	96.3
Aged 75 to 79	55	100.0	0.4	2.1	0.4	96.6
Aged 80 to 84	43	100.0	0.2	2.4	0.4	96.4
Aged 85 or older	36	100.0	0.2	2.5	0.4	96.4

	total		Asian	black	Hispanic	non-Hispanic white
	number	percent				
Wisconsin	**5,687**	**100.0%**	**2.7%**	**7.1%**	**5.9%**	**83.3%**
Under age 5	358	100.0	4.6	12.5	12.3	69.9
Aged 5 to 9	369	100.0	4.1	11.1	10.9	72.9
Aged 10 to 14	376	100.0	3.7	10.8	9.0	75.5
Aged 15 to 19	399	100.0	3.8	10.3	7.6	77.0
Aged 20 to 24	387	100.0	4.2	8.6	7.5	78.5
Aged 25 to 29	372	100.0	4.1	8.0	8.4	78.4
Aged 30 to 34	349	100.0	3.5	7.8	8.6	79.1
Aged 35 to 39	345	100.0	3.1	7.5	7.4	80.9
Aged 40 to 44	380	100.0	2.3	6.3	5.3	84.9
Aged 45 to 49	438	100.0	1.7	5.4	3.6	88.2
Aged 50 to 54	436	100.0	1.3	5.0	2.8	89.8
Aged 55 to 59	386	100.0	1.2	4.5	2.2	91.2
Aged 60 to 64	314	100.0	1.1	3.9	1.9	92.3
Aged 65 to 69	227	100.0	1.0	3.4	1.6	93.2
Aged 70 to 74	173	100.0	1.0	3.2	1.4	93.7
Aged 75 to 79	141	100.0	0.8	2.8	1.2	94.6
Aged 80 to 84	117	100.0	0.6	2.2	1.0	95.9
Aged 85 or older	119	100.0	0.5	1.6	0.7	96.8
Wyoming	**564**	**100.0**	**1.2**	**1.3**	**8.9**	**85.9**
Under age 5	40	100.0	1.5	2.5	14.8	77.5
Aged 5 to 9	37	100.0	1.5	2.0	13.9	78.8
Aged 10 to 14	36	100.0	1.5	2.0	12.7	80.1
Aged 15 to 19	38	100.0	1.4	2.0	11.1	81.9
Aged 20 to 24	40	100.0	2.1	2.2	11.0	81.8
Aged 25 to 29	41	100.0	1.6	1.3	11.0	83.3
Aged 30 to 34	36	100.0	1.4	1.2	10.7	84.0
Aged 35 to 39	34	100.0	1.5	1.1	9.9	84.6
Aged 40 to 44	33	100.0	1.2	1.0	8.4	86.4
Aged 45 to 49	39	100.0	0.9	0.9	6.9	88.7
Aged 50 to 54	44	100.0	0.8	0.8	5.6	90.6
Aged 55 to 59	41	100.0	0.8	0.6	4.7	91.9
Aged 60 to 64	33	100.0	0.6	0.5	4.4	92.4
Aged 65 to 69	23	100.0	0.5	0.4	4.0	93.2
Aged 70 to 74	17	100.0	0.5	0.5	4.3	92.9
Aged 75 to 79	12	100.0	0.5	0.6	4.2	93.1
Aged 80 to 84	9	100.0	0.4	0.5	3.7	94.3
Aged 85 or older	9	100.0	0.4	0.6	3.0	95.1

Note: Asians and blacks are those who identify themselves as being of the race alone and those who identify themselves as being of the race in combination with other races. Numbers do not add to total because not all races are shown, some mixed-race individuals are counted more than once, and Hispanics may be of any race. Non-Hispanic whites are those who identify themselves as being white alone and not Hispanic.
Source: Bureau of the Census, 2010 Census, American Factfinder, Population Estimates, Internet site http:// factfinder2.census.gov/faces/nav/jsf/pages/index.xhtml; calculations by New Strategist

9

Spending

■ The average household cut its spending by 8 percent between 2006 (the year overall household spending peaked) and 2010, after adjusting for inflation. The spending of householders aged 35 to 44 fell by a larger 10 percent.

■ Householders aged 35 to 44 reduced their spending on mortgage interest by 19 percent between 2006 and 2010, after adjusting for inflation, as some lost their homes and others entering the age group bought cheaper homes or decided to rent rather than buy.

■ Households headed by people aged 35 to 44 spent 16 percent more than the average household in 2010—or $55,946. Householders aged 35 to 44 spend significantly more than average on items commonly purchased by parents with children under age 18. They also spend more on mortgage interest.

The Spending of Householders Aged 35 to 44 Has Fallen

Gen Xers spent less in 2010 than their counterparts did in 2000.

Gen Xers are perhaps the generation hardest hit by the Great Recession. Between 2006 and 2010, the average household headed by a 35-to-44-year old (Generation X was aged 34 to 45 in 2010) slashed its spending by a substantial 10 percent, after adjusting for inflation. Householders aged 35 to 44 spent 2 percent less in 2010 than their counterparts did in 2000.

Householders aged 35 to 44 spent an average of $55,946 in 2010, down from $62,168 in 2006, after adjusting for inflation. One factor that accounts for the decline is the drop in spending on mortgage interest. Many Gen Xers bought homes during the housing bubble. The average annual spending of householders aged 35 to 44 on mortgage interest rose as high as $6,397 in 2006, fully 17 percent more than in 2000. Between 2006 and 2010, however, mortgage interest payments by householders in the age group fell 19 percent, to $5,196, as some lost their homes and others entering the age group bought cheaper homes or decided to rent rather than buy. Because of the Great Recession, householders aged 35 to 44 have had to cut their spending on discretionary items such as food away from home, alcoholic beverages, and entertainment. Meanwhile, out-of-pocket health insurance expenses for the age group rose 11 percent between 2006 and 2010. Their spending on water and other public services rose 12 percent, and vehicle maintenance and repairs increased 10 percent.

■ The Great Recession has been a setback for Gen Xers, and it will take years for them to recover.

The average Gen X household spends more than $50,000 a year

(average annual household spending by age of householder, 2010)

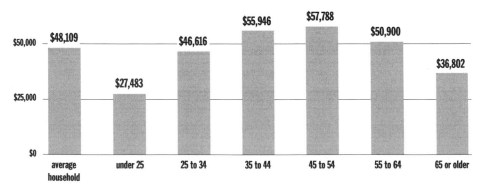

Table 9.1 Average Household Spending, 2000 to 2010

(average annual spending of consumer units on products and services, 2000 to 2010; percent change for selected years; in 2010 dollars)

	average spending			percent change		
	2010	2006	2000	2006–10	2000–06	2000–10
Number of consumer units (in 000s)	121,107	118,843	109,367	1.9%	8.7%	10.7%
Average annual spending of consumer units	$48,109	$52,349	$48,176	–8.1	8.7	–0.1
FOOD	**6,129**	**6,610**	**6,532**	**–7.3**	**1.2**	**–6.2**
Food at home	**3,624**	**3,696**	**3,825**	**–1.9**	**–3.4**	**–5.3**
Cereals and bakery products	502	482	574	4.1	–15.9	–12.5
Cereals and cereal products	165	155	198	6.7	–21.7	–16.5
Bakery products	337	329	376	2.5	–12.6	–10.4
Meats, poultry, fish, and eggs	784	862	1,007	–9.1	–14.4	–22.1
Beef	217	255	301	–15.0	–15.3	–28.0
Pork	149	170	211	–12.3	–19.7	–29.5
Other meats	117	114	128	3.0	–11.2	–8.5
Poultry	138	153	184	–9.5	–16.9	–24.8
Fish and seafood	117	132	139	–11.3	–5.3	–16.0
Eggs	46	40	43	14.9	–7.0	6.8
Dairy products	380	398	412	–4.5	–3.3	–7.7
Fresh milk and cream	141	151	166	–6.9	–8.7	–15.0
Other dairy products	240	247	244	–2.7	0.9	–1.8
Fruits and vegetables	679	640	660	6.0	–2.9	2.9
Fresh fruits	232	211	206	10.0	2.2	12.4
Fresh vegetables	210	209	201	0.6	3.7	4.3
Processed fruits	113	118	146	–4.2	–19.0	–22.4
Processed vegetables	124	103	106	20.7	–3.4	16.6
Other food at home	1,278	1,311	1,174	–2.5	11.7	8.9
Sugar and other sweets	132	135	148	–2.4	–8.7	–10.9
Fats and oils	103	93	105	10.7	–11.5	–2.0
Miscellaneous foods	667	678	553	–1.6	22.6	20.5
Nonalcoholic beverages	333	359	317	–7.3	13.4	5.2
Food prepared by consumer unit on trips	43	47	51	–7.5	–8.2	–15.1
Food away from home	**2,505**	**2,914**	**2,706**	**–14.0**	**7.7**	**–7.4**
ALCOHOLIC BEVERAGES	**412**	**538**	**471**	**–23.4**	**14.1**	**–12.5**
HOUSING	**16,557**	**17,702**	**15,599**	**–6.5**	**13.5**	**6.1**
Shelter	**9,812**	**10,463**	**9,008**	**–6.2**	**16.1**	**8.9**
Owned dwellings	6,277	7,048	5,827	–10.9	20.9	7.7
Mortgage interest and charges	3,351	4,059	3,342	–17.4	21.5	0.3
Property taxes	1,814	1,784	1,442	1.7	23.7	25.8
Maintenance, repair, insurance, other expenses	1,112	1,206	1,045	–7.8	15.4	6.4
Rented dwellings	2,900	2,801	2,576	3.5	8.8	12.6
Other lodging	635	613	605	3.5	1.3	4.9
Utilities, fuels, and public services	**3,660**	**3,674**	**3,152**	**–0.4**	**16.6**	**16.1**
Natural gas	440	551	389	–20.1	41.6	13.2
Electricity	1,413	1,369	1,154	3.2	18.7	22.5
Fuel oil and other fuels	140	149	123	–6.2	21.5	14.0

	average spending			percent change		
	2010	**2006**	**2000**	**2006–10**	**2000–06**	**2000–10**
Telephone	$1,178	$1,176	$1,111	0.2%	5.9%	6.1%
Water and other public services	489	429	375	13.9	14.6	30.5
Household services	**1,007**	**1,025**	**866**	**−1.8**	**18.4**	**16.3**
Personal services	340	425	413	−20.0	3.0	−17.6
Other household services	667	600	453	11.1	32.4	47.1
Housekeeping supplies	**612**	**692**	**610**	**−11.6**	**13.4**	**0.3**
Laundry and cleaning supplies	150	163	166	−8.2	−1.5	−9.6
Other household products	329	357	286	−7.8	24.7	15.0
Postage and stationery	132	172	160	−23.2	7.8	−17.3
Household furnishings and equipment	**1,467**	**1,847**	**1,961**	**−20.6**	**−5.8**	**−25.2**
Household textiles	102	167	134	−38.8	24.1	−24.0
Furniture	355	501	495	−29.1	1.1	−28.3
Floor coverings	36	52	56	−30.7	−6.8	−35.4
Major appliances	209	261	239	−19.8	8.9	−12.7
Small appliances and miscellaneous housewares	107	118	110	−9.2	7.0	−2.9
Miscellaneous household equipment	657	750	926	−12.3	−19.0	−29.0
APPAREL AND RELATED SERVICES	**1,700**	**2,027**	**2,350**	**−16.1**	**−13.8**	**−27.7**
Men and boys	**382**	**480**	**557**	**−20.5**	**−13.8**	**−31.4**
Men, aged 16 or older	304	382	436	−20.4	−12.3	−30.2
Boys, aged 2 to 15	78	98	122	−20.8	−19.0	−35.8
Women and girls	**663**	**812**	**918**	**−18.4**	**−11.5**	**−27.8**
Women, aged 16 or older	562	680	769	−17.4	−11.5	−26.9
Girls, aged 2 to 15	101	132	149	−23.5	−11.7	−32.4
Children under age 2	**91**	**104**	**104**	**−12.4**	**0.0**	**−12.4**
Footwear	**303**	**329**	**434**	**−7.9**	**−24.3**	**−30.2**
Other apparel products and services	**261**	**303**	**337**	**−13.8**	**−10.1**	**−22.5**
TRANSPORTATION	**7,677**	**9,202**	**9,392**	**−16.6**	**−2.0**	**−18.3**
Vehicle purchases	**2,588**	**3,700**	**4,328**	**−30.1**	**−14.5**	**−40.2**
Cars and trucks, new	1,219	1,945	2,032	−37.3	−4.3	−40.0
Cars and trucks, used	1,318	1,696	2,241	−22.3	−24.3	−41.2
Gasoline and motor oil	**2,132**	**2,409**	**1,635**	**−11.5**	**47.3**	**30.4**
Other vehicle expenses	**2,464**	**2,547**	**2,888**	**−3.3**	**−11.8**	**−14.7**
Vehicle finance charges	243	322	415	−24.6	−22.4	−41.5
Maintenance and repairs	787	744	790	5.8	−5.8	−0.4
Vehicle insurance	1,010	958	985	5.4	−2.7	2.5
Vehicle rentals, leases, licenses, other charges	423	521	698	−18.9	−25.3	−39.4
Public transportation	**493**	**546**	**541**	**−9.7**	**1.0**	**−8.8**
HEALTH CARE	**3,157**	**2,992**	**2,616**	**5.5**	**14.4**	**20.7**
Health insurance	1,831	1,585	1,245	15.6	27.3	47.1
Medical services	722	725	719	−0.4	0.8	0.4
Drugs	485	556	527	−12.8	5.5	−7.9
Medical supplies	119	127	125	−6.0	0.9	−5.1
ENTERTAINMENT	**2,504**	**2,570**	**2,359**	**−2.6**	**8.9**	**6.1**
Fees and admissions	581	655	652	−11.4	0.5	−10.9
Television, radio, and sound equipment	954	980	788	−2.6	24.4	21.1
Pets, toys, and playground equipment	606	446	423	36.0	5.4	43.3
Other entertainment products and services	364	488	498	−25.4	−2.0	−26.9

	average spending			percent change		
	2010	2006	2000	2006–10	2000–06	2000–10
PERSONAL CARE PRODUCTS, SERVICES	**$582**	**$633**	**$714**	**–8.0%**	**–11.4%**	**–18.5%**
READING	**100**	**127**	**185**	**–21.0**	**–31.5**	**–45.9**
EDUCATION	**1,074**	**960**	**800**	**11.8**	**20.0**	**34.2**
TOBACCO PRODUCTS, SMOKING SUPPLIES	**362**	**354**	**404**	**2.3**	**–12.4**	**–10.4**
MISCELLANEOUS	**849**	**915**	**983**	**–7.2**	**–6.9**	**–13.6**
CASH CONTRIBUTIONS	**1,633**	**2,022**	**1,509**	**–19.2**	**33.9**	**8.2**
PERSONAL INSURANCE AND PENSIONS	**5,373**	**5,700**	**4,261**	**–5.7**	**33.8**	**26.1**
Life and other personal insurance	318	348	505	–8.7	–31.1	–37.1
Pensions and Social Security*	5,054	5,352	–	–5.6	–	–
PERSONAL TAXES	**1,769**	**2,631**	**3,947**	**–32.8**	**–33.4**	**–55.2**
Federal income taxes	1,136	1,851	3,051	–38.6	–39.3	–62.8
State and local income taxes	482	561	712	–14.1	–21.1	–32.3
Other taxes	151	218	185	–30.9	18.2	–18.3
GIFTS FOR PEOPLE IN OTHER HOUSEHOLDS	**1,029**	**1,248**	**1,371**	**–17.6**	**–9.0**	**–25.0**

Because of changes in methodology, the 2006 and 2010 data on pensions and Social Security are not comparable with earlier years.

Note: The Bureau of Labor Statistics uses consumer unit rather than household as the sampling unit in the Consumer Expenditure Survey. For the definition of consumer unit, see the glossary. Spending on gifts is also included in the preceding product and service categories..

Source: Bureau of Labor Statistics, 2000, 2006, and 2010 Consumer Expenditure Surveys, Internet site http://www.bls.gov/cex/; calculations by New Strategist

Table 9.2 Average Spending by Householders Aged 35 to 44, 2000 to 2010

(average annual spending of consumer units (CUs) headed by people aged 35 to 44, 2000 to 2010; percent change for selected years; in 2010 dollars)

	average spending			percent change		
	2010	2006	2000	2006–10	2000–06	2000–10
Number of CUs aged 35 to 44 (in 000s)	21,912	23,950	23,983	–8.5%	–0.1%	–8.6%
Average annual spending of consumer units	$55,946	$62,168	$57,172	–10.0	8.7	–2.1
FOOD	**7,483**	**7,929**	**7,714**	**–5.6**	**2.8**	**–3.0**
Food at home	**4,255**	**4,465**	**4,412**	**–4.7**	**1.2**	**–3.6**
Cereals and bakery products	607	598	672	1.5	–11.0	–9.7
Cereals and cereal products	212	200	241	5.9	–16.8	–11.9
Bakery products	395	399	432	–1.0	–7.6	–8.5
Meats, poultry, fish, and eggs	896	1,041	1,162	–13.9	–10.5	–22.9
Beef	230	294	342	–21.8	–14.0	–32.7
Pork	172	201	236	–14.5	–14.6	–27.0
Other meats	140	142	152	–1.2	–6.8	–7.9
Poultry	168	200	225	–16.0	–11.2	–25.5
Fish and seafood	132	155	160	–14.7	–3.1	–17.3
Eggs	54	49	47	10.9	3.9	15.3
Dairy products	458	489	485	–6.3	0.8	–5.6
Fresh milk and cream	177	194	199	–8.6	–2.6	–11.0
Other dairy products	281	295	286	–4.8	3.2	–1.8
Fruits and vegetables	787	726	699	8.4	3.8	12.6
Fresh fruits	273	237	214	15.3	10.7	27.6
Fresh vegetables	233	224	208	4.1	7.8	12.2
Processed fruits	134	142	158	–5.4	–10.5	–15.3
Processed vegetables	146	123	116	18.4	5.8	25.3
Other food at home	1,508	1,612	1,394	–6.4	15.6	8.2
Sugar and other sweets	154	157	186	–1.8	–15.7	–17.3
Fats and oils	119	105	114	13.4	–7.9	4.4
Miscellaneous foods	798	858	656	–7.0	30.8	21.7
Nonalcoholic beverages	384	442	380	–13.2	16.5	1.1
Food prepared by consumer unit on trips	53	49	58	8.9	–16.4	–9.0
Food away from home	**3,227**	**3,464**	**3,301**	**–6.9**	**4.9**	**–2.2**
ALCOHOLIC BEVERAGES	**497**	**536**	**532**	**–7.4**	**0.9**	**–6.6**
HOUSING	**20,041**	**21,960**	**19,135**	**–8.7**	**14.8**	**4.7**
Shelter	**12,139**	**13,461**	**11,308**	**–9.8**	**19.0**	**7.3**
Owned dwellings	8,149	9,697	8,146	–16.0	19.0	0.0
Mortgage interest and charges	5,196	6,397	5,448	–18.8	17.4	–4.6
Property taxes	1,975	2,095	1,578	–5.7	32.8	25.2
Maintenance, repair, insurance, other expenses	978	1,205	1,119	–18.8	7.6	–12.6
Rented dwellings	3,475	3,178	2,617	9.4	21.4	32.8
Other lodging	515	585	545	–12.0	7.5	–5.4
Utilities, fuels, and public services	**4,077**	**4,169**	**3,558**	**–2.2**	**17.2**	**14.6**
Natural gas	497	605	443	–17.8	36.4	12.1
Electricity	1,567	1,535	1,278	2.1	20.1	22.6
Fuel oil and other fuels	105	170	123	–38.2	38.3	–14.5

	average spending			percent change		
	2010	**2006**	**2000**	**2006–10**	**2000–06**	**2000–10**
Telephone	$1,364	$1,375	$1,289	–0.8%	6.6%	5.8%
Water and other public services	544	486	425	12.0	14.1	27.9
Household services	**1,414**	**1,493**	**1,135**	**–5.3**	**31.6**	**24.6**
Personal services	735	877	686	–16.2	27.8	7.1
Other household services	679	615	448	10.3	37.3	51.5
Housekeeping supplies	**663**	**823**	**722**	**–19.5**	**14.0**	**–8.1**
Laundry and cleaning supplies	184	204	199	–10.0	2.8	–7.4
Other household products	332	447	355	–25.7	26.0	–6.4
Postage and stationery	148	172	168	–13.9	2.1	–12.1
Household furnishings and equipment	**1,748**	**2,016**	**2,414**	**–13.3**	**–16.5**	**–27.6**
Household textiles	111	151	157	–26.7	–3.6	–29.3
Furniture	447	580	632	–22.9	–8.2	–29.3
Floor coverings	42	43	67	–2.9	–35.5	–37.4
Major appliances	262	294	268	–10.9	9.6	–2.4
Small appliances and miscellaneous housewares	105	122	118	–14.1	3.8	–10.8
Miscellaneous household equipment	780	824	1,173	–5.4	–29.7	–33.5
APPAREL AND RELATED SERVICES	**2,040**	**2,561**	**2,942**	**–20.4**	**–12.9**	**–30.7**
Men and boys	**487**	**622**	**698**	**–21.7**	**–10.9**	**–30.2**
Men, aged 16 or older	320	436	465	–26.6	–6.2	–31.1
Boys, aged 2 to 15	166	186	233	–10.8	–20.2	–28.8
Women and girls	**765**	**997**	**1,184**	**–23.3**	**–15.8**	**–35.4**
Women, aged 16 or older	555	726	876	–23.5	–17.2	–36.7
Girls, aged 2 to 15	210	271	306	–22.6	–11.4	–31.5
Children under age 2	**117**	**138**	**133**	**–15.5**	**4.1**	**–12.0**
Footwear	**414**	**437**	**508**	**–5.3**	**–13.9**	**–18.5**
Other apparel products and services	**258**	**366**	**419**	**–29.4**	**–12.8**	**–38.4**
TRANSPORTATION	**8,763**	**10,791**	**11,019**	**–18.8**	**–2.1**	**–20.5**
Vehicle purchases	**2,905**	**4,388**	**5,060**	**–33.8**	**–13.3**	**–42.6**
Cars and trucks, new	1,341	2,162	2,183	–38.0	–1.0	–38.6
Cars and trucks, used	1,478	2,134	2,783	–30.7	–23.3	–46.9
Gasoline and motor oil	**2,537**	**2,851**	**1,997**	**–11.0**	**42.8**	**27.0**
Other vehicle expenses	**2,776**	**2,947**	**3,390**	**–5.8**	**–13.1**	**–18.1**
Vehicle finance charges	310	405	514	–23.4	–21.3	–39.7
Maintenance and repairs	889	805	897	10.5	–10.2	–0.8
Vehicle insurance	1,074	1,056	1,119	1.7	–5.7	–4.1
Vehicle rentals, leases, licenses, other charges	503	683	861	–26.3	–20.7	–41.6
Public transportation	**545**	**605**	**571**	**–9.9**	**5.9**	**–4.6**
HEALTH CARE	**2,583**	**2,470**	**2,246**	**4.6**	**10.0**	**15.0**
Health insurance	1,453	1,313	1,076	10.7	22.0	35.0
Medical services	681	686	703	–0.7	–2.4	–3.1
Drugs	340	373	360	–8.9	3.8	–5.5
Medical supplies	109	97	108	12.0	–9.6	1.3
ENTERTAINMENT	**3,058**	**3,208**	**3,120**	**–4.7**	**2.8**	**–2.0**
Fees and admissions	849	907	905	–6.4	0.2	–6.2
Audio and visual equipment and services	1,078	1,138	999	–5.3	13.9	7.9
Pets, toys, hobbies, and playground equipment	716	538	571	33.2	–5.9	25.4
Other entertainment products and services	414	625	645	–33.8	–3.0	–35.8

	average spending			percent change		
	2010	2006	2000	2006–10	2000–06	2000–10
PERSONAL CARE PRODUCTS, SERVICES	**$682**	**$744**	**$815**	**–8.4%**	**–8.7%**	**–16.4%**
READING	**80**	**121**	**191**	**–34.0**	**–36.6**	**–58.2**
EDUCATION	**963**	**927**	**779**	**3.9**	**19.0**	**23.7**
TOBACCO PRODUCTS, SMOKING SUPPLIES	**358**	**383**	**541**	**–6.5**	**–29.2**	**–33.8**
MISCELLANEOUS	**922**	**1,020**	**1,079**	**–9.6**	**–5.5**	**–14.5**
CASH CONTRIBUTIONS	**1,532**	**1,846**	**1,270**	**–17.0**	**45.4**	**20.6**
PERSONAL INSURANCE AND PENSIONS	**6,944**	**7,669**	**5,787**	**–9.5**	**32.5**	**20.0**
Life and other personal insurance	280	394	522	–28.9	–24.5	–46.3
Pensions and Social Security*	6,664	7,275	–	–8.4	–	–
PERSONAL TAXES	**1,992**	**3,426**	**4,906**	**–41.8**	**–30.2**	**–59.4**
Federal income taxes	1,242	2,428	3,817	–48.9	–36.4	–67.5
State and local income taxes	650	786	929	–17.3	–15.4	–30.1
Other taxes	100	211	160	–52.6	32.2	–37.3
GIFTS FOR PEOPLE IN OTHER HOUSEHOLDS	**732**	**838**	**1,268**	**–12.7**	**–33.9**	**–42.3**

Because of changes in methodology, the 2006 and 2010 data on pensions and Social Security are not comparable with earlier years.

Note: The Bureau of Labor Statistics uses consumer unit rather than household as the sampling unit in the Consumer Expenditure Survey. For the definition of consumer unit, see the glossary. Spending on gifts is also included in the preceding product and service categories.

Source: Bureau of Labor Statistics, 2000, 2006, and 2010 Consumer Expenditure Surveys, Internet site http://www.bls.gov/cex/; calculations by New Strategist

Householders Aged 35 to 44 Spend More than Average

Most households in the age group include children, which accounts for their above-average spending.

Householders aged 35 to 44 spend more than most other age groups—$55,946 in 2010 and 16 percent more than the average household. The age group controls 21 percent of household spending. Householders aged 35 to 44 spend significantly more than average on items commonly purchased by parents with children under age 18. They spend 26 percent more than the average household on milk and about twice the average on children's clothing. Many in this age group bought homes during the housing bubble, which explains why their mortgage interest payments are 55 percent above average.

Householders aged 35 to 44 spend less than average on some surprising items. They spend just below average on women's clothing, 21 percent less on out-of-pocket health insurance expenses, and 29 percent less on gifts for people in other households.

■ The spending of householders aged 35 to 44 is determined by children, which reduces their spending on other items.

Householders aged 35 to 44 spend more than the average household on cereal

(indexed spending of householders aged 35 to 44 on selected items, 2010)

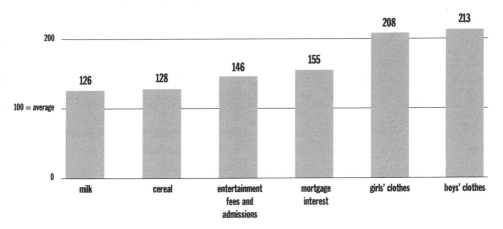

Table 9.3 Average, Indexed, and Market Share of Spending by Householders Aged 35 to 44, 2010

(average annual spending of total consumer units and average annual, indexed, and market share of spending by consumer units headed by people aged 35 to 44, 2010)

	total consumer units	consumer units headed by 35-to-44-year-olds		
		average spending	indexed spending	market share
Number of consumer units (in 000s)	121,107	21,912	–	18.1%
Average annual spending	$48,109	$55,946	116	21.0
FOOD	6,129	7,483	122	22.1
Food at home	3,624	4,255	117	21.2
Cereals and bakery products	502	607	121	21.9
Cereals and cereal products	165	212	128	23.2
Bakery products	337	395	117	21.2
Meats, poultry, fish, and eggs	784	896	114	20.7
Beef	217	230	106	19.2
Pork	149	172	115	20.9
Other meats	117	140	120	21.6
Poultry	138	168	122	22.0
Fish and seafood	117	132	113	20.4
Eggs	46	54	117	21.2
Dairy products	380	458	121	21.8
Fresh milk and cream	141	177	126	22.7
Other dairy products	240	281	117	21.2
Fruits and vegetables	679	787	116	21.0
Fresh fruits	232	273	118	21.3
Fresh vegetables	210	233	111	20.1
Processed fruits	113	134	119	21.5
Processed vegetables	124	146	118	21.3
Other food at home	1,278	1,508	118	21.3
Sugar and other sweets	132	154	117	21.1
Fats and oils	103	119	116	20.9
Miscellaneous foods	667	798	120	21.6
Nonalcoholic beverages	333	384	115	20.9
Food prepared by consumer unit on trips	43	53	123	22.3
Food away from home	2,505	3,227	129	23.3
ALCOHOLIC BEVERAGES	412	497	121	21.8
HOUSING	16,557	20,041	121	21.9
Shelter	9,812	12,139	124	22.4
Owned dwellings	6,277	8,149	130	23.5
Mortgage interest and charges	3,351	5,196	155	28.1
Property taxes	1,814	1,975	109	19.7
Maintenance, repair, insurance, other expenses	1,112	978	88	15.9
Rented dwellings	2,900	3,475	120	21.7
Other lodging	635	515	81	14.7
Utilities, fuels, and public services	3,660	4,077	111	20.2
Natural gas	440	497	113	20.4
Electricity	1,413	1,567	111	20.1
Fuel oil and other fuels	140	105	75	13.6

	total consumer units	consumer units headed by 35-to-44-year-olds		
		average spending	indexed spending	market share
Telephone	$1,178	$1,364	116	20.9%
Water and other public services	489	544	111	20.1
Household services	**1,007**	**1,414**	**140**	**25.4**
Personal services	340	735	216	39.1
Other household services	667	679	102	18.4
Housekeeping supplies	**612**	**663**	**108**	**19.6**
Laundry and cleaning supplies	150	184	123	22.2
Other household products	329	332	101	18.3
Postage and stationery	132	148	112	20.3
Household furnishings and equipment	**1,467**	**1,748**	**119**	**21.6**
Household textiles	102	111	109	19.7
Furniture	355	447	126	22.8
Floor coverings	36	42	117	21.1
Major appliances	209	262	125	22.7
Small appliances and miscellaneous housewares	107	105	98	17.8
Miscellaneous household equipment	657	780	119	21.5
APPAREL AND RELATED SERVICES	**1,700**	**2,040**	**120**	**21.7**
Men and boys	**382**	**487**	**127**	**23.1**
Men, aged 16 or older	304	320	105	19.0
Boys, aged 2 to 15	78	166	213	38.5
Women and girls	**663**	**765**	**115**	**20.9**
Women, aged 16 or older	562	555	99	17.9
Girls, aged 2 to 15	101	210	208	37.6
Children under age 2	**91**	**117**	**129**	**23.3**
Footwear	**303**	**414**	**137**	**24.7**
Other apparel products and services	**261**	**258**	**99**	**17.9**
TRANSPORTATION	**7,677**	**8,763**	**114**	**20.7**
Vehicle purchases	**2,588**	**2,905**	**112**	**20.3**
Cars and trucks, new	1,219	1,341	110	19.9
Cars and trucks, used	1,318	1,478	112	20.3
Gasoline and motor oil	**2,132**	**2,537**	**119**	**21.5**
Other vehicle expenses	**2,464**	**2,776**	**113**	**20.4**
Vehicle finance charges	243	310	128	23.1
Maintenance and repairs	787	889	113	20.4
Vehicle insurance	1,010	1,074	106	19.2
Vehicle rentals, leases, licenses, other charges	423	503	119	21.5
Public transportation	**493**	**545**	**111**	**20.0**
HEALTH CARE	**3,157**	**2,583**	**82**	**14.8**
Health insurance	1,831	1,453	79	14.4
Medical services	722	681	94	17.1
Drugs	485	340	70	12.7
Medical supplies	119	109	92	16.6
ENTERTAINMENT	**2,504**	**3,058**	**122**	**22.1**
Fees and admissions	581	849	146	26.4
Audio and visual equipment and services	954	1,078	113	20.4
Pets, toys, hobbies, and playground equipment	606	716	118	21.4
Other entertainment products and services	364	414	114	20.6

	total consumer units	consumer units headed by 35-to-44-year-olds		
		average spending	indexed spending	market share
PERSONAL CARE PRODUCTS AND SERVICES	$582	$682	117	21.2%
READING	100	80	80	14.5
EDUCATION	1,074	963	90	16.2
TOBACCO PRODUCTS AND SMOKING SUPPLIES	362	358	99	17.9
MISCELLANEOUS	849	922	109	19.6
CASH CONTRIBUTIONS	1,633	1,532	94	17.0
PERSONAL INSURANCE AND PENSIONS	5,373	6,944	129	23.4
Life and other personal insurance	318	280	88	15.9
Pensions and Social Security*	5,054	6,664	132	23.9
PERSONAL TAXES	1,769	1,992	113	20.4
Federal income taxes	1,136	1,242	109	19.8
State and local income taxes	482	650	135	24.4
Other taxes	151	100	66	12.0
GIFTS FOR PEOPLE IN OTHER HOUSEHOLDS	1,029	732	71	12.9

Note: The Bureau of Labor Statistics uses consumer unit rather than household as the sampling unit in the Consumer Expenditure Survey. For the definition of consumer unit, see the glossary. Spending on gifts is also included in the preceding product and service categories. "–" means not applicable.
Source: Bureau of Labor Statistics, 2010 Consumer Expenditure Survey, Internet site http://www.bls.gov/cex/; calculations by New Strategist

10

Time Use

■ People aged 35 to 44 have the least amount of leisure time because most are juggling work and family responsibilities.

■ The middle aged spend the most time at work. Men aged 35 to 44 spend 4.93 hours per day working versus the 3.65 hours spent working by the average man.

■ Women aged 35 to 44 spend nearly twice as much time as the average woman caring for household children. They spend 29 percent more time than the average woman at work.

■ Women aged 35 to 44 have 22 percent less leisure time than the average woman. Men aged 35 to 44 have 20 percent less leisure time than the average man.

Gen X Spends More Time at Work than at Play

People aged 35 to 44 spend 33 percent more time than the average person at work.

Time use varies sharply by age. The middle aged are the ones who spend the most time at work and the least time at play, according to the Bureau of Labor Statistics' American Time Use Survey. Men aged 35 to 44 spend 4.93 hours per day working versus the 3.65 hours spent working by the average man.

Women aged 35 to 44 spend 29 percent more time working than the average woman. They spend nearly twice as much time as the average woman caring for household children.

People aged 35 to 44 have the least amount of leisure time because most are juggling both work and family responsibilities. Women aged 35 to 44 have 22 percent less leisure time than the average woman. Men in the age group have 20 percent less leisure time than the average man.

■ As their children grow up, Gen Xers will have more leisure time.

Time at work peaks in middle age

(average number of hours per day men spend working, by age, 2010)

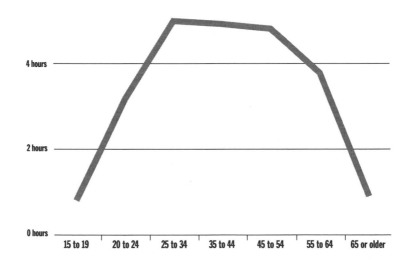

Table 10.1 Detailed Time Use of People Aged 35 to 44, 2010

(hours per day spent in primary activities by total people aged 15 or older and people aged 35 to 44, index of age group to total, and number and percent of people aged 35 to 44 participating in activity on an average day, 2010)

	average hours per day for total people	average hours per day for people aged 35 to 44	index, 35 to 44 to total	people aged 35 to 44 participating in activity	
				number (in 000s)	percent
Total, all activities	**24.00**	**24.00**	**100**	**40,089**	**100.0%**
Personal care activities	9.45	9.12	97	39,994	99.8
Sleeping	8.67	8.40	97	39,950	99.7
Grooming	0.69	0.66	96	32,684	81.5
Health-related self-care	0.09	0.04	44	1,109	2.8
Household activities	1.82	1.94	107	31,919	79.6
Housework	0.57	0.68	119	15,197	37.9
Food preparation and cleanup	0.56	0.65	116	24,401	60.9
Lawn, garden, and houseplants	0.21	0.19	90	3,577	8.9
Animals and pets	0.10	0.10	100	5,584	13.9
Vehicles	0.04	0.04	100	1,026	2.6
Household management	0.19	0.14	74	9,412	23.5
Financial management	0.03	0.01	33	1,253	3.1
Household and personal organization and planning	0.09	0.08	89	5,730	14.3
Household and personal mail and messages (except email)	0.02	0.01	50	1,242	3.1
Household and personal email and messages	0.05	0.04	80	2,768	6.9
Caring for and helping household members	0.43	0.91	212	19,949	49.8
Caring for and helping household children	0.36	0.77	214	18,314	45.7
Caring for household adults	0.01	0.01	100	625	1.6
Helping household adults	0.01	0.01	100	1,654	4.1
Caring for and helping people in other households	0.15	0.11	73	4,014	10.0
Caring for and helping children in other households	0.07	0.03	43	1,623	4.0
Caring for adults in other households	0.01	0.00	0	112	0.3
Helping adults in other households	0.07	0.08	114	2,426	6.1
Working and work-related activities	3.22	4.29	133	23,368	58.3
Working	3.14	4.17	133	22,052	55.0
Job search and interviewing	0.05	0.08	160	1,221	3.0
Educational activities	0.45	0.12	27	1,401	3.5
Taking class	0.28	0.04	14	553	1.4
Homework and research	0.16	0.08	50	1,047	2.6
Consumer purchases	0.37	0.39	105	17,512	43.7
Grocery shopping	0.10	0.11	110	6,229	15.5
Shopping (except groceries, food, and gas)	0.24	0.24	100	8,983	22.4
Professional and personal care services	0.08	0.08	100	3,374	8.4
Medical and care services	0.05	0.04	80	1,122	2.8
Eating and drinking	1.13	1.07	95	38,463	95.9
Socializing, relaxing, and leisure	4.63	3.67	79	37,327	93.1
Socializing and communicating	0.63	0.52	83	12,895	32.2
Attending or hosting social events	0.08	0.08	100	1,091	2.7

	average hours per day for total people	average hours per day for people aged 35 to 44	index, 35 to 44 to total	people aged 35 to 44 participating in activity	
				number (in 000s)	percent
Relaxing and leisure	3.84	2.98	78	35,014	87.3%
Television and movies	2.73	2.22	81	30,265	75.5
Playing games	0.21	0.12	57	2,465	6.1
Computer use for leisure (except games)	0.20	0.19	95	5,166	12.9
Reading for personal interest	0.30	0.17	57	6,495	16.2
Arts and entertainment (other than sports)	0.08	0.08	100	1,209	3.0
Attending movies	0.03	0.03	100	559	1.4
Sports, exercise, and recreation	0.33	0.32	97	7,420	18.5
Participating in sports, exercise, and recreation	0.31	0.28	90	6,995	17.4
Attending sporting or recreational events	0.03	0.04	133	573	1.4
Religious and spiritual activities	0.16	0.14	88	3,244	8.1
Volunteer activities	0.15	0.14	93	2,831	7.1
Telephone calls	0.10	0.06	60	4,559	11.4
Traveling	1.19	1.34	113	36,231	90.4

Note: Primary activities are those respondents identified as their main activity. Other activities done simultaneously are not included. Travel related to activities is reported separately. Numbers do not sum to total because not all activities are shown. The index is calculated by dividing time spent by age group by time spent by the average person and multiplying by 100. Source: Bureau of Labor Statistics, unpublished tables from the 2010 American Time Use Survey, Internet site http://www.bls .gov/tus/home.htm

Table 10.2 Detailed Time Use of Men Aged 35 to 44, 2010

(hours per day spent in primary activities by total men aged 15 or older and men aged 35 to 44, index of age group to total, and number and percent of men aged 35 to 44 participating in activity on an average day, 2010)

	average hours per day for total men	average hours per day for men aged 35 to 44	index, 35 to 44 to total	men aged 35 to 44 participating in activity number (in 000s)	percent
Total, all activities	**24.00**	**24.00**	**100**	**19,847**	**100.0%**
Personal care activities	9.24	8.91	96	19,752	99.5
Sleeping	8.56	8.29	97	19,713	99.3
Grooming	0.58	0.56	97	15,523	78.2
Health-related self-care	0.08	–	–	411	2.1
Household activities	1.44	1.47	102	14,001	70.5
Housework	0.26	0.32	123	4,445	22.4
Food preparation and cleanup	0.32	0.37	116	9,307	46.9
Lawn, garden, and houseplants	0.31	0.27	87	2,065	10.4
Animals and pets	0.08	0.09	113	2,240	11.3
Vehicles	0.08	0.07	88	817	4.1
Household management	0.16	0.12	75	3,698	18.6
Financial management	0.02	0.01	50	594	3.0
Household and personal organization and planning	0.07	0.07	100	2,041	10.3
Household and personal mail and messages (except email)	0.01	0.00	0	345	1.7
Household and personal email and messages	0.05	0.03	60	1,008	5.1
Caring for and helping household members	0.28	0.67	239	8,443	42.5
Caring for and helping household children	0.23	0.59	257	7,511	37.8
Caring for household adults	0.01	–	–	323	1.6
Helping household adults	0.01	0.02	200	1,029	5.2
Caring for and helping people in other households	0.14	0.13	93	1,669	8.4
Caring for and helping children in other households	0.05	0.02	40	502	2.5
Caring for adults in other households	–	0.00	–	57	0.3
Helping adults in other households	0.08	–	–	1,151	5.8
Working and work-related activities	3.75	5.07	135	12,864	64.8
Working	3.65	4.93	135	12,194	61.4
Job search and interviewing	0.06	0.12	200	714	3.6
Educational activities	0.44	0.06	14	376	1.9
Taking class	0.30	0.00	0	85	0.4
Homework and research	0.13	0.05	38	349	1.8
Consumer purchases	0.30	0.32	107	7,972	40.2
Grocery shopping	0.08	0.08	100	2,472	12.5
Shopping (except groceries, food, and gas)	0.19	0.21	111	3,878	19.5
Professional and personal care services	0.06	0.08	133	1,567	7.9
Medical and care services	0.04	0.04	100	573	2.9
Eating and drinking	1.17	1.13	97	19,194	96.7
Socializing, relaxing, and leisure	4.88	3.92	80	18,492	93.2
Socializing and communicating	0.61	0.52	85	5,849	29.5
Attending or hosting social events	0.07	0.09	129	511	2.6

	average hours per day for total men	average hours per day for men aged 35 to 44	index, 35 to 44 to total	men aged 35 to 44 participating in activity	
				number (in 000s)	percent
Relaxing and leisure	4.11	3.23	79	17,322	87.3%
Television and movies	2.94	2.47	84	15,604	78.6
Playing games	0.27	0.14	52	1,217	6.1
Computer use for leisure (except games)	0.20	0.20	100	2,387	12.0
Reading for personal interest	0.25	0.12	48	2,291	11.5
Arts and entertainment (other than sports)	0.09	0.07	78	434	2.2
Attending movies	0.03	0.02	67	156	0.8
Sports, exercise, and recreation	0.45	0.40	89	3,862	19.5
Participating in sports, exercise, and recreation	0.42	0.36	86	3,680	18.5
Attending sporting or recreational events	0.03	0.04	133	272	1.4
Religious and spiritual activities	0.13	0.14	108	1,373	6.9
Volunteer activities	0.12	0.10	83	1,015	5.1
Telephone calls	0.07	0.04	57	1,499	7.6
Traveling	1.22	1.33	109	18,270	92.1

Note: Primary activities are those respondents identified as their main activity. Other activities done simultaneously are not included. Travel related to activities is reported separately. Numbers do not sum to total because not all activities are shown. The index is calculated by dividing time spent by age group by time spent by the average man and multiplying by 100. "–" means sample is too small to make a reliable estimate.

Source: Bureau of Labor Statistics, unpublished tables from the 2010 American Time Use Survey, Internet site http://www.bls .gov/tus/home.htm

Table 10.3 Detailed Time Use of Women Aged 35 to 44, 2010

(hours per day spent in primary activities by total women aged 15 or older and women aged 35 to 44, index of age group to total, and number and percent of women aged 35 to 44 participating in activity on an average day, 2010)

	average hours per day for total women	average hours per day for women aged 35 to 44	index, 35 to 44 to total	women aged 35 to 44 participating in activity number (in 000s)	percent
Total, all activities	**24.00**	**24.00**	**100**	**20,242**	**100.0%**
Personal care activities	9.66	9.32	96	20,242	100.0
Sleeping	8.76	8.50	97	20,238	100.0
Grooming	0.79	0.75	95	17,161	84.8
Health-related self-care	0.10	0.05	50	698	3.4
Household activities	2.18	2.40	110	17,917	88.5
Housework	0.87	1.02	117	10,753	53.1
Food preparation and cleanup	0.79	0.92	116	15,094	74.6
Lawn, garden, and houseplants	0.12	0.11	92	1,512	7.5
Animals and pets	0.11	0.10	91	3,345	16.5
Vehicles	0.01	–	–	209	1.0
Household management	0.22	0.16	73	5,714	28.2
Financial management	0.04	0.01	25	659	3.3
Household and personal organization and planning	0.11	0.09	82	3,689	18.2
Household and personal mail and messages (except email)	0.03	0.01	33	898	4.4
Household and personal email and messages	0.05	0.04	80	1,760	8.7
Caring for and helping household members	0.58	1.14	197	11,506	56.8
Caring for and helping household children	0.48	0.94	196	10,803	53.4
Caring for household adults	0.02	–	–	302	1.5
Helping household adults	0.01	0.01	100	625	3.1
Caring for and helping people in other households	0.16	0.09	56	2,345	11.6
Caring for and helping children in other households	0.08	0.03	38	1,122	5.5
Caring for adults in other households	0.02	0.00	0	54	0.3
Helping adults in other households	0.06	–	–	1,275	6.3
Working and work-related activities	2.73	3.52	129	10,503	51.9
Working	2.66	3.43	129	9,859	48.7
Job search and interviewing	0.03	0.05	167	507	2.5
Educational activities	0.45	0.18	40	1,025	5.1
Taking class	0.26	0.07	27	467	2.3
Homework and research	0.18	0.11	61	698	3.4
Consumer purchases	0.44	0.46	105	9,539	47.1
Grocery shopping	0.13	0.14	108	3,756	18.6
Shopping (except groceries, food, and gas)	0.28	0.28	100	5,105	25.2
Professional and personal care services	0.10	0.07	70	1,807	8.9
Medical and care services	0.06	0.03	50	549	2.7
Eating and drinking	1.09	1.02	94	19,269	95.2
Socializing, relaxing, and leisure	4.39	3.43	78	18,835	93.0
Socializing and communicating	0.65	0.53	82	7,046	34.8
Attending or hosting social events	0.08	0.07	88	580	2.9

	average hours per day for total women	average hours per day for women aged 35 to 44	index, 35 to 44 to total	women aged 35 to 44 participating in activity	
				number (in 000s)	percent
Relaxing and leisure	3.59	2.74	76	17,691	87.4%
Television and movies	2.52	1.98	79	14,661	72.4
Playing games	0.15	0.10	67	1,248	6.2
Computer use for leisure (except games)	0.19	0.18	95	2,779	13.7
Reading for personal interest	0.35	0.21	60	4,203	20.8
Arts and entertainment (other than sports)	0.08	0.09	113	775	3.8
Attending movies	0.03	0.05	167	402	2.0
Sports, exercise, and recreation	0.23	0.24	104	3,558	17.6
Participating in sports, exercise, and recreation	0.20	0.20	100	3,315	16.4
Attending sporting or recreational events	0.03	0.04	133	301	1.5
Religious and spiritual activities	0.18	0.13	72	1,871	9.2
Volunteer activities	0.18	0.17	94	1,817	9.0
Telephone calls	0.13	0.09	69	3,060	15.1
Traveling	1.16	1.34	116	17,961	88.7

Note: Primary activities are those respondents identified as their main activity. Other activities done simultaneously are not included. Travel related to activities is reported separately. Numbers do not sum to total because not all activities are shown. The index is calculated by dividing time spent by age group by time spent by the average woman and multiplying by 100. "–" means sample is too small to make a reliable estimate.
Source: Bureau of Labor Statistics, unpublished tables from the 2010 American Time Use Survey, Internet site http://www.bls .gov/tus/home.htm

11

Wealth

■ Median household net worth among householders aged 35 to 44 is well below $100,000, at $69,400 in 2009. This figure is 29 percent below the $97,100 of 2007 and represents the second-largest decline among age groups.

■ The median financial assets of householders aged 35 to 44 rose by 8 percent between 2007 and 2009, to $27,500 after adjusting for inflation—the only age group to make gains.

■ Householders aged 35 to 44 owned a median of $196,500 in nonfinancial assets in 2009. The median value of their nonfinancial assets fell 15 percent between 2007 and 2009, after adjusting for inflation—a loss of more than $35,000. This decline is the reason for the lower overall net worth of the age group.

■ Gen Xers reduced their debt between 2007 and 2009. The median amount owed by householders aged 35 to 44 fell 4 percent during those years, after adjusting for inflation. The percentage of Gen X households with debt (87.7 percent in 2009) increased slightly.

■ Gen Xers are worried about retirement. In 2012, only 16 percent of workers aged 35 to 44 were "very confident" they would have enough money to live comfortably throughout retirement.

Net Worth Fell Sharply during the Great Recession

Every age group lost ground during the economic downturn.

Net worth is what remains when a household's debts are subtracted from its assets. During the Great Recession, which officially lasted from December 2007 until June 2009, the value of houses, stocks, and retirement accounts fell sharply. At the same time, debt increased. Consequently, net worth fell 23 percent between 2007 and 2009, after adjusting for inflation. These data come from a unique follow-up to the 2007 Survey of Consumer Finances. The survey is taken only every three years. Because of the severity of the Great Recession, however, the Federal Reserve Board arranged for the 2007 respondents to be re-interviewed in 2009 to determine the impact of the Great Recession on household assets, debt, and net worth.

The impact was severe. Net worth fell in every age group. It declined the most—by 37 percent—among householders under age 35, many of them recent homebuyers who bought at the peak. It fell by the smallest percentage, 12 percent, among householders aged 65 to 74, many of whom bought their house decades ago.

■ Net worth typically rises with age as people pay off their debts. That pattern has not changed. In 2009, median household net worth peaked in the 55-to-64 age group at $222,300.

Net worth peaks among householders aged 55 to 64

(median household net worth by age of householder, 2009)

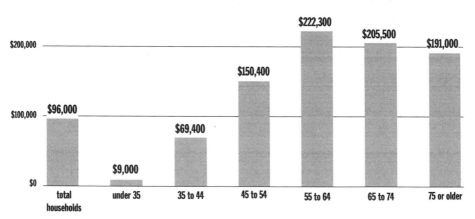

Table 11.1 Net Worth of Households, 2007 and 2009

(median net worth of households by age of householder, 2007 and 2009; percent change, 2007–09; in 2009 dollars)

	2009	2007	percent change
Total households	**$96,000**	**$125,400**	**–23.4%**
Under age 35	9,000	14,200	–36.6
Aged 35 to 44	69,400	97,100	–28.5
Aged 45 to 54	150,400	203,000	–25.9
Aged 55 to 64	222,300	257,700	–13.7
Aged 65 to 74	205,500	232,700	–11.7
Aged 75 or older	191,000	228,900	–16.6

Source: Federal Reserve Board, 2007-09 Panel Survey of Consumer Finances, Internet site http://www.federalreserve.gov/econresdata/scf/scf_2009p.htm; calculations by New Strategist

Financial Asset Value Declined in Most Age Groups

Householders aged 35 to 44 gained ground, however.

Most households own financial assets, which range from transaction accounts (checking and saving) to stocks, mutual funds, retirement accounts, and life insurance. The median value of the financial assets owned by the average household stood at $29,600 in 2009, down by a relatively modest 5 percent since 2007 after adjusting for inflation. Householders aged 35 to 44 were the only ones to make gains in the value of their financial assets between 2007 and 2009.

Transaction accounts, the most commonly owned financial asset, are held by 92 percent of households. Their median value was just $4,000 in 2009—slightly lower than the $4,100 of 2007. Retirement accounts are the second most commonly owned financial asset, 56 percent of households having one. Most retirement accounts are not large, however, with an overall median value of just $48,000 in 2009. This figure is 5 percent lower than the $50,600 of 2007, after adjusting for inflation.

Only 18.5 percent of households owned stock directly in 2009 (outside of a retirement account). The median value of stock owned by stockholding households was just $12,000 in 2009, 35 percent less than the value in 2007 after adjusting for inflation.

■ The median value of financial assets peaked in the 55-to-64 age group, at $72,500 in 2009.

The value of retirement accounts is modest, even in the older age groups

(median value of retirement accounts owned by households, by age of householder, 2009)

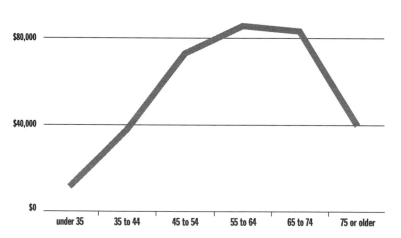

Table 11.2 Ownership and Value of Financial Assets, 2007 and 2009

(percentage of households owning any financial asset and median value of financial assets for owners, by age of householder, 2007 and 2009; percentage point change in ownership and percent change in value, 2007–09; in 2009 dollars)

	2009	2007	percentage point change
PERCENT OWNING			
Total households	**94.6%**	**94.3%**	**0.3**
Under age 35	91.4	90.2	1.2
Aged 35 to 44	92.3	93.5	–1.2
Aged 45 to-54	96.0	94.1	1.9
Aged 55 to 64	97.0	97.9	–0.9
Aged 65 to 74	97.8	96.1	1.7
Aged 75 or older	95.8	98.1	–2.3

	2009	2007	percent change
MEDIAN VALUE			
Total households	**$29,600**	**$31,300**	**–5.4%**
Under age 35	7,400	7,400	0.0
Aged 35 to 44	27,500	25,500	7.8
Aged 45 to 54	58,500	64,300	–9.0
Aged 55 to 64	72,500	78,200	–7.3
Aged 65 to 74	48,000	63,900	–24.9
Aged 75 or older	39,000	41,400	–5.8

Source: Federal Reserve Board, 2007-09 Panel Survey of Consumer Finances, Internet site http://www.federalreserve.gov/econresdata/scf/scf_2009p.htm; calculations by New Strategist

Table 11.3 Households Owning Transaction Accounts, Life Insurance, and CDs, 2007 and 2009

(percentage of households owning transaction accounts, cash value life insurance, and certificates of deposit, and median value for owners, by age of householder, 2007 and 2009; percentage point change in ownership and percent change in value, 2007–09; in 2009 dollars)

	transaction accounts			cash value life insurance			certificates of deposit		
	2009	2007	percentage point change	2009	2007	percentage point change	2009	2007	percentage point change
PERCENT OWNING									
Total households	**92.3%**	**92.6%**	**−0.3**	**24.3%**	**23.2%**	**1.1**	**15.9%**	**15.4%**	**0.5**
Under age 35	88.5	88.0	0.5	13.1	12.4	0.7	7.9	6.5	1.4
Aged 35 to 44	89.8	91.8	−2.0	16.8	17.1	−0.3	9.4	8.9	0.5
Aged 45 to 54	94.1	92.8	1.3	25.3	22.0	3.3	13.9	14.5	−0.6
Aged 55 to 64	95.3	96.5	−1.2	33.4	35.7	−2.3	20.2	19.5	0.7
Aged 65 to 74	95.0	95.0	0.0	36.3	34.6	1.7	24.8	23.0	1.8
Aged 75 or older	94.2	95.1	−0.9	34.2	29.2	5.0	35.2	36.8	−1.6

	transaction accounts			cash value life insurance			certificates of deposit		
	2009	2007	percent change	2009	2007	percent change	2009	2007	percent change
MEDIAN VALUE									
Total households	**$4,000**	**$4,100**	**−2.4%**	**$7,300**	**$8,300**	**−12.0%**	**$20,000**	**$20,700**	**−3.4%**
Under age 35	2,300	2,600	−11.5	2,500	3,600	−30.6	9,000	4,900	83.7
Aged 35 to 44	3,000	3,500	−14.3	7,000	8,300	−15.7	10,000	5,200	92.3
Aged 45 to 54	5,000	4,800	4.2	8,000	10,400	−23.1	18,000	18,600	−3.2
Aged 55 to 64	5,500	5,600	−1.8	10,000	10,400	−3.8	25,000	20,700	20.8
Aged 65 to 74	5,500	7,000	−21.4	10,000	10,600	−5.7	27,700	22,800	21.5
Aged 75 or older	7,000	6,200	12.9	8,000	5,200	53.8	31,400	31,100	1.0

Source: Federal Reserve Board, 2007-09 Panel Survey of Consumer Finances, Internet site http://www.federalreserve.gov/econresdata/scf/scf_2009p.htm; calculations by New Strategist

Table 11.4 Households Owning Retirement Accounts and Stocks, 2007 and 2009

(percentage of households owning retirement accounts and stocks, and median value for owners, by age of householder, 2007 and 2009; percentage point change in ownership and percent change in value, 2007–09; in 2009 dollars)

	retirement accounts			stocks		
	2009	2007	percentage point change	2009	2007	percentage point change
PERCENT OWNING						
Total households	**56.2%**	**55.6%**	**0.6**	**18.5%**	**18.4%**	**0.1**
Under age 35	48.4	44.9	3.5	12.6	14.6	–2.0
Aged 35 to 44	61.2	59.4	1.8	18.9	17.0	1.9
Aged 45 to 54	68.2	68.0	0.2	20.3	18.4	1.9
Aged 55 to 64	62.7	64.3	–1.6	21.3	21.2	0.1
Aged 65 to 74	51.8	53.3	–1.5	21.9	21.0	0.9
Aged 75 or older	29.5	31.3	–1.8	18.6	22.8	–4.2

	retirement accounts			stocks		
	2009	2007	percent change	2009	2007	percent change
MEDIAN VALUE						
Total households	**$48,000**	**$50,600**	**–5.1%**	**$12,000**	**$18,500**	**–35.1%**
Under age 35	11,400	10,400	9.6	3,000	3,100	–3.2
Aged 35 to 44	38,000	38,300	–0.8	12,000	15,500	–22.6
Aged 45 to 54	73,000	81,400	–10.3	11,700	19,700	–40.6
Aged 55 to 64	85,600	103,600	–17.4	16,000	24,900	–35.7
Aged 65 to 74	83,200	79,700	4.4	25,000	36,200	–30.9
Aged 75 or older	40,000	36,200	10.5	35,000	101,500	–65.5

Note: Stock ownership is direct ownership outside of a retirement account or mutual fund.
Source: Federal Reserve Board, 2007-09 Panel Survey of Consumer Finances, Internet site http://www.federalreserve.gov/econresdata/scf/scf_2009p.htm; calculations by New Strategist

Table 11.5 Households Owning Pooled Investment Funds and Bonds, 2007 and 2009

(percentage of households owning pooled investment funds and bonds, and median value for owners, by age of householder, 2007 and 2009; percentage point change in ownership and percent change in value, 2007–09; in 2009 dollars)

	pooled investment funds			bonds		
	2009	2007	percentage point change	2009	2007	percentage point change
PERCENT OWNING						
Total households	**10.8%**	**11.5%**	**−0.7**	**2.6%**	**1.7%**	**0.9**
Under age 35	5.4	5.8	−0.4	0.5	0.2	0.3
Aged 35 to 44	10.0	11.7	−1.7	1.3	0.7	0.6
Aged 45 to 54	13.2	12.6	0.6	2.4	1.1	1.3
Aged 55 to 64	14.5	14.1	0.4	3.3	2.4	0.9
Aged 65 to 74	11.5	13.8	−2.3	6.2	4.5	1.7
Aged 75 or older	12.6	15.1	−2.5	5.5	3.9	1.6

	pooled investment funds			bonds		
	2009	2007	percent change	2009	2007	percent change
MEDIAN VALUE						
Total households	**$47,000**	**$58,700**	**−19.9%**	**$50,000**	**$62,100**	**−19.5%**
Under age 35	10,000	15,000	−33.3	–	–	–
Aged 35 to 44	35,000	27,300	28.2	5,000	103,600	−95.2
Aged 45 to 54	35,000	51,800	−32.4	27,000	127,600	−78.8
Aged 55 to 64	70,400	115,000	−38.8	65,000	82,800	−21.5
Aged 65 to 74	100,000	155,300	−35.6	86,000	51,600	66.7
Aged 75 or older	70,000	77,700	−9.9	37,400	96,500	−61.2

Note: Pooled investment funds exclude money market funds and indirectly held mutual funds. They include open-end and closed-end mutual funds, real estate investment trusts, and hedge funds. "–" means sample is too small to make a reliable estimate.
Source: Federal Reserve Board, 2007-09 Panel Survey of Consumer Finances, Internet site http://www.federalreserve.gov/econresdata/scf/scf_2009p.htm; calculations by New Strategist

Nonfinancial Assets Are the Basis of Household Wealth

The average household saw the value of its nonfinancial assets fall during the Great Recession.

The median value of the nonfinancial assets owned by the average American household stood at $204,000 in 2009, far surpassing the $29,600 median in financial assets. Between 2007 and 2009, the value of the nonfinancial assets owned by the average household fell 13 percent, after adjusting for inflation. Nearly every age group saw its nonfinancial assets fall in value, primarily because of the decline in housing values. Householders under age 35 were the only ones who made gains.

Eighty-seven percent of households own a vehicle, the most commonly held nonfinancial asset. The value of the vehicles owned by the average household fell steeply (down 26 percent) between 2007 and 2009, after adjusting for inflation. Behind the decline was the reluctance of households to buy new vehicles during the Great Recession.

The second most commonly owned nonfinancial asset is a home, owned by 70 percent. Homes are by far the most valuable asset owned by Americans, and they account for the largest share of net worth. In 2009, the median value of the average owned home was $176,000, 15 percent below the median of $207,100 in 2007 (in 2009 dollars). Housing prices have continued to decline, driving median home values even lower than the numbers shown here.

■ The continuing decline in housing values may have reduced average household net worth below the 2009 figure.

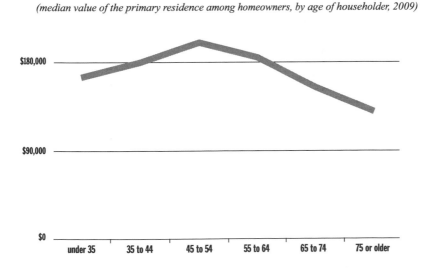

Median housing value peaks in the 45-to-54 age group

(median value of the primary residence among homeowners, by age of householder, 2009)

Table 11.6 Ownership and Value of Nonfinancial Assets, 2007 and 2009

(percentage of households owning any nonfinancial asset and median value of nonfinancial assets for owners, by age of householder, 2007 and 2009; percentage point change in ownership and percent change in value, 2007–09; in 2009 dollars)

	2009	2007	percentage point change
PERCENT OWNING			
Total households	**92.6%**	**92.7%**	**–0.1**
Under age 35	89.5	88.1	1.4
Aged 35 to 44	92.3	91.8	0.5
Aged 45 to 54	95.0	95.2	–0.2
Aged 55 to 64	95.5	96.1	–0.6
Aged 65 to 74	96.0	95.3	0.7
Aged 75 or older	86.2	90.4	–4.2

	2009	2007	percent change
MEDIAN VALUE			
Total households	**$204,000**	**$234,800**	**–13.1%**
Under age 35	52,800	44,400	18.9
Aged 35 to 44	196,500	232,000	–15.3
Aged 45 to 54	289,500	326,600	–11.4
Aged 55 to 64	308,000	361,900	–14.9
Aged 65 to 74	253,000	306,200	–17.4
Aged 75 or older	193,100	238,900	–19.2

Source: Federal Reserve Board, 2007-09 Panel Survey of Consumer Finances, Internet site http://www.federalreserve.gov/econresdata/scf/scf_2009p.htm; calculations by New Strategist

Table 11.7 Households Owning Primary Residence, Other Residential Property, and Nonresidential Property, 2007 and 2009

(percentage of households owning primary residence, other residential property, and nonresidential property, and median value for owners, by age of householder, 2007 and 2009; percentage point change in ownership and percent change in value, 2007–09; in 2009 dollars)

	primary residence			other residential property			nonresidential property		
	2009	2007	percentage point change	2009	2007	percentage point change	2009	2007	percentage point change
PERCENT OWNING									
Total households	**70.3%**	**68.9%**	**1.4**	**13.0%**	**13.9%**	**–0.9**	**7.6%**	**8.3%**	**–0.7**
Under age 35	44.6	40.5	4.1	7.1	5.3	1.8	3.1	3.1	0.0
Aged 35 to 44	68.9	66.6	2.3	11.4	12.5	–1.1	7.0	7.9	–0.9
Aged 45 to 54	78.1	77.3	0.8	14.4	15.5	–1.1	9.5	10.0	–0.5
Aged 55 to 64	81.9	82.2	–0.3	18.6	21.0	–2.4	10.9	11.5	–0.6
Aged 65 to 74	86.8	85.5	1.3	17.9	19.2	–1.3	11.1	10.9	0.2
Aged 75 or older	77.2	79.2	–2.0	11.2	14.3	–3.1	5.7	9.0	–3.3

	primary residence			other residential property			nonresidential property		
	2009	2007	percent change	2009	2007	percent change	2009	2007	percent change
MEDIAN VALUE									
Total households	**$176,000**	**$207,100**	**–15.0%**	**$150,000**	**$141,700**	**5.9%**	**$69,000**	**$78,800**	**–12.4%**
Under age 35	165,000	186,400	–11.5	100,000	62,100	61.0	30,000	51,800	–42.1
Aged 35 to 44	180,000	212,300	–15.2	155,700	155,300	0.3	28,600	59,000	–51.5
Aged 45 to 54	200,000	238,200	–16.0	176,000	163,800	7.4	90,000	79,000	13.9
Aged 55 to 64	185,000	207,100	–10.7	150,000	155,300	–3.4	100,000	103,600	–3.5
Aged 65 to 74	155,000	191,600	–19.1	149,500	139,800	6.9	100,000	103,600	–3.5
Aged 75 or older	130,000	155,300	–16.3	160,000	103,600	54.4	60,000	103,600	–42.1

Source: Federal Reserve Board, 2007-09 Panel Survey of Consumer Finances, Internet site http://www.federalreserve.gov/econresdata/scf/scf_2009p.htm; calculations by New Strategist

Table 11.8 Households Owning Vehicles and Business Equity, 2007 and 2009

(percentage of households owning vehicles and business equity, and median value for owners, by age of householder, 2007 and 2009; percentage point change in ownership and percent change in value, 2007–09; in 2009 dollars)

	vehicles			business equity		
	2009	2007	percentage point change	2009	2007	percentage point change
PERCENT OWNING						
Total households	**86.8%**	**87.9%**	**−1.1**	**11.9%**	**12.4%**	**−0.5**
Under age 35	87.2	85.8	1.4	7.7	7.1	0.6
Aged 35 to 44	87.6	87.9	−0.3	15.4	15.8	−0.4
Aged 45 to 54	90.6	91.1	−0.5	15.0	15.1	−0.1
Aged 55 to 64	90.5	92.5	−2.0	15.9	17.2	−1.3
Aged 65 to 74	88.3	90.8	−2.5	9.1	10.1	−1.0
Aged 75 or older	67.6	74.3	−6.7	3.8	5.4	−1.6

	vehicles			business equity		
	2009	2007	percent change	2009	2007	percent change
MEDIAN VALUE						
Total households	**$12,000**	**$16,200**	**−25.9%**	**$94,500**	**$103,600**	**−8.8%**
Under age 35	10,500	14,500	−27.6	41,300	46,600	−11.4
Aged 35 to 44	15,000	18,100	−17.1	70,000	98,700	−29.1
Aged 45 to 54	15,000	18,600	−19.4	80,000	103,600	−22.8
Aged 55 to 64	15,000	17,800	−15.7	150,000	152,500	−1.6
Aged 65 to 74	12,000	15,200	−21.1	500,000	517,800	−3.4
Aged 75 or older	7,900	9,700	−18.6	250,000	258,900	−3.4

Source: Federal Reserve Board, 2007-09 Panel Survey of Consumer Finances, Internet site http://www.federalreserve.gov/econresdata/scf/scf_2009p.htm; calculations by New Strategist

Most Households Are in Debt

Among households with debt, the amount owed increased between 2007 and 2009.

Seventy-eight percent of households have debt, owing a median of $75,600 in 2009. The median amount of debt owed by the average debtor household increased by 7.5 percent between 2007 and 2009, after adjusting for inflation. The percentage of households in debt fell slightly, however.

Householders aged 35 to 54 are most likely to be in debt, with 87 to 88 percent owing money. Debt declines with age, falling to a low of 35 percent among householders aged 75 or older.

Four types of debt are most common—debt secured by the primary residence (mortgages), which is held by 47 percent of households; credit card debt (43 percent); vehicle loans (34 percent); and education loans (18 percent). Mortgages account for the largest share of debt. The median amount owed by the average homeowner for the primary residence stood at $113,500 in 2009. Education loans are second in size, the average household with this type of debt owing a median of $15,000—more than the $12,400 owed by (the more-numerous) households with vehicle loans. Credit card debt is tiny by comparison, the average household with a credit card balance owing only $3,300.

■ Americans are attempting to pay down their debts, reducing consumer demand.

Education loans are common among young and middle-aged householders

(percent of households with education loans, by age of householder, 2009)

Table 11.9 Debt of Households, 2007 and 2009

(percentage of households with debt and median amount of debt for debtors, by age of householder, 2007 and 2009; percentage point change in households with debt and percent change in amount of debt, 2007–09; in 2009 dollars)

	2009	2007	percentage point change
PERCENT WITH DEBT			
Total households	**77.5%**	**79.7%**	**−2.2**
Under age 35	84.6	85.4	−0.8
Aged 35 to 44	87.7	87.3	0.4
Aged 45 to 54	86.6	88.1	−1.5
Aged 55 to 64	77.7	83.4	−5.7
Aged 65 to 74	62.1	68.5	−6.4
Aged 75 or older	35.0	36.2	−1.2

	2009	2007	percent change
MEDIAN AMOUNT OWED			
Total households	**$75,600**	**$70,300**	**7.5%**
Under age 35	51,000	37,800	34.9
Aged 35 to 44	109,500	113,700	−3.7
Aged 45 to 54	100,200	103,500	−3.2
Aged 55 to 64	62,000	64,300	−3.6
Aged 65 to 74	48,100	41,800	15.1
Aged 75 or older	8,200	20,000	−59.0

Source: Federal Reserve Board, 2007-09 Panel Survey of Consumer Finances, Internet site http://www.federalreserve .gov/'econresdata/scf/scf_2009p.htm; calculations by New Strategist

Table 11.10 Households with Residential Debt, 2007 and 2009

(percentage of households with residential debt, and median amount of debt for debtors, by age of householder, 2007 and 2009; percentage point change in households with debt and percent change in amount of debt, 2007–09; in 2009 dollars)

	secured by residential property								
	secured by primary residence			home equity line of credit			other residential debt		
	2009	2007	percentage point change	2009	2007	percentage point change	2009	2007	percentage point change
PERCENT WITH DEBT									
Total households	**46.6%**	**47.8%**	**–1.2**	**10.5%**	**8.7%**	**1.8**	**5.1%**	**5.7%**	**–0.6**
Under age 35	39.8	37.4	2.4	4.3	3.7	0.6	3.3	3.2	0.1
Aged 35 to 44	60.0	60.0	0.0	10.2	8.5	1.7	6.0	7.0	–1.0
Aged 45 to 54	62.2	64.3	–2.1	14.0	12.3	1.7	6.7	7.7	–1.0
Aged 55 to 64	46.8	51.9	–5.1	17.1	12.8	4.3	6.6	8.3	–1.7
Aged 65 to 74	34.9	37.4	–2.5	11.9	10.3	1.6	4.7	4.3	0.4
Aged 75 or older	11.5	13.4	–1.9	4.3	3.8	0.5	0.9	0.6	0.3

	secured by residential property								
	secured by primary residence			home equity line of credit			other residential debt		
	2009	2007	percent change	2009	2007	percent change	2009	2007	percent change
MEDIAN AMOUNT OWED									
Total households	**$113,500**	**$113,900**	**–0.4%**	**$21,500**	**$22,800**	**–5.7%**	**$130,000**	**$98,400**	**32.1%**
Under age 35	144,600	140,100	3.2	20,000	20,300	–1.5	118,000	80,800	46.0
Aged 35 to 44	127,800	128,300	–0.4	20,000	24,900	–19.7	150,000	110,600	35.6
Aged 45 to 54	111,600	113,900	–2.0	30,000	25,900	15.8	115,000	86,000	33.7
Aged 55 to 64	95,000	93,200	1.9	20,000	21,900	–8.7	155,000	110,900	39.8
Aged 65 to 74	80,000	81,800	–2.2	28,000	15,500	80.6	115,000	116,000	–0.9
Aged 75 or older	49,000	33,900	44.5	13,000	25,900	–49.8	23,000	51,800	–55.6

Source: Federal Reserve Board, 2007-09 Panel Survey of Consumer Finances, Internet site http://www.federalreserve.gov/econresdata/scf/scf_2009p.htm; calculations by New Strategist

Table 11.10 Households with Credit Card Debt, Vehicle Loans, and Education Loans, 2007 and 2009

(percentage of households with credit card, vehicle, and education debt, and median amount of debt for debtors, by age of householder, 2007 and 2009; percentage point change in households with debt and percent change in amount of debt, 2007–09; in 2009 dollars)

	credit card balances			vehicle loans			education loans		
	2009	2007	percentage point change	2009	2007	percentage point change	2009	2007	percentage point change
PERCENT WITH DEBT									
Total households	**43.2%**	**47.8%**	**−4.6**	**33.9%**	**36.0%**	**−2.1**	**17.7%**	**16.3%**	**1.4**
Under age 35	42.8	50.6	−7.8	43.1	46.0	−2.9	36.8	35.7	1.1
Aged 35 to 44	49.6	52.6	−3.0	44.7	44.1	0.6	19.7	15.7	4.0
Aged 45 to 54	50.5	54.1	−3.6	35.5	38.3	−2.8	18.0	14.8	3.2
Aged 55 to 64	44.6	50.4	−5.8	30.8	35.5	−4.7	9.9	11.3	−1.4
Aged 65 to 74	35.0	38.7	−3.7	21.3	21.9	−0.6	1.9	1.9	0.0
Aged 75 or older	20.2	21.8	−1.6	5.5	7.2	−1.7	0.0	0.5	−0.5

	credit card balances			vehicle loans			education loans		
	2009	2007	percent change	2009	2007	percent change	2009	2007	percent change
MEDIAN AMOUNT OWED									
Total households	**$3,300**	**$3,100**	**6.5%**	**$12,400**	**$11,200**	**10.7%**	**$15,000**	**$12,400**	**21.0%**
Under age 35	3,000	1,900	57.9	12,200	11,300	8.0	15,000	14,500	3.4
Aged 35 to 44	3,000	3,600	−16.7	13,000	12,300	5.7	16,000	12,400	29.0
Aged 45 to 54	4,000	3,700	8.1	13,000	10,900	19.3	15,000	10,700	40.2
Aged 55 to 64	4,500	4,100	9.8	12,000	9,600	25.0	12,000	7,300	64.4
Aged 65 to 74	2,900	3,200	−9.4	10,000	12,500	−20.0	–	–	–
Aged 75 or older	2,000	800	150.0	9,500	7,600	25.0	–	–	–

Note: "−" means sample is too small to make a reliable estimate.
Source: Federal Reserve Board, 2007-09 Panel Survey of Consumer Finances, Internet site http://www.federalreserve.gov/ econresdata/scf/scf_2009p.htm; calculations by New Strategist

Retirement Worries Are Growing

Few workers are "very confident" in having enough money for a comfortable retirement.

Only 14 percent of workers are very confident in their ability to afford a comfortable retirement, according to the 2012 Retirement Confidence Survey. The 14 percent figure is well below the 23 percent who felt very confident in 2002. There is little variation in retirement confidence by age.

Reality may be dawning on many workers. Since 2002, the expected age of retirement has climbed. The percentage of all workers expecting to retire at age 65 or older (including those who say they will never retire) increased from 52 to 70 percent between 2002 and 2012. Among workers aged 55 or older, fully 74 percent expect to retire at age 65 or older.

One reason so many are putting off retirement is that they have little in the way of retirement savings. Among workers approaching retirement—those aged 55 or older—the 60 percent majority has saved less than $100,000 for retirement (not counting the value of their home).

■ Nearly one-third of workers aged 55 or older have saved less than $10,000 for retirement.

Most workers are not planning on an early retirement

(percent of workers aged 25 or older who expect to retire at age 65 or older, by age, 2012)

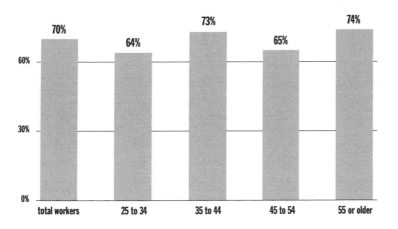

Table 11.11 Retirement Confidence, 2002 and 2012

(percentage of workers aged 25 or older who are "very confident" in financial aspects of retirement, by age, 2002 and 2012; percentage point change, 2002–12)

	total workers	25 to 34	35 to 44	45 to 54	55 or older
You will have enough money to live comfortably throughout your retirement years					
2012	14%	13%	16%	12%	16%
2002	23	26	20	21	25
You will have enough money to take care of basic expenses during retirement					
2012	26	26	27	25	27
2002	38	40	38	39	32
You are doing a good job of preparing financially for retirement					
2012	19	22	21	14	18
2002	23	26	23	21	24
You will have enough money to take care of medical expenses during retirement					
2012	13	14	15	11	14
2002	20	19	17	19	26
You will have enough money to pay for long-term care during retirement					
2012	9	10	11	8	8
2002	13	15	14	10	14
The Social Security system will continue to provide benefits of at least equal value to the benefits received by retirees today					
2012	6	4	4	4	12
2002	6	1	4	7	16
The Medicare system will continue to provide benefits of at least equal value to the benefits received by retirees today					
2012	4	2	3	6	7
2002	5	3	4	5	15

Source: Employee Benefit Research Institute, Retirement Confidence Surveys, Internet site http://www.ebri.org/surveys/rcs/2012/

Table 11.12 Expected Age of Retirement, 2002 and 2012

(expected age of retirement among workers aged 25 or older, by age, 2002 and 2012; percentage point change, 2002–12)

	2012	2002	percentage point change
ALL WORKERS			
Before age 60	8%	17%	–9
Aged 60 to 64	16	22	–6
Age 65	26	29	–3
Aged 66 or older	37	18	19
Never retire	7	5	2
Don't know/refused	5	9	–4
AGED 25 TO 34			
Before age 60	15	21	–6
Aged 60 to 64	16	20	–4
Age 65	27	33	–6
Aged 66 or older	34	17	17
Never retire	3	4	–1
Don't know/refused	4	5	–1
AGED 35 TO 44			
Before age 60	5	16	–11
Aged 60 to 64	15	27	–12
Age 65	29	30	–1
Aged 66 or older	35	14	21
Never retire	9	6	3
Don't know/refused	6	8	–2
AGED 45 TO 54			
Before age 60	10	21	–11
Aged 60 to 64	18	17	1
Age 65	22	28	–6
Aged 66 or older	34	21	13
Never retire	9	7	2
Don't know/refused	6	6	0
AGED 55 OR OLDER			
Before age 60	1	6	–5
Aged 60 to 64	15	25	–10
Age 65	23	23	0
Aged 66 or older	44	26	18
Never retire	7	2	5
Don't know/refused	8	18	–10

Source: Employee Benefit Research Institute, Retirement Confidence Surveys, Internet site http://www.ebri.org/surveys/rcs/2012/

Table 11.13 **Retirement Savings by Age, 2012**

(percent distribution of workers aged 25 or older by savings and investments, not including value of primary residence, by age, 2012)

	total	25 to 34	35 to 44	45 to 54	55 or older
Total workers	**100%**	**100%**	**100%**	**100%**	**100%**
Less than $10,000	48	57	51	46	31
$10,000 to $24,999	12	19	10	8	9
$25,000 to $49,999	10	12	11	9	8
$50,000 to $99,999	10	6	14	9	12
$100,000 or more	20	6	15	29	40
$100,000 to $249,999	10	5	12	12	18
$250,000 or more	10	1	3	17	22

Source: Employee Benefit Research Institute, 2012 Retirement Confidence Survey, Internet site http://www.ebri.org/surveys/rcs/2012/

Glossary

adjusted for inflation Income or a change in income that has been adjusted for the rise in the cost of living, or the consumer price index (CPI-U-RS).

age Classification by age is based on the age of the person at his/her last birthday.

American Community Survey The ACS is an ongoing nationwide survey of 250,000 households per month, providing detailed demographic data at the community level. Designed to replace the census long-form questionnaire, the ACS includes more than 60 questions that formerly appeared on the long form, such as language spoken at home, income, and education. ACS data are available for areas as small as census tracts.

American Housing Survey The AHS collects national and metropolitan-level data on the nation's housing, including apartments, single-family homes, and mobile homes. The nationally representative survey, with a sample of 55,000 homes, is conducted by the Census Bureau for the Department of Housing and Urban Development every other year.

American Indians Include Alaska Natives (Eskimos and Aleuts) unless those groups are shown separately.

American Time Use Survey Under contract with the Bureau of Labor Statistics, the Census Bureau collects ATUS information, revealing how people spend their time. The ATUS sample is drawn from U.S. households that have completed their final month of interviews for the Current Population Survey. One individual from each selected household is chosen to participate in the ATUS. Respondents are interviewed by telephone only once about their time use on the previous day.

Asian Includes Native Hawaiians and other Pacific Islanders unless those groups are shown separately.

Baby Boom Americans born between 1946 and 1964.

Baby Bust Americans born between 1965 and 1976, also known as Generation X.

Behavioral Risk Factor Surveillance System The BRFSS is a collaborative project of the Centers for Disease Control and Prevention and U.S. states and territories. It is an ongoing data collection program designed to measure behavioral risk factors in the adult population aged 18 or older. All 50 states, three territories, and the District of Columbia take part in the survey, making the BRFSS the primary source of information on the health-related behaviors of Americans.

black The black racial category includes those who identified themselves as "black" or "African American."

Consumer Expenditure Survey The CEX is an ongoing study of the day-to-day spending of American households administered by the Bureau of Labor Statistics. The CEX includes an interview survey and a diary survey. The average spending figures shown in this book are the integrated data from both the diary and interview components of the survey. Two separate, nationally representative samples are used for the interview and diary surveys. For the interview survey, about 7,500 consumer units are interviewed on a rotating panel basis each quarter for five consecutive quarters. For the diary survey, 7,500 consumer units keep weekly diaries of spending for two consecutive weeks.

consumer unit *(on spending tables only)* For convenience, the term consumer unit and households are used interchangeably in the spending section of this book, although consumer units are somewhat different from the Census Bureau's households. Consumer units are all related members of a household, or financially independent members of a household. A household may include more than one consumer unit.

Current Population Survey The CPS is a nationally representative survey of the civilian noninstitutional population aged 15 or older. It is taken monthly by the Census Bureau for the Bureau of Labor Statistics, collecting information from more than 50,000 households on employment and unemployment. In March of each year, the survey includes the Annual Social and Economic Supplement, which is the source of most national data on the characteristics of Americans, such as educational attainment, living arrangements, and incomes.

disability As defined by the National Health Interview Survey, respondents aged 18 or older are asked whether they have difficulty in physical functioning, probing whether respondents can perform nine activities by themselves without using special equipment. The categories are walking a quarter mile; standing for two hours; sitting for two hours; walking up 10 steps without resting; stooping, bending, kneeling; reaching over one's head; grasping or handling small objects; carrying a 10-pound object; and pushing/pulling a large object. Adults who report that any of these activities is very difficult or they cannot do it at all are defined as having physical difficulties.

dual-earner couple A married couple in which both the householder and the householder's spouse are in the labor force.

earnings A type of income, earnings is the amount of money a person receives from his or her job. *See also* Income.

employed All civilians who did any work as a paid employee or farmer/self-employed worker, or who worked 15 hours or more as an unpaid farm worker or in a family-owned business, during the reference period. All those who have jobs but who are temporarily absent from their jobs due to illness, bad weather, vacation, labor management dispute, or personal reasons are considered employed.

expenditure The transaction cost including excise and sales taxes of goods and services acquired during the survey period. The full cost of each purchase is recorded even though full payment may not have been made at the date of purchase. Average expenditure figures may be artificially low for infrequently purchased items such as cars because figures are calculated using all consumer units within a demographic segment rather than just purchasers. Expenditure estimates include money spent on gifts for others.

family A group of two or more people (one of whom is the householder) related by birth, marriage, or adoption and living in the same household.

family household A household maintained by a householder who lives with one or more people related to him or her by blood, marriage, or adoption.

female/male householder A woman or man who maintains a household without a spouse present. May head family or nonfamily households.

foreign-born population People who are not U.S. citizens at birth.

full-time employment Thirty-five or more hours of work per week during a majority of the weeks worked.

full-time, year-round Fifty or more weeks of full-time employment during the previous calendar year.

Generation X Americans born between 1965 and 1976, also known as the baby-bust generation.

Hispanic Because Hispanic is an ethnic origin rather than a race, Hispanics may be of any race. While most Hispanics are white, there are black, Asian, and American Indian Hispanics.

household All the persons who occupy a housing unit. A household includes the related family members and all the unrelated persons, if any, such as lodgers, foster children, wards, or employees who share the housing unit. A person living alone is counted as a household. A group of unrelated people who share a housing unit as roommates or unmarried partners is also counted as a household. Households do not include group quarters such as college dormitories, prisons, or nursing homes.

household, race/ethnicity of Households are categorized according to the race or ethnicity of the householder only.

householder The person (or one of the persons) in whose name the housing unit is owned or rented or, if there is no such person, any adult member. With married couples, the householder may be either the husband or wife. The householder is the reference person for the household.

householder, age of Used to categorize households into age groups such as those used in this book. Married couples, for example, are classified according to the age of either the husband or wife, depending on which one identified him or herself as the householder.

housing unit A house, an apartment, a group of rooms, or a single room occupied or intended for occupancy as separate living quarters. Separate living quarters are those in which the occupants do not live and eat with any other persons in the structure and that have direct access from the outside of the building or through a common hall that is used or intended for use by the occupants of another unit or by the general public. The occupants may be a single family, one person living alone, two or more families living together, or any other group of related or unrelated persons who share living arrangements.

Housing Vacancy Survey The HVS is a supplement to the Current Population Survey, providing quarterly and annual data on rental and homeowner vacancy rates, characteristics of units available for occupancy, and homeownership rates by age, household type, region, state, and metropolitan area. The Current Population Survey sample includes 72,000 housing units—61,200 occupied and 10,800 vacant.

housing value The respondent's estimate of how much his or her house and lot would sell for if it were for sale.

iGeneration Americans born from 1995 to the present. Also known as the Plurals.

immigration The relatively permanent movement (change of residence) of people into the country of reference.

in-migration The relatively permanent movement (change of residence) of people into a subnational geographic entity, such as a region, division, state, metropolitan area, or county.

income Money received in the preceding calendar year by each person aged 15 or older from each of the following sources: (1) earnings from longest job (or self-employment), (2) earnings from jobs other than longest job, (3) unemployment compensation, (4) workers' compensation, (5) Social Security, (6) Supplemental Security income, (7) public assistance, (8) veterans' payments, (9) survivor benefits, (10) disability benefits, (11) retirement pensions, (12) interest, (13) dividends, (14) rents and royalties or estates and trusts, (15) educational assistance, (16) alimony, (17) child support, (18) financial assistance from outside the household, and other periodic income. Income is reported in several ways in this book. Household income is the combined income of all household members. Income of persons is all income accruing to a person from all sources. Earnings are the money a person receives from his or her job.

industry The industry in which a person worked longest in the preceding calendar year.

job tenure The length of time a person has been employed continuously by the same employer.

labor force The labor force tables in this book show the civilian labor force only. The labor force includes both the employed and the unemployed (people who are looking for work). People are counted as in the labor force if they were working or looking for work during the reference week in which the Census Bureau fields the Current Population Survey.

labor force participation rate The percent of the civilian noninstitutional population that is in the civilian labor force, which includes both the employed and the unemployed.

married couples with or without children under age 18 Refers to married couples with or without own children under age 18 living in the same household. Couples without children under age 18 may be parents of grown children who live elsewhere, or they could be childless couples.

median The amount that divides the population or households into two equal portions: one below and one above the median. Medians can be calculated for income, age, and many other characteristics.

median income The amount that divides the income distribution into two equal groups, half having incomes above the median, half having incomes below the median. The medians for households or families are based on all households or families. The median for persons are based on all persons aged 15 or older with income.

Medical Expenditure Panel Survey MEPS is a nationally representative survey that collects detailed information on the health status, access to care, health care use and expenses and health insurance coverage of the civilian noninstitutionalized population of the U.S. and nursing home residents. MEPS comprises four component surveys: the Household Component, the Medical Provider Component, the Insurance Component, and the Nursing Home Component. The Household Component is the core survey, is conducted each year, and includes 15,000 households and 37,000 people.

metropolitan statistical To be defined as a metropolitan statistical area (or MSA), an area must include a city with 50,000 or more inhabitants, or a Census Bureau-defined urbanized area of at least 50,000 inhabitants and a total metropolitan population of at least 100,000 (75,000 in New England). The county (or counties) that contains the largest city becomes the "central county" (counties), along with any adjacent counties that have at least 50 percent of their population in the urbanized area surrounding the largest city. Additional "outlying counties" are included in the MSA if they meet specified requirements of commuting to the central counties and other selected requirements of metropolitan character (such as population density and percent urban). In New England, MSAs are defined in terms of cities and towns rather than counties. For this reason, the concept of NECMA is used to define metropolitan areas in the New England division.

Millennial generation Americans born between 1977 and 1994.

mobility status People are classified according to their mobility status on the basis of a comparison between their place of residence at the time of the March Current Population Survey and their place of residence in March of the previous year. Nonmovers are people living in the same house at the end of the period as at the beginning of the period. Movers are people living in a different house at the end of the period than at the beginning of the period. Movers from abroad are either citizens or aliens whose place of residence is outside the United States at the beginning of the period, that is, in an outlying area under the jurisdiction of the United States or in a foreign country. The mobility status for children is fully allocated from the mother if she is in the household; otherwise it is allocated from the householder.

National Ambulatory Medical Care Survey The NAMCS is an annual survey of visits to nonfederally employed office-based physicians who are primarily engaged in direct patient care. Data are collected from physicians rather than patients, with each physician assigned a one-week reporting period. During that week, a systematic random sample of visit characteristics are recorded by the physician or office staff.

National Compensation Survey The Bureau of Labor Statistics' NCS examines the incidence and detailed provisions of selected employee benefits in private sector establishments and state and local governments. Each year BLS economists visit a representative sample of establishments across the country, asking questions about the establishment, its employees, and their benefits.

National Health and Nutrition Examination Survey The NHANES is a continuous survey of a representative sample of the U.S. civilian noninstitutionalized population. Respondents are interviewed at home about their health and nutrition, and the interview is followed up by a physical examination that measures such things as height and weight in mobile examination centers.

National Health Interview Survey The NHIS is a continuing nationwide sample survey of the civilian noninstitutional population of the U.S. conducted by the Census Bureau for the National Center for Health Statistics. Each year, data are collected from more than 100,000 people about their illnesses, injuries, impairments, chronic and acute conditions, activity limitations, and the use of health services.

National Hospital Ambulatory Medical Care Survey The NHAMCS, sponsored by the National Center for Health Statistics, is an annual national probability sample survey of visits to emergency departments and outpatient departments at non-Federal, short stay and general hospitals. Data are collected by hospital staff from patient records.

National Household Education Survey The NHES, sponsored by the National Center for Education Statistics, provides descriptive data on the educational activities of the U.S. population, including after-school care and adult education. The NHES is a system of telephone surveys of a representative sample of 45,000 to 60,000 households in the U.S.

National Survey of Family Growth The 2002 NSFG, sponsored by the National Center for Health Statistics, is a nationally representative survey of the civilian noninstitutional population aged 15 to 44. In-person interviews were completed with 12,571 men and women, collecting data on marriage, divorce, contraception, and infertility. The 2002 survey updates previous NSFG surveys taken in 1973, 1976, 1988, and 1995.

National Survey on Drug Use and Health Formerly called the National Household Survey on Drug Abuse, this survey, sponsored by the Substance Abuse and Mental Health Services Administration, has been conducted since 1971. It is the primary source of information on the use of illegal drugs by the U.S. population. Each year, a nationally representative sample of about 70,000 individuals aged 12 or older are surveyed in the 50 states and the District of Columbia.

Native Hawaiian and other Pacific Islander Beginning with the 2000 census, this group was identified as a racial category separate from Asians. In most survey data, however, the population is included with Asians.

net migration Net migration is the result of subtracting out-migration from in-migration for an area. Another way to derive net migration is to subtract natural increase (births minus deaths) from total population change in an area.

net worth The amount of money left over after a household's debts are subtracted from its assets.

nonfamily household A household maintained by a householder who lives alone or who lives with people to whom he or she is not related.

nonfamily householder A householder who lives alone or with nonrelatives.

non-Hispanic People who do not identify themselves as Hispanic are classified as non-Hispanic. Non-Hispanics may be of any race.

non-Hispanic white People who identify their race as white and who do not indicate a Hispanic origin.

nonmetropolitan area Counties that are not classified as metropolitan areas.

occupation Occupational classification is based on the kind of work a person did at his or her job during the previous calendar year. If a person changed jobs during the year, the data refer to the occupation of the job held the longest during that year.

occupied housing units A housing unit is classified as occupied if a person or group of people is living in it or if the occupants are only temporarily absent—on vacation, example. By definition, the count of occupied housing units is the same as the count of households.

outside principal cities The portion of a metropolitan county or counties that falls outside of the principal city or cities; generally regarded as the suburbs.

own children Sons and daughters, including stepchildren and adopted children, of the householder. The totals include never-married children living away from home in college dormitories.

owner occupied A housing unit is "owner occupied" if the owner lives in the unit, even if it is mortgaged or not fully paid for. A cooperative or condominium unit is "owner occupied" only if the owner lives in it. All other occupied units are classified as "renter occupied."

part-time employment Less than 35 hours of work per week in a majority of the weeks worked during the year.

percent change The change (either positive or negative) in a measure that is expressed as a proportion of the starting measure. When median income changes from $20,000 to $25,000, for example, this is a 25 percent increase.

percentage point change The change (either positive or negative) in a value which is already expressed as a percentage. When a labor force participation rate changes from 70 percent of 75 percent, for example, this is a 5 percentage point increase.

poverty level The official income threshold below which families and people are classified as living in poverty. The threshold rises each year with inflation and varies depending on family size and age of householder.

primary activity In the time use tables, primary activities are those respondents identify as their main activity. Other activities done simultaneously are not included.

proportion or share The value of a part expressed as a percentage of the whole. If there are 4 million people aged 25 and 3 million of them are white, then the white proportion is 75 percent.

race Race is self-reported and can be defined in three ways. The "race alone" population comprises people who identify themselves as only one race. The "race in combination" population comprises people who identify themselves as more than one race, such as white and black. The "race, alone or in combination" population includes both those who identify themselves as one race and those who identify themselves as more than one race.

regions The four major regions and nine census divisions of the United States are the state groupings as shown below:

Northeast:
—New England: Connecticut, Maine, Massachusetts, New Hampshire, Rhode Island, and Vermont
—Middle Atlantic: New Jersey, New York, and Pennsylvania

Midwest:
—East North Central: Illinois, Indiana, Michigan, Ohio, and Wisconsin
—West North Central: Iowa, Kansas, Minnesota, Missouri, Nebraska, North Dakota, and South Dakota

South:

—South Atlantic: Delaware, District of Columbia, Florida, Georgia, Maryland, North Carolina, South Carolina, Virginia, and West Virginia

—East South Central: Alabama, Kentucky, Mississippi, and Tennessee

—West South Central: Arkansas, Louisiana, Oklahoma, and Texas

West:

—Mountain: Arizona, Colorado, Idaho, Montana, Nevada, New Mexico, Utah, and Wyoming

—Pacific: Alaska, California, Hawaii, Oregon, and Washington

renter occupied *See* Owner occupied.

Retirement Confidence Survey The RCS, sponsored by the Employee Benefit Research Institute (EBRI), the American Savings Education Council (ASEC), and Mathew Greenwald & Associates (Greenwald), is an annual survey of a nationally representative sample of 1,000 people aged 25 or older. Respondents are asked a core set of questions that have been asked since 1996, measuring attitudes and behavior towards retirement. Additional questions are also asked about current retirement issues.

rounding Percentages are rounded to the nearest tenth of a percent; therefore, the percentages in a distribution do not always add exactly to 100.0 percent. The totals, however, are always shown as 100.0. Moreover, individual figures are rounded to the nearest thousand without being adjusted to group totals, which are independently rounded; percentages are based on the unrounded numbers.

self-employment A person is categorized as self-employed if he or she was self-employed in the job held longest during the reference period. Persons who report self-employment from a second job are excluded, but those who report wage-and-salary income from a second job are included. Unpaid workers in family businesses are excluded. Self-employment statistics include only nonagricultural workers and exclude people who work for themselves in incorporated business.

sex ratio The number of men per 100 women.

suburbs *See* Outside central city.

Survey of Consumer Finances A triennial survey taken by the Federal Reserve Board. It collects data on the assets, debts, and net worth of American households. For the 2007 survey, the Federal Reserve Board interviewed a representative sample of 6,500 households.

unemployed Those who, during the survey period, had no employment but were available and looking for work. Those who were laid off from their jobs and were waiting to be recalled are also classified as unemployed.

white The "white" racial category includes many Hispanics (who may be of any race) unless the term "non-Hispanic white" is used.

Youth Risk Behavior Surveillance System The YRBSS was created by the Centers for Disease Control to monitor health risks being taken by young people at the national, state, and local level. The national survey is taken every two years based on a nationally representative sample of 16,000 students in 9th through 12th grade in public and private schools.

Bibliography

Agency for Healthcare Research and Quality
Internet site http://www.ahrq.gov/
    —Medical Expenditure Panel Survey, Internet site http://meps.ahrq.gov/mepsweb/ survey_comp/household.jsp

Bureau of the Census
Internet site http://www.census.gov
    —2010 American Community Survey, American FactFinder, Internet site http://factfinder2 .census.gov/faces/nav/jsf/pages/index.xhtml
    —2010 Census, American Factfinder, Internet site http://factfinder2.census.gov/faces/nav/ jsf/pages/index.xhtml
    —2010 Census, Internet site http://2010.census.gov/2010census/data/
    —A Child's Day: 2009, Internet site http://www.census.gov/hhes/socdemo/children/data/ sipp/well2009/tables.html
    —American Housing Survey National Tables: 2009, Internet site http://www.census.gov/ housing/ahs/data/ahs2009.html
    —Educational Attainment, CPS Historical Time Series Tables, Internet site http://www .census.gov/hhes/socdemo/education/data/cps/historical/index.html
    —Educational Attainment, Internet site http://www.census.gov/hhes/socdemo/education/
    —Families and Living Arrangements, Internet site http://www.census.gov/population/www/ socdemo/hh-fam.html
    —Fertility of American Women: 2010, Detailed Tables, Internet site http://www.census .gov/hhes/fertility/data/cps/2010.html
    —Geographical Mobility, Internet site http://www.census.gov/hhes/migration
    —Health Insurance, Internet site http://www.census.gov/hhes/www/hlthins/
    —Historical Health Insurance Tables, Current Population Survey Annual Social and Economic Supplements, Internet site http://www.census.gov/hhes/www/hlthins/data/ historical/HIB_tables.html
    —Historical Income Tables, Internet site http://www.census.gov/hhes/www/income/data/ historical/index.html
    —Housing Vacancies and Homeownership Survey, Internet site http://www.census.gov/ hhes/www/housing/hvs/hvs.html
    —Income, Current Population Survey, Internet site http://www.census.gov/hhes/www/ income/data/index.html
    —Number, Timing, and Duration of Marriages and Divorces: 2009, Current Population Reports P70-125, 2011, Internet site http://www.census.gov/hhes/socdemo/marriage/data/ sipp/index.html
    —Population Estimates, Internet site http://www.census.gov/popest/data/index.html
    —Poverty, Current Population Survey, Internet site http://www.census.gov/hhes/www/ poverty/index.html
    —School Enrollment, Historical Tables, Current Population Survey Annual Social and Economic Supplements, Internet site http://www.census.gov/population/www/socdemo/ school/.html
    —School Enrollment, Internet site http://www.census.gov/hhes/school/

Bureau of Labor Statistics

Internet site http://www.bls.gov

—Consumer Expenditure Surveys, various years, Internet site http://www.bls.gov/cex/home.htm

—2010 American Time Use Survey, Internet site http://www.bls.gov/tus/home.htm

—Characteristics of Minimum Wage Workers, 2011, Internet site http://www.bls.gov/cps/minwage2011tbls.htm

—College Enrollment and Work Activity of 2010 High School Graduates, Internet site http://www.bls.gov/news.release/hsgec.nr0.htm

—Employee Tenure, Internet site http://www.bls.gov/news.release/tenure.toc.htm

—Employment Projections, Internet site http://www.bls.gov/emp/

—Employment and Unemployment among Youth Summary, Internet site http://bls.gov/news.release/youth.nr0.htm

—Employment Characteristics of Families, Internet site http://www.bls.gov/news.release/famee.toc.htm

—Labor Force Statistics from the Current Population Survey—Annual Averages, Internet site http://www.bls.gov/cps/tables.htm#empstat

—National Compensation Survey, Internet site http://www.bls.gov/ncs/ebs/home.htm

—Table 15. Employed persons by detailed occupation, sex, and age, Annual Average 2011 (Source: Current Population Survey), unpublished table received from the BLS by special request

Centers for Disease Control and Prevention

Internet site http://www.cdc.gov

—Behavioral Risk Factor Surveillance System, Prevalence Data, Internet site http://apps.nccd.cdc.gov/brfss/

—Cases of HIV/AIDS and AIDS in the United States and Dependent Areas, 2009, Internet site http://www.cdc.gov/hiv/surveillance/resources/reports/2009report/

—Youth Risk Behavior Surveillance–United States, 2009, Internet site http://www.cdc.gov/HealthyYouth/yrbs/index.htm

Employee Benefit Research Institute

Internet site http://www.ebri.org/

—Retirement Confidence Surveys, Internet site http://www.ebri.org/surveys/rcs/

Federal Interagency Forum on Child and Family Statistics

Internet site http://childstats.gov

—America's Children: Key National Indicators of Well-Being, 2011, Internet site http://www.childstats.gov/

Federal Reserve Board

Internet site http://www.federalreserve.gov/econresdata/scf/scfindex.htm

—*Surveying the Aftermath of the Storm: Changes in Family Finances from 2007 to 2009*, Appendix tables, Internet site http://www.federalreserve.gov/econresdata/scf/scf_2009p.htm

Homeland Security
Internet site http://www.dhs.gov/index.shtm
> —Yearbook of Immigration Statistics, Internet site http://www.dhs.gov/files/statistics/publications/yearbook.shtm

National Center for Education Statistics
Internet site http://nces.ed.gov
> —*The Condition of Education 2011*, Internet site http://nces.ed.gov/programs/coe/
> —*Digest of Education Statistics: 2011*, Internet site http://nces.ed.gov/programs/digest
> —National Household Education Survey, Internet site http://nces.ed.gov/nhes/

National Center for Health Statistics
Internet site http://www.cdc.gov/nchs
> —*Anthropometric Reference Data for Children and Adults: United States, 2003–2006*, National Health Statistics Reports, Number 10, 2008, Internet site http://www.cdc.gov/nchs/products/pubs/pubd/nhsr/nhsr.htm
> —Birth Data, Internet site http://www.cdc.gov/nchs/births.htm
> —*Complementary and Alternative Medicine Use Among Adults and Children: United States, 2007*, National Health Statistics Report, No. 12, 2008, Internet site http://www.cdc.gov/nchs/products/nhsr.htm
> —*Health Characteristics of Adults 55 Years of Age and Over: United States, 2004–2007*, National Health Statistics Reports, No. 16, 2009, Internet site http://www.cdc.gov/nchs/nhis.htm
> —Mortality Data, Internet site http://www.cdc.gov/nchs/deaths.htm
> —*National Ambulatory Medical Care Survey: 2009 Summary Tables,* Internet site http://www.cdc.gov/nchs/ahcd/web_tables.htm#2009
> —*National Hospital Ambulatory Medical Care Survey: 2008 Emergency Department Summary,* Internet site http://www.cdc.gov/nchs/ahcd/web_tables.htm#2009
> —*National Hospital Ambulatory Medical Care Survey: 2008 Outpatient Department Summary,* Internet site http://www.cdc.gov/nchs/ahcd/web_tables.htm#2009
> —*Health, United States,* various editions, Internet site http://www.cdc.gov/nchs/hus.htm
> —*Sexual Behavior, Sexual Attraction, and Sexual Identity in the United States: Data from the 2006–2008 National Survey of Family Growth,* National Health Statistics Reports, No. 36, 2011, Internet site http://www.cdc.gov/nchs/nsfg/new_nsfg.htm
> —*Summary Health Statistics for U.S. Adults: National Health Interview Survey, 2010*, Series 10, No. 252, 2012, Internet site http://www.cdc.gov/nchs/nhis.htm
> —*Summary Health Statistics for U.S. Children: National Health Interview Survey, 2010*, Series 10, No. 250, 2011, Internet site http://www.cdc.gov/nchs/nhis.htm
> —*Summary Health Statistics for the U.S. Population: National Health Interview Survey, 2010*, Series 10, No. 251, 2011, Internet site http://www.cdc.gov/nchs/nhis.htm

National Sporting Goods Association
Internet site http://www.nsga.org
> —Sports Participation, Internet site http://www.nsga.org

Substance Abuse and Mental Health Services Administration
Internet site http://www.samhsa.gov
    National Survey on Drug Use and Health, 2010, Internet site http://www.samhsa.gov/data/
    NSDUH/2k10ResultsTables/Web/HTML/TOC.htm

University of California, Berkeley, Survey Documentation and Analysis, Computer-assisted Survey Methods Program
Internet site http://sda.berkeley.edu/
    —General Social Surveys 1972-2010 Cumulative Data Files, Internet site http://sda.berkeley
    .edu/cgi-bin/hsda?harcsda+gss10

University of Michigan, Monitoring the Future Study
Internet site http://monitoringthefuture.org
    —Monitoring the Future Study, Data Tables and Figures, Internet site http://
    monitoringthefuture.org/data/data.html

Index